THUS HE LAY BROODING OVER HIS GRIEF.

Frontispiece.

JOHN MILTON

AND HIS TIMES.

AN HISTORICAL NOVEL.

BY

MAX RING.

TRANSLATED FROM THE GERMAN, BY

F. JORDAN.

COMPLETE IN ONE VOLUME.

With Illustrations by Gaston Fay.

NEW YORK:
D. APPLETON & CO., 90, 92 & 94 GRAND STREET.
1868.

CONTENTS.

BOOK I.

BOOK II.

BOOK III.

JOHN MILTON AND HIS TIMES.

BOOK I.

CHAPTER I.

LOST IN HAYWOOD FOREST.

Two young noblemen, accompanied by their sister, rode in the most beautiful month of spring through Haywood Forest, one of those splendid woods which formerly adorned Old England so charmingly, and which are fast disappearing from the surface of the country. They had paid a visit to their relatives at Harefield, the noble house of Derby, and were now returning to Ludlow Castle, the residence of their father, who was no other than the Earl of Bridgewater, at that time Lord President of Wales. The earl was the son of Thomas Egerton, the celebrated jurist, who, under the reigns of Queen Elizabeth and her successor, had held the responsible and commanding positions of Lord Keeper of the Seal and Chancellor of England with the greatest distinction to an advanced period of his life.

The descendants of this eminent man were not unworthy of him. His grandsons, mere youths at the time at which our story opens, had not become degenerate; and charming Lady Alice Egerton was considered everywhere one of the most beautiful and amiable young ladies in Merry Old England. She and her brothers were in the full bloom of youth, beauty, and vivacity. They were tenderly attached to each other, and no calamitous event had hitherto disturbed the clear and even current of their lives. Joy and hilarity beamed from their sparkling eyes and blooming cheeks.

Thus they rode, chatting gayly and carelessly, through the verdant, fragrant forest. Merry jests, such as only the young know and like, caused them from time to time to burst into ringing laughter, in which the birds of the forest joined now and then harmoniously with their sweet warbling and chirping. Haywood forest, like the larger portion of the county of Hereford, in which it is situated, consists of a series of undulating knolls and heights, densely covered with tall, gigantic oaks and beeches. The highway, on which the travellers were riding at the time, led them first past a deep gorge, and then along the base of a precipitous hill, from which a small rivulet rushed noisily into the depth below. Many a by-path intersected the road and penetrated deeper and deeper into the thicket. There were still remote parts of the forest which human feet had rarely or never trodden, and into which no murderous axe had yet penetrated—virginal sanctuaries, clad with all the weird charms of lonely and undefiled nature.

The three travellers had entered one of these by-paths, in the eagerness of their conversation, without noticing that they had left the highway. The wonderful charms of this beautiful wilderness fascinated them. Oh, how glorious was this verdant solitude of the forest! There stood those primeval oaks, the patriarchs of creation, spreading their knotty arms, as if to bless the forest, over the younger generations of slender birch, maple, and chestnut trees. Flexible ivy encircled their gigantic trunks with tender gracefulness; and on their bark grew long-haired, silver-colored mosses, resembling gray beards, light-brown mushrooms, and the mysterious mistletoe, parasitic plants deriving life and nourishment from this curious soil. On the ends of the branches gleamed reddish shoots like quivering flames, symptoms of the still undiminished vigor of the trees.

"Those are splendid fellows," remarked Thomas Egerton, the younger brother, pointing gayly to the giants of the forest. "I do not remember ever having seen here such beautiful oaks, although I have passed through Haywood Forest more than fifty times."

"I believe we have strayed from the highway and penetrated too far into the forest," replied John, the elder brother, who, during his father's lifetime, bore the name and title of Lord Brackley. "This part of the forest is entirely unknown to me."

"But it is gloriously beautiful," exclaimed fair Alice, who was riding on her white palfrey between her two brothers, with radiant eyes. "I should like to stay here all day."

"Like Celia in the play," said Thomas, jestingly. "That remark is characteristic of my dear sister, who always thinks of her Shakespeare. Very well, I am at your service; let us stop here. I shall be your Orlando, if our melancholy Jaques does not object to it."

The merry youth applied this name from Shakespeare's "As You Like It" to his graver brother, who, as the first-born son, according to the custom of the country, exercised a certain authority over his younger brother and sister. However, far from availing himself of his authority now, John yielded to their wishes, although their straying from the highway rendered him more uneasy than he admitted to them.

"Very well," he said, with seeming carelessness, "if you are tired, we may rest here for an hour or so. The sun is yet high in the heavens, and I hope we shall reach the highway again. Let us, in the mean time, take our dinner here in the forest, like Robin Hood, and encamp in the shade of these trees."

"You speak as though you were Solomon himself," exclaimed Thomas, merrily. "I say, like Orlando: 'If this uncouth forest yield any thing savage, I will either be food for it, or bring it for food to thee.'"

With this classical quotation from the well-known old poet, the vivacious youth jumped from his horse and hastened to offer his services as equerry to his beloved sister, while he left to his more sedate brother John the care of fastening the reins of the horses to a tree, and unpacking the provisions which they had brought with them. The young travellers were not accompanied by their servants, as the two youths were sufficient for the protection of their sister, and would not tolerate any vexatious companions near them.

The merry company sat down on the soft green turf, in the shade of one of the primeval oaks, to partake of the frugal repast. The brothers had converted their cloaks into a pleasant seat for Alice, whom they treated in every respect with the kindest attention and solicitude. In their conduct toward her, they combined the tone of fraternal love with the then customary delicate gallantry which dated from the times of Queen Elizabeth, when all England lay admiringly at the feet of the Maiden Queen. The homage rendered to the foremost lady of the world was soon transferred to the whole female sex, and became a matter of fashion. The gentlemen adopted a most sentimental demeanor toward the ladies, and addressed them only in terms of peculiar delicacy and politeness. This exaggerated language of courtesy imparted a certain fantastic charm to the conversation of the brothers with their sister, and added to their mutual sallies the piquancy of a pleasant, arch irony. Thomas, the younger brother, excelled particularly in this respect. He played with evident relish the assumed part of a knight-errant and sentimental shepherd, and it was undeniable that his performance was highly successful. He treated his sister precisely like an imaginary mistress, and lavished on her the most tender and nicely-constructed love-phrases, which he borrowed very happily from the fashionable authors of that period, Sir Philip Sidney and Sir Walter Raleigh.

"Noble lady," he said, placing a dish before her, and speaking in a tone slightly tinged with merry sarcasm, "will you not partake of this tender venison pie? This wing of the grouse longs to make the acquaintance of your sweet lips. Can you be so cruel as to refuse it that favor?"

Laughing and gayly entering into his jest, Alice thanked him exactly in the spirit of the rôle of a romantic young lady.

"What! you are not hungry?" he asked. "Noble lady, is there a secret grief gnawing at your heart, and have you lost your heart with your appetite? Is it the fair-haired Carbury, the cavalier from Wales, who has robbed me of your affections? or is it our philosopher, Sir Kenelm Digby, who, by his magic arts, has inmeshed already many a female heart, although he still plays the heart-broken widower? Answer, or, by Jove! this weapon, which has just carved the juicy mutton ham, will put an end to my miserable existence if you deprive me of all hopes."

"Stop!" cried Alice, with feigned terror. "I swear by chaste Diana and all her nymphs, that neither Carbury nor our cousin Digby is nearer to my heart than you."

"But no third admirer, either? There was at the house of our good aunt Derby a young poet, with so pretty and sentimental a face, that I felt inclined to take him for a girl in disguise, an Arcadian shepherdess. This poet paid the most particular attention to my sweet little sister, and he did not once avert his fiery and eloquent eyes from her charming face."

"I really do not know whom you refer to," said the blushing girl, in evident confusion.

"O Dissimulation, thy name is woman!" exclaimed the youth, in a tone of mock gravity. "Can you really not have noticed at the house of our aunt, the Countess of Derby, a certain John Milton, the poet of the *Arcades?*"

"I did, of course," replied Alice, with seeming indifference. "I have even exchanged a few words with him. He seemed to me taciturn and misanthropic."

"Say rather awkward and clumsy, like most men who hold more intercourse with their books than with the world and men," remarked the elder brother, who had hitherto listened to their conversation in silence.

"I do not consider this awkwardness by any means ridiculous," replied the beautiful girl, in a tone of slight irritation. "Poets are like nightingales; they are silent in a noisy crowd, and sing most beautifully in solitude."

"Well said," remarked Thomas, playfully. "But I prefer this roast pheasant to all your poetical nightingales and similar useless singing-birds."

Alice scoffed, smilingly, at her brother's prosy nature, while he derided merrily and gracefully her predilection for poets and poetry. The elder brother listened for some time to this exchange of witty and amusing sallies, but without forgetting his habitual caution. Already more than once he had anxiously interrupted the playful conversation by the request to put an end to it and start again, as time was passing by with winged speed.

"Only a quarter of an hour yet," begged his lovely sister, who could not make up her mind to leave the delightful spot already.

In fact, Nature had lavished her choicest charms on the place where they were reposing. The green turf and soft moss formed a most beautiful carpet, while the primeval oak arched like a splendid canopy over their youthful heads. Wild rose-bushes covered with fragrant blossoms, snow-white blackthorns, and evergreen laurels formed the neat and graceful border of this natural dining-hall. Aromatic thyme, mint, and the whole countless host of forest herbs and flowers, impregnated the balmy air with sweet perfumes. Vernal air and vernal life filled the beautiful green forest. Finches and linnets vied with each other in singing, and enlivened the silence of nature. At a distance the cuckoo sounded its monotonous yet sweet melancholy notes, and the thrush warbled boldly from lofty tree-tops. Blue and yellow butterflies flitted past, turning around the cups of the flowers and sipping their sweet nectar with their long, fine tongues from golden bowls. Lady-birds with red outside wings, dotted with black, were climbing up the flexible twigs and practising their break-neck acrobatic feats; while a brown squirrel was rocking itself in the highest branches of a slender white birch, and curiously looking down with its piercing eyes. At times a pliable lizard slipped through the soft moss, and a sunbeam gilded its greenish, lustrous body. All these beings were moving in the bright sunshine, and rejoicing in the bliss of their existence; and the young people reposed in the midst of this blessed solitude, themselves the happiest and most contented creatures in the glorious forest. All three were young, handsome, and as yet undefiled by the contact of life and the world, children of Spring, blossoms of May. Therefore, they felt glad and happy in these kindred surroundings. Free from all restraints, they surrendered willingly to the charms of the forest, which they were so loth to leave. Hours glided by like moments, and when they were at length obliged to set out, it seemed to them as though they were parting with their paradise.

The elder brother had to exhort them repeatedly and urgently before the little cavalcade resolved to continue the journey. Even the horses, which had found here a splendid pasture, shook their heads, as it were, disapprovingly, and allowed themselves to be saddled again reluctantly, and amid loud, indignant neighs. Especially did Alice's white palfrey seem to share the predilection of his mistress for this romantic spot. More than once he turned back his head toward the rich pasture which had pleased him so well. At times he even stopped, contrary to his habit, to nibble with his rosy lips at a few herbs and low shrubs on the wayside. Alice willingly permitted these little diversions of her palfrey, and from time to time turned her lovely face toward the cozy nook where she had passed such blissful hours.

Her sensible brother John led the way with restless haste. He did not yet give up the hope of reaching again the highway with which he was thoroughly familiar; but the further they advanced, the stranger and more alarming appeared to him the path which they had taken. Moreover, it soon became quite narrow and impassable. Dense thorn-bushes and rankling weeds bordered it on both sides, and naked roots crept across it like black snakes. The landscape had gradually lost its graceful character, and became gloomier and gloomier. Sombre pines had taken the places of the leafy trees, and shed a melancholy twilight on the scene. The most profound silence reigned far and near; for even the tread of the horses sounded weird and dull on the ground, which was covered with pointed leaves, and, by its slipperiness frequently caused the usually sure feet of the animals to stumble. The apprehension that they had lost their way became soon a certainty in the mind of the anxious leader of the cavalcade.

"We cannot get through here, and must return to the former path," said John.

"We must retrace our steps, eh?" replied the bolder Thomas, who was attracted by every adventure. "By the memory of our great ancestor Robert Malpas, who fought in the battle of Hastings, the motto of our house sounds otherwise: '*Sic donec!*'"

A slight stroke of the riding-whip incited the fiery horse on which the youth was mounted to renewed efforts. Alice kept close behind him, and the more prudent John was obliged to follow the two, contrary to his better conviction. In the outset, fortune seemed to favor the daring brother and sister. The path became for some time again sufficiently broad and convenient, so that the travellers were able to follow it without any special difficulty for more than half a mile. Already they indulged in the pleasant hope that they were in a fair way of reaching the highway again, but they were doomed to a sad disappointment. The insidious path terminated suddenly in close proximity to a gorge which had probably been the bed of a sylvan rivulet. It was in vain that the three turned their eyes with prying glances in all directions. After long and fruitless search, they discovered a narrow footpath which was barely wide enough to afford to a single daring horseman room to penetrate through a labyrinth of thorny hedges and rankling weeds and shrubs. It was impossible for the brothers to expose their delicate sister to the fatigues and even dangers of such a road.

After a brief consultation, John resolved to follow the path, which, in his opinion, would lead him to some human habitation, the hut of a charcoal-burner or the lonely house of a game-keeper. There he hoped to find a guide through this intricate wilderness. Thomas was to remain with his sister, whom he was not to leave under any circumstances. The elder brother enjoined the rash youth repeatedly not to violate this order, and then set out, accompanied by the heart-felt wishes of his brother and sister.

Thomas and Alice remained with their horses near the gorge, which presented a by no means inviting spectacle to their eyes. The traces of the destruction which the swollen forest rivulet caused every spring were distinctly visible all around. The country far and near looked barren and sandy, and covered with the fragments which the furious waters had detached from the mountains. Scanty, dwarfed herbs and ferns cropped out between these *débris*. Sparse and isolated pines and firs of wretched appearance stood here and there. The insidious waters had laid bare the roots, and the fragile trees awaited their downfall whenever a livelier breeze should spring up. Other trees had already succumbed to the violence of the equinoctial storms and the rising waters. These tree-corpses lay broken, with dead branches, and half-rotten. From the moist, decayed bark cropped out poisonous mushrooms, and impudent crows skipped with dismal croaking round the sear, withered twigs.

This gloomy scenery could not but exert a sombre effect on the spirits of Alice and Thomas. The witticism, by which Thomas strove to amuse his sister became somewhat forced. The conversation soon ceased entirely, and both awaited impatiently the return of their brother John. Time hung heavy upon them, and minutes seemed like hours.

"I know brother John," said the youth, after a long pause, almost angrily. "He is always so slow, and I bet he has arrived at some cross-road, and he is so irresolute which direction to take, that he does not stir from the spot."

"You do him injustice," replied Alice, gently. "His caution is praiseworthy, at all events, and he does not deserve your censure. If we had followed his advice and retraced our steps as soon as he asked us to do so, we should doubtless have got back to the right road, and we should have been spared the *ennui* of waiting here."

Notwithstanding the gentle tone in which his sister uttered these words, they were sufficient to irritate and sadden the passionate youth. He accused himself with exaggerated impetuosity of his former folly, and would have shrunk from no danger in order to extricate his beloved sister from the disagreeable predicament in which his rashness had involved her. Moreover, the inactive part assigned to him was highly distasteful. His whole nature urged him to take quick and resolute steps. He jumped up uneasily from the stone on which he had sat hitherto, and paced the brink of the dismal gorge with a nervous step in order to discover another path. Now he looked at the footpath which John had taken, now his eyes turned in the opposite direction, which at all events would lead them somewhere. Pride and ambition filled him with passionate excitement. He wished alone to save them all. The longing for distinction slumbered unknown to him in his young soul. More than once, in his childlike dreams, he had seen himself at the head of a large army and performed miracles of valor. The chivalrous spirit of his times and the thirst for adventures for which his countrymen were noted at that period, filled his bosom. He wished to excel all by his courage and intrepidity, and especially his elder brother, whose preponderance, based as it was on birth and custom, he acknowledged only with the greatest reluctance.

Thus this youthful heart concealed, under the deceptive cover of rashness and recklessness, a burning ambition and thirst for distinction. Vainly did Alice, who often exercised a great deal of authority over him, and stood as a mediatrix between the two brothers, exhort him to be quiet and patient.

"What matters it," she said, soothingly, "if we have to stay here another hour? We shall reach Ludlow Castle even then in time. The day is so fine, and we shall be at home before sundown."

"And there I shall be scolded again," replied the youth, in a tone of irritation. "John will be praised for his prudence, and father will scold me for my rashness."

"We may say that we left aunt's house at an advanced hour of the day. Father shall not learn from us that we lost our way. What good would it do? He would get unnecessarily excited, and would not allow us again to travel alone. And is not this very adventure delightful? We owe to it the charming hours which we passed among the oaks. Come, Orlando, give me your hand, and do not look so gloomy, which does not sit well on you, and which I do not like at all."

In this amiable manner the lovely sister tried to soften the anger of the sullen youth. But that which she had formerly always succeeded in accomplishing was frustrated this time by her brother's intense mortification. He started up at the slightest noise, and listened with eager suspense to every distant sound. Now he believed he heard approaching footsteps, now the sound of human voices.

"Do you hear nothing?" he asked his sister, vehemently. "There must be men here, and, moreover, close by. The sounds I hear proceed distinctly from the gorge yonder."

"Perhaps you are deceived by the rustling of the wind, or the notes of a bird."

"No, no. There are men in the gorge. I will ascertain from them how we may get back to the highway, and will return to you in a few moments."

Before Alice could prevent him, the impatient youth had already disappeared. He pursued his object with a quick step. In the outset Thomas hastened along the dry bed of the rivulet, which afforded him a very convenient path. But fragments of rocks and large heaps of sand soon obstructed the path, and rendered it almost impassable. The youth was obliged to leave it again. However, these obstacles only incited his zeal to redoubled efforts instead of deterring him. On the crest of a neighboring hill which he climbed, he found the distinct traces of many human footsteps. These traces soon increased in number, and intersected each other in different directions. Finally all the footsteps led back to the dry bed of the rivulet, which became passable again. Thomas satisfied himself more and more that human hands had made this hidden path. It did not escape his keen eyes that even the fragments of the rocks had been intentionally piled up in such a manner as to arrest the progress of the uninitiated. This unexpected discovery warned him to be on his guard, and caused him to hesitate; his intrepid heart, however, did not so easily shrink from a dangerous adventure. On the contrary, his daring spirit found only fresh fuel in all these circumstances, and the secret which was concealed here excited his curiosity to the last degree.

Hence, he bravely advanced without further hesitation. The deeper he penetrated into the gorge, the more it expanded at his feet, and it seemed to terminate in a deep, round cleft. However, he was prevented by groups of tall trees and almost impenetrable shrubbery from obtaining a full view of it. A natural hedge of closely interwoven thorn-bushes and young shoots and shrubs seemed suddenly to put a stop to his further progress. Already he had drawn his sword, which, according to the custom of the period, never left his side, in order to open himself a passage through the thicket, when he discovered an artificial door, skilfully concealed behind ivy and pine-branches.

The youth hesitated for a moment, and reflected, contrary to his usual habit, before resolving to penetrate into the mysteries of the wilderness. Poachers and gangs of daring robbers were by no means rare in those days, and perhaps they carried on their unlawful profession in this inaccessible solitude. It was, therefore, unadvisable for a single man to plunge recklessly into such a danger. Besides, Thomas had often heard of secret meetings and illicit organizations of such religious sects as were ruthlessly persecuted by the government. His own father, Lord President of Wales, had been instructed by the government, more than once, to break up such conventicles by main force. Bloody scenes had sometimes ensued, for the Puritans, Separatists, or whatever their names might be, offered a bold and even desperate resistance to their assailants, whenever they were numerous enough to cope with them. Thomas thought also of his sister Alice, whom he had rashly left in the forest all alone and without protection.

All these considerations would have probably induced him to turn back and retrace his steps, had he not been irresistibly captivated at this moment by the loud and swelling notes of a solemn anthem. It was a simple but touching melody which all at once broke the profound silence of the wilderness in so wonderful a manner. He listened breathlessly to the impressive anthem which penetrated in subdued notes to him from a distance. These notes seemed to proceed from choirs of spirits, and not from human lips. He was carried away by them in spite of himself. With a quick motion he opened the mysterious door, and his eyes glanced over the wonderful spectacle suddenly exhibited to his view.

CHAPTER II.

THE FOREST CONVENTICLE.

At his feet the extensive gorge lay now plainly visible. Bordered on all sides by dark beeches and majestic oaks, it formed a natural church, a cathedral which the power of the Creator had erected with invisible hands. The magnificent trees loomed up like imposing Gothic pillars, and their green tops seemed to be the gigantic organ animated by the Lord's breath. The softened rays of the setting sun stole through the foliage, as if through painted church-windows, filling the gorge now with a golden light, now with a purple glow. The soft turf was a comfortable carpet, and in its centre welled forth a sparkling spring as a baptismal font. The first Christians of England had, perhaps, celebrated their secret rites at the same spot when dangers were still besetting them on all sides. To-day their successors were compelled to resort to the same hiding-places. The whole life of humanity is but a repetition, and one page of the history of the world often bears a most striking resemblance to another.

A numerous crowd had assembled here to worship the Lord in the open air and after their own fashion. They were Christians, hated and persecuted by Christians. Their only crime consisted in their refusal to acknowledge the Episcopal Church of England, and in basing their creed exclusively on the Bible and its teachings. Hence, they were obliged to repair to this hiding-place; but God Himself had built for them the church which was refused to them by man, their king, and the then powerful bishops. They had fled hither with their stubborn, immovable courage and faith in God. Men, women, and children, lay around in picturesque groups. On one side a rude pulpit had been constructed with gray slabs of slate piled one above another. On it stood the worthy preacher with silvery hair and beard. His tall, emaciated form was wrapped in a black Genevan coat, devoid of any other marks of distinction. He never would have donned the surplice of the Anglican clergy; for it was an abomination in his eyes, because it reminded him of Babylon and Antichrist, which were the titles he applied to the Roman Catholic Church and the detested Pope. The pale face of the preacher bore distinct traces of profound sufferings and the prison air which he had breathed for a long time. But all these persecutions had been unable to damp his zeal, and no sooner had the faithful pastor been released than he had returned to his anxious flock, ready at any moment to suffer the same martyrdom for the sake of his faith. The Rev. Samuel God-will-be-my-help (such was the name which he had assumed in accordance with the custom of the Puritans of that time) awaited the conclusion of the psalm which his congregation was singing, when he delivered one of those impassioned sermons so well calculated to fire the hearts of his audience, and render them proof against the persecutions of the government and the bishops.

Round the pulpit and the preacher stood or sat groups of the most different aspect. Thomas, who was concealed merely by the trunk of a tree, was able to distinguish the several persons from his stand-point. Most of those present were poor people, of lowly condition; but among them was to be seen here and there the form of a wealthier farmer or a well-to-do commoner.

It is true, the difference of their costumes was but slight. Nearly all wore plain black woollen doublets and breeches, white stockings, and shoes on which rosettes of dark-colored ribbons filled the places of silver buckles. Their heads were covered with pointed hats, likewise devoid of any ornaments. There were no waving plumes, no golden clasps, or bright-colored trimmings, such as were required by the ostentatious taste of that period. Their hair was clipped even and short around their heads. At that time, when long and neatly-curled ringlets were deemed peculiarly becoming, and were generally worn, the reverse could not but be the more surprising, and therefore called forth the nickname of "Roundheads," which was applied to the members of this denomination by their enemies. They called themselves children of God, or the chosen people. In full harmony with this sombre simplicity of dress was an air of gloomy fanaticism prevailing in the whole assembly. Almost all faces exhibited the same expression of sullen defiance and self-conscious energy. Sufferings of every description had aroused their power of resistance, and the firm conviction of the truth of their principles, and the ultimate victory of the good cause, had imparted to them a pride which was not devoid of haughtiness, and which greatly increased the exasperation of their enemies. It was plainly to be seen that these strong, heavy-built men submitted to circumstances only with inward rage, and that they were waiting impatiently for the day of retribution. A close observer might have read in their faces, besides the marked expression of piety, an almost savage determination; and while their lips were singing the psalm with great unction, their eyes shot fire whenever the words alluded to the adversaries of the Lord—a designation which they applied, of course, to their own hated enemies.

This austere and repulsive impression was somewhat softened by the presence of the women and children. Even among the former, there were not wanting sombre forms, with hard, disagreeable features; the majority, however, and particularly the younger generation among them, were distinguished for a certain mild enthusiasm, which lent an additional charm to their generally fresh and beautiful faces. Their dress, too, notwithstanding its Puritanic simplicity, was not so monotonous and sombre as that of the men. Female vanity and coquetry found even under the most unfavorable circumstances a way of skilfully adding here a ribbon, there a pretty little knot. The small white, close-fitting caps imparted even a singularly prepossessing appearance to many a youthful face, and worldly feeling cropped out now and then notwithstanding the semblance of austere piety. Thomas, who possessed a most refined taste in such matters, noticed among the young girls several who might have risked a comparison with his beautiful sister Alice.

The youth made such observations from his hiding-place only long after the notes of the anthem, which had attracted him so powerfully, had died away. After a brief pause, the preacher was about to begin his sermon. The congregation thronged closer round the pulpit, probably to hear better what the worthy minister would say to them. Curiosity, and his adventurous spirit, induced Thomas likewise to leave his safe hiding-place. He stole, slipping along cautiously between the trees, toward the side of the gorge where the pulpit had been erected. This was not noticed by anybody, and the first success restored his former boldness to the daring youth. He had long wished to hear a sermon from a Puritan preacher, and his merry spirit depicted to him the intense enjoyment which he would derive from the speaker's nasal tone and ridiculous gestures; for, in accordance with the universal belief of the Episcopalians, he thought every Puritan minister must preach in that style.

After the usual murmuring and hemming, which are heard in all large assemblies on such occasions, had died away, the Rev. Samuel God-will-be-my-help commenced speaking, amidst a silence so profound, that the rustling of the foliage in the breeze and the bubbling of the spring were distinctly to be heard. The men looked grave and gloomy, and even the female part of the congregation manifested unusual attention. It was evident that these people yearned sincerely for the Word of God, for the sake of which they had come from distant parts of the country, and were incurring the greatest dangers.

"People of Israel, listen to me," said the minister, in a low, tremulous voice, which, during the progress of the sermon, became louder and louder. "Your enemies are increasing from day to day, and the number of your adversaries is legion; but fear not, for the Lord is with you. He will be your protector, and strike down your adversaries with the strength of His arm. A king has arisen in our midst worse than Pharaoh, who oppressed the chosen people, and imposed the most laborious services on them; but we still likewise have a Moses, who will strike him down with the keen edge of his sword, and bury him and his whole host in the deep bed of the sea. Bear with patience the sufferings which you have to endure, and resist the temptations to which you are exposed; for the plagues of Egypt will come upon the tyrant and his evil advisers. He is intent on compelling you to worship the foreign idols, and bend your knees after the fashion of Rome. His bishops are strutting about in unholy vestments, and smell of superstition and idolatry. Woe to them! They leave untried no means to induce the pious flock to deviate from the right path. They threaten the true believers with shackles and imprisonment, and lacerate their backs with sharp scourges. Who is there among us that could not bear testimony to their cruel rigor?"

A low murmur of assent broke the solemn stillness for a moment. On remembering the oppressions which they had undergone, the men clinched their fists involuntarily, and their threatening faces betrayed only too plainly the rage which they restrained with difficulty.

"Heavy penalties in person or property," continued the aged minister, "have been inflicted more or less upon us all; but the sun will sooner deviate from his course, and rise in the west instead of the east, than we should prove recreant to the Lord and His commandments. He will not forsake His faithful believers, but raise them from the dust to greater splendor. Only a brief space of time, and all Israel will rise as one man, and wreak vengeance on his tormentors. I tell you, and the Lord speaketh out of my mouth, the day will soon dawn when the children of God shall enter the New Jerusalem. Then the chosen people will rejoice exceedingly, and the impious wretches will tremble on account of their ruthlessness. Therefore, be glad and hopeful, bear new burdens with patience, until the moment comes when you may throw them off. But we will not await the day of retribution in vain idleness. Let the peasant grind his scythe, for the harvest is drawing nigh; let the warrior whet his sword for the bloody work which is in store for us. Up, up, my people; prepare for the day of retribution; arm your hands, and unfurl your holy standard!"

The preacher paused again, exhausted by his effort. His fragile body was no longer sufficient for the fiery zeal of this soul, exasperated by all sorts of sufferings and persecutions. He tried to gather fresh strength, in order to continue in the same violent strain. While he was speaking, his deep-lying eyes, concealed under the gray shaggy brows, shot fire, and his emaciated form seemed to grow in size. His words fired the sufficiently prepared and susceptible hearts of his audience. The whole congregation was carried away and plunged into a state of violent excitement. Old and new wrongs which they had endured rankled in the breasts of the men, and they remembered with gnashing teeth the tortures which they had suffered but recently.

Somewhat different was the impression which the sermon produced upon the youth who happened to have fallen among these enthusiasts.

He could not laugh at it as he had expected at first, for his own position was too alarming for that, and the bearing of the whole assembly was too grave and stern. A mixture of sympathy and repugnance captivated him in spite of himself. The son of the Lord President of Wales had been educated in the strictest principles of loyalty and attachment to his king and the Episcopal Church of England, and he shared, moreover, the prejudices of his age, and of most of the members of his class, against the votaries of Puritanism. Their austere, morose bearing, and their simple, sombre costume were looked upon as hypocrisy, and were by no means calculated to enlist the sympathies of merry youths and overbearing courtiers. The seditious words of the preacher wounded his loyal feelings; nevertheless, he could not deny that what he heard and saw exhibited a certain dignity and simple grandeur. He was fascinated in spite of himself, and disregarded the requirements of caution, so far as to give up his reserve, and approach gradually closer and closer to the circle of the audience. While the worthy minister was speaking, his sermon engrossed the attention of the congregation so exclusively, that they overlooked the appearance of the young newcomer. It was only during the pause now ensuing that the immediate bystanders perceived him. The presence of a stranger, whose rich and striking dress, and defiant bearing, seemed to indicate that he was an impudent intruder and an enemy of the children of God, was sufficient to inflame still further the excitement already prevailing among the Puritans. The rage and hatred of the assembly had suddenly found a definite target. The rash youth was immediately surrounded by a threatening crowd; wild and distrustful glances met him, and loud imprecations burst forth in whatever direction he tried to turn. The universal exasperation increased from second to second. Already some of the men had stretched out their arms toward him; already Thomas, who awoke only now to a full sense of his dangerous position, had put his hand on the hilt of his sword, in order, if need be, to repel violence by violence, even though without any prospect of success; when, all at once, a vigorous gentleman of distinguished and almost chivalrous bearing, ordered the excited crowd to be still. The preacher, too, being prevented by the sudden uproar from resuming the thread of his sermon, had descended from the pulpit and hastened to the scene of the disturbance as quickly as his infirmity permitted.

"Who is this youth, and what does he want here?" asked the before-mentioned gentleman, who seemed to exercise a certain authority over the Puritans.

"A spy who has watched us and intends to betray us," cried the men on all sides.

"You lie!" replied Thomas, courageously. "An accident has brought me hither and made me a witness of your meeting. What should your cant and sanctimonious doings concern me otherwise? I care not so much as that about them."

"Hear the impious rascal!" roared the furious crowd. "Down with the wretch, down with the son of Belial!"

The imprudent words which the rash youth had uttered had aggravated his danger materially. Vainly did the aged minister and his companion endeavor to allay the fury of the excited congregation. Some of the men laid their hands upon Thomas, who, with quick determination, now unsheathed his sword. However, before he had been able to make a dangerous use of his weapon, it had already been wrested from his hand. Thus disarmed, the youth was exposed to the wrath of his exasperated adversaries. He stamped angrily with his foot, and his impotent rage drew a tear from his eye. Thus he stood, with glowing cheeks and defiant face, in the midst of the crowd. The women, too, had hastened to the spot, and were now contemplating, with a mixture of compassion and anxiety, the handsome youth, who seemed to them by no means so dangerous as he did to the rude and distrustful men.

The sight of the flashing blade, which fortunately had done no further harm, had filled them with increased rage. The imprecations and threats levelled at the intruder became more violent from minute to minute. Only the presence of the worthy minister and the other gentleman protected Thomas from corporal injuries. After reëstablishing some degree of order, these two held a brief consultation. They spoke in a low whisper of the entirely unexpected incident which, to them also, seemed fraught with danger. While this consultation was going on, the congregation observed a grave and measured attitude toward the prisoner, whose arms were held by two strong men, for the purpose of rendering it impossible for him to escape or offer further resistance.

After a short pause, during which Thomas had had an opportunity to indulge in not over-pleasant reflections upon the predicament in which he was placed, the gentleman who seemed to be leader or elder of the congregation approached and addressed him.

"You have intruded in a manner entirely uncalled for into this asylum," he said to the youth, with calm dignity. "Our safety requires me to put to you some questions which you will answer frankly and truthfully. Above all things give me your name."

"I do not know with what right you dare subject me to a regular examination," replied Thomas, whose defiant spirit was not broken, but rather strengthened by the danger.

"Our right is the right of the stronger, and we make the same use of it to-day as our adversaries. Take the advice of an older and more experienced man, and do not aggravate your position by such untimely superciliousness. I request you once more, sir, to give me your name."

"I shall not do so before you have told me yours."

This bold reply excited another outburst of indignation among the Puritans, and it required all the authority of their leader to quiet the exasperated men. After he had succeeded in so doing, he turned with a smile to the rash youth.

"I do not know," he replied, "why I should conceal my name from you. It is Overton."

"Overton, Sir John Overton!" exclaimed the youth, in surprise. "Your name is not unknown to me. If I am not mistaken, I have heard it mentioned repeatedly, and with great respect, at my father's house. You are, therefore, a cavalier like myself."

"Now you will certainly not hesitate to comply with my request, and will no longer conceal your name from me."

"My name is Thomas Egerton."

"Son of the Lord President of Wales."

"And I can bear witness that the young man tells you the truth," interposed a deep, grave voice, which issued from the mouth of a gloomy-looking old man.

Thomas turned his eyes involuntarily to the side where stood the speaker, whom he had not hitherto noticed in the crowd. He likewise now recognized the old man, by whose side was standing a lovely young girl in the costume of the rural population. Her blue eyes met the dark ones of the youth, and a sudden blush suffused the fine and highly-expressive face of the beautiful girl. No one in the assembly took any notice of this brief *intermezzo*, and yet it was a significant meeting after a long separation. The features of the young girl awakened many feelings and reminiscences in the soul of the youth. Lucy Henderson (that was the name of the old man's daughter) had been Alice's foster-sister and the playmate of her brothers while they were children. At that time she passed whole days at the castle of the Egertons, and participated in all the games and amusements of the highborn young people. She even attended their lessons very frequently, and in this manner Lucy had received an education such as is to be found only in exceptional cases among persons of her class. Her father, morose old Henderson, had arrived here years ago from a distant country, and settled in the neighborhood of Ludlow Castle. His wife, who had died since then, had nursed Alice Egerton in her infancy; and thus the two girls, of the same age, grew up together. Their friendship continued even after Mrs. Henderson's death; but for a long time past these intimate relations had been interrupted. The older Mr. Henderson became, the more stubborn and sombre became his temper, which had always been strongly tinctured with melancholy. The neighbors attributed this change, which did not escape them, to the loss of his beloved wife; for while she was alive he was by far more sociable and kind in his own peculiar way toward his fellow-men. Gradually, however, he retired more and more from the world, and broke off all intercourse with the inmates of Ludlow Castle, who had done nothing to justify such neglect. The Countess of Bridgewater especially had always manifested the greatest kindness toward the Henderson family, and lavished favors and presents on little Lucy. These kindnesses were rejected now by the rough widower with insulting haughtiness; and he allowed his daughter no longer to hold intercourse with her aristocratic playmates and friends.

Despite her tears and objections, she was finally obliged to yield and give up the intercourse which was so dear to her. Years had elapsed since then, and Lucy had become a blooming young girl, while her friend Thomas, whom she had always preferred to his elder and graver brother, was now a vigorous and fine-looking youth. Under circumstances so altered occurred the first meeting of the formerly so intimate young friends after their long separation.

This was neither the right place nor the right time for them to give expression to their mutual surprise. The two greeted each other silently with a scarcely perceptible nod of the head, accompanied by a tender glance on the part of the youth, and a sweet blush and joyous tremor on that of the lovely Lucy. The old acquaintances renewed their former friendship on this strange occasion without exchanging their sentiments, and engraved each other's portraits on their hearts. Had they been at liberty to give expression to their feelings, they would certainly have burst out into the exclamation: "Oh, how handsome and tall you have grown!"

In the presence of this large assembly, however, they were obliged to repress any such utterances; but the more silent their lips remained, the more eloquent was the language of their eyes.

Under such circumstances, a moment often decides the course of a whole human life, and the inclination violently repressed for the time soon seeks and finds an opportunity to reveal itself in its full extent and irrepressible intensity. Never before had the young girl appeared so charming and desirable to the youth; never had lovely Lucy had an inkling of the passion with which the unexpected aspect of her former playmate filled her heart. Both longed to approach each other after so long a separation; both felt irresistibly drawn toward each other. No one in the whole assembly, and least of all old Henderson, suspected what was taking place in these young hearts. Only a remnant of his former gratitude, perhaps, induced the old Puritan to intercede in behalf of the youth.

Thomas was so embarrassed on account of his wonderful meeting with Lucy, that he forgot its immediate cause and his still by no means pleasant position. Henderson's words, however, had evidently produced an effect decidedly favorable to him. The immediate bystanders assumed a more peaceable attitude toward him, and no longer uttered any threats against him. Both the reverend minister and the chivalrous Overton even fixed looks of sympathy on the more rash than guilty youth.

"I am glad," said Overton, "that so good a man as our friend Henderson bears testimony to the truthfulness of your words; but this does not yet explain or excuse your uncalled-for intrusion into this asylum. How did you get here?"

"That is easily explained. I lost my way in Haywood Forest."

"I believe you, as your whole bearing breathes youthful sincerity, and as I cannot imagine that you have come hither for the purpose of watching or even betraying our meeting."

"Sir, I believe my name alone is sufficient to protect me from any such suspicion," cried Thomas, vehemently.

"I will admit that," replied Overton, whose calmness and firmness contrasted strikingly with the rash vehemence of the youth. "But who warrants us that you will not betray hereafter what you have seen here? You may purposely or rashly communicate to others what an accident made you discover."

"Sir John Overton!" exclaimed Thomas, crimsoning with indignation, "only my present helplessness allows you to use such unchivalrous language. By the escutcheon of my ancestors, had I my sword at my side, I should call you to a bloody account for this insult."

"You would do better to repress your somewhat proud and impertinent language. Look around; these good people here are not in a very playful humor, as you have found out already. Their safety, their property, nay, perhaps their lives are at stake, for the cruelty of their tormentors knows no compassion. For this reason, you cannot blame either them or myself, if we ask of you some better security than the mere name of Egerton and the worm-eaten escutcheon of your ancestors."

"I hope you will be satisfied with a nobleman's word of honor," replied the youth, gnashing his teeth, and scarcely able to restrain another outburst of his rage.

"A nobleman's word of honor, perhaps, might satisfy me; but those men yonder will demand additional security. They know what it is worth since the first nobleman of England, King Charles, has broken his word and violated his sacred pledges more than ten times."

This was too much for the deeply-mortified youth. Brought up in sentiments of unbounded loyalty, he could sooner bear insults heaped on himself than the least attack upon the honor of his king. With a cry of rage, he broke loose from the men who held him, and rushed upon Overton, after having previously wrested his sword from the hands of the Puritan who had taken it from him. Overton avoided the impetuous lunge of the furious youth by a skilful turn. At the next moment he had likewise unsheathed his sword, and one who beheld the firmly-knit form of the man, his strong arm, the coolness and composure of his whole bearing, and compared it with the blind fury and scarcely-developed form of the youth, could not for a moment entertain the slightest doubt as to the issue of this unequal contest.

Only the predilection which the English entertain at all times for scenes of this description, and respect for courage and manly deportment, prevented the assembly from interfering between the two. Despite their Puritan austerity, these grave men had preserved their former relish for such spectacles. The circle widened at once, that the two fencers might have sufficient room. The duellists, so unlike each other, stood in the centre and crossed their flashing swords. All around reigned anxious silence, which even the worthy minister did not venture to break by a word of peace. Thomas attacked his adversary with his customary wild impetuosity, so that Overton had enough to do to ward off the strokes and thrusts showered down upon him in rapid succession. At first the calmer Overton seemingly intended to remain entirely on the defensive; but no sooner had the impetuous youth rashly exhausted his strength, than the practised swordsman turned this advantage to account and gave up his passive attitude.

The spectators followed the course of the contest with increasing suspense, and their flashing eyes and flushed faces plainly indicated that a majority of them were no strangers to the profession of arms. A murmur of applause burst from the crowd whenever Overton parried a stroke of his adversary with the coolness peculiar to him, or skilfully evaded one of his furious lunges; just acknowledgments were likewise rendered to the courage of the youth, but the homage thus paid to him was blended with expressions of the dissatisfaction felt at his haughty conduct. But no one contemplated the scene with more intense agitation than charming Lucy Henderson. She had advanced as close as possible to the duellists, and watched them with flushed cheeks, trembling limbs, and breathless suspense.

The decision was still in doubt. What was wanting to the youth in strength and practice, he made up for by his impetuosity, while Overton supplied his lack of fire by his caution and skill. It was a wonderful spectacle to behold the blooming Thomas, with his waving blonde ringlets, his flushed face, and his slender form, fighting with the heavy-set Overton, whose face did not betray even the slightest emotion. No greater contrast could be imagined than that presented by the impetuosity of the one and the calmness of the other. Youth and mature manhood seemed to measure their strength in this arena. Neither could hardly find again worthier representatives of their respective advantages.

The contest had lasted a considerable time, when the cool Overton thought it was best to put a stop to it. In doing so, however, he by no means intended to inflict great bodily harm on our courageous Thomas. With keen-eyed sagacity, he seemed to account the many advantages which the rash valor of his adversary offered to him. He parried quietly and skilfully the stroke which Thomas levelled at him, and then, with his full strength, struck the sword from the youth's hand before the latter was able to prevent it. In doing this, he could not avoid inflicting on Thomas a slight wound, whence the red warm blood trickled down and fell in dark drops on the green turf.

No sooner did Lucy perceive that the friend of her youth was wounded, than she uttered a piercing cry, and sank, fainting and with eyes closed, into the arms of the bystanders.

The vanquished Thomas stood blushing and disarmed before his triumphant adversary. Overton, however, was not inclined to follow up the advantage which he had obtained. He magnanimously lowered his sword, which he sheathed with his wonted calmness. His chivalrous conduct did not fail to exert a soothing effect upon the youth. Overton had given him his life, which had been at his mercy. The feeling of gratitude which animated him, however, was dimmed by the mortification of his wounded vanity.

"You have spared me," he said, in a tremulous voice. "According to the old-established custom, I am in your debt. You may fix the amount of my ransom."

"Let the silence which you will observe in regard to what you have seen here be your ransom. You will give me your word of honor as a cavalier that you will do so."

"I promise upon honor not to betray you."

"You must not inform anybody of this mysterious hiding-place which an accident caused you to discover, nor even speak of it to your nearest relatives. Whenever and wherever one of those present here may meet you, you swear that you will feign not to know him?"

"I swear."

"And now you are free, and may leave the place, and return by the same road by which you came."

The youth proceeded immediately to avail himself of the permission thus given to him, and leave the meeting which he had disturbed. It was with the most varied feelings filling his heart that he set out to retrace his steps. Shame and mortification at his discomfiture took the foremost place among these feelings. Though obliged to render homage to Overton's magnanimous conduct, he wished to meet him soon again, sword in hand, and measure his strength with him under more favorable circumstances. His prejudices against the sectarianism of the Puritans had been increased rather than lessened by his meeting with them. Only the image of lovely Lucy Henderson shed a pleasant light on all the clouds rising in his soul. He thoughtfully entered the path which was to lead him back to his sister Alice.

The pious congregation, too, was in a state of anxious suspense and absence of mind. The service had been interrupted and disturbed by the events that had taken place. Some of the Puritans were not at all satisfied with Overton's conduct. In their opinion, he ought not to have contented himself with the mere parole of the haughty youth, but should have demanded of him a solemn oath on the Bible. The more fanatical in the assembly went further, and censured Overton for allowing Thomas to depart on any conditions. There were among them men who did not even shrink from the thought of a bloody deed. They would have unhesitatingly committed a crime when their safety was at stake. They murmured aloud now, and it required Overton's whole authority and the soothing eloquence of the venerable minister to prevent them from taking further steps. They wished to pursue Thomas and yet carry out their cruel purpose. To justify this, they quoted a number of passages from the Bible, especially the Old Testament, which they interpreted after their peculiar fashion.

While the men were discussing in this manner, the compassionate women attended to Lucy, who had not yet recovered from her swoon. They fetched water from the neighboring spring in the vessels which they had brought with them, and sprinkled with it the pale cheeks and forehead of the young girl. A few experienced matrons, in the mean time, rubbed fragrant forest-herbs, by whose piquant ethereal odor they wished to arouse her slumbering vital spirits. At length their united efforts succeeded in restoring Lucy to consciousness. She opened her eyes wonderingly, and turned her first glance to the spot where the duel had just taken place.

"Where is he?" she breathed, in a faint voice, on not beholding the youth.

The wondering women deemed this, to them, incomprehensible question a new wandering of her mind, and were unable to answer it, or even interpret it correctly. It was only from the lips of her father that Lucy learned the fate of her playmate, and that he had left the place without sustaining any severe injuries. This agreeable news brought about her speedy recovery, and she was able to accompany her father when he departed with the whole congregation and returned to his home.

ALICE

p. 21.

CHAPTER III.

ALICE AND COMUS.

In the mean time, Alice awaited in solitude the return of her brother. His sudden disappearance occasioned her at first but little uneasiness, as she was already familiar with the impetuosity of his proceedings. She believed, moreover, that he could not have gone very far, and would be back in the course of a few minutes. It was not until he had stayed away much longer than she had expected, that she became seriously alarmed. She possessed as much courage as any woman would have under similar circumstances, and soon succeeded, therefore, in overcoming her rising apprehensions. She sought and found an occupation to divert her idle thoughts. She had discovered on the edge of the gorge a few flowers, forget-me-nots and pansies, which she resolved to gather and make a wreath of them. She went quickly to work, and it was not long before she was done. With childlike joy she placed the pretty wreath on her blond head after removing the inconvenient barret-cap. But Thomas had not yet returned, and she gave way again to her anxiety, although she tried to overcome it by deriding it and thinking of other and more pleasant subjects. In the first place, she remembered the beautiful hours which she had passed at the hospitable house of her relatives. The castle of her aunt, the Countess of Derby, had always been the rendezvous of the high aristocracy and the neighboring gentry. In its high and ancient halls reigned a cheerful tone of refined sociability and culture. Alice had there made the acquaintance of ladies and gentlemen of eminent accomplishments and fascinating manners, and had found among the latter many an admirer of her budding charms. Although no one had made a deeper impression on her innocent heart, she had not been insensible to the attentions and homage rendered to her. With feminine, but certainly venial vanity, she now dwelt in her recollections mostly upon those who had distinguished her in this manner. There appeared before her excited imagination now the image of the nobleman from Wales to whom her brother Thomas had alluded, now the expressive face of Kenelm Digby, a gentleman then already famous both for his eccentricities and his learning—a relative of the Derby family, who had abducted, married, and lost by her speedy death a daughter of the noble house, the beautiful and eccentric Lady Venetia Stanley. The various rumors which Alice had heard in regard to the eminent gentleman, were in themselves calculated to excite her liveliest interest in him and his strange doings. Moreover, he was surrounded by a certain veil of mystery which always inflames the susceptible imagination of women and interests their sentimental hearts.

A third gentleman played a prominent part in her recollections. It was a modest poet, named John Milton, with delicate, almost girlish features, of great intellectual beauty. Only in moments of enthusiasm and inspiration did he overcome his innate timidity, and display a wealth of sublime and charming ideas which could not but surprise the listener the more, the less he had previously suspected him to be possessed of such faculties. It had not escaped Alice that his dreamy hazel eyes followed her whenever they could do so without being noticed. Besides, she herself had witnessed the triumph which his poetical genius had achieved. A charming mask, entitled "The Arcades," and written by Milton, was performed at the aunt's house and received with rapturous applause by the whole audience. Only Kenelm Digby did not seem to share the favorable opinion of all others; but Alice was delighted with the melodious verses and their poetical sentiments. She deemed it even incumbent on her to express her joy to the poet, and her heart-felt praise had called a blush of modesty to his cheeks, paled by nocturnal studies. But modesty, perhaps, was not the only cause of his blushing: it was occasioned even more by his rising love for the sweet girl. Like the poets of all times, young Milton possessed a heart susceptible of the power of love. Whether the charming Alice perceived or even shared his affection, we venture to decide the less, as she herself, not yet fully conscious of her own sentiments, resembled a bud, filled much more with vague anticipations and longing than well-defined wishes and thoughts.

All these recollections did not assume a definite shape, but passed before the girl's soul like dissolving views and fleeting shadows. This dreaming with open eyes, something by no means unusual in young persons of the hopeful age of seventeen, soon passed into a real, gentle slumber. The long journey and unwonted sojourn in the open air had rendered Alice tired and exhausted. Her weariness was increased by the stillness surrounding her, broken only by the monotonous rustling of the wind in the tree-tops, or the mournful notes of a bird which had strayed into this melancholy wilderness. Vainly she struggled against her sleepiness; her beautiful eyes closed gradually, and her fair head sank down to the soft turf. The images and ideas of her fancy became confused and dissolved like thin clouds, from which the fantastic god of dreams shaped all sorts of wonderful forms. As echo renders the real tone, these dissolving views echoed the events of her immediate past. Before the closed eyes of the girl appeared the lofty halls of Castle Derby, with its pinnacles and towers glistening in the rays of the setting sun. The sunbeams were transformed into devouring flames which seized her dress, and threatened to burn her. Already she believed herself irretrievably lost, when a heavenly form bearing the familiar features of John Milton flitted down to her. With a strong arm he lifted her from the burning ruins, rising with her above the smoke and the hissing flames, and borne aloft by the powerful silver wings growing from his shoulders. Only after reaching a golden star did he repose with his sweet burden; sacred music received them there; choirs of angels intoned hymns sweeter than she had ever heard before. Her Saviour, too, seized a harp hanging on a golden pillar, and the most sublime melodies fell from His lips. The poet grew taller and taller, his whole form glowed with the light of transfiguration, and the strings of the harp turned into radiant rivers flowing from heaven down to earth. His words became figures and assumed now human, now supernatural forms. A man and a woman stood under a tree full of tempting fruits; but coiled around its trunk she saw the serpent, whose head bore the features of the famous Kenelm Digby. Suddenly the modest Carbury approached, unsheathed his sword, and sundered the head of the serpent with a powerful blow from the trunk; but from the drops of its blood sprang countless infernal demons, who were dancing with horrible grimaces and scornful laughter about the terrified girl.

Louder and louder grew the laughter of the demons, and, blended with it, she seemed to hear the notes of wild music. Alice opened her eyes wonderingly, but she thought she was dreaming on, for the demons whom she had seen in her slumbers surrounded her couch. It was a troop of wild, daring fellows in all sorts of fantastic costumes. The procession was headed by a band of strangely-dressed musicians, who made an infernal noise with their instruments. Some of them were disguised as Moors, and had blackened their faces; in their hands they held small drums, tambourines, and cymbals, which they were striking together. Others were dressed in the skins of wild beasts, and had placed wreaths of young oak-leaves and evergreen ivy on their shaggy heads; they were playing on the shawm or sounding well-known street-airs on squeaking pipes.

The longer Alice stared at these strange forms, the faster returned her consciousness. Her fear of the demons soon gave place to a still greater anxiety. She perceived at once that she was in the midst of a merry, drunken gang of so-called May-dancers, who were returning from some rural festival, and into whose hands she had fallen alone and defenceless. . A majority of the band consisted of young peasant-lads who would treat a solitary young girl with little or no delicacy. Escape was not to be thought of; hence, Alice submitted to her fate, firmly resolved to ward off all undue familiarities of the dancers by her determined bearing, and by mentioning her name and position.

The band had surprised the fair sleeper under the trees and awakened her by their deafening noise. Alice had jumped up in terror; with flushed cheeks, and her heart throbbing with anxiety, she awaited the result of the dangerous adventure. She yet wore the wreath of forget-me-nots on her blond hair, which had become loosened during her slumber, and was flowing in golden ringlets round her forehead and her white neck. Her slender, sylph-like form was wrapped in a green hunting-dress, and a short silken mantilla of the same color waved on her shoulders in the breeze. She had hastily picked up the riding-whip, the only weapon with which she could defend herself. On the ground lay her barret-cap with the waving plume, and her white palfrey and the horse of her absent brother were grazing close by.

Whether it was owing to the surpassing beauty of the young girl, whose appearance made a fairy-like impression upon the beholder, or the expression of innocence and noble dignity animating her features, the rude band seemed to hesitate at first and keep aloof respectfully, feeding their eyes with the beautiful spectacle so suddenly presented to them. Even vulgar persons feel in such moments the majesty surrounding the head of an innocent maiden, as if with a protecting halo, and the power of true beauty is so great that it strikes even vulgar men like a revelation from above, and silences all worldly desires. A murmur of applause greeted the fair girl.

"By St. George," exclaimed one of the dancers, "there stands the fairy of Haywood Forest."

"I will accost her," said another.

"Beware! Do you not see that she holds her magic wand in her hands? If you irritate her, she will transform you into a donkey."

"And you into a sheep."

"Let me manage it," shouted a stout lad, who seemed to be the leader of the band. "I shall speak a confidential word to the beauty of the forest, and I will bet a rose-noble that she will not bewitch me for it immediately. You do not know how to speak to spirits and sylphs."

"Yes, Billy knows it," cried the first speaker; "his grandmother was an old witch, and he learned it from her."

"And your grandmother is the devil's cousin. Attention now, and see how I am going to manage it."

The merry lad now advanced toward Alice with all sorts of odd leaps and laughable bows. He was about twenty-four years old; his form was short and wiry; two exceedingly shrewd black eyes flashed in his keen face. His red nose indicated an intimate acquaintance with the bottle, and his full, fleshy cheeks, as well as his round paunch, showed that he was an epicure of the lowest class. His low forehead and shaggy hair were covered with a green cap, which he wore on his ears, and on which the long plume of a peacock was waving. The short doublet which he wore was held together by a broad leathern belt, in which hung a large soup-ladle in place of a sword. His thick neck and broad breast were covered with a very short cloak, which was trimmed with lambs' tails instead of princely ermine, and set all over with diminutive bells, tinkling merrily at every step he made. In his hands he held a half-emptied bottle and a brown staff, the top of which was a fool's head, rudely carved out of the wood. This queer figure rested, moreover, on two crooked legs, loosely encased in white stockings, covering only a part of his plump hairy calves.

This fellow now approached Alice, who was by no means reassured at his sight. Distorting his large mouth, which was dotted with white, pointed teeth, into a broad grin, he saluted her with exaggerated and ludicrous politeness.

"Most beautiful of all fairies," he said to her, "pardon me if I take the liberty of approaching you; but it would be wrong in me not to render homage to so extraordinary a beauty. Permit me, therefore, to drink first your health out of this bottle, and then hand it to you, that you may do likewise."

So saying, he raised the bottle to his thick lips and drank a long draught from it, after which he presented it to her. She pushed back his rude hand with a gesture of horror, so that the bottle fell to the ground and broke noisily in pieces.

"Aha!" cried the fellow, angrily; "you are proud, and refuse to drink with me. Do you know, my little sweetheart, my supercilious fairy princess, whom you have insulted? I am at least as good as you, if not better. You behold in my person the king of all fools, the prince of folly, the sovereign of all merry people, the king of jest. Just distend your lovely eyes, and however disdainfully you may turn up your tiny nose, however contemptuously you may curl your sweet cherry-lips, you will whistle another tune so soon as you have heard my name, rank, and title; for there stands before you no other than Comus, the god of festive joy and mirth, whose rule is acknowledged by all England. Condescend, therefore, to pledge me."

At a beck which the man made to his companions, another bottle was brought to him. He presented it to the girl. In order not to increase his anger, Alice resolved reluctantly to comply with his request, and, bowing slightly, she raised the bottle to her lips.

"That is right," said the extemporized god. "I see that you are submissive, and I hope we shall get along very well with each other. It was my intention long since to give up my bachelor life and marry a lady of equal rank. Your heavenly appearance has kindled the flame of love in my heart, and I feel that its ardor is increasing every minute. Fair Gloriana, most beautiful of fairies! give me your soft white hand, that we may form an everlasting union. I place you on my throne. From this hour you shall share my crown and be the queen of the kingdom of fools."

Alice's situation became more and more painful; she did not know what to reply, or what course she ought to adopt under such circumstances. After a brief reflection, she deemed it best to join in the jolly tone of the dancers, and converse with them in the same strain. The fellow who had addressed her displayed, despite his rudeness and impertinence, uncommon wit and a jolly kindheartedness which somewhat reassured her; and she resolved to gain him by her complaisance, instead of irritating him by ill-advised defiance. Above all things, it was important for her to gain time, as she might momentarily look for the return of her absent brothers. All these reasons induced her to adopt a conciliatory manner, and turn the unpleasant adventure into a joke. She, therefore, replied as follows:

"Great and powerful Comus! your proposals take me so much by surprise that I really feel embarrassed. Your power and rank are well known to me; for all England is aware that you are one of the most distinguished gods. Your realm is certainly the largest in the world, for fools will never be wanting to it. The renown of your exploits has penetrated to my ears, and I have often heard of you and the brilliant court which you hold in various parts of this island, and particularly in Oakley Park. I bless my star, therefore, for permitting me to see you and your peers face to face, and obtain the conviction that the fame of your courteous manners, gallantry, and wit, is by no means undeserved. But as for your honorable proposals, I must confess that I consider myself unworthy to share the throne of so powerful a ruler and to live by the side of a god. I am no fairy, and least of all the famous Gloriana. My parents are only poor mortals, and I myself am a plain young girl, and by no means worthy to become the consort of so powerful a spirit."

"Hold on," cried the young fellow, with an ecstatic grin. "Your words only serve to fan the flame of my love. Whoever you may be, whether the fairy of this forest, or the daughter of a sooty charcoal-burner, your beauty and understanding have fascinated me so much that I will never part with you. You shall be queen of the fools, and receive immediately the homage of my lords and my other subjects. Kneel down, you rogues, blackguards, and fools! Shout with me: 'Long live our Queen!'"

"Long live our queen! Long live the great Comus!" roared the chorus of the merry lads.

At the same time the band struck up again its noisy music. The drums rolled, the fifes squeaked, and all expressed their assent to, and delight at, the selection which Comus had made, by the most ludicrous leaps and deafening cheers.

"Come, bring me the throne," commanded the leader, whom the others willingly obeyed.

A few lads made a sort of chair of branches which they cut quickly from the trees. Alice was requested to seat herself on it. Before she was able to object or desist, strong arms lifted her up easily and softly. She sat on the shoulders of her bearers, and had to submit to being carried by them in triumphant procession. Her white palfrey was led after her, while the leader of the band mounted her brother's horse and rode by her side.

The strange procession was headed by the masked musicians, who struck up a noisy march. Behind them followed a number of masks dressed in the skins of wild beasts. They formed, as it were, the body-guard, and carried for this purpose large staves adorned with flowers and ribbons. Then came various dancers in their gay costumes and covered all over with small bells; they danced on both sides, and performed all sorts of ludicrous leaps. Alice was carried on the quickly-extemporized throne in their midst. The golden rays of the setting sun illuminated the sweet picture. Nothing more beautiful and graceful could be traced by a painter's pencil. A mixture of girlish anxiety and childlike archness brought a smile of confusion and hilarity to her sweet lips and rosy cheeks. The merry spirits of jest and mirth played round her charming dimples and her finely-chiselled chin. Her blond ringlets fell down on her green riding-dress, which chastely veiled her exquisite form. The wreath on her head imparted a queenly appearance to her, and was suitable to the part which had been forced upon her. A last vestige of embarrassment and anxiety remained in her eye, which she dropped, thus adding to her beauty the still greater charm of modesty and humility.

Gradually this anxiety wore off, and Alice regained her usual courage. Her merry spirit even delighted to some extent in the unexpected adventure. She appeared to herself a queen travelling triumphantly through her realm, and receiving homage at the hands of her subjects. She yielded unwittingly to the fantastic charms of the place, and the whole wonderful scenery surrounding her. The dancers treated her with studied politeness, and before long she had acquired more confidence in them. These rude lads were as if fascinated by the power of beauty, and the wild outbursts of their rough and unbridled humor assumed more and more the shape of jovial and even graceful witticisms. The stout carriers strutted about, evidently proud of their fair burden; Comus, the god, rode slowly by her side, and devoted himself now to maintaining good order in the procession, now to amusing his intended consort. Even the wildest dancers tried to impart a chaster character to their somewhat indecent leaps. All without exception endeavored visibly to please their new queen, who manifested her gratitude by pleasant glances and kind words.

Notwithstanding this favorable turn of her adventure, Alice longed for the return of her brothers, as the thought of what would be the end of all this filled her with serious misgivings. Dangers might threaten her every moment, alone and unprotected as she was amidst this horde of lads flushed with wine, mirth, and licentiousness. Moreover, the procession moved farther and farther away from the spot where her brothers would look for her. Her confusion therefore increased at every step; but she took care to conceal her embarrassment from her companions. With ardent impatience she turned her eyes in the direction in which she thought her brothers would approach, but not a trace was to be discerned of them. She overcame her dejection, however, for she was still in hopes that she would speedily be extricated from her embarrassing position.

CHAPTER IV.

THE RESCUE.

At the same time two young men were wandering in a similar direction through Haywood Forest. They were friends, nearly of the same age, and had been tenderly attached to each other for many years. One of them, who was a little older than his companion, presented a refined and aristocratic appearance. Slender and tall, his whole bearing indicated a certain firmness, and the distinguished manners which the sons of wealthy and aristocratic families assume so easily. His dress likewise betokened the wealth of his family. His high forehead and carefully-curled dark hair were covered with a plumed hat, which was adorned with a golden agraffe set with brilliants. His dark, well-kept beard, which, after the fashion of that period, was perfumed with fragrant oil, surrounded his blooming, bronzed cheeks. An air of careless gayety played round his finely-chiselled mouth, and happiness and content beamed from his dark eyes. His doublet, of costly Dutch velvet, and the golden chain encircling his neck, completed the picture of a wealthy young nobleman of that time. Fortune seemed to have been less favorable to his younger companion, the unusual neatness of whose burgher-like dress made up for the plainness of the stuff of which it was made. His shorter, and almost girlish form, moreover, presented a not very advantageous contrast with that of his fine-looking friend. But a glance at his noble face, at his high, expansive forehead, and his deep, unfathomable eyes, satisfied attentive observers at once that he was a man of extraordinary genius. Despite the delicacy of these features, which made him appear much younger than he really was, they indicated a rare ripeness of the mind. The color of his cheeks, without being sickly, showed the traces of his nocturnal studies and exhausting meditations. An indescribable charm played round his finely-chiselled lips, and an air of intellectual beauty illuminated the whole expressive face, in whose delicate yet sharp lineaments feminine gentleness was coupled with manly, earnest, and even stubborn firmness.

The two young wanderers were homeward-bound from one of their usual excursions. They were very fond of roaming during the fine season hand-in-hand through the forests and fields. They shortened the length of the roads by conversations alike instructive and entertaining. Already at the University of Cambridge Edward King, the only son of a distinguished government officer, had become very fond of his younger friend Milton, whose father was a lawyer. The two youths studied together the treasures of classical antiquity, whose ardent admirers they were. The works of the noble Greeks and Romans kindled in their souls an ardent enthusiasm for all that is great and beautiful. Especially young Milton distinguished himself by the zeal and earnestness with which he yielded to the spirit of antiquity and rendered himself familiar with it. He had soon obtained a thorough knowledge of the writings of the greatest philosophers and poets of Athens and Rome, and mastered the difficulties of both languages so well that he himself was able to write beautiful poetry in them. But his indefatigable industry did not content itself with this: profoundly impressed with the sublime beauties of the Bible, he devoted himself to the arduous study of the Hebrew language, and, after incessant toils, he succeeded to his utmost joy in reading and understanding "God's Word" in the original.

A rare good fortune preserved him from the lamentable pedantry which so often clings to learned men. His lively imagination protected him from confining himself to one-sided studies, and always led him back from his dusty study to the forest and fields, and to the bustle of the world. Art, too, shielded him from such aberrations. Milton's father was an excellent musician, and communicated to his son at an early age a taste for harmonious beauty. Neither did young Milton neglect bodily exercise, and the young *savant* was as well skilled in the practice of arms and in horse manship as he was at home in his books and manuscripts. Under such circumstances friends and distinguished patrons could not be wanting to him.

For the rest, that period was a decidedly prosperous one for the poets and learned men of England. Science and literature, which, after reawakening in the fifteenth century from that lethargy in which they had been long sunk, spread from Greece and Italy throughout Europe, found here an especially fertile and susceptible soil. After terrible civil wars and struggles between the hostile factions, England had at length found a durable peace. The nation's energy turned to the ocean surrounding this much-favored island-realm on all sides. The commerce of the country soon became very extensive, and the treasures of the most remote countries poured into the coffers of Great Britain. Important discoveries and territorial acquisitions in distant parts of the world added to the wealth and prosperity of the people. While haughty Spain, owing to her gloomy intolerance and indolence, was declining more and more, the greatness and commerce of England, under the sceptre of the sagacious and powerful Elizabeth, had been constantly on the increase. The more enlightened spirit of Protestantism fostered and promoted this grand development of the country, and aroused the moral and material energy of the people. The progress of commerce and prosperity had considerable influence in awakening the desires of the people for increased culture and education. Elizabeth herself was a lover and protectress of science and poetry. At her court were to be found the most eminent scholars and poets—Bacon, the father and restorer of modern science, Sir Walter Raleigh, and many others. At that time the great Shakespeare wrote his immortal plays, and enjoyed the protection of his queen, the acquaintance and friendship of the most distinguished noblemen, and the love and admiration of his contemporaries. Under Elizabeth's successor, the pedantic but learned James I., science and culture were treated with the highest distinction. In this way it happened that the whole nation took a lively part in the awakening of this taste for science and culture, and men of scholarly attainments occupied a distinguished position in public and social life. The most aristocratic families opened their hospitable mansions to them, and the nobility of the mind marched henceforth hand-in-hand with the nobility of birth.

In this manner Milton, by his talents, had obtained access to the noble house of the Earl of Derby, and this was also the reason why the aristocratic and wealthy Edward King felt highly honored and flattered by his friendship for, and intercourse with, the young poet and *savant*. Their mutual friendship had grown more ardent from day to day, and it was still constantly on the increase. Whenever they could, the friends passed their time together, exchanging their views and feelings. They liked best to roam in the country on sunny days, and feast their eyes on the beauty of the landscape and the varied scenery of Nature. Such walks seemed to both exceedingly delightful and refreshing. Now they traversed the green forest, engaged in a most animated conversation; now they reposed on the soft moss in the shade of a tall oak, and partook of the repast which they had brought with them, and with which they drank water from the bubbling spring. At times they had on such occasions some little adventure which gave them additional topics of conversation. By means of these delightful excursions they became intimately acquainted with the whole neighborhood. During their trips they often met with solitary shepherds, sooty charcoal-burners, and simple-minded farm-laborers, and did not disdain to walk with them for a while. In this manner they obtained a better insight into the peculiarities of the different classes, their simple mode of life, their views, wishes, and wants. The ever-attentive poet received at these meetings many a poetical subject, and learned popular songs which had hitherto been unknown to him. At other times they visited the clients of Milton's father, well-to-do-farmers, who received them with open-handed hospitality.

The most delightful hours, however, they passed in the solitude of the forest. Here all the great events of the past arose before them, and their lively imaginations revelled in recalling the beauties of ancient Hellas and the power and grandeur of Rome. They lived then in the past, and the present disappeared from their eyes. They felt transformed, as it were, and their surroundings seemed to assume the stamp of remote times and countries. Over their heads rustled the sacred oaks of Dodona, and in the whispers of their foliage they fancied they heard the voice of the Oracle. At other times they walked with Plato through the groves of the Academy, and listened to the wise teachings of his divine mouth. The mountain in the neighborhood assumed the shape of Helicon, and the brook at their feet became the Castalian spring. Thus they confounded their surroundings with the creations of their imagination. Even their friendship received the peculiar stamp of classical antiquity. Orestes and Pylades, Damon and Pythias, were the models whom they strove to emulate. Their ordinary names sufficed them no longer, and they adopted in their stead the euphonic ones of Thyrsis and Lycidas, by which they called each other henceforth. In doing so, they thought of the friendships of faithful shepherds, such as Virgil and Theocritus celebrated in their bucolics.

With these symbolic fancies, however, they coupled a lofty earnestness, and the zealous endeavor not only to equal those sublime models, but to surpass them. Both were at that happy age when the mind soars from earth toward the stars, and seeks its ideals there. Nothing seemed henceforth impossible to them, and they thought they could reach the highest goals. As yet friendship and poetry filled the whole realm of their thoughts and feelings, and these benign genii accompanied them everywhere.

The animated conversation of the two friends was unexpectedly interrupted by the deafening notes of music which resounded very near them. The dense shrubbery surrounding them prevented their seeing the cause of the uproar.

"What does this mean?" asked Milton, dropping the previous subject of their conversation.

"It must be a chorus of Bacchantes," replied his friend, still continuing in their former strain.

"You are right, my Lycidas. I hear distinctly the noisy pipe of goat-footed Pan, and the loud drum and ringing cymbals of the furious Mænades. Evoe Bacche! Do you not hear the rejoicings of the jubilant chorus? I should not wonder if Dionysus himself, crowned with ivy and vine-leaves, and seated in his chariot drawn by panthers, were to issue from the thicket and turn round yonder corner of the forest."

"Let us hasten, then, to greet the god, lest we suffer the fate of those who once laughed at his distress. To you, my Thyrsis, the meeting with the furious Bacchantes might be especially dangerous; for you know that they once tore the immortal Orpheus in pieces. As a poet you might easily suffer a similar fate, which would, of course, leave me inconsolable."

"So far as I am concerned, you need not be afraid," replied Milton, entering with a pleasant smile into his friend's jest. "I am as yet any thing but so famous a bard as Orpheus was. The notes of my lyre neither stay the course of the rivers, nor do they tame the wild beasts of the forest. At the best, they gain for me the applause of my too indulgent Lycidas, whose love kindles in my heart the liveliest gratitude toward the gods."

So saying, Milton led the way, anxious to discover the source of the noisy music which broke the silence of the forest so suddenly. King likewise accelerated his steps, and both reached almost at the same time a small clearing where they were able to survey the spectacle so unexpectedly exhibited to them. The procession, in whose midst they beheld the god Comus and Alice, moved past them at a distance of a few yards. The wonderful scene surprised the two observers greatly. Indeed, their jocular words seemed to be realized, and their reminiscences of the feast of Bacchus appeared to be verified. The dancers, in their masks and skins of wild beasts, with their false whiskers and wreaths of oak-leaves on their heads, reminded them strikingly of the goat-footed chorus of the god of wine. Even old Silenus seemed to be present; for on a small donkey hung a fat, bloated drunkard, with a red copper-face, whom his weary, tottering feet were no longer able to support. The strangely-dressed musicians, too, were rending the air with thoroughly pagan strains from their drums, fifes, and shawms. The astonishment of the two friends, however, soon turned into the highest admiration when they beheld the charming Alice seated on her throne of branches and green leaves. She occupied her lofty seat with the bearing of a young queen, illuminated by the purple glow of the setting sun. The sweetest of fairies, the most ravishing sylph, seemed embodied in her to fascinate every mortal eye. The dazzling light prevented Milton at first from recognizing the features which were so well known to him, while his companion believed he was beholding the most beautiful of the wonders of antiquity.

"By Jove!" exclaimed Edward King, enthusiastically, "we are at Naxos, and the lovely girl yonder can be no other than Ariadne, whom the servants of Bacchus are carrying in triumphal procession."

Milton made no reply, but suddenly ran down the small knoll on which the friends were standing, and hastened toward the procession.

"What is the matter?" asked King, wonderingly.

"It is she, it is she!" panted Milton, breathlessly, dragging his surprised friend by the hand with him.

Alice heard his loud exclamation, and turned her lovely head in that direction; a new gleam of hope colored her cheeks and lit up her blue eyes. She thought she had recognized the voice of a friend, nor was she mistaken. In a few moments Milton and his faithful friend, Edward King, stood before her.

"Lady Alice Egerton, Lady Alice!" exclaimed Milton.

"It is I," said Alice, to dispel his doubts.

"And what are you doing here in the midst of these men?"

"For God's sake, extricate me from this dreadful position," she cried, in an anxious voice.

The beautiful girl had to confine herself to these vague words. She had no time for a more extended explanation, for the fellow who was playing the part of Comus, and riding by her side, was becoming impatient.

"Halloo, my little dove," he growled angrily, "you mean to violate your plighted faith and fly away! But that will not do. Stand aside, gentlemen, and render homage to the god Comus and his suite. If you do not clear the way immediately, you stand a chance to become acquainted with his wand and the fists of his subjects."

So saying, the speaker brandished the staff with the fool's head, and the body-guard likewise threatened the friends with their sticks. This was too much for young King's chivalrous courage. He thought he was able to cope all alone with the rabble, whose numerical strength did not frighten him in the least. He unsheathed his sword quickly, and penetrated resistlessly close up to Alice.

"Knock him down!" roared the leader to his men.

But before the latter had time to recover from their surprise, the bold youth had dragged the fellow from his horse, and threatened him with his flashing sword.

"If one of this rabble touches me with the tip of his finger, you are a dead man!"

This threat had the desired effect. The god's suite kept at a respectful distance, and Comus himself made no effort to extricate himself from his adversary's grasp. Meanwhile, Milton had likewise hastened to the spot, in order, if possible, to prevent bloodshed. He devoted his first attention, however, to the frightened girl, who was watching this new incident tremblingly from her throne.

"Put down the lady," he said, imperatively, to the carriers.

The latter obeyed immediately, and, with Milton's assistance, Alice's feet touched the ground again. After rendering her this service, he turned to the group surrounding him. The loud music had ceased, and the performers stood about with faces half confused and half anxious. The body-guard of the god had lowered their staves, and the half-intoxicated subjects had fallen back in dismay. Comus himself lay on the ground, and his former grandiloquence had given way to the most abject cowardice. His red face had suddenly turned very pale, and his shrewd eyes glanced anxiously from one of the bystanders to another. On his fat paunch rested one foot of his victorious adversary, whose left hand firmly grasped the fellow's throat, while his right hand held the sword at his breast. The imminent peril wrung a heavy sigh from the frightened Comus, and he durst not stir for fear of irritating his adversary. It was in this unpleasant predicament that Milton found the poor fellow when he turned his attention to him, and was not a little astonished on recognizing an old acquaintance.

"Billy Green!" he exclaimed, in surprise.

"Yes, 'tis I, your honor," groaned the fellow, in ludicrous despair. "Dear Mr. Milton! get me out of this difficulty, and I will be forever bound to you."

"I do not know whether it is advisable to release so notorious a gallows-bird, poacher, and scapegrace. Your conduct toward this lady deserves the severest castigation."

"Ask herself if I have addressed an insulting word to her. I took the liberty of joking her a little, that was all. And then I did not know who and what she was.—Noble lady, just say if I have offended you in any manner whatever, and pray intercede with these gentlemen in my behalf. A word from your beautiful lips, and a glance of your flashing eyes, will be sufficient to make poor merry Billy Green your everlasting debtor."

This request, uttered in the most contrite tone, excited Alice's compassion, and, turning to her deliverer with a graceful smile and a sweet blush, she said:

"Noble sir, pardon me, if I couple a request with my thanks. You have acted toward me with true chivalry, and manifested your bravery in the most striking manner. But do not forget that virtue which always accompanies true chivalry, to wit, pity for the vanquished. I confirm what he says to you. It is true, he joked me in an unbecoming manner, but did not insult me. As I pardon him, you must no longer be inexorable. Allow him to rise and withdraw immediately with his companions."

The tone of these words, her sweet voice, and her lovely features, made a powerful impression upon the youth, who now saw Alice for the first time. Though usually not at a loss for words, he needed a few moments to recover his presence of mind.

"Noble lady," replied Edward King, after a short pause, "your thanks make me blush, because I do not deserve them. Neither courage nor bravery was required to deliver you from such hands. First give me an opportunity to deserve your gratitude by shedding my blood and risking my life for you, and then you may thank me. This fellow is unworthy of your intercession in his behalf, but should be punished severely for his impudence. However, your request of course prevents me from chastising him. I will only make him pledge us his word, for the safety of us all, that neither he nor his companions will molest us any more. My friend Milton seems to be acquainted with him, and if he will be his security, the rascal may go, after first asking your pardon on his bended knees. He will not cheat the gallows anyhow."

"A thousand thanks," grinned Billy Green, evidently not a little relieved. "I shall take care not to fulfil your honor's prophecy."

"Dear Edward," added Milton, "I have known the fellow for a long time. He often comes to our house, and my father has repeatedly saved him from a punishment which, as a notorious poacher, he has deserved more than once. However, I believe he is a fool and jester rather than a rogue; and as Lady Alice has already spoken in his behalf, I will add my intercession to hers. Let him pledge his word that he will not molest us any more, and then let him withdraw with his companions."

"The devil take me," cried the delighted

god, "if I ever forget what you have done for me. I always said that Mr. Milton deserved a special seat in heaven. If you need me either by day or by night, just send for merry Billy Green. For your sake, I would willingly rob a church, if need be."

Even the grave Edward King could not help smiling a little at this well-meant effusion.

"Well, be it so," he said. "I submit to the orders of the lady and the prayers of my friend. Rise, you scoundrel! First, however, swear on your bended knees that you repent of what you have done, and will do so no more."

"I swear, and may God punish me if I break my oath," said Billy Green, making an effort to look grave and solemn.

King thereupon withdrew his hand from the fellow's throat, which he had grasped until then. The released Comus jumped with a wild leap from the ground, and hastened to the lady and to Milton in order to thank them. He gazed at Alice with mock melancholy and waved his green cap humbly before her. The peacock-plume had been broken and torn off during the scuffle.

"Farewell, beautiful fairy," he cried, with laughable emotion. "Our union lasted only a brief spell, but it was the happiest time of my life. I see now that you are too sensible to remain the queen of the realm of fools. 'Tis a pity! I am afraid the reign of folly will soon be at an end in merry Old England, and the god Comus will no longer be permitted to dwell on this island. Our time makes a serious face, and the world hangs its head. The drawling Puritans are becoming more numerous from day to day. In their eyes every jest is a sin, and every witticism dooms him who utters it. They detest dancing and hate merry songs. If this goes on much longer, merry Old England will soon be as silent as the grave. Hence, I prefer to renounce my throne of my own accord, and abdicate as you did. In place of this wand, I will take a hymn-book in my hand, and exchange my fool's crown for a round head. For the time being I shall intrust you with the emblems of my power. Keep them until I ask you to return them to me. This folly will come to an end too, as all folly does on earth. Good-by, then, until we meet in better times."

The fellow burst into tears in the midst of his queer address; but no one could tell whether his tears were natural or only simulated. He laid down his cap and wand sobbingly at Alice's feet. When Milton stooped to pick up these emblems of folly, the dethroned god added:

"It is right in you, Mr. Milton, to take charge of these things. I know that you are a scholar and a poet, that is to say, a twofold fool; therefore you deserve to be my successor. Share my inheritance with the beautiful lady. And now, musicians, strike up once more a merry march, before they beat your heads with your fiddles. They will soon have a very different dance in England, and the drums and fifes will play a crazier tune than was ever heard before. Forward, boys; dance for the last time! Who knows if you will be permitted to dance any longer to-morrow?"

The dancers were not less surprised at the strange mood and sudden sadness of their leader than the lady and the two friends. The musicians, however, struck up a merry march as he had ordered. Amidst its stirring notes the procession moved on, the leader walking at its head with a tottering step, from time to time wiping away the tears running down his fat cheeks. Gradually the procession disappeared among the trees, veiled by the twilight which was fast setting in. The notes of the music grew fainter and fainter, until they finally died away entirely. The pale sickle of the moon rose in the west, and profound silence reigned again in the forest.

CHAPTER V.

THE RETURN.

Alice was now alone with the two friends, of whom only the young poet was slightly acquainted with her. Milton now introduced chivalrous Edward King to her. The timid girl soon overcame her embarrassment, and gave her deliverers a full account of the strange adventure which had befallen her.

"And what do you intend to do now?" asked Milton, sympathetically.

"I really do not know," replied Alice.

"We are at your command," said King, with officious zeal. "We shall not leave you until you are perfectly safe."

"Certainly not," affirmed his friend. "So long as you have need of us, we will, if you permit it, remain with you. The question is now whether you prefer taking the direct route to Ludlow Castle, or intend remaining here until your brothers have returned."

"I deem it more prudent for you," remarked King, "to leave the forest and return to the highway."

"But my brothers," objected Alice, "will seek me, and if they find me no longer in the forest, they will be needlessly anxious on my account. Moreover, I should not like to trouble you, gentlemen, any more than I have already done. I am sure that your route lies in a different direction from mine."

"We know of no other duty just now," replied King, politely, "but to serve an unprotected lady; and it is of no consequence whatever whether we get home an hour earlier or later. But you, noble lady, must no longer expose yourself to the inconveniences and dangers of this wilderness. The fatigues of the day must have exhausted your strength, and you need physical and mental repose. Moreover, your absence will doubtless occasion the liveliest anxiety to your parents. As to your brothers, I believe we shall meet with them a great deal sooner on the highway than here in the forest. They have deserved some punishment for being such bad custodians of such a treasure."

As Milton assented to the opinion of his friend, Alice resolved to adopt the well-meant advice. With King's assistance, she mounted the palfrey, which had been taken from the dancers, while the young man, leading her brother's horse by the bridle, and John Milton, walked on either side. Both were sufficiently familiar with the road, and the gentle rays of the moon illuminated the tolerably smooth path. It was a splendid, fragrant May night; a gentle breeze murmured in the young foliage; the blooming birches exhaled delicious perfumes, and the nightingales sang the joys and woes of love in long, melting notes. The young wanderers yielded silently to the exquisite charms of Nature; the mysterious fascinations of Spring, the time of buds and flowers, floated round them and filled their hearts with longing and delight.

Alice at length broke the silence, which almost filled her with anxiety. She turned in the first place to Milton, with whom she had already been acquainted. She spoke with him of her aunt's house, and of the last festival which she had witnessed there.

"I envy my Aunt Derby," she said, in the course of the conversation, which became more and more animated, "for being able to gather around her a circle of ladies and gentlemen such as perhaps is not to be found anywhere else. What delightful amusements she manages to prepare for her guests. I shall never forget the days which I passed at her house, and which glided away unfortunately only too rapidly."

"Let me assure you," said Milton, significantly, "that I likewise remember them with grateful emotion. A new life dawned upon me in that house."

He paused suddenly, to the great regret of Alice, who longed to hear more from him, especially as to what and whom he referred to in speaking of a "new life." She was almost afraid lest he would relapse into his bashful reserve, which he seemed to overcome here in the green forest with greater ease than in the proud halls of her aunt's castle. Fortunately his friend now took up the thread of the conversation.

"If I am not mistaken," he said, "a mask, written by you, was presented at the country-seat of the noble Countess-dowager of Derby. As usual, you have not yet told me any thing about its success; hence, I must apply for particulars about the performance to you, beautiful lady."

"I suppose you refer to 'The Arcades?'" asked Alice, kindly.

"That is the name of the mask, of which I have hitherto heard only detached fragments."

"A trifle hardly worth mentioning," interposed the modest poet.

"You do injustice to yourself and your work," said Alice, almost indignantly. "But as you, like an unjust and cruel father, expose and disown your own child, I shall have mercy on it, and cherish and foster it in accordance with its merits."

"Your irony is cruel. I wish you would forget the ungainly child."

"I cannot, sir; and, to prove how deeply its beautiful features are engraved upon my mind, I will quote some lines which struck me as particularly beautiful."

"Pray, don't," murmured Milton, blushing.

But the amiable girl did not heed his objections, and commenced as follows:

"Such sweet compulsion doth in music lie,
To lull the daughters of Necessity,
And keep unsteady Nature to her law,
And the low world in measured motion draw
After the heavenly tune, which none can hear
Of human mould, with gross unpurgéd ear."

"Is it not beautiful?" said Alice, interrupting her recitation, and turning inquiringly to Edward King, who had listened to her attentively. "Do not these lines themselves sound like music."

"They certainly do in your mouth."

In the mean time Milton was so much fascinated that he could not utter a word. Could there be any thing more blissful for the poet than to hear his own words and thoughts from the lips of his beloved? It was the first time that praise had intoxicated him. It is true he was as yet far from giving another interpretation to her homage, and reading in it the hidden confession which it conveyed; but her words filled the poet's heart with an indescribable ecstasy, betokening more than the mere feeling of gratified vanity. His heart was too full for utterance; dreaming blissfully, he walked by the side of the fair horsewoman, looking up to her stealthily from time to time, as if to the heavenly muse herself, which she had become for him at this hour.

His friend was not less sensible of the charms of the beautiful girl. By his position, King had obtained a more extensive acquaintance with distinguished ladies than his bashful friend Milton; nevertheless, he was obliged to confess to himself that he had never met with so perfect a beauty either at court or in society. Alice combined with her youthful charms an intellectual grace which Nature grants only to her special favorites. Her whole bearing breathed an indescribable loveliness, and imparted a peculiar charm to her most insignificant words and actions. Even the most trivial sayings sounded attractive from her lips, and the listener believed he had never heard any thing like it. This surpassing grace was only the reflection of a highly-gifted mind, in which the most delicate feelings were coupled with a firm will, and great lucidness of understanding with the liveliest imagination. And all these surpassing gifts had been harmoniously cultivated and perfectly balanced by a most careful education.

Her young companion had time enough and an excellent opportunity to become acquainted with her accomplishments during this prolonged conversation. The strange meeting in the forest, the magnificent spring night, were well calculated to add to the susceptibility of his heart and imagination. He felt that he could never forget the noble, beautiful face to which the moon's silver light lent an additional charm. The sweet tone of her voice vied with the nightingale, and her slender form on the palfrey constantly reminded him of the wonders of fiction and of the world of fairies. When she bent over the neck of her palfrey and caressed the faithful animal with her soft hand, King wished he were in its place; when her ringlets touched his flushed cheek, a sweet shudder passed through his frame. The whole journey seemed to him a heavenly dream from which he was afraid he should be aroused too soon.

After her first embarrassment had worn off, Alice turned with confiding familiarity, in the innocence of her pure heart, now to one of her companions, now to the other. This beautiful flower disclosed her accomplishments to them more and more unreservedly. Those were moments such as never return in a lifetime—blissful moments capable of making amends for long years of suffering; for is there any thing more delightful on earth than such chaste and intimate intercourse between noble youths and a charming girl? As yet no other feeling than the purest benevolence mixed with their conversation. The inclination slumbering unconsciously in the young hearts had not yet assumed a definite shape, and did not mar the confiding familiarity of their intercourse

Distant heat-lightning flashed up from time to time near the dark horizon, and the low thunder of a rising spring-storm admonished the wanderers to make haste. Soon after, they succeeded in reaching the highway.

"Oh, I know the road now," said Alice; "we must be at Ludlow Castle in half an hour."

"Then we shall reach it just in time to escape the thunder-storm," replied King.

"How splendidly the flashes of lightning cross each other! I am not afraid of the thunder-storm, but you, gentlemen, cannot possibly get home to-night. My father will be glad to tender the hospitality of his house to you. My deliverers will certainly be welcome to him."

The friends tried vainly to decline her polite invitation. Alice insisted upon it, and they had to promise her to stay at Ludlow Castle at least till the following morning. The nearer Alice approached her home, the merrier became the turn which she managed to give to the conversation. With the perfect security which she began to feel again, returned also her good humor and exuberant spirit.

"I am delighted," she said, smilingly, "with the adventure which has ended so agreeably. Like an errant lady, I come back now, accompanied by a valiant knight and an excellent minstrel. Suppose, sir minstrel, you write an epic poem on our meeting?"

"I will bet," said King, "that he has already finished it in his head. I know his ways. When he does not speak, he makes poetry."

"It is true," said Milton, entering into the jest, "the whole occurrence resembles a poem; but I scarcely feel able to treat the beautiful subject in a becoming manner."

"Oh, pray try it," said the charming girl, beseechingly. "But in doing so, you must not omit your own part in the adventure. We must all appear in your poem, my brother, my deliverers, and Comus, the god, who frightened me so badly."

As Milton made no reply, she added anxiously:

"What, you are silent? I hope my childish wish does not offend you. It is true, I can imagine that a poet who writes such elegant Latin verses as you do—verses which I unfortunately do not understand, but which I have been told are very beautiful—must deem it beneath his dignity to celebrate so insignificant an event in plain English."

"You are mistaken, noble lady," replied the poet in a grave tone. "From my first years it was found that whether aught was imposed upon me by them that had the overlooking, or betaken to of my own choice, in English or other tongue, prosing or versing, but chiefly the latter, the style, by certain vital signs it had, was likely to live. Perceiving at a later time that some trifles which I had composed met with acceptance above what was looked for, I began thus far to assent to divers of my friends, and not less to an inward prompting, which now grew daily upon me, that by labor and intent study, which I take to be my portion in this life, joined to the strong propensity of nature, I might perhaps leave some so written to aftertimes as they should not willingly let it die. These thoughts at once possessed me, and these other, that if I were certain to write as men buy leases, for three lives and downward, there ought no regard be sooner had than to God's glory, by the honor and instruction of my country. For which cause I applied myself to the resolution to fix all the industry and art I could unite to the adorning of my native tongue; not to make verbal curiosities the end, that were a toilsome vanity; but to be an interpreter and relater of the best and safest things among my own citizens throughout this island in the mother dialect. The kind of poetry to which I aspire is a work not to be raised from the heat of youth or the vapors of wine, like that which flows at waste from the pen of some vulgar amorist, or the trencher-fury of a rhyming parasite; nor to be obtained by the invocation of Dame Memory and her siren daughters; but by devout prayer to that Eternal Spirit, who can enrich with all utterance and knowledge, and sends out His seraphim with the hallowed fire of His altar, to touch and purify the lips of whom He pleases. Now you know my heart and its aspirations."

"And you will succeed," said Alice, profoundly moved, and carried away by the poet's enthusiasm. "I see already the laurels which will one day wreathe your brow. The name of Milton will be placed by the side of those of Shakespeare and Spenser."

"Hold!" replied Milton. "I am not worthy as yet to unloose the shoestrings of these great men, and least of all those of Shakespeare, the immortal genius of England. What have I accomplished hitherto that would permit me to lift my eyes to him?"

"You are young, and the blossom ripens into the fruit only in the course of years."

"Was Shakespeare older than I when he wrote 'Romeo and Juliet,' the song of songs of love?"

"Every plant has its own time of development and maturity. Yours will come too."

"Oh, I would you were a true prophetess! How gladly would I devote day and night to this sublime object! Before you, noble lady, and my friend here, I may speak frankly, for I know that you will not misunderstand me. You may hear it, but let me whisper my confession into your ear, lest I should blush. Yes, I long for immortality. I am exercising and strengthening my wings and preparing for a bold flight; but as yet the wings of my Pegasus are too feeble to soar as high as I would like. Hence, I believe I must be content with less lofty aspirations."

The noise of horses and loud shouts interrupted the effusions of the poet, who had suddenly become so eloquent. At the head of a number of servants, whom the anxious parents had sent out, appeared now young Lord

Brackley in search of his sister. On perceiving her, he uttered a loud, joyful cry. Alice introduced the friends as her deliverers to her brother, who thanked them cordially, and invited them likewise, on account of the rising thunder-storm, to stay overnight at Ludlow Castle. Only Thomas was missing yet, but his brother and sister were not over-anxious on his account, for the courageous youth often returned late at night from his excursions and hunts. However, another party of servants had been dispatched into Haywood Forest in search of him.

The young lord was soon on very friendly terms with the companions of his sister, of whom only King was unknown to him, as he had already met with the poet at his aunt's house. At a beck from him, horses were brought for the friends; the servants, with their torches, led the way, and the whole cavalcade moved toward Ludlow Castle, which they reached before the threatening thunder-storm had burst forth.

The parents received their guests in the hall of the castle with old English politeness and hospitality. An ample repast was served up, and Alice, who was seated between the friends, had to relate her adventure once more. In doing so, she said as little as possible about the imprudent conduct of her absent brother; but he was nevertheless universally censured. Great was the praise accorded to the chivalrous conduct of the two friends. Their noble host conversed with them in the most cordial manner, and requested them to spend several days at the castle, the modest demeanor and the intelligent answers of his young guests having made a very favorable impression upon him. As is usual on such occasions, it turned out during their conversation that there were many points of mutual interest between them. The Lord President of Wales had formerly been acquainted with King's father. They had often met at court and in London society, and had now and then exchanged friendly words, so that the son was received with increased cordiality on this account. Milton, too, quite unexpectedly, met at the table with an old acquaintance. Opposite him sat a young man who taught music in the family of the Earl of Bridgewater. The poet recognized the features of his neighbor, though he had not seen him for several years, and did not hesitate to greet him as his former fellow-student, Henry Lawes. Alice was the more delighted with this incident, as the modest and able teacher was a special favorite of hers. The recognition gave rise to reminiscences by which the young lady, who listened attentively to the conversation of the friends, learned many interesting events which had taken place in the early years of the poet. Lawes alluded particularly to a former adventure which had happened to Milton, and the recollection of which seemed to embarrass the modest poet.

"Do you remember the nickname which we gave to you at school?" said the musician to his friend.

"Oh, certainly," replied Milton, blushing.

"What nickname was it?" asked Alice.

"We called friend Milton only 'the Lady of the College,'" replied the musician, gayly. "This nickname was applied to him on account of his delicate, girlish appearance. Indeed, what with his slight form, his rosy cheeks, and bashful demeanor, he resembled a timid young lady rather than the wild, impetuous boys who sat in the same class with him. We teased him for this reason very often, but at the bottom we were very fond of him, for he was the best-hearted fellow in the world. Nor was he lacking in courage, for all his softness and delicacy. When we teased him too much, he defended himself bravely, and made up by his agility and skill for what he lacked in brute strength. I would not have advised anybody to challenge him. In wrestling, fencing, and horsemanship he possessed extraordinary skill. Nevertheless, we always called him 'the Lady;' there was still another reason for our doing so."

Milton signed vainly to his fellow-student, whom the joy of meeting his old friend, and a few glasses of wine, had excited a little.

"Ah, you need not motion to me," continued the merry musician; "Lady Alice shall hear that story in spite of your objections. It sounded at the time so beautiful and wondrous, that I felt almost tempted to believe that you had dreamed, or had one of your usual poetical visions."

"You really excite my curiosity," interposed Alice, who seemed to be delighted with the poet's confusion.

"One day," related the loquacious musician, "friend Milton lay under a tree in the college garden, and fell asleep. An Italian lady, who was on a visit to Cambridge, is said to have seen the slumbering youth, and to have been so intensely delighted with his appearance, that she dropped on him a rose which she held in her hands. Round the stem was tied a piece of paper, which contained a few beautiful lines in Italian on the sleeping Endymion."

"Do you still remember those lines?" asked Alice, archly.

"I do. If I am not mistaken, they were of the following purport:

'Oh, fairest eyes, ye orbs of blissful light,
If closed, ye such power wield,
What could my heart, if ye were open, shield?'"

"I think these lines are really charming," remarked the young lady, "though they seem to me more suitable to a woman than a man."

"That is what the whole class thought, and henceforth we called Milton 'the Lady of the College' more than ever before."

"And you heard nothing further from the unknown lady?" said Alice to the confused poet.

"How should I?" he replied. "Perhaps the whole occurrence was only a poor joke of my fellow-students. I should have liked best to consider the whole event only a dream of my lively imagination, had I not, on awaking, found the rose with those lines carefully wrapped round the stem. Moreover, I really thought I had, on opening my eyes, seen a female form hurrying rapidly from the garden. Nay, I even remembered her name, for I thought I heard an older lady, accompanying her, calling out to her, 'Leonora!' I confess frankly that this strange affair engrossed my mind for some time afterward."

"Maybe you will meet the lady at some future time," said Alice, playfully. "Did you never entertain this desire?"

"In former times I did, but it is a long while since I forgot the whole occurrence, until Lawes just now reminded me of it. I look upon the adventure now only as a rather bold jest on the part of the unknown lady, and who knows whether I ought to desire to meet the Signora again? The reality would probably undeceive me, as is usually the case under such circumstances. As it is, she lives at least in my imagination as a picture of the Muse who visited her votary in his dreams."

"And you are afraid lest your Muse, on meeting you again, should be old and ugly? You may be right, so far as that is concerned," added Alice, smilingly.

In the mean time, the condescending host conversed with young King on the affairs of the king, and on what was going on at court. The noble earl spoke with a great deal of moderation on these topics. He made no secret of his apprehensions in regard to the quarrels between Charles I. and his Parliament. He expressed his hope and earnest desire, however, that these dissensions might be amicably settled. At the conclusion of the conversation, the Lord President of Wales took up the goblet standing before him.

"God grant," he said, raising his voice,

"peace and tranquillity to our country! But let me once more heartily welcome you, my dear guests, to Ludlow Castle, and repeat my invitation to you to stay at my house as long as you like it."

Thereupon he rose, thereby indicating that the repast was at an end. The earl's steward had prepared rooms in the side-wing of the castle for the reception of the friends. Preceded by a footman, and accompanied by the kind-hearted musician, they retired after bidding the earl's family good-night.

CHAPTER VI.

A MORNING AT LUDLOW CASTLE.

A SPLENDID spring morning awakened the sleepers, who had enjoyed the most delightful repose after the fatigues of the previous day. Even the thunder-storm had been unable to disturb their sleep. It had burst forth at midnight, but passed away very soon, and the only traces it had left behind were the heavy raindrops now hanging on every blade of green, and sparkling magnificently in the golden sunshine. Milton was the first to awake, and had stepped immediately to the open bay-window. At his feet lay the large garden, with the carefully and ingeniously arranged flower-beds, whose sweet perfumes were wafted up to him by the morning breeze. A whole sea of flowers and blossoms spread out before his eyes; the warm shower of the thunder-storm had called forth countless buds, and transformed the cherry and apple trees into fragrant white snowballs. Amidst them glistened the reddish blossoms of the chestnuts and apricots, and the young foliage in all its variegated colors, from yellow and green to the deep black of the sombre cypresses, the whole resembling the palette of an industrious painter. The fresh morning breeze swept merrily over it, and, like a color-grinder, produced new and surprising combinations of these different tints, while the hanging drops fell from the foliage to the ground like a rain of flashing diamonds. Adjoining the luxuriant garden was the park, with its mighty trees, whose tops seemed entirely bathed in the morning light; beyond it extended the landscape with its green meadows and fields, isolated groups of trees and sparse cottages, from which blue smoke was rising in straight lines. A gentle, sloping chain of hills, adorned here and there with an imposing structure, or the ruins of a castle, dating from the period of the Romans, bordered the horizon. There could be no more beautiful view than this fertile and withal picturesque landscape in the full splendor of the glorious May-time. The azure sky was clear and limpid; not a cloudlet dimmed its noble vault, and the first vigorous sunbeams shed so bright a lustre, that even the broad shades of the dewy fields resembled large golden stripes, embroidered with pearls and diamonds. At the same time, morning had filled the wide world with new life. At a distance, the cock of the barn-yard uttered its loud notes; the lark warbled up from the clover-field, or rang its sweet morning greetings down from the clouds; the industrious swallows were building their nests chirpingly on a decayed wall, and all the other sweet singers of the forest and the fields joined in the early concert of creation.

Amidst this beautiful and fertile landscape rose Ludlow Castle, a proud structure in the Norman-Gothic style. Situated on a precipitous rock, this imposing edifice, which dated from the times of William the Conqueror, commanded a splendid view of the adjoining country; according to the chronicler Leland, its walls had a circuit of nearly a mile. Fortified ramparts and drawbridges protected it from hostile attacks. By the enormous entrance-gate one penetrated into the large inner court-yard, which was surrounded by a number of side-buildings used for various purposes. Further back the visitor beheld the imposing front of the ancient castle, which the hands of giants seemed to have built of tremendous blocks of stone, and which had defied the corrosive power of centuries. Two enormous towers rose from it, menacingly and imperiously; they contained embrasures, and were crowned with slender pinnacles. Joined to the main building, in picturesque angles and projections, were the wings, which were of later origin than the old structure, to which they had been added from time to time. These additions imparted to the whole the charm of variety, combined with massiveness and extraordinary extent. The heavy Norman lines and forms of the original building were covered and interrupted by the handsome Gothic arches, pillars, and spires, without lessening the grandeur and dignity of the castle. Nature and art had thus combined in rendering it a truly royal residence, and the sovereigns of England had indeed owned it since the death of its first owner, Roger Montgomery, and had often personally resided there. It was not until the reign of Henry VIII. that Ludlow Castle had been assigned as the official residence of the Lord President of Wales. At the present time the Earl of Bridgewater, who filled that distinguished position, and his family, occupied this magnificent country-seat. A large number of officers, such as every nobleman of his rank and position kept about him at that period, occupied a part of the wings and outbuildings. Besides, there was a small garrison at the castle, to defend it, if need be, against foreign or domestic foes. Numerous guests, in those days of liberal hospitality, met with a welcome reception in the extensive suites of apartments, of which there was no lack.

Milton feasted his æsthetic eyes long and wonderingly on the imposing pile. A charming *clare-obscure* floated round the gray old walls. Above the western tower yet stood the pale silver sickle of the moon, while the pinnacles were sparkling like golden crowns in the bright morning sun. From thence the rays glided down the projections and pillars, here illuminating a Gothic window, there lighting up a rose of stone or a jutting oriel. Other parts, however, were still veiled in the shade, until the lustre of the victorious sun gradually divested them of their gloomy physiognomy. In the depth below flashed the waters of the Teme, which surrounded the ramparts of the castle in picturesque meanderings and reflected its proud pinnacles.

Gradually various sounds issued from the interior of the castle, and indicated the re-awakening of life. In the neighboring stables neighed horses, and pointers and setters barked in the court-yard; doors opened noisily, and many footsteps resounded on the pavement. At first busy servants passed hastily under Milton's window; next came the steward with his grave air, scolding the loiterers and brandishing threateningly his staff with the large silver top, whenever his words were not promptly listened to. Buxom servant-girls, their cheeks still flushed with sleep, stood at the well, chatting gayly and cleaning the earthen and copper vessels of the remnants of last night's supper, or filling the wooden buckets with water from the bubbling spring. Others stepped from the stables, preceded by the stately housekeeper, and carrying the new milk on their heads. Idle footmen and hunting-grooms jested with them, which excited the anger of the old housekeeper and caused her to tell them indignantly to go to work. The cook and his assistants returned from the store-room, loaded with venison and meat as if they had to prepare a wedding-banquet. At the head of this culinary procession was carried the wild boar which the Lord President had killed with his own hands a few days before, and whose gilded head was to be the chief ornament of to-day's dinner-table. In the midst of all these persons moved grave-looking clerks and the bailiff, rent-roll in hand, to receive the rent from a farmer or the taxes from an humble peasant who took off his hat in the presence of the stern gentleman. The bustle in the court-yard was constantly on the increase. The corpulent chaplain walked yawningly from his rooms to the hall of the castle to say grace at the breakfast-table. On passing the cook and his assistants, he cast a longing glance on the fat boar and the meats which were carried by. The agreeable prospect of a sumptuous dinner imparted a highly-benevolent expression to his face. With a pleasant smile he thanked the steward, who greeted the clergyman with profound respect.

"A fine morning," he said, trying to open a conversation with the chaplain. "Splendid weather. The cornfields look twice as nice after the shower as they did yesterday. With God's assistance we shall have good crops this year."

"Yes, yes, God's goodness and patience with sinful humanity are great," replied the clergyman, clasping his hands.

"Well, well, the world is not so very bad."

"What, not so bad?" said the chaplain, indignantly. "Have you not heard that the dissenters and contemners of our Church are daily on the increase? Not so bad, you say, Mr. Buller? And in our own vicinity there are swarms of sectarians, Brownists, Anabaptists, Familists, Antinomians, Socinians, Puritans, and whatever may be the names of the blasphemous scoundrels. And what is worse yet, they are performing their infamous rites quite unconcernedly."

"You do not say so!" replied the worthy steward, shaking his head incredulously.

"What I say is as true as that it is now broad daylight. I have been credibly informed that they hold in all sorts of out-of-the-way hiding-places, in caves and forests, their clandestine meetings and conventicles, where they inveigh against the Church of England, and preach rebellion against the anointed head of the king. But this is the consequence of the untimely patience and forbearance of our authorities. I would proceed against them with fire and sword, if I had the power of our gracious master, the Lord President."

"He is a good master, God bless him!" replied the loyal steward, taking off his hat.

"But his goodness is entirely out of place here. This is a time when nothing but severity will be of any avail to extirpate the growing evil of heresy. Some members of my congregation begin also to deviate from the true path. I must speak a word in dead earnest with the noble earl, that he may put a stop to the growing mischief, and that the faithful sheep may not be infected by the shabby ones. Henderson is one of the latter."

"James Henderson from Huntington? I know him well; he is an industrious, prompt, and reliable man; only he is a little sullen and morose since his wife's death."

"Say rather seditious and rebellious against God and his king. I know this industrious James Henderson better. Industrious he is, to be sure, but only in blasphemy, and prompt in disobedience. Did he not assert the other day, loudly and in the presence of a great many others, that no one ought to pay ship-money and the tax on soap? The rascal said these new taxes were illegal, inasmuch as they were collected without the approval of Parliament. Illegal, indeed! As if the king could do wrong; and even though he should, is a subject allowed to resist him? Does not the Bible command the people to be obedient to their rulers? Did not the Saviour Himself say, 'Render unto Cæsar the things which are Cæsar's?' And that Cæsar was a heathen and not a confessor of the true faith, like King Charles, whom God bless and preserve for many years to come!"

"But what do we have a Parliament for?" timidly objected the steward, who, like most

Englishmen, was filled with profound reverence for the ancient constitution of his country. "According to Magna Charta, no additional taxes can be imposed upon the people without the approval of Parliament."

"H'm," murmured the clergyman, in a milder tone. "Parliament is a good institution, and I will say nothing against it. God forbid that I should deny its privileges and prerogatives! But we do not speak of that just now, but of the accursed James Henderson, who speaks disrespectfully of our most gracious king, and who has not been at church, nor listened to my sermons, for upward of a year. It is on his account that I wish to speak a word in earnest with our earl. As Lord President and representative of his majesty, he must inflict well-merited punishment on this Henderson on account of his infamous sayings and doings. If he followed my advice, he would order Henderson to be whipped and confined in the deepest dungeon."

"You forget that Henderson has a powerful protectress. His daughter is the foster-sister of our young lady."

"I do not care for that. I shall do my duty regardless of her protection. It will not avail him before God."

So saying, the zealous chaplain proceeded, as the breakfast-hour had struck in the mean time. The delicious odor of fresh-baked pies which issued from the hall allayed his holy wrath somewhat, and damped his eagerness to persecute the Brownists, Anabaptists, and other sects, which were so remorselessly persecuted and punished by the Church and government of England. The steward followed him hastily, in order to miss neither the blessing nor the breakfast.

This conversation, to which Milton had listened, transferred the enthusiastic poet at once from the contemplation of blooming Nature to the dreary religious troubles and dissensions of his times. Protestantism in England had not resulted, as in Germany, from the intelligence of the people, and their conviction that a change was indispensable. The quarrel of Henry VIII. with the pope in regard to his divorce had brought about the rupture between England and the Roman Catholic Church. In direct opposition to the German Reformation, which was based on the principle of religious freedom, and strove for it alone, the English Reformation had been forced, at least, upon a part of the people by the arbitrary decrees of a tyrannous king. Luther, the simple, inspired monk, ventured upon his struggle against all-powerful Rome with no other support than that of public opinion and the Bible. Henry VIII., on the contrary, profited by his royal authority and the power which was at his command. Personal considerations and worldly advantages were the motives of the latter, while the German Reformer commenced and finished his immortal work solely in the name of truth and the freedom of conscience. The King of England took the place of the pope in his country, but in most essential points he remained a zealous Catholic, and, with the exception of the pope's supremacy in secular affairs, and of the monastic system, he made few important changes in the old dogmas of his Church. Thus the two Reformations differed materially at the outset. They started from opposite points, and pursued ever afterward a widely different course. The religious current which originated in Germany rose from below upward, from the people up to the nobility and princes, who promoted the Reformation partly from inward conviction, partly, like Henry VIII., for the sake of worldly advantages. The reverse was the case in England; the religious movement here extended from the summit to the base, from the throne down to the lower strata of the people. The latter soon took in hand the reformation of their faith, not as a secular, but as an exclusively divine affair. Regardless of the motives which had prompted the king in his defection from Rome, the people, instead of the earthly riches for which the crown had principally longed, sought for the eternal boons of toleration and freedom of conscience. From the rich inheritance of the Roman Catholic clergy, from the treasuries of the convents, they chose, in place of the golden vessels, the precious trinkets, and the estates of the Church, nothing but the Bible, which had hitherto been withheld from them. From the Word of God they derived an exuberance of information and an entirely novel view of the government of the world. The Bible became, in the hands of the people, the powerful weapon with which they achieved their ultimate victory over tyranny, and conquered, at length, religious and political freedom. From this time on arose the struggle against the king's authority, which had so arbitrarily arrogated the place of that of the pope. The successors of Henry VIII. acted more or less in the same spirit. His great daughter, Queen Elizabeth, established the Church of England npon that firmer footing which it has retained to the present day, and left its supervision in the hands of the bishops and archbishops. By virtue of this arrangement, the sovereigns always remained the head of the Church and exercised supreme power in it; their power in this respect was supported by the bishops, who seconded the king's authority on these conditions by all means at their command. Thus originated the so-called Anglican or Episcopal Church. The king had taken the place of the pope, and the bishops were only dependent officers of unlimited authority in all clerical affairs. Such a system could not possibly satisfy the newly-awakened religious cravings of the people, and it met at the very outset with determined opposition. The doctrines of the great Swiss reformer, Calvin, had penetrated from Geneva to England, and with them the liberal political views which usually prevail in small republics. Every religious reformation is accompanied by a similar movement in the sphere of politics. Hence, the crown was threatened with a twofold danger; not only its spiritual prerogatives, but even its political privileges, were disputed by the people. In opposition to the Episcopal Church, which was based upon the authority of the king and the delegated power exercised by the bishops, the popular religious party demanded the free election of their clergymen and superintendents, who were called presbyters or elders, whence their adherents were afterward styled Presbyterians. The people demanded the right of regulating their own religious affairs, and in justification quoted the precepts of the Bible and the example of the first Christian congregations. Besides, most of the Presbyterians rejected all the rites and usages of the Catholic service, which the Episcopal Church had partially retained, and which reminded them of hateful Rome. Hence, they were called Puritans. This sectarian spirit had made especial headway in Scotland, where many of Calvin's disciples preached their dogmas and enlisted the liveliest sympathies of the people.

The religious parties were soon arrayed in open hostility against each other. The persecutions of the government aroused the resistance of the people. The greater the pressure became on one side, the more intense grew the zeal on the other, soon bursting into the devouring flames of irresistible fanaticism. At the head of the Episcopal Church stood the well-known Laud, Bishop of London, who exerted a most deplorable influence over the king. He was the soul of those relentless persecutions, and the dreaded Star-Chamber, which tried all religious offenders, proceeded, under his leadership, with inexorable severity and cruelty against the dissenters. But neither the most exorbitant fines, nor long imprisonment, nor the whole host of penalties of every description, were able to set bounds to the religious zeal and enthusiasm of the people. The sufferers were extolled as martyrs by the people, and their examples were constantly imitated by others. With admirable courage they braved the most cruel persecutions, ready and willing to give up their lives rather than their convictions.

All these facts stood before Milton's soul, after he had listened to the conversation between the Episcopal chaplain and the earl's steward. He himself was an adherent of religious freedom, although he was entirely destitute of fanaticism and zealotry. From the example set him by his own father, he had learned to appreciate toleration and moderation. Old Mr. Milton had embraced the Protestant faith, and been disinherited by his bigoted Catholic parent. The poet knew of no greater boon than freedom of conscience. This was the sole reason why he had given up the study of theology, and renounced the clerical career, which offered to him at that time, on account of his talents and industry, the most brilliant prospects. "On perceiving," he wrote in his own justification, "that the despotism to which the Church'laws compel him who takes orders to subscribe his own servitude, and moreover impose on him an oath which only men of easy conscience can take, I preferred a blameless silence to what I considered servitude and forswearing."

These considerations had induced Milton, despite his father's earnest wishes, to give up the study of theology and choose another career. He had replaced the Fathers of the Church by the poets and prose writers of classical antiquity, but, nevertheless, he took the liveliest interest in the religious struggles of his times; and, whenever he was reminded of them, he sided with the oppressed and persecuted.

The conversation to which he had just listened filled him anew with intense aversion to the arrogance and intolerance of the Episcopal Church, and he would not have been a poet had he not taken sides with the more liberal faith, and approved of the position taken by its adherents. All these reflections which arose in his soul imparted to his surroundings a different and much gloomier color. The beautiful landscape lost its charms in his eyes, and the magnificent castle no longer excited his enthusiasm. His vivid imagination conveyed him to the lowly cottages of the people, where poor peasants were worshipping behind locked doors. He saw Henderson, the accused, torn from his bed, loaded with chains, and standing tremblingly before his stern judge. The splendid edifice, which had filled him a few minutes ago with heart-felt admiration, seemed now transformed into a vast prison, in whose deepest dungeons the tormented dissenters were groaning. He felt an irrepressible desire to become their defender, and to speak a great word and perform a deed of deliverance for the freedom of religion and the rights of the oppressed people.

Such ideas had already arisen from time to time in the poet's soul, but his love of the sciences, and his occupation with the ideal creations of antiquity and with poetry, had silenced them, and the splendor of the past had made him forget the sufferings and troubles of the present. As yet the time had not come for him to take the active part in the political and religious struggles of his country which he did at a later period of his life. At this moment, too, his thoughts were soon led into a different channel.

A beautiful girl stepped from a side-gate leading into the garden. He recognized Alice immediately, although she wore an entirely different costume. She had exchanged her splendid riding-dress of gold-embroidered green velvet for a light white morning-gown, which floated like a silver wave round her charming figure in the gentle morning breeze. Instead of the handsome barret-cap, with the waving plume, a veil surrounded her youthful head, concealing only partially the luxuriant exuberance of her golden ringlets. By her side stood a lady's maid, bearing a basket filled with all sorts of grain. From time to time Alice plunged her white hands into it and strewed a part of its contents on the ground, uttering at the same time a sweet, gentle call. It was not long before the spot where she was standing was filled with the feathered tribe, and even the quadrupeds of the courtyard. Voracious chickens, headed by the stately rooster, and ducks of all sorts, gathered round their benefactress. From the sunny height of the roof and the pinnacles, cooing doves flitted down, and the proud peacock strutted about amidst all this poultry, displaying its magnificent tail, and uttering its disagreeable notes. A tame white roe hastened likewise to its mistress, and plucked her gown to remind her not to forget it.

The poet watched this charming scene with indescribable delight. He thought he had never beheld a sweeter spectacle. Amidst this crowing, chirping, and cooing crowd stood the lovely girl, like a goddess distributing their daily bread with blessed hands among all these creatures. A cheerful smile of content played round her lips, and she often burst into a peal of laughter when one of the animals, in its too great eagerness, fell down, or when the grains intended for it were snatched away by another right under its nose. At the next moment, however, she indemnified the sufferers by liberal offerings. No one was allowed to depart hungry from her banquet. Even from the melancholy turkey she drew those deep, guttural notes, by which it indicates its satisfaction and gratitude; nay, it forgot its pride and ill-humor so far as to mingle, at her call, among the common rabble of barn-yard fowls, to which, however, it did not vouchsafe a glance. It pounced hastily upon the share allotted to it, swallowed it, and then withdrew, moving its wings disdainfully from the company so unworthy of the proud bird's presence. Alice treated with especial liberality her favorites; the hen, with its little ones, and the doves, which were flitting caressingly around her. The white roe was much better off than any of the others, for it was permitted to take its breakfast from its mistress's hands, which it kissed gratefully. Soon the ample contents of the basket were emptied, and Alice handed it back to her maid. She then clapped her hands, and the whole flock dispersed. The doves rose like a silver cloud from the ground, and rocked to and fro in the air, until they disappeared. Only the white roe followed with its wonted fidelity the kind mistress, who went into the garden to pay her daily morning visit to her flowers.

CHAPTER VII.

ALICE AND MILTON.

The human heart, and especially that of a poet, is a wonderful thing. It sways to and fro like a reed in the breeze, moved by the slightest gust of air. A glance from two beautiful eyes, a word from sweet lips, the waving of a blond ringlet, the springing step of a slender form, and all our resolutions and purposes are gone, and we see the world in a different light. Where a dark cloud stood a moment ago, beams now the most radiant sunshine; where we saw only sharp thorns, we behold now a wealth of blooming roses. What a magician is our imagination! what a foolish thing the human heart, which is guided by it!

This is what happened to Milton, whom Alice's appearance suddenly withdrew from all his former thoughts. All at once he was again a poet, intoxicated with the charming spectacle which he had just enjoyed. After the lovely girl had disappeared in the direction of the garden, he suddenly felt an irrepressible desire to enjoy the beautiful morning in the open air. Now, nowhere did Nature seem to him lovelier, the air balmier, or the sun brighter, than in the garden, where he knew Alice was. He was about carrying his resolution into effect, but at the last moment an inexplicable embarrassment seized him. He felt as though he were about to commit a crime. For a few moments he was as undecided as Hercules at the cross-roads, but finally he succumbed to the temptation. He cast a glance on his friend, who was still fast asleep, and then left the room. He descended the broad staircase of sandstone very slowly, considering at every step whether it was becoming in him to follow the fair magician who drew him after her so irresistibly. His way led him through a long gallery, whose walls were adorned with the portraits of the ancestors of the house. Casting a fugitive glance on the fine-looking men and richly-attired ladies, among whom were the highest dignitaries and greatest beauties of the country, he felt for the first time the almost impassable gulf separating him from the descendant of these august persons. He seemed to read a decided disapproval of his steps in the proud features of these noble lords and pious prelates, some of whose portraits were masterpieces of illustrious Dutch painters. Only when he had walked through the gallery, and stood at the open gate leading into the garden, did this embarrassment, mixed as it was with a feeling of awe, wear off.

The fragrant odor of the flowers, and the sweet notes of the birds, speedily dissipated the poet's apprehensions. How differently and more freely throbbed his heart under the rustling trees than in the high halls, whose immense pile threatened to crush him! Had he found Alice there, how different would have been his meeting with her; he would have scarcely ventured to address her! Here in the garden he lacked neither courage nor desire to do so. A considerable while elapsed, however, before he was able to attain his object. The carefully-kept gravel-walks led in the most various directions, of which Alice could have taken only one. Hence, Milton traversed a labyrinth of flower-beds, cozy bosquets, and shady alleys, before he succeeded in finding the beautifnl girl. The garden was laid out in accordance with the taste of that time; it was of vast dimensions, and divided into several sections. As yet the French style of landscape gardening was in its infancy in France itself, and its stiff forms had not been adopted in England. By far more prevalent was the Italian style, adapted to the peculiarities of the country, in the gardens of the aristocracy. A special portion of the grounds was allotted as a kitchen-garden, another for the culture of the most important medicinal plants, and then followed the pleasure-garden. Several steps led up to it, as it ascended in terraces the hill on which the castle was situated. Long lines of orange and lemon trees, then far more rare than they are now, bordered the main avenue. Between the trees stood some statues, made by English sculptors after Greek models, and bearing witness that this branch of art, hitherto neglected, was now cultivated with much zeal and success. To be sure, the flower-beds could not bear a comparison with the highly-developed culture of the present time, as they were mostly confined to domestic plants, and were destitute of the beautiful exotics which are to be found everywhere nowadays. But this defect was made up for by the luxuriant bosquets, and several groups of trees of extraordinary beauty. A rivulet, bubbling from the rock, meandered through the whole garden, and spread everywhere a refreshing coolness. It fell noisily into a pond, in the midst of which was to be seen a group of bathing nymphs and swimming Tritons, blowing shells. Round the edge of the pond had been fixed benches of sandstone, surrounded everywhere by shady shrubbery. Those seated in this cozy nook enjoyed at the same time a splendid view of the castle, and the prospect of the fertile landscape, visible between the neighboring hills. This spot was the favorite resort of Alice, and here it was that the poet found her at length, after traversing the garden in all directions.

Her delicate form in the white dress reminded him of the nymph of the spring. He approached her timidly and with a hesitating step. She rose from her seat, and a gentle blush suffused her cheeks on meeting him so unexpectedly after the events of the previous day.

"Pardon me," said Milton, bowing deeply, "if I disturb you in your solitude. The splendid morning and the beauty of the garden tempted me, and, finding the gate open, I entered without permission. Do not be angry at my boldness. I will withdraw at once."

"You do not disturb me," she replied, not without embarrassment. "As a guest of our house, you are welcome everywhere, and I am glad if you like our garden. I presume you have already looked around a little, but you do not yet know the most beautiful points. I will show them to you."

Before Milton could thank her, she was already by his side. The tame roe, which had hitherto lain at her feet, now leaped gracefully by her side, and all three sauntered through the fragrant garden. At first their conversation was somewhat incoherent, but both soon surmounted the bashfulness so natural under such circumstances. Alice was the first to recover her presence of mind. As hostess, she conducted her guest from one of her favorite spots to another, and called his attention to the numerous beauties of the landscape and the garden. Now he had to admire a surpassingly splendid tree, now a flower which she herself had planted, now the prospect of a ruin dating from the era of the Romans, or a decayed stronghold of the ancient Britons. At times, such a sight excited her enthusiasm again, and she interrupted the just started conversation more than once by exclaiming: "Oh, how magnificent! how charming!" Milton never failed to share her transports, and, with his refined and poetical spirit, did the fullest justice to the beauty of the landscape and the castle. Both always agreed in their appreciation of the scenery, and that which carried her away was sure to delight the enthusiastic poet. Never before had he discovered and enjoyed so many beauties of nature as by the side of his lovely companion. Indeed, the garden seemed to him a paradise, where he conferred in his mind the parts of Adam and Eve upon himself and Alice. Thus they passed, as if in a dream, the fragrant flower-beds, the white marble statues, and walked through shady alleys formed by luxuriant vine-leaves. They ascended slowly to the terrace, where, leaning against the balustrade of stone, they scanned thoughtfully the varied scene. At their feet extended the sunny valley, with its scattered houses and huts. The quiet river flowed amidst luxuriant meadows and waving cornfields. Driven by its waters, the mill-wheel revolved rapidly, and the spray dashed from its spokes sparkled in the bright morning light like strings of diamonds and pearls. A boat glided gently on the water, and the morning bells of the Cathedral of Ludlow, which was concealed from their eyes, penetrated like distant spirit-voices to their ears.

Here they enjoyed moments such as never return in life, moments of the most unalloyed happiness. What Alice said to Milton sounded to him like a revelation. The wondrously beautiful surroundings, the glorious May-day, unlocked the innermost recesses of her soul.

She had quickly learned to repose full confidence in the poet, and did not hesitate to communicate her innermost thoughts and feelings to him. What he discovered here resembled that nature which surrounded him. The delight and ecstasy of spring surged in her bosom, sunny brightness and clearness filled her soul, and the fragrant charm of innocence bloomed in her heart. Her highly-cultivated mind revelled with him in the wondrous realm of poetry. The poets of her native country had been her perpetual friends and companions; but foreign authors, nay, even those of classical antiquity, were no strangers to her. Alice, like many noble ladies of that time, had enjoyed a more careful education than most ladies of the present age. She had read Ariosto and Tasso in the original, and even tried to read Virgil and Horace in their own tongue. Such accomplishments were not unusual among the higher classes in the days of the reawaking of science and literature, and among them was to be found many a lady who combined with true feminine grace and amiability profound learning and a more than superficial knowledge of classical antiquity. The daughters of Sir Thomas More, Lady Jane Grey, and Queen Elizabeth, vied in this respect with the most learned men of their times. Alice, who, in compliance with her father's wishes, had taken part in the lessons of her brothers, likewise surprised Milton by displaying a wealth of sound knowledge which could not but add to the admiration with which the young *savant* looked upon her.

How delighted he was in hearing from such beautiful lips now a classical quotation, now the melodious verse of Tasso's "Jerusalem Delivered," or Ariosto's "Orlando Furioso;" and how her eyes flashed when he expatiated on the beauties of ancient literature, the epics of Homer, and the sublime tragedies of Æschylus! She was able to follow him everywhere, and manifested the most intimate familiarity with a world generally so foreign to a young girl. Insensibly she became a pupil hanging enthusiastically on the lips of her new teacher. As Abélard and Héloïse in times of yore drew the sweet poison of love from the cup of science and investigation, so here, too, the growing affection stole under the mask of thirst for learning and intellectual improvement into the hearts of Milton and Alice. The verses and strophes of the ancient poets resembled the seeds which are found in the old tombs of Egypt, and which, sown in fertile soil, germinate, blossom, and bear fruit.

But not only did the ideas of Greek and Roman antiquity offer them countless points of contact; but the present with its exciting religious troubles called forth an exchange of opinions regarding the gravest questions of humanity. Alice, like most of the women of her time, was deeply imbued with the eternal truths of Christianity. Faith in the divine Redeemer and enthusiastic admiration for His teachings and His example were the keynotes of her soul. The former tutor of her brothers, Jeremy Taylor, who afterward became one of the most illustrious divines of England and the chief ornament of the Episcopal Church, had, at an early day, strengthened and given a firm direction to Alice's religious sentiments. She was an ardent adherent of the Church of England, while Milton already inclined to the more liberal views of the persecuted dissenters. The opposite course which the two pursued in this respect was for them rather a point of attraction than otherwise. Mutually endeavoring to convince and convert each other, they imparted an extraordinary ardor to their conversation, and, in defending their principles, felt that the personal esteem and affection which they entertained for each other were constantly on the increase.

The spectacle offered by these two young persons was certainly as remarkable as it was attractive. In accordance with the spirit of those days, although their hearts were filled with love, they did not exchange their tender feelings in the face of blooming Nature, but subtle views and ideas concerning the most abstruse theological questions. A holy zeal colored the cheeks of the lovely girl and lit up the flashing eyes of the poet, when, stimulated by his love of liberty, he gave vent in enthusiastic words to his indignation at the tyrannous conduct of the government and the bishops.

"No, no," he said, vehemently. "You cannot deny, noble lady, that the Episcopal Church is becoming more and more Romanized from day to day, and that it is striving to force Catholicism, with all its iniquity and idolatry and the horrors of the inquisition, upon us."

"God forbid!" replied Alice, with the unaffected dismay of a fervent Protestant of that time.

"Have they not dared already," added Milton, "to lay hands on the sacred palladium which we have enjoyed only for so short a time? They grudge us the Bible, which was sought out of the dusty corners where profane falsehood and neglect had thrown it. At the same time the schools were opened, and divine and human learning raked out of the embers of forgotten tongues; princes and cities gathered apace under the new-erected banner of salvation; and martyrs, with the irresistible might of weakness, shook the powers of darkness and stormed the fiery rage of the old red dragon. And is all this to be in vain now? Are not these symptoms significant enough for those who have ears to hear and eyes to see? What is the Episcopal Church but Catholicism in disguise?"

"You go too far. The king is a good Protestant, and will never betray our dear-bought faith."

"And did he not promote the growth of this fearful evil to the best of his power by choosing a Catholic consort? He will perceive the error of his ways only when it is too late. The bishops have always been the enemies of royalty in this country. Have they not been as the Canaanites and Philistines to this kingdom? What treasons, what revolts to the pope, what rebellions, and those the basest and most pretenceless, have they not been chief in! What could monarchy think, when Becket durst challenge the custody of Rochester Castle and the Tower of London as appertaining to his seigniory, to say nothing of his other insolences and affronts to regal majesty, until the lashes inflicted on the anointed body of the king washed off the holy unction with his blood drawn by the polluted hands of bishops, abbots, and monks? What good upholders of royalty were the bishops when, by their rebellious opposition against King John, Normandy was lost, he himself deposed, and this kingdom made over to the pope! When the Bishop of Winchester durst tell the nobles, the pillars of the realm, that there were no peers in England, as in France, but that the king might do what he pleased, what could tyranny say more? Witness also the rendering up of Tournay by Wolsey's treason, the excommunications, cursings, and interdicts upon the whole land. To be sure, the bishops openly affirm the dogma, no bishop no king. A trim paradox, and that you may know where they have been a begging for it, I will fetch you the twin brother to it out of the Jesuits' cell: they, feeling the axe of God's reformation hewing at the old and hollow trunk of popery, and finding the Spaniard their surest friend and safest refuge, to encourage him in his dream of a fifth monarchy, and withal to uphold the decrepit papacy, have invented this superpolitic aphorism, as one may term it, one pope and one king. Amongst many secondary and accessary causes that support monarchy, these are not of least reckoning, though common to all other states:

the love of the subjects, the multitude and valor of the people, and store of treasure. In all these things has the kingdom been of late sorely weakened, and chiefly by the prelates. Their principal weapon is religious persecution. What numbers of faithful and freeborn Englishmen, and good Christians, have been constrained to forsake their dearest home, their friends and kindred, whom nothing but the wide ocean and the savage deserts of America could hide and shelter from the fury of the bishops! Oh, if we could but see the shape of our dear mother England, how would she appear, think you, but in a mourning weed, with ashes upon her head, and tears abundantly flowing from her eyes, to behold so many of her children exposed at once, and thrust from things of dearest necessity, because their conscience could not assent to things which the bishops thought indifferent!"

"I certainly deplore with you," said Alice, deeply moved by the eloquent words of the poet, "these proceedings, which every one must disapprove. My father has openly denounced them at the risk of displeasing the court. So far as it is in his power, he pursues a mild and indulgent course toward the dissenters; but are not these Puritans and Presbyterians to blame for their own fate? Are they not, in their unbridled longing for a mistaken political and religious freedom, intent on overthrowing the foundations on which our whole political fabric is based? Do they not threaten alike the sacred majesty of the king and the authority of the Church?"

"Pardon me, noble lady; you speak like most of the adherents of the Episcopal Church. The priesthood, from time out of memory, has striven to make men believe that it was the Church, or rather identical with faith and religion. But the two things are as materially different from each other as the vessel is from its contents, the gold from the miner who digs it, or the workman who shapes it. Wine is wine, whether it is contained in earthen cups or golden goblets, and gold does not lose its solid value by being set with this or that substance. It is not the letter that gives life, but the spirit and idea."

"But the idea needs a definite form, without which it cannot exist or maintain itself."

"This form exists; it is that which Christ, the Saviour and Redeemer of the world, gave us Himself. The Puritans, who are so grossly misrepresented, are precisely bent on purifying this genuine gold from all earthly dross. They go back to the fountain-head of Christianity, and derive their faith from the sacred books which the Apostles have bequeathed to us. Say yourself if this is not necessary here in England. Where do you find here Christian charity, toleration, and self-abnegation? The court is the embodiment of haughtiness and arrogance, and vice stalks unblushingly near the king's anointed person. His courtiers exhibit the most demoralizing spectacle by their dissipated life and shameless conduct. The bishops, who call themselves successors of the Apostles, are far from following their example. They would laugh at your folly, if you were to ask them to live in poverty and endure the privations of their holy predecessors. They revel in the riches which they extort from the poor people. If they had one thought upon God's glory and the advancement of Christian faith, instead of lavishing their great resources upon senseless ostentation and luxury, they would provide for the building of churches and schools where none now exist, and for their increase where now there are too few; for the suitable maintenance of laborious ministers who can now scarcely procure bread, while the prelates revel like Belshazzar, with goblets and vessels of gold torn from God's temple. What a mass of money is drawn from the veins into the ulcers of the kingdom by such execrable, such irreligious courses!"

"And your Puritans are going to abolish all these abuses? What will they put in their place?"

"God and liberty!" exclaimed the poet, enthusiastically. "If, under a free and untrammelled monarch, the noblest, worthiest, and most prudent men, with full approbation of the people, have in their power the supreme and final determination of the highest affairs, there can be nothing more appropriate than that under the sovereign prince, Christ's vicegerent, using the sceptre of David, according to God's law, the godliest, the wisest, the most learned ministers in their several charges should have the instructing and disciplining of God's people, by whose full and free election they are consecrated to that holy and equal aristocracy. If they follow faithfully the example set them by their predecessors and draw their faith from the same sources as they did, Christianity will be restored to its pristine purity, and it will fill the hearts of all believers with justice, truth, love, and toleration. Then, amidst the hymns and hallelujahs of saints, some one may perhaps be heard offering, in new and lofty measures, to sing and celebrate the mercies and marvellous judgments of Providence in this land throughout all ages; and this great and warlike nation, instructed in and inured to the fervent and continual practice of truth and righteousness, will become the soberest, wisest, and most Christian people."

"Would to God you rwords were verified!" replied Alice, with radiant eyes; "would to God this wish were fulfilled! If I cannot assent to all you have said, I long with you at least for the time when an era of mutual toleration and forbearance shall dawn upon us. How often have I heard similar words from the mouth of my revered teacher, Jeremy Taylor! He is likewise opposed to persecution of any description, and, though an orthodox divine of the Episcopal Church, yet full of mildness and forbearance toward dissenters. How wonderful! When I listen to you, Mr. Milton, I always feel as though he were standing before me. You are animated with the same enthusiasm, you possess the same poetical and flowery peculiarity of expressing your thoughts as that excellent man; and even the tone of your voice reminds me of him. He would have made more satisfactory replies to your arguments than I, an ignorant girl, have been able to do. For he is a very learned man, and, above all things, a profound divine. He would certainly be a foeman worthy of your steel. What a pity that he is no longer here, for, despite your contrary opinions, you would assuredly become warm friends. Noble and generous men, I have often heard him say, oppose, but do not persecute each other. Only God Himself knows the truth; hence, it is wrong in men to arrogate the position of its judges and avengers. The most different roads may lead to the goal where the good of all times and countries, from what opposite points soever they may have started, will meet in the end to join hands in love and peace. Let us do the same, although I see that we differ in regard to many essential points; and, wherever we may meet, let our motto of recognition be: 'Toleration and charity, friendship and love.'"

The lovely girl whispered in a low voice the last words, which, in her mouth, contained another and sweeter meaning for the happy poet. Milton took the hand which she extended to him, and held it long in his own, like a pledge which he was determined never to give up again. Thus the hostile parties anticipated in the blooming garden the sacred festival of reconciliation which England was to celebrate only after long and bloody civil wars. Human and divine love, wonderfully blended and interwoven, accomplished in a moment the sublime task at which the statesmanship of the most skilful politicians, the persuasive eloquence of the most impassioned orators, and the exertions of a great and powerful people were vainly toiling for many years in succession. A fleeting moment realized that which decades were unable to bring about, and filled up the gulf which the parties thought insurmountable.

Alice left her hand willingly to the poet. Thus they stood on the terrace, leaning against the balustrade, now looking into the sweet valley at their feet, now gazing deeply into each other's eyes. Their enthusiasm had silenced them. What could they say to each other after such words? Any additional conversation would only have marred the sacred beauty of this hour and the sublime gravity of the previous moment. Only the dying notes of the church-bells, proclaiming peace and joy to the people, joined harmoniously in the devout and inspired feelings of the young hearts which celebrated to-day their resurrection, the Easter-morn of their sweet young love.

CHAPTER VIII.

RENDEZVOUS OF THOMAS AND LUCY.

On her way back to the castle Alice met with her younger brother. Thomas had reached Ludlow Castle much later than the others, and the midnight hour had struck long before he arrived there. After being told by a servant that Alice and the two friends had arrived before him, he immediately retired in a not very pleasant frame of mind. His agitation was such that he could not sleep for a long while. The recollection of his adventure with the Puritans, and the prospect of his being scolded by his parents and his more prudent brother, kept him awake in his bed. Nevertheless, he rose at an early hour, and Alice met him already fully dressed in the court-yard. The youth stood in the midst of a pack of setters and pointers, which were jumping and barking around him in a caressing, delighted manner. A groom held his horse, which was neighing and stamping its hoof impatiently, and which Thomas was just going to mount in order to take a ride.

"Good-morning, Orlando!" shouted Alice to him, kindly, from a distance. "Oh, is that right? You are going to leave me without greeting me? You have not even inquired about my health, and what adventures befell me since you forsook me so faithlessly and imprudently? Do you know, then, that I am quite angry with you?"

"That was the very reason why I wished to leave. I cannot stand these eternal reproaches."

"You wild boy! have I reproached you, then, with any thing? You are decidedly too sensitive. To punish you, I want you to stay here and tell me what fairy or beautiful magician met you and enticed you so deep into the forest that you forgot to return to your sister."

"I can do that in a very few words," replied the youth, with the blush which always accompanies a first lie. "On leaving you, I really thought I had heard human voices in the gorge. It was an illusion, however. The farther I advanced, the farther receded these seductive sounds. It was unfortunately too late, when I found out my mistake. I wished to retrace my steps immediately, but I had now lost my way entirely. Thus I wandered through the wilderness for several hours without knowing where I was until I met with some peasants, with whose assistance I got back to the highway. I hastened at once back to the place where I thought I should find you yet. However, you had disappeared. I vainly shouted your name, no one replied to me. An indescribable terror seized me, and I passed a long time in search of you. Finally I met the servants whom father had sent out. They reassured me as to your fate, and I started with them for Ludlow Castle. I soon learned the particulars of your rescue by two young men, of whom one at least is no stranger to you."

"And now you are going to leave us again, and roam no one knows where."

"I give you my reasons for it. I cannot bear being censured on all sides. To-morrow I may be better able to endure it. The thunder-storm which has gathered over my head must pass away a little before I shall return. It is true, you have good reason to be angry with me; but you are not, and I am sure you have forgiven me long since."

"Yes, I have, you wild madcap; and if you will stay here, I will intercede with father in your behalf."

"Not to-day," said the youth, beseechingly. "I should play too sorry a part among you. Spare me this confusion in presence of the strangers, and let me go."

"Well, I do not care, incorrigible one; but I will let you go only on condition that you return before nightfall. I will excuse your absence as well as I can."

"Do so," replied the youth, vaulting into the saddle and galloping away.

Alice looked after him until he disappeared; she then went to her room, where she engaged in company with her mother in needlework, which gave her the best opportunity for thinking undisturbedly of the absent poet and the grave conversation she had held with him.

Meanwhile Thomas was galloping with his dogs toward the neighboring forest. But a close observer would soon have perceived that the youth was not intent on hunting to-day; this had been only a pretext to cloak, in his own eyes, the disquietude which drove him away from home. No sportsman rides so carelessly through the fields and forest as he did. Before long he left to his horse the task of finding the way, seeming to be entirely indifferent as to the direction which the noble animal took. He hung carelessly in the saddle, holding the reins loosely in his hands. At times a blossoming branch touched his hat and cheek, but he paid no attention to it. The dogs trotted at first merrily by his side and barked a little whenever they scented game, but the sullen hunter did not hear them. He was following an entirely different scent. His game was a slender young girl with hazel eyes and dark ringlets. Beautiful Lucy Henderson engrossed all his thoughts, and he pursued her image, or rather it pursued him on his way. He knew her dwelling, which lay in the valley below, near the bank of the Teme. An irresistible longing drew him thither, but his aversion to meeting the austere Puritan prevented him from riding directly toward the place. The closer he came up to the cottage occupied by old Henderson and his daughter, the more audibly throbbed the heart in the youth's bosom.

Already he saw the small dwelling in the midst of the blossoming fruit-trees. How often had he played there with his brother, his sister, and little Lucy, and playfully called her his little bride! The happy days of innocent childhood were over, and more ardent longings and desires now filled the heart of the fiery youth. How much he would have given for permission to be together with her as quietly and undisturbedly as he was but a few years ago! Now he was quite close to the entrance-gate, but he was not bold enough to ask admittance. He halted his horse on the opposite bank of the river, and looked with longing eyes at the cottage where lived the fair friend of his childhood. Like a thief, he crept close up to it, hidden by the dense willows and alders on the river-bank. From time to time he cast a furtive glance on the cottage, but its door remained closed, and no white hand drew back the bolt, no blooming girlish face appeared at the window.

At no great distance from Thomas, and entirely unnoticed by him, there lay a man stretched out on the turf amidst the shrubbery. He looked with seeming carelessness at the fishing-rod which he held in his hand, but the shrewd twinkling of his squint-eyes showed that the presence of the young man had not escaped him. The angler watched him cautiously, but with great attention and curiosity. He saw very well what Thomas was after, and why he watched old Henderson's cottage so closely. At times a sneering air overspread the broad, shrewd face of the rough-looking fellow.

"Hem!" he murmured to himself. "I warrant the young nobleman is not watching here for nothing. If I am not mistaken, the old Puritan has a pretty daughter well worth committing a little sin. A sweet morsel for such a hunter! I will see how the fowler will manage to catch this little bird. Attention, Billy Green! perhaps there is something for you to do here. Lovers are generous, and my pockets are as empty as my stomach. What if I offered him my assistance? I know the necessary little tricks ten times better than any one else."

So saying, Billy Green, who is no stranger to us, raised himself from his comfortable posture. The noise which he made caused the dogs to bark, which aroused Thomas from his reverie.

"Who is there?" he said to the fellow, who stood suddenly before him.

"Your servant," replied Billy Green, humbly, taking off his cap. "My name is of no consequence, and cannot be useful to you, but my person can. He whom you see before you is the best sleuth-hound in the whole country. I will drive up the game you are hunting for."

"Take this," said the youth, dropping a small coin into the fellow's cap. "You see that I want to be alone. Go, therefore; I have no use for your services, and dogs, you see, are not wanting to me."

"Oh, you are rather gruff, sir. But you ought to know that there is a difference between dogs. Your dogs know only how to scent lean rabbits or half-starved grouse; but I can find the most beautiful girl in the whole country for you. I know here a nice little girl named Lucy Henderson, who is surely worth hunting for."

"Fellow," cried the youth, eagerly, "what do you know about the girl? Speak!"

"Aha! I see that I am on the right trail, for you are as eager for it as a hunter is to get sight of a fat deer with sixteen branches. Well, it will not be my fault if you do not catch your game this very day."

"No bad jokes, if you please. Tell me plainly, do you know the girl?"

"How should I not know the flower of the valley, the fairest rose of Herefordshire? But take care. The old proverb says, 'No rose without thorns,' and morose old Henderson is a whole thorn-bush protecting the sweet little rose from profane hands. Unless you are, at least, a saint or an archangel, with your hair cropped like that of the Roundheads, he will slam his door in your face. Besides, he is desperate enough to send after you from his old blunderbuss some blue pills that might make it impossible for you ever to call again. The old Puritan dog is not a man to be joked with; he will snap and bite in the same breath."

"I know, I know," murmured Thomas; "and yet I must see Lucy even though all hell with a legion of devils should guard her. Will you do me a favor?"

"Two for one," replied the fellow, gayly; "that is to say, if you pay me two prices."

"I will pay you liberally. Take these two crowns on account."

"So a poor devil like me gets two crowns when the king has but one; but I doubt not that one often presses more heavily on his head than my two. Tell me now what I am to do; for I am sure you did not give me this money merely for the sake of my fine face.

Billy Green is not a beggar of the highway, but an honest fellow who will fight the devil himself if he gets paid for it."

"I will trust you, though I do not know any thing about you. You seem to be a shrewd, smart fellow."

"Just give me a chance to show my shrewdness and smartness, and you will see wonders. I suppose you are in love with pretty Lucy Henderson? Just let me manage it, and you shall see her speedily. By Heaven, I know of no greater fun than to play a trick on such a canting, sanctimonious, psalm-singing Puritan! Just think of what he did the other day! Meeting me on Sunday, not in a very sober condition, I must confess, he called me a ruthless Sabbath-breaker, a son of Antichrist and of Babylon; in short, he gave me all sorts of hard names, and all for being a little merry on Sunday. The devil take these Puritanic scoundrels, who want to deprive every merry fellow of his little amusements!"

"You may vent your bile another time, and curse the Puritans as much as you like. I will not prevent you from so doing, but join in it with all my heart. But now you have no time to lose if you intend to redeem your promise."

"There you are right; but, above all things, I must know how far you have conquered the girl's heart; whether you are at the A or the Z of love; whether the little bird is only casting furtive glances on the berries, or has already tasted the forbidden fruit."

"What does that concern you, fellow? You use language which I do not want to hear again."

"All right, sir; but that will render my task more difficult. I know the girls and the birds, for Billy Green is no novice so far as that sort of sport is concerned. Lucy will not believe me, unless you give me a token which will satisfy her that the message I bring comes from you. Lovers have a cant of their own. I must bring her some such mysterious greeting, else she will not trust me. Is there not some word or motto that is only known to her and you? Let me hear it."

Thomas, who perceived the sagacity of what Billy said, reflected a few moments. A long time had elapsed since he had spoken with the young girl. How was she to recognize, then, that it was he who wished to see her? Fortunately he remembered a little ditty which both had sung very often in their youth, and whose last lines were as follows:

"He raised the maiden on his steed,
He bore her to his castle proud,
For ah, he loved her well!"

It was not difficult for Billy Green to remember the words of this old song, and the melody which the youth sang to him in a low voice. Thus prepared, Billy set out, promising to obtain an interview with beautiful Lucy Henderson, and return speedily with a reply from her. He approached cautiously the house of the Puritan, with whom he did not wish to meet, because he knew that the morose old man was not in the habit of treating such idlers and good-for-nothings very kindly or considerately. The shrewd fellow prowled for some time around the closed court-yard like a fox intending to visit a dove-cot. He hoped to find somewhere an open side-gate, by which he might slip stealthily into the cottage; but he very soon found that this was impossible. The distrustful and misanthropic Henderson had taken means to prevent strangers from penetrating into his house. A high and substantial wall, surmounted with stout spikes, surrounded the whole building. Billy Green was not very eager to endanger his limbs, or to receive a wound. Nothing, therefore, remained for him but to knock loudly at the entrance-gate, and demand admittance. His ingenuity had already suggested to him an excellent excuse in case he should meet the Puritan, and he took care to impart to his face as grave and sanctimonious an expression as possible.

He had knocked already for some time without attracting any one to the gate. The house seemed entirely deserted; not a voice resounded in response to his calls; not a foot, not a hand stirred to open the gate to him. He almost gave up the hope of succeeding in delivering his message to the beautiful Lucy. He was upon the point of withdrawing and retracing his steps, when he determined to make a final desperate effort before returning to Thomas. He was bent on mischief, and his ambition also prompted him to persist; and he resolved to force his way into the house, even at the risk of getting a sound whipping. For this purpose he commenced shouting with all his might: "Fire! fire! Help! help!"

This last resort had the desired effect. He heard persons moving in the house. An elderly woman and a young girl rushed anxiously into the court-yard, and a laborer hurried up from the stable. All three had heard the shouts, and looked for the man who had uttered them, but who took good care to conceal himself, in order to await the effect of his stratagem. He had already seen enough to be satisfied that old Henderson, of whom he was more afraid than of any one else, was not present. The frightened inmates of the house soon arrived at the conviction that some passer-by had fooled them; for, notwithstanding the most careful researches, they were unable to discover any traces of fire. Lucy and the old housekeeper were about to return into the house, but the laborer was not yet willing to drop the matter.

"I will pay the fool for this," he cried, with clinched fist. "I bet he is concealed close by. I'll pay him for the fright he gave us."

Before the women, who were still excited and anxious, could prevent him, he had drawn back the bolt from the gate and rushed out. Billy Green rubbed his hands gleefully in his hiding-place, for there was no longer any thing to prevent him from entering the house. As soon as the laborer, in the eagerness of his pursuit, was sufficiently distant from the house, Billy left his hiding-place, and stepped boldly into the court-yard. At the sight of the stranger, whose appearance was by no means reassuring, the timid housekeeper uttered a loud cry, and ran away. Lucy, who was a courageous girl, stood still and waited for the new-comer to tell his errand.

"What do you want?" she inquired, fearlessly. "My father is not at home. If you want to see him, you must come again to-morrow, when he will be back from his trip to the neighboring city."

"I am glad to hear that, for now I can deliver my message without being interfered with by him."

"Your message? To whom?" she asked, in surprise, and starting back a few steps, as the stranger's conduct aroused her suspicion.

"To whom but yourself, beautiful Lucy?"

"I do not know who could send me a message."

"A young man whom you know, and who loves you."

"You are a rogue and villain to address such words to me. Begone, or I will have you driven ignominiously from the place."

"Do not get excited," said Billy, with an impudent leer, "although your indignation sits very well on you. You cannot deceive me, for I know all about it. *We* all know what girls will do."

"Silence, sirrah! There comes our laborer, and he shall punish you for your impudence."

"You will change your mind before he gets here. If you are determined not to hear my message, let me sing a nice little ditty to you:

'He raised the maiden on his steed,
He bore her to the castle proud,
For ah, he loved her well!'

Well, how do you like that?"

Lucy had immediately recognized the words and the melody, which Green hummed to her in an undertone, and accompanied by expressive ludicrous gestures. He looked at her at the same time so archly, and watched her so closely, that her agitation could not escape him.

"I see already that I have struck the right note this time," he added, smilingly. "Well, why do you stand staring as though some miracle had happened to you?"

"How do you come to know that song?" faltered out Lucy.

"Great heavens! she asks me how I come to know that song! A merry bird sang it to me under the willows; and as I liked it, I remembered it easily."

"No, no, *he* taught it to you. Do not torment me, but tell me the truth: is the commission which you have for me from *him?*"

"If you mean by *he* and *him* a slender young hunter of aristocratic appearance, distinguished manners, a face like milk and blood, and a pretty little black mustache, you are right?"

"And you say that he is quite close by?"

"Not much beyond the range of a good rifle. With your nimble feet you can reach him in five minutes, and be in the arms of your beloved.

'And thus they sat, and thus they lay,
In the green field, in the green field;
They sat, and, ah, forgot that day,
The whole wide world, the whole wide world!'"

"Pray, stop this nonsense. Our servant may return at any moment, and, besides, we are watched by the housekeeper, who is only prevented by her terror from gratifying her curiosity."

"Very well, make haste then, and give me a favorable reply to take to your lover."

"What does he want of me, then?"

"Oh, these girls! Like kittens they sniff round the hot soup, which they would like so well to taste. The young nobleman wants to see, embrace, and kiss you. If you do not come, he will commit suicide. He is dying of longing and impatience. Perhaps he has already, driven to despair by my long delay, plunged into the cold waters of the Teme to cool his ardent love."

"He wants to see me, did he say?"

"He said so, and swore and raved, as all lovers do; for he is head over ears in love with you. I can bear witness to that. His loud sighs aroused me from my sleep, and it was nothing but compassion for his sufferings that caused me to become his messenger. But now make up your mind quick, for I really see that boor of a servant coming toward us, after ransacking every shrub, and looking for me behind every blade. What am I to tell your lover?

'My love, my love, oh come to me,
Beneath the shade I wait for thee:
The trees our joys will not betray,
The little stars are mute as they!'"

Although Lucy had perceived the approach of her father's servant, and saw that there was no time to be lost, she hesitated yet to make a reply. She was afraid of old Henderson's severity, and besides, a feeling of girlish timidity deterred her. But the very puritanic retirement and restraint to which she had been so long subjected, had aroused longings for freedom in her bosom. For a long time her mind had secretly revolted at the narrow bounds which had been set to it. She yearned for the wide world, from which she was shut out. By forbidding her to visit Ludlow Castle and its inmates, Henderson had sorely chafed her rebellious spirit. Her last meeting with Thomas had produced a truly feverish effect upon her warm blood. She had dreamed all night of her former playmate, and even in the daytime his image was ever present to her soul. Now he had taken the first step, and come to her; could she resist any longer?

The servant was scarcely fifty steps from

the gate, and the housekeeper's head was to be seen at the window. Lucy had no time to lose.

"Go," she whispered to Billy Green, "and tell him who sent you that I will see him. My father is absent on business, and will not be back before to-morrow; but, notwithstanding his absence, I am watched like a prisoner. I shall not be able to steal away until after dinner. Let him await me then at the old tombstone near the three pines. Every child knows the place; he will easily find it by inquiring for it."

"I myself will conduct him thither, and stand guard lest any one should overhear you."

"Do so, good man, and take this for your trouble."

Billy Green pocketed with a chuckle the small coin which Lucy handed to him, and vowed in return, without being asked for it, eternal fidelity and silence; and he really intended to redeem his promise, in order to gratify his hatred against the Puritan. He passed the returning servant with a smile of great satisfaction.

"Did you find the man you were looking for?" he asked him, maliciously.

The servant contented himself with eying Billy distrustfully.

"Let me give you a piece of good advice," said Billy to him. "On leaving the yard henceforth, you had better lock the gate lest a fox should steal your Puritan chickens while you are pursuing his trail!"

He disappeared with a peal of laughter behind the shrubbery on the bank, before the servant was able to make a fitting reply to him. The stone which he hurled after the vagabond fell noisily into the water, and excited anew the mirth and sneers of Billy Green, who was very proud of having so completely fooled the servant.

CHAPTER IX.

THE MEETING.

Lucy waited with feverish suspense the moment when, after their long separation, she was to see her former playmate again undisturbedly. The hours seemed to creep along with snail-like slowness; the hands of the clock would not move on. At dinner she was scarcely able to swallow a morsel, so that the old housekeeper asked her anxiously if she was unwell, and what ailed her. She sought to appear gay and unconcerned, although she hardly succeeded in doing so. At last the servant went to work again after carefully bolting the gate; the old housekeeper seemed to have fallen asleep in her easy-chair. Now was the time for Lucy to steal away. She slipped noiselessly on tiptoe to the door, and then anxiously looked back. The housekeeper had her eyes open again, and asked, dreamily, "Where are you going, Lucy?"

"Into the garden," said the girl. "I am going to look after the new plants."

"Go, my child. But do not stroll farther away from the house, for you know that your father does not like you to do so, especially in his absence. If he should learn of such a thing, he would scold us both."

"I shall remain in the garden."

"Very well, very well," murmured the old woman (a relative of Henderson), and fell once more into her doze.

Lucy, as she had said, went in the first place to the garden. It consisted of a few modest flower-beds and a small orchard. On one side were to be seen the beehives, to which old Henderson devoted particular attention. Their industrious inmates swarmed in great numbers past Lucy toward the neighboring forest, where they sought for richer spoils of honey. The daughter of the house was well known to the sagacious insects. A bold little bee seated itself on Lucy's hand, which it had taken, perhaps, for a white blossom; but, probably finding out its mistake, it soon unfurled its brown wings and sped forward, as if to show her the way. A gate led from the garden into the open fields; closed on the inside with a wooden bolt. The girl drew it back with a trembling hand, as though she were about to commit a great crime. Thus she had crossed the threshold of her paternal home, and stood still for a moment, hesitating whether to proceed or not. Indescribable anxiety filled her once more. The little bee was still humming before her, and flew on boldly and carelessly, filled with no such apprehensions, and, if it thought at all, thinking only of the sweet honey which was in store for it. Suddenly a swallow darted down out of the air, and the little bee paid with its life for its first sally into the fields. Lucy had not noticed the occurrence, for she was too much engrossed in her own thoughts; otherwise, perhaps, it might have served as a caution to her. But, as it was, passion and hot blood carried the day, and she was bound to see Thomas, even though it should cost her life.

Young as the girl was, she possessed a strength of will bordering on obstinacy. Something of old Henderson's puritanic stubbornness was to be found in her character. His severe treatment had aroused her indignation, and she was determined to bear no longer the restraint imposed upon her. She had formerly become acquainted with another and more brilliant life than that she was compelled to lead now at the quiet house, in the company of her old relative, and under the surveillance of her morose father. At that time, when her mother still lived, and she was yet allowed to hold daily intercourse with the inmates of Ludlow Castle, she had been the partner of their joys and manifold amusements. For days she was permitted to play in the sumptuous apartments of the castle, surrounded by all sorts of precious and gorgeous objects. The stern orders of old Henderson had suddenly put an end to all this. How many tears had the privations imposed on her all at once wrung from her! She thought night and day of those charming times, and every thing beautiful and magnificent was associated in her mind with Ludlow Castle. There lay the country she was yearning for, the lost paradise of her childhood.

It was for this reason that her meeting with Thomas in Haywood Forest had made so deep an impression upon her. All the old wounds commenced bleeding afresh, and memory fanned her slumbering love into a bright flame. Nothing was needed but an opportunity, a beck, and Lucy would leave her hateful paternal home and return into the arms of her former playmate. The imagination of this girl of seventeen looked upon the youth as a savior and deliverer from the jail in which she felt herself imprisoned. The warm life-blood circulating through her veins, throbbed for enjoyment and pleasure, which had so long been denied to her. The gloomy Puritan allowed his daughter none of the amusements for which young persons so justly yearn; even the most innocent joys were forbidden to her. She was not permitted to go out, except in the company of her father, or under other surveillance, nor ever to attend a rural festival. Old Henderson detested the notes of a bagpipe or violin; he considered dancing a terrible sin, and every other harmless pleasure a heavy crime. This was in keeping with the spirit of the times, and with the views of those sectarians. Lucy was not even permitted to sing, and yet she was famous for her fresh and charming voice. Mr. Lawes, the music-teacher at the castle, after hearing her, had been so delighted as to offer, of his own accord, to give her the necessary instruction and cultivate her voice. The surly Puritan would not even permit this, and had rejected the offer under the pretext that the human voice was destined only to praise the Lord, and that no instruction was necessary for this purpose. Lucy had borne all this long enough, in her opinion—his exaggerated severity, her joyless loneliness, the rude and oppressive treatment she had to endure, and the privation of the most innocent amusements. The moment had come for her now to indemnify herself to some extent. Her heart was unconsciously filled with longings for liberty, and for some change in this tedious and monotonous life.

Her friend's message reached her when such was her frame of mind. She felt like a prisoner whose cell is opened by a compassionate hand, and rushed rashly out of the garden. It was not until she had left it that she began to reflect, and bashfulness stole upon her heart. Her anxiety increased at every step as she moved from her father's house. Every tree by the wayside seemed to her a spy, and behind every shrub she thought she saw some one watching her. She had to fear the worst from her father's severity in case he should ever learn that she had disregarded his orders in such a manner. Her heart felt no love for, but only intense fear of him; but it was not this feeling alone that deterred her now. Her conscience, her virgin shame, raised their warning voices in her bosom. Both advised her against the step she was taking; they spoke to the hesitating girl softly, it is true, but impressively enough. Her heart throbbed with tumultuous agitation and threatened to burst her close-fitting black bodice. All sorts of objections arose in her soul, and more than once she turned her eyes back toward the house which lay so quiet in the noonday sun. So long as Lucy saw this house where she was born, and at the door of which she had so often sat with her lamented mother, concealing her curly head in the lap of the kind-hearted matron, she still felt tempted to return. The windows seemed to her like eyes looking anxiously after her, and the smoking chimney like a finger cautioning her against what she was about to do. She seemed to hear a well-known voice calling her back in plaintive tones. These remembered tones pierced her heart; her knees trembled involuntarily, and her feet seemed nailed to the ground. But the next moment she thought of the promise she had given to the friend who was waiting for her, and turned her back resolutely upon her home and the spirits of her domestic hearth, which were following her warningly. Once more she turned before setting foot on the small bridge that was to lead her to the opposite bank. The house had disappeared and was concealed from her eyes. It seemed to her as though she had no longer a home.

She crossed the bridge with a rapid step, and breathed freely again only after reaching the opposite bank. Behind her lay the gloomy past, and before her the flowery meadows and the mute forest, where her lover was waiting for her under the pines. How lovingly did her heart throb toward him! But her home seemed not yet willing to give her up; it sent after her a faithful messenger who pursued her steps with stubborn perseverance. She heard a panting sound behind her, but was not courageous enough to turn. The pursuer came nearer and nearer, howling and barking, spying and seeking. It was the faithful watch-dog that had hastened after her. Now he jumped up to her, and gave vent to his joy at finding her in loud barking and wonderful leaps. Evidently out of breath he pressed his shaggy head against her airy form, and looked at her with his sagacious, good-natured eyes. She was unable to bear his glance, which seemed a silent reproach to her. This unexpected witness was a burden to her. Vainly did she drive the animal from her side; the dog, usually so obedient, refused to leave her; he returned to her again and again; neither her prayers nor her threats were of any avail.

From her earliest childhood he had been her constant companion; he had grown up with her, always a friend, a careful guardian, and now, perhaps, more than ever. This thought presented itself again to Lucy, and yet she would not suffer the dumb monitor near her. She begged and scolded, she threatened and entreated, but the dog did not move from the spot. At the best, he remained a few steps behind, and trotted after her mournfully and hanging his head. The girl would not tolerate his company at any cost. It was almost with tears in her eyes that she ordered him to go home; but it was all in vain, he stuck to her heels like the warning voice of conscience. Her impatience caused her to forget everything—his fidelity and love, his long, long services, and her old affection for him. She picked up a stone and hurled it at the faithful animal. The dog uttered a loud howl, and limped off with a bleeding foot. Her head began to swim, and she thought she would faint. On looking up again, she discovered that the dog had already disappeared.

She hastened forward now to make up lost time, but she still seemed to hear the panting of the faithful dog behind her, and to see the reproachful glance which he cast on her when the hand which had hitherto always caressed him raised the stone against him. She felt a load weighing down her heart as if she had committed a crime. Her conscience raised its warning voice once more, but it was again in vain. She could already see her destination, the three lonely pines and the old tomb. The last scene had heated her warm blood still more, and added to her obstinacy. Her cheeks were flushed, her pulse was throbbing, a sort of wild frenzy had seized her soul. Thus she rushed toward her fate.

Thomas waited likewise with feverish excitement for the arrival of the girl, for whom so ardent a love had arisen in his heart overnight. He had hunted during the morning in the forest only to kill the time till the hour of meeting, but the game had been safe from his bullets. His thoughts were engrossed in something else, and Lucy's charming image stood constantly before his eyes. She was the prey which he had chosen, and the description which Billy Green had given him of her beauty only added to the flame burning in his heart. It was not love, but a wild intoxication that had seized his senses, an infatuating fascination which suddenly changed the whole character of the hitherto innocent youth.

The designated spot lay somewhat off the highway, on a hill, where one could not be seen, and yet, shielded by the dense shrubbery, could survey the whole neighborhood. A gray, moss-grown slab covered the grave of an unknown knight, who had fallen here several centuries ago in a duel, or by the hands of assassins. The inscription had long since become illegible, and the name had been forgotten, but the legend had stuck to the bloody spot, and did not even allow the slain knight to find rest in his grave. Passers-by asserted that they had often seen a pale youth seated on the slab, surrounded by his dogs. The superstitious peasantry of the neighborhood avoided the road leading past the grave. It was but rarely that any one ventured to set foot on this weird spot, and even the birds seemed to shun it. Profound silence reigned all around. The heavy branches of the sombre pines did not move, and the tall grass murmured almost inaudibly. Such was the spot which Lucy had chosen for her interview with Thomas; she was sure that no one would watch and disturb them here. She herself was not afraid, for old Henderson had remained free from the superstition of the common peasantry, and had educated his daughter in this spirit.

A shrill whistle uttered by Billy Green informed the impatient youth of the girl's arrival. Soon after she stood before him, breathless, and unable to utter a word. Thomas signed to Billy Green, who disappeared at once in the shrubbery, and the lovers were alone.

"At last! At last!" cried Thomas. "I was already afraid you would not come."

"Was I not obliged to come after you had called me?" she replied, affectionately. "I should have come even though it had cost my life."

"Lucy, do you love me?"

"Ask me, rather, if I ever ceased to love you. All my thoughts have always been with you and your sister at Ludlow Castle. Oh, how I have longed to meet with one of you, and unbosom the grief weighing down my heart! At length I saw you yesterday in Haywood Forest. My heart throbbed impetuously toward you, but I could not utter a syllable in that hateful crowd. What did I suffer for your sake on seeing you exposed to such deadly peril! Thank God, you were saved, they did not kill you."

"You see I got off tolerably well. But let us no longer speak of me, and, least of all, of my adventure yesterday. I hope I shall one day get even with the rabble, and wreak vengeance on them for the contumely which they heaped on me. Tell me, rather, about your affairs, your life. We have not seen each other for so long; it has been almost an eternity for me."

"Really? Oh, would that I could believe you!"

"Did I ever tell you a falsehood? Were you not always my dearest friend since my earliest childhood? Come, sit down; let us chat together as we used to do in former times."

He took her hand, and drew her down to his side on the moss-grown slab. He folded her to his heart, and she did not prevent him from imprinting glowing kisses on her lips and cheeks.

"You want to know about my life during these latter years?" she asked, with a sigh, after a pause. "Alas! Since my dear mother's death I have not had a single merry hour. My father became more morose from day to day, and held intercourse with no one. You know that he joined the Puritans, and, like them, is at variance with the whole world. He reads all day long in the Bible, which he carries constantly about him; he looks, with sullen hatred, upon every thing that is not in keeping with his austere notions. I am obliged to follow his example, although this kind of life is so odious to me that I long for death every day. I am kept at home like a prisoner, and am watched at every step. No matter what I may do, it is always a sin in father's eyes, and he pronounces every pleasure a bait of hell. I cannot bear it any longer. If I had not met you, I should surely have carried my resolve into effect."

"What resolve?"

"To throw myself into the Teme where it is deepest."

"Oh, you bad girl! Would you really have been capable of doing that?"

"Yes, I would, and you know that I was already in my childhood able to take firm resolutions. But since I have found you again, and since you have told me that you love me yet, I will live. Oh, I love this life so dearly, when it smiles at me so gayly from your eyes!"

"Yes, we will live," said Thomas, pressing the girl's slender form to his heart. "To live and enjoy shall be our motto. Away with the morose teachings of the hypocritical Puritans! What do their gloomy sermons concern us? God did not create the beautiful world in vain. He did not vouchsafe us our joyous youth in vain. Despite all canting, sanctimonious villains, we will enjoy the present. What does the flower bloom for, if we are not allowed to pluck it; what does the wine grow for, if we are not to drink it? Our lips are created for something else besides singing tedious psalms all the time. Kiss me, my sweet love, and I will absolve you from this sin by another kiss."

By such tender jests the youth dissipated the misgivings which still rose from time to time in the girl's heart. He preached likewise, but it was the gospel of enjoyment and love, to which she lent only too willing an ear. Against the gloomy spirit of Puritanism he called up the merry spirits of pleasure and enjoyment. Lucy was unable to resist him. She shared neither the fanaticism of her father nor his austere views of the life of this world; her whole nature rebelled against them. Youth and love revolted in her heart at a creed which was in constant opposition to the desires of her warm blood. "Renounce!" said to her the creed that was forced upon her. "Enjoy!" whispered love into her ear. She followed the sweet voice of the tempter.

The everlasting struggle between mind and matter, between resignation and enjoyment, to which Christianity gave rise, was never carried on in England with greater zeal and fanaticism than in those days. On one side stood the extravagant court, with the rich and overbearing cavaliers. There reigned in those circles the greatest splendor and luxury, surpassing by far all that the present has to compare with it. Buckingham, the favorite of two kings, may be justly looked upon as the representative. His extravagance knew no longer any bounds. His palaces and country-seats were the centres of fashion and dissipation; the value of his diamonds and other gems exceeded the sum of two hundred thousand pounds sterling. He was the first Englishman who rode in an equipage drawn by six horses, and he was the first also to use a sedan-chair, an innovation which exasperated the people greatly and was generally denounced, because men had to perform in it the services of beasts of burden. His whole life was in keeping with this extravagance. Countless *liaisons*, the most notorious of which was that with the Queen of France were attributed to him. His example was imitated by most of the younger courtiers. Love-affairs of the most immoral character were even deemed meritorious, and the most heartless and revolting actions were not only glossed over, but more frequently praised and extolled. A spirit of open, unbounded licentiousness reigned in these circles; *liaisons*, carousals, and gambling were the rule, and not the exception. The courtiers were leading this most objectionable life under the very eyes of the king and queen. Even the reviving arts, and especially poetry, were drawn into this vortex. The poets, such as Waller and Davenant, were either themselves dissipated courtiers, or hirelings of immorality and extravagance. The Muse had lost her chastity, and occupied the degrading position of a *soubrette*.

In the face of this extravagance and luxury the Puritans, who were gaining new adherents with astounding rapidity, denounced with stern austerity and wild fanaticism all the pleasures of this world, which they looked upon only as seductions of hell. In their blind zeal they demanded the abolition of all amusements. They were the sworn enemies of luxury, and preached the greatest simplicity of dress and conduct. Their favorite colors were dark-brown or black, and they were intent on imparting this sombre hue, this monotonous, joyless, and forbidding character, to their own lives and those of others. They detested music and dancing, and deemed the fine arts not only superfluous, but pernicious. From their midst had risen that gloomy enthusiast William Prynne, who demonstrated in a thick folio volume, called *Histriomastix*, with a great display of absurd learning, the sinfulness of theatrical amusements, plays, masques, etc. His book was received with rapturous applause by his fellow-dissenters, and the author, whom the court persecuted for this reason, and upon whom unjust and ignominious penalties were inflicted, was adored and revered as a martyr by the masses of the people.

Thus the hostile parties were more at variance than ever before: on one side, the licentiousness of the cavaliers; on the other, the austere stoicism of the Puritans. Both were wrong, owing to their excesses and one-sidedness. What with the alternate triumphs and victories of either party in the course of time, England presented now the spectacle of a voluptuous wanton, now that of a stern, stony-hearted matron. These striking contrasts have not yet entirely disappeared, and although they are no longer as greatly at variance as they were then, but exist peaceably, side by side, yet the whole nation is even yet affected injuriously by the consequences of these two opposite currents. With a prudery bordering on the extremely ridiculous, the greatest licentiousness frequently goes hand in hand, and Puritan austerity paralyzes only too often the wings of free investigation and the development of genius. Lord Byron, the greatest poet of modern times, was most injuriously affected by these moral ills of his native country.

Every one unconsciously bore at that time the stamp of the party to which he belonged, and shared its sins and weaknesses. Thus Thomas was a cavalier from head to foot; brave and courageous, loyal to the king and Church of England, but also overbearing, reckless, and destitute of firm moral principles. He had inhaled the poison of his time and his class; for, as in the midst of the plague every one bears the germ of infection more or less within his body, so even the best men were not entirely free from the general corruption of their surroundings. The germ was in the rash and reckless youth, and it needed only an opportunity to burst forth. It was to such hands that the inexperienced Lucy intrusted her fate, her innocence, and honor. She yielded willingly to his dangerous caresses, and listened to the blandishments which he whispered to her. He was handsome; his carefully-dressed blond ringlet floated round his proud, aristocratic forehead; his soft mustache and goatee shaded the finely-chiselled mouth and chin; a white lace collar surrounded his breast and neck; his magnificent gold-embroidered dress was in striking contrast with the sombre, monotonous costume of the Puritans, which she saw every day. How refined were his manners! how sweet sounded his words when he spoke to her of his love, or told her of the amusements and festivals at Ludlow Castle! She did not tire of listening to him, and did not notice how swiftly the time was passing.

The setting sun admonished her to return; she was afraid that she might reach home too late, and that her old relative might notice her prolonged absence and inform her father of it. It was with great reluctance that she tore herself from his arms; she left her heart with him.

"When shall I see you again?" he asked, beseechingly.

"Soon, as soon as possible, even though it should cost my life. My father is frequently absent from home. I do not know what he is doing, but he is often away for several days in succession. So soon as he is absent again I will give you a signal, and we will meet at the same place."

"I shall die of longing until then. I will send my messenger to you."

"The same man who called me hither?"

"He is shrewd, and I believe close-mouthed. You may always send me word by him."

"But I must go now. Dusk has already set in; detain me no longer, or you will get me into trouble. Farewell!"

A long, long kiss united the lovers; Lucy then tore herself from the impetuous embrace of the youth, and hastened back to her home like a chased roe. Thomas looked after her until her slender form had disappeared among the trees; then he whistled to his dogs and set out for Ludlow Castle.

"Good luck!" shouted Billy Green to him. "And if you need again a fellow to rouse the bounding prey for you, just inquire for me at the tavern of the 'Three Pigeons.'"

So saying, he stooped to pick up the coin which Thomas threw to him on going away. He eyed the treasure with greedy eyes, and put it into his pocket.

"I did not suppose that the pious Puritan girl would go so fast to the devil," he murmured, smilingly. "But what do I care for that? I always serve him who pays me best."

CHAPTER X.

SIR KENELM DIGBY.

A NEW guest had arrived at Ludlow Castle. Sir Kenelm Digby deemed it incumbent on him to pay, on his return trip to London, a visit to the Earl of Bridgewater, who was nearly related to him. Perhaps he combined still another object with this act of courtesy, for Sir Kenelm never did any thing without some secret purpose. The reception with which he met at the hands of the noble family was in keeping both with its far-famed hospitality and the reputation of the eminent man. Kenelm Digby was the son of Sir Everard Digby, a wealthy knight. His father, an ardent Catholic, had been executed as an accomplice in the famous gunpowder-plot.

His orphan son was educated in the Protestant religion, in order to save at least a part of the fortune which the crown had confiscated already. His guardian was the well-known Archbishop Laud, then Dean of Gloucester. The talented boy gave promise of a remarkable career at an early age, and made extraordinary progress in all branches of knowledge. When he became a youth, his mother, who was a very zealous Catholic, placed him under the guidance of the learned Thomas Allen, and caused him to travel in France and Italy. After his return the rumor spread, and met with general belief, that he had forsworn at Rome the Protestant religion, which had been forced upon him; he himself, however, denied this strenuously for some time afterward. At a court festival, given in honor of the marriage of the Princess Elizabeth with the Count Palatine Frederic, afterwards King of Bohemia, he became acquainted with beautiful Venetia Stanley, the daughter of Sir Edward Stanley, whose mother was a Percy, and who, therefore, belonged to the highest nobility of the kingdom. Notwithstanding all obstacles, he succeeded in gaining the love of the young lady, who was only sixteen years old, but whose reputation, according to the testimony of her contemporaries, was none of the best. Before marrying her, he was obliged to take up his abode for some time at Paris. His fine appearance and his extraordinary understanding excited the greatest sensation at the French court, and even the queen, that lovely and frail Anne of Austria, fell in love with him and entered into a *liaison* with him. From the queen's arms, however, he hastened back to his beloved Venetia, who, if the unanimous verdict of the authors of her times is to be believed, was one of the most amiable and seductive women in England. It was not until he had forcibly abducted and secretly married her, that he obtained full possession of his beloved. Ambition and thirst for adventures led him back to the court and the bustle of the world. He accompanied the extravagant Buckingham on his embassy to France. To defray the expenses of this journey, his beloved Venetia had to pawn her valuable jewelry, which she did readily and willingly. At a later date he armed and equipped several vessels in the war which King Charles waged against France. As commander of these vessels, he courageously attacked the united galleys of the French and Venetians, and achieved a brilliant victory.

He returned triumphantly to England, and devoted himself during the peaceful years which ensued exclusively to his love and to science. His favorite study was chemistry, with which, by the most indefatigable industry, he acquired a familiarity such as few of his contemporaries could boast of. His wife died in the fifth year of their wedded life. Her death was so sudden, that suspicions of her being poisoned were aroused, and that her husband was accused of having murdered her in a fit of jealousy; for Venetia was believed to have been faithless to him, which, considering her former life, was not so very strange. However, his conduct after this loss bordered almost on insanity. For months he locked himself up in his laboratory, and shut himself entirely out from daylight. With unkempt hair and beard, he stared into vacancy, and gave way to boundless despair. It was not until a year afterward that he appeared again at court, where he obtained the special favor of the Catholic Queen. Charles I. made him his confidant, and appointed him his chamberlain. The whole appearance and bearing of the knight were in keeping with this eventful life of him who was at the same time a warrior, thinker, and courtier. His athletic form indicated extraordinary strength and energy. His gigantic neck, however, was surmounted by a most expressive and prepossessing head, proclaiming the supremacy of the mind over this Herculean frame. The high, strongly-arched forehead showed that he was a keen and able thinker. The glance of his dark-gray eyes was as clear and bright as a mirror of burnished steel, and indicated the preponderance of the intellectual faculties. In striking contrast with their expression was his voluptuous, soft mouth, round which an air of dreamy enthusiasm constantly played. His curly hair was black and glossy, but it was already quite thin, and a part of the head was bald. A dark beard fringed his pale cheeks and flowed down on his breast, imparting to the face, notwithstanding its intellectual stamp, a weird and ghostly expression. His whole appearance combined so many contradictions, that it could not but arouse some distrust in the beholder's mind. Voluptuousness and fanatical austerity, cold reason, and an eccentricity bordering on insanity, were to be read in his keen features. The various rumors which had been circulated in regard to him, were well calculated to add to the strange and mysterious impression of his person. Like many persons of a peculiarly intellectual character, the suppressed feelings of his heart, and his restrained imagination, burst forth with redoubled violence in unguarded moments. His impetuousness then knew no bounds, and the outbursts of his eccentricity resembled destructive storms and fatal thunder-bolts.

Both his social position and near relationship to the family of the Earl of Bridgewater secured him an exceedingly kind reception. The lord president retired with his guest soon after his arrival to converse with the experienced and accomplished courtier on the condition of the king and the court. The earl's private cabinet lay in one of the Gothic towers, and commanded a delightful view of the valley and the hills of Herefordshire. Soft carpets were spread on the floor to dampen every loud noise. The stamped leathern hangings contained representations from the Old Testament. On one wall was to be seen Abraham, about to sacrifice his only son; close to them stood the ram, and over the altar flitted the saving angel with gilded wings. Another picture showed the Israelites in the desert, worshipping the golden calf; on a knoll stood Moses, with an angry face, and holding the tables of stone in his hands. In this manner the religious spirit of the period showed itself everywhere in the study of a wealthy nobleman. Furniture, hangings, and every thing destined for household use were at that time in strict keeping with the views and notions prevailing among the people. Even the seats and easy-chairs were covered with Biblical embroideries. Close to the window stood the earl's old-fashioned writing-table, laden with books and papers. Thick folio volumes, bound in hog-skin or parchment, filled the places of our modern neat octavo and duodecimo volumes; and instead of the official documents of our times, were to be seen everywhere heavy metal cases, enclosing the parchments and preserving the large seals from injury.

It was in this room that the two men conversed now, undisturbed by the presence of witnesses. The Lord President of Wales was already an aged man, with dignified features. Like his father, Chancellor Egerton, who gained such great celebrity during the reigns of Elizabeth and James I., he had devoted himself to the study of the law, and, like him, given all his life evidence of the most unwavering fidelity to duty, and a most stubborn sense of justice. Notwithstanding his attachment to the royal house, he was unable to approve of the last measures of the government. The oppressions and extortions of the Star-Chamber, the unjustifiable dissolution of Parliament, the arbitrary taxation brought about by this measure, had rendered him justly apprehensive of the future of the country. He now uttered his fears, though in a guarded manner, to his new guest, but his innate loyalty frequently came into conflict with his conscience on this occasion.

"Believe me," he said, in the course of the conversation, "the people hereabouts are every day more difficult to manage. The king must call a new Parliament, unless he desires to provoke an extremely grave state of affairs. You live at court near his person, and are therefore able to tell me what he intends to do."

"Charles will try to govern as long as possible without Parliament. Having once tasted the joys of unlimited sovereignty, he is unwilling to part with them without a struggle. For the time being no other system is to be thought of; and so long as he has sufficient funds at his command, he will take good care not to convoke a new session of those morose taskmasters and canting preachers."

"But the extravagant expenditures in which the court is indulging at the present time will soon exhaust the royal exchequer."

"Leave that to old Noy. That shrewd fellow is poring night and day over worm-eaten parchments and dusty title-deeds. Wherever he finds an iota of an ancient claim of the government, a mere vestige of a tax collected by the crown in former times, he follows it up and manages to coin money out of it. He is racking his brain night and day to devise additional taxes and imposts of an apparently legal character. He is so cunning in this respect, he knows every nook and corner of our ancient laws so well, that no one is able to refute him. Does not the king owe to him the invention of the soap-tax, to which some old statute of the time of the Conqueror gave rise? It is true the people are grumbling because they can no longer wash so often as formerly; but what does that amount to? The Puritans set a higher value on a pure heart and blameless life than a clean shirt and well-washed hands."

"You are jesting, when I and all the true friends of the king are filled with the gloomiest forebodings."

"You are wrong to yield to any such misgivings, noble earl," replied Sir Kenelm Digby, with a sinister smile. "I see that, living in the country, you no longer know what is going on at court. No one there has any fears of the future. Only the pleasures of the moment are thought of, and every day brings a new festival. We all have our hands full of balls, masquerades, and similar amusements. The queen has taken Buckingham's palace, and I pledge you my word that we are amusing ourselves just as delightfully as when the great duke still lived. Poor Buckingham! Who would have thought that you would meet with so premature an end at the hands of an assassin? No sooner were your remains in the grave, than you were already forgotten. Such is the course of the world."

"God grant him eternal peace!" replied the pious lord president, clasping his hands. "He is most to blame for the present confusion and troubles, but death atones for a great many things. Had the king listened less readily to the advice of his favorite, and had he not always defended him so obstinately, he would have been on better terms with Parliament, and it would have been unnecessary for him to dissolve it."

"Amen!" exclaimed his guest, with a sneer. "However, the king gets along very well without Parliament. As yet he has plenty of money; the revenue raised by the soap-tax, and the ship and tonnage money, is sufficient to defray all royal expenses. The Star-Chamber also sees to it that the penalties and fines imposed on the dissenters keep the royal exchequer well filled. A thousand pounds more or less do not startle it at all, and when a poor devil is unable to pay his fine, he is imprisoned at the pleasure of his majesty. He may deem himself happy if his ears are not cut off at the pillory, as was justly done in the case of that impudent fellow Prynne. I myself witnessed the scene, and admired the courage which the rascal displayed on that trying occasion. During the bloody operation he made a violent speech to the people, and even the executioner was unable to shut his mouth. I tell you the scoundrel acted like a martyr, and stood there as though he expected every moment to be proclaimed patron saint of England."

"All you tell me only adds to my fears. I have been told that a great many men of the highest respectability, merchants and country gentlemen, have already refused to pay the ship-money and tonnage-impost, because it is raised without the consent of Parliament. If their example should be imitated by many others, the king would have to yield. Unfortunately, he could do so then only by lowering his dignity. Parliament would act only the more boldly, and demand new privileges besides those which it has already, whereby additional bounds would be set to the power of his majesty."

"It is true, where there is no money, there is no courage either. '*Point d'argent, point de Suisses*,' say the French. For the time being, however, those who refuse to pay taxes are imprisoned until they do pay. A jail is the best means in the world to make such obstinate persons pliable and submissive. In it blows an air well calculated to quiet and cool down such hot-headed fellows. A few days' sojourn in the Tower or at Newgate is often amply sufficient to tame the wildest of them. Hitherto the remedy has never failed in effecting a speedy cure."

"But suppose the judges should refuse to lend their hands to such persecutions; suppose there should yet be in England men who value justice higher than the good graces of the court, what would happen then?"

"Pshaw! The king will get along in spite of them. They will be deposed in the most unceremonious manner. With some energy all such obstacles are easily surmounted. Our minister, Lord Wentworth, showed us very handsomely how true this is. He is a man of great energy, strikes terror into the hearts of the rebels, and maintains law and order in the country. He knows how to do so, for he himself was formerly one of the rebellious members of the dissolved Parliament; hence, he is most familiar with the tricks, devices, and weaknesses of his former colleagues. In India, I have been told, they use trained elephants for the purpose of catching wild ones. Believe me, apostates are the wood out of which the most relentless persecutors of men of their own class may be carved. A former democrat may be transformed immediately into an adherent of the government, provided the latter knows how to arouse and satisfy his ambition. They are all venal, and Wentworth is governing now with a rigor and recklessness upon which none of the old adherents of the king would have ventured. It is said he intends even to organize a standing army. If this master-stroke should prove successful, it would be unnecessary for the king to convene Parliament."

"But in that case all the liberties of the people would be lost, and none of us would be better off than the slaves in Turkey. The nobility, which is at the head of society, will feel the change first. We shall become nothing but tools and servants of the crown, while at present the King of England is only chief among equals, the peer of his peers. Just look at France, where Richelieu is governing despotically in the name of King Louis! Are you desirous of having a similar state of affairs brought about in our own country? The proud cardinal is putting his foot on the necks of the noblest families, and cuts off the most aristocratic heads whenever he pleases."

"The vigorous rule of one is by far preferable to the many-headed government of the people. You know that I am a naturalist; well, then, I have learned from Nature that the members of a whole must be subject to the will of the head. The stronger one coerces the weaker, that is a law which cannot be overthrown. In chemistry the various powers struggle with each other until one is in the ascendent, whereupon the others submit to it willingly. Even among metals a certain system like this is to be found. Gold is king, iron is servant. It was so from the beginning, and will always be so."

"I do not deny it, but I should think that, between a Christian king and a despotic tyrant, there is as much difference as between a ploughshare and a sword. One spreads blessings and prosperity, the other ruin and destruction. Our fathers were wise enough to perceive this, and therefore divested royalty of its arbitrary character, without detracting from its dignity. Parliament is the natural bulwark against royal tyranny. Are we ourselves to aid in tearing down this bulwark? Tell me, what protection would be left to us in that event?"

"The Church!" replied Sir Kenelm Digby, emphatically. "It always was the best counterpoise to the encroachments of the temporal power. The popes always protected the nations from the oppressions of their rulers. It is the greatest bane of the Reformation that it broke the power of the Church and took from it the weapons with which it always effectually opposed the encroachments of tyranny. The thunderbolts of Rome caused the kings to tremble on their thrones."

"One who hears you talk in this strain cannot but believe that you have really turned Catholic, as a great many persons have asserted from time to time. I have hitherto refused to credit these rumors."

"Can one not be a good Protestant, then, and yet not shut his eyes against the great advantages of the Roman Church? Will you deny that Catholicism was a bulwark to the nations? I do not think you are one of those prejudiced men who break into imprecations as soon as Rome and the Pope are mentioned. You always seemed to me destitute of prejudice. Hence, you will be obliged to admit that the Reformation was by far more advantageous to the princes than to the people. The Catholic Church was free and independent. Its clergy formed a consecrated army, a state within the state, with almost a republican constitution. Its head, the pope himself, is elected to his office, and the lowest priest can reach this exalted position, if he possesses the necessary talents. This secures at once the supremacy of the mind over brute force. In this sense Rome always resisted the encroachments of the princes, and its dreaded thunderbolts deterred the most powerful monarchs from high-handed violence. What did the Reformation bring us for all this? It enriched the kings and impoverished the people. The clergy lost its independence, and thereby its influence; from being a free order, it sank to the low condition of servitude. The property of the Church fell into the hands of the princes, and not into those of the people, and added greatly to their power. Who is to shield the people now from the arbitrary proceedings of the princes, since they have lost their best protector? Brute force has taken the place of intellectual and spiritual supremacy, and the justly odious Inquisition has been replaced by a far worse one. Or do you think that the religious tyranny of the Star-Chamber is milder, that the fines and penalties which it imposes are less painful, and that its dungeons are not as deep and cruel? I repeat it, the Reformation is the real source of our present evils and troubles."

"Hush, for God's sake, hush!" cried the anxious earl. "If any one heard you talk thus, you yourself might have to appear before the dreaded Star-Chamber, and, as a secret Catholic, suffer the most severe penalties. Even though you may be right in some respects, you must not forget that the Reformation was the very event that brought spiritual freedom to the people. It gave to the people the Bible, the unadulterated word of salvation. We have learned to read and *think*. The Roman Church is like the miser who starves his children and keeps his riches locked up in his strong box. It is true, it often protected the people from the tyranny of the princes, but it did so only in its own interest, like the shepherd who protects his sheep from the attacks of the wolf, in order to shear and kill them when he desires to get their wool or their meat. Now, mankind is not an irrational flock of sheep; it rebelled against this spiritual servitude, the worst of all tyrannies. Even though the present state of affairs may not be the happiest, it is much better for us to suffer in our property and lives than our salvation. The protection which Rome granted to the nations had to be purchased too dearly. The price was freedom of conscience and thought."

"And whither has this much-vaunted freedom led us! All England is split up into hostile sects, hating and persecuting each other with the utmost ferocity. The most absurd teachings find every day more adherents and mouth-pieces. We are like degenerate sons who are unable to agree upon the division of their father's inheritance, and lacerate and murder each other, until no one is left to enjoy the inheritance. I see farther, a great deal farther, than you think. Behind these religious dissensions I behold already the Gorgon head of civil war, of a bloody struggle threatening to overwhelm all existing institutions. The teachings of the so-called primitive Christianity begin already to bear fruit, and fanatical enthusiasts and cunning hypocrites derive from the Bible the justification of the most infamous attacks on property and the government. Have you not heard of the Anabaptists who infested parts of Germany? They demanded nothing less than the abolition of all privileges and a division of property. Our Puritans bear the greatest resemblance to their German brethren. They are said to dream of a millennium, and of the rule of the chosen people. They mean thereby neither more nor less than the unlimited rule of the rabble, the abolition of nobility, and the confiscation of our property. The chosen people of the Lord are intent on beheading us and taking our places. They consider us only a host of accursed heathens, Moabites, Edomites, etc.,who deserve no mercy, and whose property, lands, pastures, gardens, and forests, God has assigned to His true children as rewards of their merits and piety. See, that is what we owe to your Bible and freedom of conscience. Let the uneducated people get hold of this two-edged sword, and you will soon see your own life menaced."

"Unfortunately I am obliged to admit that you are right, although I do not know how the evil is to be counteracted. For this reason I should like to hear your views. You are known to me not only as a profound scholar, but as an experienced statesman. What do you advise us to do in the present state of affairs? I believe I am not mistaken in venturing upon the surmise that your journey conceals some other than its ostensible object, and that a secret mission is probably coupled with your visit. You enjoy the implicit confidence of his majesty, and are the confidential friend and adviser of the queen. Archbishop Laud was formerly your guardian, and is now your intimate friend. Be frank with me, and disclose your mission to me."

Sir Kenelm Digby kept the earl some time waiting for a positive reply. He deemed it prudent to veil himself in mysterious silence. He neither contradicted nor confirmed the surmises of his host.

"You are mistaken," he said, with a significant smile, "if you think my royal master has intrusted me with a special mission. Is any other motive for a visit to your house needed, then, than our long friendship and the bonds of relationship, which, instead of loosening, I should like to draw closer? In truth, I have communicated to you only my individual views on the condition of our country. Possibly I may be mistaken. But as you seem to attach some importance to my advice, I will not withhold it. Hippocrates says that iron cures what medicine does not heal; and where iron proves ineffectual, fire should be resorted to. In my opinion, the ills of the state require the same remedies as the diseases of the human body. First, try lenity, and, if it proves ineffectual, resort to vigorous, and even harsh measures. The sore limb must be removed before mortification seizes the whole body. It is better that a putrid part be lost than the whole. This is my sincere opinion. I believe it is the only way for us to save ourselves, and preserve, as loyal subjects, our king from injury and danger. But excuse me, if I leave you now. I have not yet waited upon the ladies of the house. If you permit, I will go to them now."

It was with great reluctance that the earl dismissed his guest, with whom he would have liked to converse further on the affairs of the country. He himself had hitherto been unable to form a definite opinion in regard to them, and he was hesitating and vacillating between his innate mildness and the fear of dangerous events. His eminent position imposed grave responsibilities upon him. He remained in his study, absorbed in his reflections, without coming to a definite resolution. Even the doubts which his visitor had aroused in his soul concerning the salutary influence of the Catholic Church had made a marked impression on his mind; and, although the Protestant convictions of the lord president revolted at the idea of Roman supremacy, he had to admit to himself that his guest had uttered some irrefutable truths.

Meanwhile Sir Kenelm Digby was walking with an air of great satisfaction through the gallery toward the apartments of the ladies. He had attained his object by the interview he had just had with the earl, and perhaps gained over another irresolute mind to his plans. He hated the Reformation from the bottom of his soul, as it had caused the death of his father. For the time being, however, he deemed it prudent not to throw off the mask and to secretly enlist friends and adherents for the Catholic Church.

CHAPTER XI.

MILTON AND DIGBY.

THE room in which the ladies were seated was sumptuously furnished in the style of that period. Mythological scenes adorned the gilded ceiling. Venus rode in a car drawn by doves and surrounded by little Cupids, who carried, with ludicrous faces, the arms of Mars, his helmet, shield, and lance. Costly hangings of crimson silk covered the walls; heavy curtains of the same stuff flowed down over the doors and windows. The high-backed chairs were carved in the most artistic manner. Near one of the arched windows stood a small table beautifully inlaid with pearl and ivory. Its upper part consisted of curiously-wrought wood, ivory, and metal, forming the most attractive figures, butterflies, flowers, and birds. A small bureau, of the same materials and workmanship, stood close by. The ladies kept in it their jewelry and similar toilet articles. Alice and her mother were seated on low chairs, occupied with needlework and embroidery; opposite them sat Milton and his friend Edward King. At some distance from them Lawes, the musician, had seated himself at the organ, then an indispensable article in the house of every aristocratic family. He had just finished a song, which he had composed at the request of the countess, and for which he was enthusiastically applauded by his whole audience. Scarcely had the conversation, interrupted by his performance, been resumed, when Sir Kenelm Digby came in and paid his respects to the ladies. His attitude and bearing indicated at once the well-bred and accomplished gentleman, who had moved with so much distinction at the prominent courts of Europe. As, in his interview with the earl, he had so advantageously displayed his statesmanship as to excite the admiration of his host, so he now delighted the ladies by his refined wit and his surpassing accomplishments. He made an especially favorable impression on the countess, who was a very handsome lady yet, and to whom he seemed to devote particular attention, without neglecting Alice even for a moment. He took part in the conversation with his habitual ease and gracefulness. Milton, without knowing the reason why, felt a most decided aversion to the guest who had come in so unexpectedly. It was not envy, not even jealousy, that arose in his bosom, and filled him with distrust of the stranger. The poet, perhaps, was displeased with the superiority and ill-concealed egotism of the new-comer; or, maybe, the mysterious atmosphere surrounding Sir Kenelm Digby made such a disagreeable impression upon him. There was something demoniacal in his appearance and bearing. Milton could not help thinking of those magnificent but poisonous flowers, which exhale narcotic odors, and, notwithstanding their beauty, make an unpleasant impression on the beholder. The dissimilitude of the two characters, destitute of a single point of contact, was probably the principal cause of this aversion.

Alice perceived, first of all, with the keen eye of young love, the poet's aversion to Sir Kenelm Digby, and she tried to draw him again into the conversation, after he had been silent for some time.

"Well, Mr. Milton," she said, playfully, "you are probably reflecting at this moment on the promise you gave me and your friend Lawes."

"What promise?" asked the poet, absently, starting up from his reverie.

"Why, I should not have thought you so forgetful. Do you no longer remember that you consented to immortalize our adventure in Haywood Forest?"

"I do, indeed," faltered out Milton, in great confusion, "and I shall redeem my promise."

"Loquacious Fame," interposed Sir Kenelm, "has informed me of your adventure, noble lady, and I envy the young gentlemen who were fortunate enough to render you so chivalrous a service. The author of 'The Arcades,' for I am happy to recognize him, in my opinion cannot make a better use of his talents than to dedicate charming verse to beauty and innocence. This is the only place I assign to poetry; otherwise I think very little of it."

"And may I inquire how the Muses have incurred your aversion?" asked Alice, displeased with the sneering tone of the guest.

"Because they circulate nothing but lies and falsehoods in the world. Most of the poets are ignorant of real life, and put in its place their fanciful dreams and the deceptive creations of their imagination. Their mind calls up before their readers nothing but dissolving views, which, on closer contemplation and examination, turn out to be empty vagaries. Especially injurious is the influence of poetry to young persons, because it misleads the reason, shows every thing in a false light, and fills the heart and the head with fanciful ideas and feelings. Like the divine Plato, I should exile the poets from the state."

Milton had listened to this unjustifiable attack with flushed cheeks and eyes flashing with indignation. His pride rebelled against the reviler of poetry, which he valued highest among all arts. To him the Muse was not a mere pastime, not an earthly servant, destined only for pleasure and enjoyment. A poet, in his eyes, was equivalent to a prophet; hence, he could not suffer such scornful allusions to his calling, and least of all in the presence of his beloved. He had suddenly lost his former bashfulness; he had jumped up from his seat, and now stood in the full ardor of his enthusiasm in front of the reviler of poetry.

"No matter what Plato says!" he exclaimed indignantly. "I believe that poetry is one of the greatest blessings vouchsafed to mankind What! poetry, the greatest benefactor to mankind, be injurious to the state and to society. Does it not elevate the soul by the consciousness of its relationship to all that is divine, pure, and noble? When soaring to its full height, it is fused into religion, into Christianity itself, for, like it, it spiritualizes man and nature. I grant that poetry sometimes serves vice and appears in the company of evil passions; but genius even then preserves its divine nature, and poetry, even in the service of voluptuousness or hatred, cannot entirely deny its sublime origin. Traces of pure sentiments, traits full of delicacy, pictures of innocent happiness, sympathy with the sufferings of virtue, burst from the dark cloud of wrath, from the night of despair; passages full of a lofty spirit of morality may be found even in every immoral work; and they prove, in the most striking manner, how difficult it is for a poetical mind to prove recreant to its inborn excellency; for poetry is the constant ally of our best sentiments. It delights in the beauty and grandeur both of nature and the human soul. Indeed, it depicts with terrible truthfulness the errors of passion, but only such as bear witness to a powerful nature, a strength calculated to inspire terror, and yet filling us with profound, shuddering compassion. Its principal aspiration and greatest task is to carry the mind beyond the beaten, dusty, and muddy paths of every-day life, and elevate it to purer heights, where it may breathe in an atmosphere full of noble and lofty sentiments. It reveals to us the full beauty and loveliness of nature, restores to us the freshness of youthful sensations, vivifies the joy felt in simple pleasures, and fans and preserves the sacred flame of enthusiasm, which warms the spring of our life, ennobles the love of the two sexes, excites our sympathy for all human relations and all classes of society, and, by prophetic forebodings, lays the foundations of our blissful belief in a future life."

"Splendid!" replied Sir Kenelm Digby, sardonically. "You defend your own cause with a great display of mind and imagination. But, like a true poet, you avoid my charge, and confine yourself to an encomium of poetry. You have not by any means refuted what I said against it."

"I shall do so now. You charge poetry with spreading erroneous views and false expectations of real life, filling the mind with fantastic illusions, and building up air-castles on the ruins of wisdom. I do not deny, indeed, that it combats that kind of wisdom which is exclusively based on material views, considers physical pleasures and enjoyments the highest human blessings, and accumulation of means the only task of life; yea, I do not deny it, and praise this circumstance as not the meanest service which poetry is rendering to mankind, in delivering us from the thraldom of this earth-born and worldly prudence. But I prefer not to enter into this point, and will prove only that all the charges of falsehood and deception, raised against poets, are utterly unfounded. In many poems there is more truth than is to be found in history itself, and in philosophical systems. The creations of genius are often revelations of the highest truth; they disclose to us unknown regions of thought, and shed a new light on the mysteries of life. The word itself sometimes appears false in poetry, while the spirit is imbued with the highest truth. And if truth thus lives even in the boldest flights of poetry, how much more will this be the case when the poet portrays real life; for our present life is only, as it were, the primary school of the immortal spirit, and indescribably rich in poetical elements. It is the sublime task of the bard to draw these divine elements from the coarse dross covering and surrounding them. Life is not by any means so prosy, sober, and trivial, as people generally believe. An open eye sees at once that it teems with poetry. The sentiments which it awakens in our own hearts, and scatters as seeds for the future; the powers of omnipotent passion, which seem to arm the soul with superhuman energy; the innocent and ever-new joys of youth, the blissful transports of the heart, succumbing for the first time to the sweet charms of love, and dreaming of a happiness too sublime for this world; woman with her beauty and grace, her irresistible amiability and boundless devotion; the blush of innocence, the tone, the glance of which only a mother is capable: all this is poetry. It is false to say that the poet depicts a life that does not exist in reality. He distils and concentrates the heavenly essence of life, preserves and secures its volatile aroma, unites the severed and mutilated parts of its beauty, and imparts a longer existence to its, alas! too rapidly withering blossoms. And in doing this, he is a benefactor, for it is a blessing for us to be reminded that life does not belong exclusively to the painful satisfaction of our earthly wants, but admits also of sentiments and feelings that fill us with unutterable bliss, and are worthy of a better world. This power of poetry to refine and purify our views of life and happiness should be the more carefully fostered, and is the more necessary to us, the greater the progress of society. It is necessary to us, in order to meet the arrogant assumptions of our heartless and artificial relations, which, brought about by civilization, make the world appear to us so desolate and uninteresting. It is necessary to us, in order to combat the one-sided aspirations of science, which is no longer, as formerly, taught for its own sake, but from vile covetousness and for the sake of the advantages which it holds out to greedy men. Hence, poetry must prevent men from sinking and perishing under the burden of this worldly life of the present time, which attaches the highest importance to sensual pleasures."

At the conclusion of his speech, there was in the room so profound a silence, that it almost frightened him. Enthusiasm had carried him so far away, that he forgot all his surroundings, the place where he was standing, and the persons whom he was addressing. Coloring and awaking as if from a dream, he looked at his audience, which seemed fascinated by the spell of his words. Alice had dropped her needlework on her knees, and sat in a reverential attitude, her hands clasped as if in prayer. A blissful smile played round her lips, and in her pure heart resounded yet the echoes of the words she had just heard. They had expressed her own thoughts and feelings, but had clad them in more beautiful language, and had been more profound than she had ever thought or felt them. The enthusiastic musician had risen from his feet and gratefully shook hands with the blushing poet. Even the sneering courtier dropped his sarcastic tone, and contented himself with cloaking the evident defeat which he had sustained, by adroitly extolling first of all the able manner in which, he said, the poet had defended his cause.

"You have conducted your defence so well, that I am almost obliged to admit that I am vanquished. You are not only a poet, but also a most skilful advocate. Being possessed of such talents, you may obtain the highest distinctions and honors, if you know how to profit by your accomplishments. I will not recur to our controversy, else I should advise you to give up poetry, which rewards its votaries only with crowns of thorns. The laurel always has been, and always will be, unfruitful."

"For this reason, he is the symbol of the highest glory. He who strives for the divine renounces any earthly gain."

"But as we live on earth, you would do well to turn your talents to account, and profit by them as much as possible. The civil service is open to you, and a young man of your ability will be able to reach the most eminent positions, if he is determined to do so."

"Just now, however," interposed the Countess of Bridgewater, "you must not dissuade Mr. Milton from serving the Muses. We have need of him. The birthday of my husband, the lord president, will be celebrated this month. We have resolved to present some mask or other play on this occasion, and were just going to request the poet to lend us his most valuable assistance."

"My feeble ability is at your service, gracious countess; I will assist you with all my heart," replied Milton.

"And I will furnish the music," said Henry Lawes. "I am already proud of the beautiful poem which you will write for me."

"You are doing me a great deal of honor," replied the poet; "but I am really at a loss to decide what subject would be most suitable to the occasion."

"Oh, let me help you to choose an excellent subject," exclaimed the musician. "You may kill two birds with one stone. What do you think of selecting the adventure in Haywood Forest as the subject of the mask? You might add the most charming scenes and changes to it. The persons appearing in the mask may be depicted as they really are—our gracious Lady Alice, the two brothers, and Comus, the foolish vagabond. This will save you half the trouble, and I will compose for it melodies which will delight the angels in heaven."

"The only question is," objected Milton, "whether Lady Alice and her brothers consent to be brought upon the stage in this manner. And then I do not feel equal to such a task."

"Oh, pray try it," said Alice. "You have my consent, which I grant with the greatest readiness, and my brothers will have no objections either. I impose, however, the condition that you must not idealize us too much, nor treat us with too great poetical license. You yourself said just now that poetry is destined to serve truth, and I take you at your word."

"You need not be afraid, for I shall take good care not to falsify my own words. Reality in this case is full of poetry. I shall go to work immediately, and Lawes shall receive in a few days the first verses, which he will compose"

"I thank you for your great kindness," said the countess. "And that we may represent truth as faithfully as possible, Alice and her brothers shall themselves perform on the stage the adventure which occurred to them."

"That is splendid!" exclaimed the musician, jubilantly. "The persons interested in the adventure will thus pass through it a second time."

"For the other *rôles* which you intend to add to the mask," continued the countess, "I believe we shall likewise find suitable performers. Of course, I count in the first place upon you and your friend Mr. King. As saviors of my daughter, you must, of course, appear in the mask."

"Pray do not insist on it, so far as I am concerned," said Milton, beseechingly. "I myself do not possess any theatrical talents whatever. Whenever I am to speak in public, my tongue seems paralyzed, and I am unable to utter a word. I should, therefore, play but a sorry part on such an occasion. Moreover, the honor of the rescue, if it may be called so, is due exclusively to the bravery and courage of my friend. Hence, it will be sufficient if he performs this *rôle* in the mask which is now forming in my mind."

"But who will represent the god Comus?" asked Alice.

"I will, if you permit me," replied Sir Kenelm Digby.

"What? You will do it?" exclaimed the Countess, wonderingly.

"I should like to contribute my mite to the festival, and as Nature has given me a prosy character, let me, in God's name, take upon myself the *rôle* most suitable to my peculiarities. Of all the Olympic gods, friend Comus, the god of laughter and jollity always pleased me best, and I shall take pains to do honor to him, provided you and the poet do not object to it. I am sure Mr. Milton will not treat friend Comus with a niggardly hand, but bestow a good share of wit and humor on him. In this case, I will allow him even to encroach a little upon truth, and not represent the awkward, sneering fellow entirely in accordance with nature. On the other hand, he must not be entirely destitute of malice and irony; for they impart the real zest to life, and will add to the attractions of the mask."

"I am obliged to you for this hint," replied the poet, "and shall profit by it to the best of my ability. You will have no cause to complain of me; I shall certainly follow your suggestions."

"But what is to be the name of the mask?" asked the musician.

"Alice; or, Rescued Innocence," replied Edward King, who had hitherto been silent, absorbed in thinking only of the lovely girl.

"You do me too much honor," objected Alice. "Let the name of the mask rather be 'Comus.'"

"Your request is equivalent to an order," replied the poet; "I myself like this title best, and will go to work immediately. I hope to finish the mask in the course of a few days."

"And I shall be on hand in time," said Sir Kenelm Digby, "and learn and play my part conscientiously."

"We will take you at your word," replied the countess. "Of course you will all promise to keep the matter secret, as it is to be a surprise for my husband."

The conversation soon took a more general direction. Sir Kenelm Digby was requested to speak of his travels, and he did so in a manner which delighted his hearers. He had seen the greater part of Europe, under the most peculiar and brilliant circumstances. He knew how to describe life at the courts of France and Spain in the most interesting and amusing manner. Owing to his personal acquaintance with the most eminent persons, he was able to impart a peculiar zest to his descriptions. Thus he traced a lifelike portrait of Cardinal Richelieu, whom he pronounced the greatest statesman in the world. He interwove his narrative with numerous witty allusions and piquant anecdotes, and did not forget to expatiate on the love of the cardinal for Queen Anne, of Austria, and her aversion to the all-powerful minister. He dwelt longest upon the wonders and beauties of Italy. Here he became himself almost a poet, and in praising the marvels of Venice, the charms of Florence, and the sublime grandeur of Rome, he was carried away by his enthusiasm, and forgot his habitual irony.

"Yes, you must go to Rome," he said, turning to the poet. "A new life will dawn upon you there. No city on earth combines in the same degree the wonders of ancient and modern times. Wherever you tread, the ground is hallowed. Here rises the Colosseum, the very ruins of which make an overwhelming impression on the mind; here you behold the majestic front and sublime dome of St. Peter's. Devout awe fills the heart in such gigantic surroundings, and when the colossal organ and the enchanting choir accompany high mass, every one bends his knees involuntarily. Temples and palaces are to be seen in endless procession, and the immortal creations of art beam in eternal beauty from their walls and in their niches. All Olympus descends to you, and you see the gods created by the teeming imagination of the Greeks. The large, grave face of Juno gazes at you; the goddess of love rises with a sweet smile before your eyes from the froth of the sea. The marble seems to live, and you expect that she will stretch out her longing arms toward you. The chaste Diana hastens past you with a quick step; you fancy you hear the arrows rattle in her quiver, and wish secretly to be kissed in your sleep, like Endymion, by these sweet virgin lips. Leaning against the tree stands Apollo, the god of music and poetry, and the prototype of manly beauty. His head seems surrounded with beams of light; ambrosial hair flows from his radiant forehead; generous pride and inspiration swells his beautiful mouth and his royal nostrils. And as if these witnesses of past splendor and glory were insufficient, new wonders emerge every day from the bowels of the earth, which faithfully concealed such treasures from the hordes of the barbarians, and restore them to a better and more civilized era which knows how to appreciate them. These relics of antiquity rekindled the love of art in Italy. It was not in vain that Raphael feasted his eyes on these sublime works of art, and that Michael Angelo's piercing glance penetrated the simplicity and grandeur of the world of the ancients; both created works striving not only to equal, but to surpass their models. The lovely splendor of colors has taken the place of the cold marble. Christianity displays treasures not less precious than pagan antiquity. How much more beautiful are these Madonnas, these saints, painted by the master-hand of a Raphael, who knows how to surround mortal loveliness with the halo of divine glory, than all those goddesses of love; how much more sublime is Michael Angelo's 'Last Judgment,' than the 'Struggle of the Titans!' And all this is surrounded by a charming wreath of villas and gardens, where the laurel grows on ruins, the vine loaded with grapes encircles the slender poplar, and the dark cypress reminds us with warning finger that every thing is perishable, and yet invites us to enjoy the delights of life."

"Oh!" exclaimed Milton, carried away by the words of the speaker, "I will some day visit this wonderful country!"

"You will be justified in doing so," added Digby, with a strange smile. "Where Virgil lived, Horace wrote, and Cicero spoke and thought, inspiration cannot be wanting to the poet. The great library of the Vatican will open to you its intellectual treasures, its books and rare manuscripts. You will find there combined, at one point, all that human genius created for ages past, an arsenal of knowledge, a treasury of the noblest kind, such as is not to be found anywhere else in the world. But the classical spirit does not alone lie dead in those books, it still lives in that wonderful country; and you will become acquainted there with many men possessed of extraordinary knowledge, and animated by the most refined humanity. Italy is, as heretofore, the dwelling-place of genius, the fatherland of the poets, and her great men are still the teachers of the whole world."

Digby spoke to Milton in this enthusiastic strain, and fanned in his bosom the wish, which he had entertained for a long time, to visit Italy, until it became a devouring flame. He had already often thought of visiting the classical country. At that time young men were sent thither to finish their education, as afterward to France and Paris. Rome and Florence were still considered the high-schools of the mind, and no cavalier was looked upon as a finished gentleman unless he had lived there for some time. Milton's father was fully convinced of the necessity of such a journey for his gifted son, and had long since given him permission to enter upon it; only no time had as yet been fixed for it, and several domestic events had compelled the son to postpone the project. Digby's descriptions reawakened the old plan, which nothing but his growing love for Alice prevented him now from carrying into effect. His affection for her had made decided progress during the few days which he had passed at Ludlow Castle. Since that meeting in the garden, every hour had drawn them closer together; and although neither the poet nor Alice had hitherto lent words to their feelings, they were nevertheless sure of their mutual happiness.

However, the parting hour struck at last. Milton and his friend could no longer stay at Ludlow Castle and enjoy the generous hospitality which was offered to them there. The grief of their separation, however, was lessened by the hope that they would soon meet again. The poet had to promise the countess once more that he would return with his work in a few days, make the necessary arrangements for the mask, and conduct the performance himself. Alice held out to him her hand, which he pressed respectfully to his lips.

"We shall soon meet again!" she whispered to the poet.

"We shall soon meet again!" he repeated, thoughtfully.

CHAPTER XII.

CATHOLIC PLANS AND PROGRESS.

Digby stayed at the castle several days after the friends had left. The presence of this gifted and interesting man was more or less welcome to all its inmates; especially was the countess delighted with his attractive conversation. The attention which he devoted to Alice filled her maternal heart with pride, and not with uneasiness. She seemed to second secretly his aim, which became more evident from day to day, to obtain the hand of her daughter. A great many ladies manifest a surprising indulgence on such occasions. Neither the by no means unblemished reputation of the suitor nor his mature age injured him in the eyes of the mother, whom he managed to gain by his refined manners and the advantages of his position. The other members of the family were also favorable to him. The impressible Thomas especially felt attracted by the fascinations of the distinguished cavalier and polished courtier. The youth listened rapturously to his enticing descriptions of the brilliant life of the aristocracy in London and at the court of Charles I. Alice alone did not share the general predilection; and although she was unable to keep entirely aloof from the charm of his conversation, she felt near him an embarrassment and anxiety which she could not explain to herself. Digby, however, did not allow himself to be deterred by her reserved bearing, and continued his courtship in so delicate and discreet a manner that she was unable to reject it without treating him with downright rudeness.

Thus the astute guest wove his net insensibly round the whole house—a net-work of schemes and purposes of various kinds. He observed here likewise the mysterious attitude which had become peculiar to him. At times he locked himself for hours in his room to write long letters to persons in different parts of the world. These letters were written in a cipher which no uninitiated person was able to read. A discreet servant forwarded them, and was almost incessantly on the road for this purpose. From time to time there arrived strangers who inquired for the guest, and with whom he had interviews to which no one else was admitted.

One day two gentlemen were announced to him. Both seemed to be foreigners, and to have just arrived after a long journey. The broad-brimmed hat of one of them concealed a very characteristic Italian face, a mixture of clerical sanctimoniousness and worldly cunning. No sooner was Digby alone with his visitors, than he gave vent to his surprise.

"Reverend father," he said, kissing the hand of the Italian, "I should sooner have expected the heavens to fall than to see you in England. Are you aware of the danger to which you are exposed here?"

"I am. I am not ignorant of the barbarous law which forbids every foreign Catholic priest under severe penalties to set foot on British soil."

"And yet you ventured to come hither?"

"This will show you the importance of the mission intrusted to me. I count upon you, as I am aware of your zeal for the good cause. Hence, I did not shrink from coming to Ludlow Castle before repairing to London; I was desirous of making sure of your assistance. I am the bearer of a letter, written to you by our holy general, the Rev. Father Vitelleschi, and I bring you also the most cordial greetings and warm recommendations from the superiors and rectors of our order. At the same time permit me to introduce to you here my assistant and substitute, our worthy brother, Signor Con. I myself intend to stay but a short time in England, as I must soon return to Rome."

"Holy Virgin!" exclaimed Digby, after reading the letter attentively, "the plan is bold, and does honor to him who conceived it. I have no doubt of its success, and will help you to carry it into effect to the best of my feeble power. You know that the Church has no more faithful servant than me. Oh, how I hate this Reformation, which caused my father's death and made me a beggar! I shall be willing to die on the day when all England forswears its false creed and returns into the bosom of our Holy Church."

"May all the saints bless your prayer! but I am afraid a long time will elapse before this will be the case."

"The state of affairs here is by far more favorable than you think, reverend father. Every thing tends to promote our plans. Since Buckingham's death, the influence of the queen has been constantly on the increase, and her zeal for the Catholic cause is well known to you. She has to be checked rather than incited, as she is yet too destitute of sagacity, and suffers herself to be hurried on to imprudent steps by her restless mind and her impatience.

Many distinguished persons in the kingdom either adhere firmly to the ancient faith, or have returned to it publicly or secretly. Some important conversions have lately taken place even among the prominent officers of the king. Lord Cottington, and Windbank, the private secretary, have turned Catholics, and the example they have set is imitated every day by others. There are even many clergymen of the Church of England who are secret friends of Rome. If we succeed in gaining the all-powerful Laud over to our side, we are sure of victory."

"And you think that he will espouse our cause?"

"His inclination toward the Catholic Church cannot be doubted. Wherever he can, he restores the ancient rites and ceremonies. His liturgy is but slightly different from our mass. He has introduced again costly vestments, altars, and images of saints; in short, he lacks nothing to be as good a Catholic as you and I but the acknowledgment of papal authority. His boundless pride has hitherto prevented him from bowing to Rome; but now that you bring him the cardinal's hat which the Holy Father has conferred on him, this last scruple will disappear also."

"You know that my own safety does not permit me to negotiate directly with Laud; nor will the Primate of the Church of England be willing to receive me. Our negotiations, therefore, must be carried on by a person who will not be suspected, and the general of our holy order has selected you to take this task upon yourself."

"I shall always treat his wishes as orders. I shall leave Ludlow Castle with you this very day, and repair to London in order to communicate your offers to the archbishop. All personal considerations must be subordinate to the interests of the order."

"You seem to leave the castle reluctantly," said the wily Jesuit. "I am sorry that I am compelled to disturb your plans, for mere pleasure does not seem to be the reason of your sojourn here."

"You may be right; but in serving my own interests, I never lose sight of those of the order. The Earl of Bridgewater, Lord President of Wales, is one of the wealthiest and most distinguished noblemen of this kingdom. I have succeeded in gaining his confidence, and sowing the seeds of doubt in his weak heart. In a few days the seeds would probably have borne some fruit already, and we should have gained another adherent to our Church. I am afraid that all will be lost again by my absence."

"He who desires to gain great things must know how to give up lesser ones. If Laud, the Primate of the Church of England, joins our side, the others will follow him, as the whole flock follows the shepherd. Your labor will not be lost for all that; it will be acknowledged both in heaven and here on earth."

"I do not desire to conceal any thing from you. The earl has a daughter."

"I understand. You are desirous of putting an end to your forlorn condition as a widower; and as a rich dower is doubtless not wanting to the lady, you intend thereby to extricate yourself from your pecuniary embarrassments. The order cannot blame you for this; nay, it approves of what you are doing, as it is important to it that the influence and social standing of its friends should be placed on a firm footing. In the first place, however, it must insist on the strict fulfilment of your duties. After performing your mission and gaining Laud over to our side, you will have plenty of time left to occupy yourself with the affairs of your heart, court the lady, and make her your wife."

"But what if another should outstrip me?"

"Then there are rivals of your suit, and competitors for her favor?"

"There is but one up to this time, so far as I know. A young poet who lives in the neighborhood seems to have made some impression upon the heart of the young lady. He is not destitute of talent, and it has occurred to me that he might become a useful instrument in our hands, although he sympathizes openly with the Puritans."

"What is his name?"

"Milton. John Milton."

"I will remember it, and the order will not lose sight of him."

The Jesuit drew from a secret pocket a note-book, in which he wrote a few words in cipher.

"For the rest," he added, in a calmer tone, "it seems to me you have little or nothing to fear from such a rival. Poets are rarely dangerous; your own experience must have taught you that, as you yourself did homage to the Muses in your early years. They are wild enthusiasts, and it is not until the vapors and mists of imagination have vanished, that they see men and things as they really are. But then it is too late for them; the opportunity is gone, and they stand empty-handed. I am astonished that a man like you should be afraid of such an enthusiast. Seize the prize boldly, and the lady cannot escape you. But we will talk of this secondary affair at some other time. We have to speak of more important matters. You mentioned the Puritans. What of them and the dissenters in general?"

"They are gaining every day numerous adherents, and are rankling like weeds in the dismal swamp of the Reformation."

"So much the better," replied the Jesuit, with a singular smile. "We cannot wish for a more faithful ally than this sectarian spirit, provided we know how to profit by it. The more numerous the sects in England, the easier will be our triumph. They are fighting and persecuting each other for us; their dissensions are sure to deliver them into our hands. You know the parable of the bundle of arrows. So long as a bond unites them, they cannot be broken, but any child can break them singly. We will look on quietly while the heretics are destroying each other. You will see it will not last much longer."

"The Catholics are to remain neutral, then?"

"Not altogether. There may soon come a time when we shall take a decisive part in the struggle. But for the time being I deem an attitude of quiet observation most advisable for us. We must break neither with the Church of England, nor with the Puritans. Who knows to-day which side may be victorious to-morrow? Besides, you will bear in mind that the interests of the Catholics in England in some points are identical with those of the Protestant dissenters."

"Of our worst enemies?" asked Digby, wonderingly.

"Yes. Are not the Puritans and similar separatists persecuted as we are? are we not both groaning under the same penal laws? In demanding freedom of conscience and toleration, the sectarians are fighting for us. Not our friends, but our enemies, must be useful to us. It will be good policy for us to go hand in hand with them so long as our own advantage requires it. After triumphing with them and through them, it will be time enough for us to drop them. Do not forget this policy, which you will, perhaps, be obliged to pursue in a very short time."

"You will find me ready at all times to obey the instructions of the order, and the commands of the Holy Church."

"Very well. Let us not lose a moment. We must leave the castle this very hour, and enter upon our most important mission. If Laud accepts the cardinal's hat, England will be ours to-morrow."

Digby at once obeyed the Jesuit, whom he

honored as his superior. He himself was a secret member of the order, and he had even received permission to remain apparently a member of the Church of England so long as his position should require it. On the other hand, he had solemnly pledged himself to strictly obey the orders of his superior. Filled from early youth with intense hatred of the Reformation, which had cost him his father's life, and a large portion of his fortune, he knew no other or higher object than the restoration of Catholicism. In these aspirations he was upheld and seconded by his bigoted Catholic mother. Already, during his sojourn in France, he had carried out the purposes which he had entertained for a long time, and had returned into the bosom of the Catholic Church. He had ever since devoted his whole activity to the interests of the order, which soon found him to be one of its most useful and energetic members.

Rome, which forgets nothing and gives up nothing, could not get over the defection of the English people. During the reign of Queen Elizabeth, the Holy See had called out the Catholic powers against the heretical princess, to reëstablish the ancient faith, sword in hand. At the bidding of Rome, Philip of Spain had equipped the proud Armada, which was shipwrecked on the shores of England. Rome was the soul of all insurrections and conspiracies against Elizabeth; the unfortunate Mary Stuart was only a welcome tool in her hands. Especially did the order of Jesuits, which had been established but a short time, display extraordinary activity and energy in this respect. After Elizabeth's death, early in the reign of James I., the Jesuits brought about Guy Fawkes's celebrated gunpowder-plot, the object of which was to blow up the Parliament-house, when the king, the queen, the king's eldest son, the lords, and the members would all be present. An accident led to the discovery of the plot, and the dreadful explosion was prevented. Almost down to the present time this event was annually celebrated in London and nearly every town of England, and a figure of Guy Fawkes was burned amid great rejoicings. All these plots and intrigues added to the hostility with which the English people were animated against Rome, and stirred up an unyielding fanaticism against the Catholic Church. The Protestant clergy thundered forth the most terrible denunciations and menaces against the pope and his adherents, and lavished on them the most offensive invectives and obscene by-words, from which that period of ardent fanaticism never shrank back. Rome was called a hot-bed of sin and lewdness, and the pope was compared with the Antichrist, the dragon, and the seven-headed beast of the Apocalypse. Thus the gulf was widening from day to day, and the hatred of the people became constantly more intense.

Notwithstanding these unfavorable prospects, the Catholic Church was not disheartened. What she had failed to accomplish by violence, she sought to obtain in a more peaceful way. Moreover, there had been in English affairs a change which seemed to encourage her to renewed activity. It is true, the hearts of the people and of Parliament were still filled with the old hatred of and aversion to Rome, which manifested themselves by the most cruel laws and bloody penalties. No Catholic was permitted to hold a public office. The priests of the Roman Church were persecuted as heretofore, imprisoned, and even executed, and conversions were rigorously prohibited. King Charles I. had married a Catholic princess, Henrietta of France, and promised her not only that she herself should be at liberty to worship God in accordance with the rites of her religion, but that such alleviations as were in his power should be granted to all the members of her Church. The queen had in her suite not only French courtiers, but also priests, and even monks. For the first time in many years, the citizens of London saw bearded capuchins in their streets. Mass was regularly celebrated in the apartments of St. James's, and even the foundations of a Catholic Church were laid in the neighborhood of the royal palace. The people contented themselves with manifesting their disapproval by low murmurs. Relying on the protection and growing influence of the young queen, the Catholic party raised its head once more, in the beginning timidly and hesitatingly, but afterward more openly and haughtily. Public and secret conversions were no longer rare occurrences, and the relentless Star-Chamber suddenly displayed much lenity and forbearance in this respect.

The Church of England, to which the king was earnestly devoted, was by no means as hostile to and different from Catholicism as the other reformed sects. It had retained many ancient rites, and outwardly differed but little from it. Laud, the primate of the kingdom, manifested even a surprising inclination toward Rome and its tenets. The more the people became imbued with Puritan principles, the more determined was the stand which the government and court took in the opposite direction. The Jesuits profited by these favorable circumstances, with their usual shrewdness and energy. Their agents, one of whom was Sir Kenelm Digby, displayed the greatest activity. They were everywhere secretly at work; they had succeeded in converting many eminent persons, and if the offer of a cardinal's hat should bring about the defection of the ambitious Laud, no insurmountable obstacles would prevent them from restoring England to the bosom of Catholicism.

For years past Digby had devoted his whole energy to this great task. Now he had been commissioned to enter into negotiations with the primate, and gain him over by holding out to him so rich a prize. Sir Kenelm did not shrink from this adventure, counting as he did upon the pride and unbridled ambition of the Episcopal prelate.

Before setting out from Ludlow Castle, he took leave of all its inmates with studied courtesy and kindness. The Earl of Bridgewater expressed great surprise and regret at his sudden departure.

"I am exceedingly sorry," he said, politely, "that you leave us so soon, as I intended to converse with you yet on many important subjects."

"I hope to return very speedily, and profit once more by your kind hospitality. Pressing business unfortunately compels me now to go to London."

"As you are going to see his majesty, you may render me an important service."

"Speak, and I will gladly do all I can for you and your house."

"In the first place, I desire you to present to his majesty the assurance of my unalterable loyalty and attachment, and likewise to the queen, your august patroness and protectress."

"Do you wish to ask a favor of their majesties?"

"Indeed I do, and yet I scarcely venture to ask for it myself, as so many proofs of the royal favor have been lavished on me that any additional demand on my part would look like an abuse of the great kindness of their majesties. I have a son, with whom you are acquainted."

"Lord Brackley?"

"I do not refer to him, but to his younger brother Thomas. He has enjoyed an excellent education, and is a young man of noble gifts, both of the mind and body. Nevertheless, I have reason not to be entirely satisfied with him. He does not profit by his fine accomplishments, but squanders his talents in deplorable idleness. Latterly, especially, I have noticed a by no means favorable change in his bearing and conduct. Instead of devoting himself to his studies, he roams about for days without any apparent purpose. He is absent-minded, inattentive, and shuns society. The greater was my surprise, on seeing him so soon on excellent terms with you, and I looked upon this as a hint given me by Fate."

"And I am glad that the youth, who is so amiable, despite your charges, had confidence in me and became immediately attached to me."

"I build my plan on this very fact, and hope that you will lend me your assistance. Already for a long time past it was my intention to send my son to the royal court. As a younger brother, he must strive in time to secure himself a position there. Hence, I am very anxious to see him become a member of the household of the king or queen."

"I believe you will meet with no obstacles in obtaining such a position for him, although a great many younger sons are flocking to court for the same purpose."

"The more necessary is it that some one should intercede in his behalf. You are an intimate friend of her majesty, and I request you, therefore, to speak favorably of him to the queen."

"What little influence I am possessed of shall be used in his behalf; however, my intercession is unnecessary. The son of the Lord President of Wales is sure of meeting with a favorable reception."

"That is not all I ask for. The inexperienced youth, besides, needs some one to watch over and guide him. If your friendship for him and myself should induce you to take upon yourself the arduous task of guiding his first steps on the slippery ground which he is about to enter, you would place me under the greatest obligations."

"Your confidence does me so much honor that I will try to deserve it to the best of my power. I shall mention the subject to the king and my august protectress immediately after my return to London. It is my firm conviction that they will receive your son most graciously, and assign him at once a suitable position. On my part, good advice shall not be withheld from him, although I may resemble certain preachers whose words are excellent, while their deeds are any thing but praiseworthy. However, I have the advantage of being very familiar with the temptations of court life; hence, I am able to caution the youth against the sirens, and protect him from the Charybdis to whose dangers I was likewise exposed."

"Then be a wise Mentor to him on his life-path. In the mean time I will prepare him for his new career, and when you return in the course of a few weeks, as you have promised, you may take with you your pupil, whom I would not intrust to any man more willingly than to you."

It was with intense joy that Digby took upon himself this task, which could not but draw closer the bonds connecting him with the earl's family. In doing so, he would, as it were, hold in his hands a pledge that would powerfully promote his schemes. For this reason he promised the earl solemnly that he would watch with the utmost solicitude over his son Thomas. The countess renewed her former invitation to him. Alice treated him with less reserve when he took leave of her.

"Do not forget Comus," she added, playfully, "and do not keep us waiting too long."

"Never fear, noble lady; I shall be here in time, and play my part as well as the best actor."

"I never doubted it," she replied, archly.

On account of his Jesuit companions Digby rejected the offer of the two brothers, who proposed to accompany him on horseback beyond the boundaries of Ludlow. After his departure the whole family concurred in extolling their well-bred and accomplished guest, and all were delighted that he would return in the course of a few weeks. Alice alone was silent and thoughtful. She alone felt an inexplicable aversion to him whom the others eulogized so enthusiastically. Innocence possesses as a shield a presentiment surpassing by far the sagacity and experience of the children of the world. Moreover, another and worthier love protected her heart from the snares of the courtier. She loved the poet.

CHAPTER XIII.

MILTON'S CHOSEN VOCATION.

Milton's father had relinquished business several years ago, and purchased a small property at Horton, in Buckinghamshire. Here he lived in moderately comfortable circumstances, which enabled him to educate his talented son with great care. He was distinguished as a musical composer, and devoted himself in his leisure hours, which were not wanting to him, to this delightful and soothing art. Milton's mother was a gentle, quiet lady, distinguished for her piety and rare benevolence. An elder brother of the poet, and a married sister, completed the family circle; and, notwithstanding their conflicting views on some subjects, all were warmly attached to each other. The dwelling was one of those old houses with a gable-roof, of modest appearance outside, but well furnished, comfortable, and cozy within. Despite the limited size of the building, the poet had a study of his own, opening upon the neighboring garden. The small window was fringed with vines and honeysuckle; when he opened it, the sweet odor of flowers penetrated into the room. The walls of the study contained no other ornaments than a large library neatly arranged and always kept in good order; for the slovenly habits of some literary men were utterly distasteful to Milton. As he was scrupulously neat and even elegant in his dress, so he took care that his room should always present a most attractive aspect. The Latin and Greek classics, poets, and philosophers, stood or lay in old-fashioned cases and on quaintly-carved shelves; and among the representatives of antiquity were to be seen also large folio editions of the fathers of the Church and the most renowned theologians. Thus there were here in contact the opposite elements from which that period derived its learning and culture; classical antiquity and Christian theology occupied the same shelves. On the plain table lay an open Hebrew Bible, always the favorite book of the poet, who drew his principal inspiration from its sacred pages.

Milton had passed here many a sleepless night in arduous study and profound meditation: for to him poetry was not the easy pastime of a versatile and vivid imagination, the passing trance of momentary and fast-vanishing enthusiasm, but the grave task of his whole life, and the quintessence of the highest and noblest creations of human genius. He intended to enter the temple of the goddess only after passing through the Propylæa of Science. He was fully alive to the great difficulties of this arduous task.

Since his return to Ludlow Castle he had laid aside his scientific studies, and occupied himself exclusively with the mask which he had promised to write. The plan was quickly arranged, and the poet went at once to work upon it with his usual energy. He rapidly wrote down several scenes and sketches of the leading persons. One day his father, who repeatedly inquired after the occupations of his son, surprised him while he was thus employed. Milton concealed nothing from his indulgent parent, but informed him frankly of the object and scope of his poem, and told him all about the adventure in Haywood Forest and his sojourn at Ludlow Castle. The enthusiastic description he gave him of the family of the Earl of Bridgewater, and especially of Alice's grace and loveliness, made his tender father thoughtful and anxious.

"You know full well," he said, in a more serious tone than usual, "that I have hitherto never interfered with your doings. Other parents would probably have insisted that a son of your age should at length choose a definite vocation and think of gaining a lucrative position. I have thus far refrained from urging you to do so."

"And I thank you for it," replied the poet, warmly, seizing his father's hand and pressing it with filial reverence to his lips. "I thank you for your forbearance, although I am sorry to say that my gratitude as yet is confined only to empty words. You have granted me rare freedom since my earliest youth, and always abstained from setting bounds to the course of my mind; nor would you allow me to enter the beaten track, strive for filthy lucre, and hunt after vain and glittering splendor. You did not compel me to take orders contrary to my conviction, and teach things against which my conscience rebelled; on the contrary, you permitted me to enrich my mind, which was thirsting for knowledge, and occupy myself in delightful solitude with my favorite studies. But few parents would have done so; therefore, I thank my fate, which gave me the best and most sagacious of fathers."

"For this reason, I suppose you will listen the more readily to my well-meant words?"

"Speak, and I shall obey you willingly, for I know that you will give me only the most judicious advice."

As Milton saw that his interview with his father would be longer than usual, he hastened to fetch him a comfortable easy-chair, and himself remained standing before him in the most respectful attitude. After a short pause his father said to him:

"You will certainly admit that I have not hindered or disapproved your predilection for poetry. I always rejoiced in your talents, and received your first works with paternal pride. Nevertheless, I am not desirous that you should devote yourself exclusively to the Muses, for in such a career you will never obtain a competence and prominent position in life. Most of the poets with whom I have been acquainted have had to struggle with care and want; their occupation gains them sometimes honor and fame, but rarely bread enough to feed them. I am willing to admit of poetry as an ornament of life, but it is not well calculated to furnish a man with sufficient means to live upon. Therefore I deem myself in duty bound to recommend another course to you. You refused to take orders, because you said you preferred a blameless silence to what you considered servitude and false teaching. I approved your decision at that time, but you cannot refuse for the same reason to aspire to a position upon the bench. The judiciary is one of our most respected classes. I will neither urge you to make up your mind at once, nor compel you to follow my advice, but give you sufficient time for reflection. You may tell me frankly what you think of my proposition."

"I must acknowledge your kindness once more," said Milton, after a short pause. "Like you, I revere Poetry so highly as to be unwilling to degrade her to a servile position and ask from her the daily bread of life. She has nothing to do with our worldly affairs, and where she is used as a means of making money she loses her divine dignity. The life of man is a twofold one. The body demands its rights as well as the mind, and the material world forces itself soon enough upon our attention. Hence, I deem your exhortation decidedly well-timed and judicious. But I should not like to aspire to a position on the bench at this juncture. No one can have a more exalted opinion of the judicial position than I, but my respect for it lasts only so long as the bench preserves its independence from external influence. When the despotism of a tyrannical government falsifies justice, violates the laws, and reduces judges by force or persuasion to mere tools, the whole order sinks even below the level of executioners; and such is unfortunately the case in England at this time. Your own experience has shown you that I speak the truth. Would you advise me, then, to become a judge, that is to say, a slave?"

"God forbid!" replied his father, with a gesture of horror. "You are right—we are living in evil times. Yet I should like to have you choose a definite vocation."

"I am going to do so, for I am obliged to acknowledge the justice of your wish; but neither theology nor the law would afford me that satisfaction which a man must find in his profession if he is to be useful to himself and others. There is still a third calling which, at this juncture, I must prefer to any other profession. Let me become a *teacher of youth.* It is only in this calling that I can be useful to the world and my native country. I know well that it is not very lucrative, but if its outward reward is small, its inward one is great. I have long been engrossed in this plan, and it has always seemed to me that the reforming of education is one of the greatest and noblest designs that can be thought of. You smile at my enthusiasm, and think perhaps of our poor schoolmasters who painfully instill the rudiments of science into the untutored minds of ignorant children, or of our professors who from their dusty treatises always repeat the same wisdom to their own disgust and that of others."

"It is true, I should not have expected that you would choose such a career, inasmuch as I am aware of your aversion to our present system of education and instruction."

"It is precisely because my own experience in regard to this matter has been a truly melancholy one that I am determined to struggle against these abuses to the best of my power. At present our schools are nothing but prisons both for the body and mind, and our universities only rob us of seven or eight of the finest years of our lives. They present their young unmatriculated novices at first coming with the most intellective abstractions of logic and metaphysics; so that they, having but newly left those grammatical flats and shallows where they stuck unreasonably to learn a few words with lamentable construction, and now on the sudden transported under another climate, to be tossed and turmoiled with their unballasted wits in fathomless and unquiet deeps of controversy, do for the most part grow into hatred and contempt of learning, mocked and deluded all this while with ragged notions and babblements, while they expected worthy and delightful knowledge; till poverty or youthful years call them importunately their several ways, and hasten them with the sway of friends either to an ambitious and mercenary or ignorantly zealous divinity; some allured to the trade of law, grounding their purposes not on the prudent and heavenly contemplation of justice and equity, which was never taught them, but on the promising and pleasing thoughts of litigious terms, fat contentions, and flowing fees; others betake them to state affairs, with souls so unprincipled in virtue and true generous breeding, that flattery and court shifts and tyrannous aphorisms appear to them the highest points of wisdom; instilling their barren hearts with a conscientious slavery, if, as I rather think, it be not feigned. Others, lastly, of a more delicious and airy spirit, retire themselves (knowing no better) to the enjoyments of ease and jollity, living out their days in feast and luxury; which indeed is the wisest and the safest course of all these, unless they were with more integrity undertaken. And these are the errors, and these are the fruits of misspending our prime youth at the schools and universities as we do, either in learning mere words, or such things chiefly as were better unlearned."

"And despite these evils you wish to become a teacher?"

"I wish to do so, because I have long since formed the design of reforming our whole system of education. This idea has long, in silence, presented itself to me, of a better education, in extent and comprehension far more large, and yet of time far shorter, and of attainment far more certain, than has been yet in practice. The end of learning is to repair the ruins of our first parents by regaining to know God aright, and out of that knowledge to love Him, to imitate Him, to be like Him, as we may the nearest by possessing our souls of true virtue, which, being united to the heavenly grace of faith, makes up the highest perfection. But because understanding cannot in this body found itself but on sensible things, nor arrive so clearly to the knowledge of God and things invisible, as by orderly conning over the visible and inferior creature, the same method is necessarily to be followed in all discreet teaching. With the elements of grammar, I will instill into the minds of my pupils the teachings of virtue and morals, for words are only the envelopes of ideas, and language is the garb of thoughts. My pupils shall learn to read and think at the same time. And after mastering the principles of arithmetic, geometry, astronomy, and geography, with a general compact of physics, they may descend in mathematics to the instrumental science of trigonometry; and in natural philosophy, they may leisurely proceed from the history of meteors, minerals, plants, and living creatures, as far as anatomy. To set forward all these proceedings in nature and mathematics, what hinders but that they may procure, as oft as shall be needful, the helpful experiences of hunters, fowlers, fishermen, shepherds, gardeners, apothecaries; and in the other sciences, architects, engineers, mariners, and physicians? When all these employments are well conquered, then will the choice histories, heroic poems, and Attic tragedies of stateliest and most regal argument, with all the famous political orations, offer themselves; which, if they were not only read, but some of them got by memory, and solemnly pronounced with right accent and grace, as might be taught, would endow them even with the spirit and vigor of Demosthenes or Cicero, Euripides or Sophocles. In which methodical course it is so supposed they must proceed by the steady pace of learning onward, as at convenient times, for memory's sake, to retire back into the middle ward, and sometimes into the rear of what they have been taught, until they have confirmed and solidly united the whole body of their perfected knowledge, like the last embattling of a Roman legion. By this time, years and good precepts will have furnished them more distinctly with that art of reason which in ethics is called proairesis; that they may with some judgment contemplate upon moral good and evil. Then will be required a special reënforcement of constant and sound indoctrinating to set them right and firm, instructing them more and amply in the knowledge of virtue and hatred of vice. But in cultivating the minds of the pupils, sight must not be lost of the development of their bodies. The leisure hours are to be devoted to repose, physical exercise, and the divine harmonies of music, which has a great power over dispositions and manners, to smooth and make them gentle from rustic harshness and distempered passions. In those vernal seasons of the year, when the air is calm and pleasant, it were an injury and sullenness against Nature, not to go out and see her riches, and partake in her rejoicing with heaven and earth. I should not, therefore, be a persuader to them of studying much then, after two or three years that they have well laid their grounds, but to ride out in companies, with prudent and staid guides, to all the quarters of the land; learning and observing all places of strength, all commodities of building and of soil for towns and tillage; harbors and ports for trade. These ways would try all their peculiar gifts of nature, and, if there were any secret excellence among them, would fetch it out, and give it fair opportunities to advance itself by, which could not but mightily redound to the good of this nation, and bring into fashion again those old-admired virtues and excellencies with far more advantage now in this purity of Christian knowledge. Nor shall we then need the monsieurs of Paris to take our hopeful youth into their slight and prodigal custodies, and send them over back again, transformed into mimics, apes, and kickshows."

"I am glad," replied his father, gravely, "that you have weighed your plan so carefully, and still more, that you think at last of choosing a vocation. To tell you the truth, your present occupations caused me to doubt it. Your associations, too, filled me with a certain distrust. It is true, the intercourse with aristocratic persons, with whom you have associated of late almost exclusively, offers some advantages, to which I attach due importance; but you must never forget that one may thereby very easily lose one's own independence, and become the sport of their whims and amusements. They foster and protect talents only so long as they serve to divert them and help them to kill their time. They are never forgetful of their higher position, and always retain their innate pride, despite their seeming condescension. So soon as you pretend to treat them on terms of equality, they will haughtily tell you that they are your superiors; and when they have no longer any need of you, they will drop you unceremoniously. I have too good an opinion of your worth to believe you could ever stoop as low as many poets of the present time have done, and become a mere parasite and sycophant of the nobles."

"Dear father, you know neither the house of the Countess of Derby, nor the noble family of Bridgewater."

"But I know the world, and especially the sentiments of the nobles, owing to my experience as a lawyer, as which I frequently came in contact with them. Of course, there are exceptions, and I am willing to regard your patrons and friends as such; nevertheless, I wish to warn you, lest you should meet sooner or later with bitter disappointments, and be rudely aroused from your dreams. I am willing to admit that our nobles are honoring poets and attracting them to their houses; but they esteem and befriend only the poet, and not the man. If the latter should be bold enough to demand real friendship, or even true love, they would soon show him that they think they are his superiors. You know the Latin proverb, '*Procul a Jove, procul a fulmine.*'"

Milton's father uttered these words so emphatically, and with so significant a glance, that the poet blushed and dropped his eyes. He felt that the secret of his heart was betrayed.

His father then left him, and Milton remained absorbed in his reflections. Before him lay the last scene of his mask *Comus*, which he had just written when his father's entrance had interrupted him. As if to quiet his agitation, he read once more the lines describing Alice's appearance in Haywood Forest. Her lovely image was before his eyes, and dispelled all at once the doubts and fears which his father's warnings had awakened in his mind. He read in a loud, sonorous voice, the lines which the lovely girl was to recite on this occasion:

"This way the noise was, if mine ear be true,
My best guide now; methought it was the sound

Of riot and ill-managed merriment,
Such as the jocund flute, or gamesome pipe,
Stirs up among the loose unlettered hinds,
When for their teeming flocks and granges full,
In wanton dance they praise the bounteous Pan,
And thank the gods amiss. I should be loath
To meet the rudeness and swilled insolence
Of such late wassailers; yet, oh! where else
Shall I inform my unacquainted feet
In the blind mazes of this tangled wood?
My brothers, when they saw me wearied out
With this long way, resolving here to lodge
Under the spreading favor of these pines,
Stepped, as they said, to the next thicket-side,
To bring me berries, or such cooling fruit
As the kind hospitable woods provide.
They left me then, when the gray-hooded Even,
Like a sad votarist in palmer's weed,
Rose from the hindmost wheels of Phœbus' wain,
But where they are, and why they came not back,
Is now the labor of my thoughts; 'tis likeliest
They had engaged their wandering steps too far;
And envious darkness, ere they could return,
Had stole them from me: else, oh thievish Night,
Why shouldst thou, but for some felonious end,
In thy dark lantern thus close up the stars,
That Nature hung in heaven, and filled their lamps
With everlasting oil, to give due light
To the misled and lonely traveller?
This is the place, as well as I may guess,
Whence even now the tumult of loud mirth
Was rife, and perfect in my listening ear;
Yet naught but single darkness do I find.
What might this be? A thousand fantasies
Begin to throng into my memory,
Of calling shapes, and beckoning shadows dire,
And airy tongues that syllable men's names
On sands, and shores, and desert wildernesses.
These thoughts may startle well, but not astound
The virtuous mind, that ever walks attended
By a strong-siding champion, Conscience.
O welcome, pure-eyed Faith, white-handed Hope,
And thou, unblemished form of Chastity!
I see ye visibly, and now believe
That He, the Supreme Good, to whom all things ill
Are but as slavish officers of vengeance,
Would send a glistering guardian, if need were,
To keep my life and honor unassailed.
Was I deceived, or did a sable cloud
Turn forth her silver lining on the night?
I did not err—"

While the poet was reading these lines, the door opened noiselessly. Unnoticed by him, his friend Edward King had entered the room and overheard at least the latter part of the lines recited. He knew at once that Alice was to recite this passage on appearing in Haywood Forest. The love which he had felt for the charming girl ever since his first meeting with her, reawoke now with redoubled strength. A sigh escaped his breast. Milton turned and perceived his friend.

"Welcome, my Lycidas!" he exclaimed. "You have kept me waiting a long time for your visit."

"I was afraid of disturbing you, as I knew you were occupied with your mask."

"I shall finish it very soon, and besides I have always time and leisure for my friends. If you have no objections, we will take a walk. I have worked all day, and a stroll with you will do me good."

The room also seemed to his friend too narrow. Both left it and entered upon their habitual walk.

CHAPTER XIV.

LOVE'S SACRIFICE TO FRIENDSHIP.

The friends walked a long while side by side, without conversing as they used to do. Their thoughts were fixed on the same distant object; the same inclination made them silent. Perhaps each suspected the other's feelings, and therefore avoided speaking to each other. A certain bashfulness prevented them from mentioning Alice's name, and alluding to their late sojourn at Ludlow Castle. Milton, who noticed the change in his friend's demeanor, and the pallor of his cheeks, broke at last the almost painful silence.

"You look very pale," he said; "what ails you, my Lycidas?"

His friend started almost in dismay from his musing.

"What ails me?" he asked, evasively. "I am as well as ever."

"And yet I think you have lately undergone a marked change. Your cheeks are pale, your glance is wild and wandering, and I have heard you sigh repeatedly, contrary to your former habit. If some secret grief weighs down your heart, communicate it to me. I long to advise and help you."

"Oh, you are so good," murmured King, "and I do wrong in concealing from you a secret that fills my whole heart. Yes, you shall know all, this very day."

"Indeed, you excite my curiosity."

"Come, let us repose here under this linden. In its fragrant shade I will confide to you what I have scarcely ventured to confess to myself. I am in love."

"You are!" exclaimed Milton, in surprise. "Oh, now I understand it all, for love is a powerful wizard, transforming us and all our peculiarities. It makes the bold bashful and timid, the wise foolish, the eloquent mute, and the mute eloquent. It saddens the glad, and gladdens the sad. No wonder is impossible to it, as it is itself the greatest wonder in which the mysterious power of Nature reveals itself to us. You are in love; now I comprehend why my once gay Lycidas creeps along like the shivering ghosts on the banks of the Acheron, and fills the woods with his lamentations."

"You depict love as though you were yourself enamoured of some fair girl. One hearing you would take it for granted that you had likewise succumbed to the tender flame."

"Who knows?" said Milton, smiling and crimsoning with confusion. "Perhaps my hour has struck too; perhaps I may likewise surprise you soon by my confessions; but first I must find out what nymph has won your coy heart. I am sure she is as shy as a young roe, endowed with a noble heart, and with all the charms that fill us with rapture, as beautiful as Venus, and as accomplished as Pallas. Such I fancy to be the woman capable of winning your heart."

"You portray her as though you knew already who she is. Well, you know her as well as I do. You have seen her, and undergone the fascination of her charms and accomplishments. No other woman can be compared with her. Language is too tame and feeble to describe her loveliness. Is it necessary for me to utter her name?"

A shudder seized Milton, his heart stood still, and consciousness threatened to leave him. He well knew that his friend alluded to Alice Egerton. It was only by a violent effort that he restrained his agitation, which escaped the speaker, who was absorbed in his own thoughts.

"Alice!" murmured the poet, in profound emotion.

"Alice! You have guessed it," said King. "I loved her the moment I saw her in Haywood Forest. At that time I fancied she was the fairy of the forest, a blessed angel descended from above. Afterward I became better acquainted with her, and every day lent new charms to her. It was not only her beauty that won my heart; a more profound impression was made upon me by the innocence surrounding her whole form like a halo, and her accomplishments, coupled as they are with the most touching modesty. Oh, she is peerless on earth!"

Every word by which his transported friend extolled the loveliness of Alice added to the grief with which this unexpected confession could not but fill the poet's heart. He almost succumbed to his agony, and succeeded, only by the most violent efforts, in mastering his emotions and restraining an outburst of his tortured feelings.

"And she returns your love?" faltered out Milton.

"Oh, I would you were the true prophet of my happiness. Hitherto I have not ventured to put such a question to her; but I may confess to you that I am not entirely destitute of hope, for what would life be worth to me in future if I could not hope? Alice did not reject my admiration, but received it with en couraging kindness. When she spoke to me, or met me, her conduct was such as to make me believe that I was not entirely indifferent to her. Her parents, too, and especially her father, seemed not to disapprove my bashful efforts to obtain their daughter's love. All this, however, does not convince me that my suit would really be agreeable to them. Your own experience has shown you, perhaps, that a lover's heart at first fluctuates between blissful transports and overwhelming despair. Now, I have come to you to obtain some certainty about it. I have no more faithful friend than you, and whom should I apply to but my Thyrsis, the playmate of my childhood and faithful companion of my youth?"

"I shall know how to deserve your friendship more than ever before," replied the poet, with all the self-abnegation of which he was capable at that moment.

"I count upon you," continued his friend, with the blind egotism of an ardent lover. "You have known Alice longer than I, and are just now on even more intimate terms with her. Perhaps you may succeed in observing her in unguarded moments, or even gaining her confidence. She knows that we are friends. A word from you now and then may do a great deal of good, and disclose the true state of her heart to me. Therefore, strive to approach her even closer than hitherto, and speak to her much and often about me, that I may learn her feelings toward me. But whatever you may bring to me, life or death, I shall always gratefully acknowledge the service which you will render me thereby."

"I will try to comply with your request," faltered out Milton, whose heart was bleeding from a mortal wound.

"And I am convinced that you will leave nothing undone to second my courtship. I implore you in the name of our friendship to aid me energetically and honestly, for I feel that I cannot live without her."

"I will assuredly do all I can, and I have no doubt that you will obtain Alice's hand."

A painful sigh escaped the poet, and now at last King perceived Milton's agitation. His deathlike pallor, the profound grief stamped on his features, could no longer escape him; but, so far from suspecting the real cause of these marked symptoms of suffering, he attributed them to an entirely different one.

"Pardon me," he said, after this discovery, "if, in speaking of my love-affair, I entirely forgot yours. If I did not misunderstand you, you alluded to a similar inclination filling your heart with grief and anxiety. Follow the example I have set you, and unbosom your sorrow to me. Speak as frankly as I have done, and command me. All that I am and have is at your disposal, and I should rejoice if I could help you to attain your object. Speak, beloved Thyrsis, and you will see that love has not deadened in my heart the sacred feelings of friendship. Let me know, too, what grieves your heart."

"Not now—no, not now," groaned Milton; "perhaps some other time."

"And why not now?" said his friend, pressingly. "I hope you do not believe that my sympathy for you and your friendship is less ardent than it was? Oh, how I grieve at the mere thought of it! You know me, you know how dearly I love you. I should be capable of giving up all for you—yes, Thyrsis, all! Have we not often sworn to each other fidelity and devotion until death; are we not, as heretofore, brothers such as Castor and Pollux were of yore—you, my Damon; I, your Pythias? Or do you think that such instances of a league of souls are to be found only in Greece and in past centuries? No, I am animated, as heretofore, by the love and enthusiasm which would make me willing to die for you."

"No, you shall not die for me," exclaimed the poet, deeply moved. "If one of us is to die, if one of us is to sacrifice himself, let it be me. I long for death more than I ever did. But you must live and enjoy the pleasures of life; for the gods have smiled upon you ever since the hour of your birth. You possess a distinguished name and rank, and all the boons which Heaven showers upon its favorites with lavish hands. Think of the brilliant future which is in store for you, of your parents whose pride and joy you are, and, above all, of your love for Alice."

"And of the friend who is dearer to me than all the treasures of the world. Come! Let us renew, at this beautiful hour, the old bond of our love. Whatever may happen, no accident, no reverse must separate us. Swear to me everlasting love and friendship, as I do to you."

Overcome by their feelings, the youths embraced each other fervently. The soft moonlight illuminated their features. On the heart of his friend Milton vowed to himself to renounce Alice and sacrifice his love to him. When he raised his pale face again, a tear was yet trembling in his eyes, the only trace of the dreadful struggle which his heart had undergone.

The sacrifice had been made.

In this hour he crushed the most precious dream of his heart for the sake of his beloved friend. He was imbued with the teachings of the ancients, and, bearing in mind the glorious examples of antiquity, he was able to achieve this victory over himself. Never was King to learn the greatness of the sacrifice he had made to him.

The friends wandered hand in hand through the silent night. King tried once more to draw Milton's secret from him; but the poet replied beseechingly:

"Do not insist on it to-day. You know that silence under such circumstances is always most welcome to me. For all that, you must not charge me with a lack of candor. Your own confession engrosses my mind so much, that I cannot give utterance to my feelings. Therefore, content yourself with the reply that I have likewise found a young girl worthy of the most ardent affection."

"And I am sure she loves you, for you are worthy of the fairest and noblest woman's love."

"I do not know it," replied the poet, restraining his feelings, "for I have not yet uttered a single word about my love. My innate timidity has always prevented me from so doing."

"But your glances, your face must have certainly revealed the secret to her. The female eye is in this respect by far more keen-sighted than ours. She knows that you love her."

"I believe not; and even though she were aware of it, what good would it do me? She stands too high, and will never condescend to give her hand to a poor poet and future schoolmaster."

"That, then, is the secret cause of your grief? It should not induce you to give up all hope. Love is omnipotent, and levels mountains obstructing its path. Every new obstacle increases its strength and impetuosity. You must not lose heart. A poet is the peer of the greatest noble in the kingdom. Your learning will open you the way to the most exalted positions. You have friends and patrons who will interest themselves in your behalf and assist you energetically. My own father loves you as his son, and his influence at court will enable him to obtain a good position for you. Then you may go boldly to your beloved, or, if you are too timid and bashful, I will ask her to give you her hand."

"I thank you from the bottom of my heart," faltered out the poet.

"After the dearest wishes of our hearts have been fulfilled, we will, with our beautiful and virtuous wives, enter upon a new life. Do you not feel, as I do, the transports filling my heart at this thought? Alice will be at my side and inspire me with enthusiasm to perform the noblest deeds, for she is endowed with a lofty spirit and a heart ardently devoted to the most sublime interests of mankind. For her sake I shall give up the idleness in which I have hitherto lived, and strive to distinguish myself. Henceforth I will devote myself earnestly to the service of my native country, and toil for it with unflagging zeal. I shall share with her every victory I shall thus achieve, and if ever a civic crown should be conferred upon me, it shall adorn the fair brow of my lovely wife. But when silent evening draws nigh, when the loud noise dies away, and business is over for the day, I shall hasten to her, the friend of my soul; the cozy roof of my *Penates* will receive me, the purest love will indemnify me for the wranglings of factions and the cares of the statesman, and her lips will greet me sweetly and gently with charming kisses and smiles. Our time will pass in the most delightful manner, and you will join us, no longer alone, but accompanied by your sweet wife. Your happiness will redouble mine. You will bring with you the gifts of the Muses, and the admiring hearers will surround the poet with sincere enthusiasm. Thus my house will be transformed into a temple of love and friendship, a quiet sanctuary where daily incense will be offered to the Muses and Graces. We will enjoy life hand in hand, not egotistically, but serving the great whole, setting an example to future generations, and handing down to our children the friendship which once united their fathers so firmly and tenderly."

The happy youth gave vent to his enthusiasm in this manner, without suspecting how deeply he wounded his friend by his words. Milton no longer betrayed by word or gesture the pain torturing his heart. He walked silently by his side, with a mortal wound in his heart.

It was not until King took leave of him, in the neighborhood of his father's house, that he gave way to his profound grief. Milton sank, faint and exhausted, on the green turf, which he moistened with his tears. It was not until now that he felt the whole bitterness of the loss he had sustained. Alice's image stood before his soul; he vainly tried to drive it away; it returned again and again, with a gentle, beseeching face. The sweet lips seemed to say to him, "Do not drive me from you," and she opened her soft arms to him longingly. All the places where he had seen her rose again in his memory—Haywood Forest in the silvery moonlight, the garden with its pond, the court-yard, and the cozy sitting-room of the ladies. His poetical imagination added to the pangs torturing his heart; it called up before his soul again and again the radiant, yet so modest and innocent, eyes of the beloved girl, her gestures and motions so full of the most charming grace, her sweet smiles and sagacious words; it depicted all this to him in the most glowing colors. She had never appeared to him so beautiful as at this moment of despair, when he was to renounce her forever, and drain the cup of his sorrow to the very dregs.

Thus he lay on the ground, brooding over his grief; the foliage of the trees murmured softly over his head, as if they wished to join in his wails; the nightingale broke the stillness of the night by its long-drawn, sobbing notes, but he did not hear the sweet bird, which seemed to lament his sorrow. He called Death in a loud voice, and wished that the green turf might open and close over him forevermore, but the angel of death flitted past the unhappy poet to strike with the point of his sword more fortunate beings, revelling in the enjoyment of all pleasures.

Milton had vowed resignation, and he was strong enough to conquer himself. After paying tribute to human weakness, he rose to that height of ancient heroism which he had found in the writings and examples of antiquity. Like the immortal Greek youth, he attached a higher importance to the faith which he had plighted than to love, although this view of friendship entailed upon him the greatest sufferings during his whole life; for all the fibres of his soul were firmly fixed in the ideas of the modern world, which grants the foremost place to love, and not to friendship. His resignation was not a natural triumph over a passion, but rather a fastidious imitation of examples, set at a remote period and amid vastly different circumstances. In sacrificing himself for his friend, he destroyed love, a higher ideal than friendship.

However, he rose victorious from the ground; only his pale, distorted face bore yet the traces of the fearful struggle through which he had passed. Day was dawning in the eastern horizon; faint red gleams colored the gray clouds. The morning breeze swept merrily through the rustling foliage and awakened sleeping Nature to renewed life. Its strong breath rent the veils of night. Already the lark was warbling in the blue air, and sending unseen its greetings from the clouds to reawaken Nature. The horizon grew brighter and brighter; the rosy streaks of the clouds turned into flaming purple and radiant gold. The last remnants of darkness fled before the victorious power of light.

After a short slumber which Milton allowed his exhausted body, he was able to resume his wonted labors. Above all things, he deemed it incumbent upon him to finish the work which could not but arouse so many mournful reminiscences in his mind. He did so with stoical self-abnegation, and it was only in rare intervals that his oppressed breast heaved a heavy sigh when he thought of his first meeting with Alice Egerton. Such reminiscences, it is true, rendered more painful the sacrifice which he was about to make to his friend, but it was impossible for him to avoid them. Lawes, the musician, came to see him from time to time in order to hasten the completion of the mask and come to a thorough understanding in regard to it with the poet. He brought him greetings and flattering invitations from the Countess of Bridgewater and her daughter. Milton had engaged to conduct the rehearsals of the mask in person, and this necessitated a sojourn of several days at the castle, which he would have preferred to avoid. However, it was impossible for him to break the promise which he had made to the countess, and, therefore, he was obliged to set out reluctantly and with heavy heart, accompanied by the musician, to Ludlow Castle.

How greatly changed were the feelings with which he beheld again the scenes of his lost happiness! On seeing the hospitable house, he felt his grief and despair burst forth with redoubled strength. He needed his whole determination in order not to be borne down by this crushing burden. The reception which he met at the hands of the noble family was exceedingly cordial, and Alice expressed her delight at his return so openly, that he was scarcely able to restrain his emotion. His changed demeanor would not have escaped her and the other inmates of the castle, had they not all been engrossed in the preparations for the festival and the arrival of numerous guests from far and near. Milton owed it to this circumstance that he remained unnoticed in the crowd. Under the pretext that it was necessary for him to revise his mask once more and make many alterations in it, he withdrew from the society of the others, and held intercourse only with Lawes, who had to confer a great deal with him in regard to the music.

The other guests, among whom were Edward King and Sir Kenelm Digby, passed the time in the most agreeable manner. Now they made an excursion in the park, which resounded with their loud laughter; now they made a trip to the more remote environs of Ludlow Castle, or went out hunting. The soul of all these diversions was Sir Kenelm Digby, who always distinguished himself as the boldest horseman, the best shot, and the most amiable story-teller. Notwithstanding these brilliant qualities, Alice seemed to shun rather than seek his presence; she avoided being alone with him, and evaded his incessant effort to gain her favor, so far as she could, without positive discourtesy. She much preferred the company of a young gentleman from Wales, with whom she had become acquainted at the house of her Aunt Derby, and who, as a neighbor, had likewise received an invitation to the celebration of her father's birthday.

Simple and unassuming in his whole bearing, Sir Robert Carbury exhibited the most striking contrast with the accomplished courtier. His frank, rosy face, his good-natured blue eyes, did not indicate a very profound mind, but an excellent heart coupled with a great deal of common-sense. A certain uncouthness caused him to appear less gifted and accomplished than he really was. He lacked neither knowledge nor judgment, after overcoming his innate bashfulness and gaining confidence in himself and the persons with whom he had to deal. His body was exceedingly strong and well built, and, as is often the case with such men, his strength was coupled with almost feminine mildness and gentleness; yet all felt that he would display extraordinary courage and great perseverance in critical moments. There was in his whole appearance something hearty and honest, qualities which are still to be found very often among the English country gentlemen, and for which this honorable class is particularly noted. His broad, Welsh dialect, and an almost childlike awkwardness, rendered Sir Robert Carbury the butt of Alice's brother and the other guests. This excited at first her compassion, and she indemnified the poor cavalier for the naughty jests of the company by her kindness, which won his whole heart. He perceived the motive of her conduct and was grateful to her. In this manner he soon became her constant companion, and Alice had sufficient opportunities to discover the excellent qualities which his plain outside concealed from the eyes of the world. She soon entered into an even closer connection with her *protégé*, by taking pains to polish his rough and angular peculiarities, and call his attention, with noble frankness, to his imperfections. She did this with the greatest delicacy, and found in him a most willing and docile pupil. The sneers presently died away, particularly as Carbury's strength and undoubted courage obliged the others to treat him with a certain degree of respect.

However, the preference which Alice gave him was not calculated to excite the jealousy of the chivalrous King, nor that of the accomplished courtier. Both continued uninterruptedly to court the beautiful girl, who, in accordance with the spirit of the times, received their homage as a tribute due to her from all gentlemen. Thus surrounded with admirers, engrossed by all sorts of amusements, Alice did not notice the poet's absence so much as she would have done under other circumstances. It was only in moments of thoughtful quiet that she missed the faithless friend, who was most congenial to her of all the men with whom she was acquainted, and who was yet so dear to her heart.

CHAPTER XV.

REHEARSAL OF THE MASK OF COMUS.

Meanwhile Milton, assisted by his friend, had in his quiet retirement given the finishing touches to his work. The parts were assigned to the performers, and the rehearsals commenced. Besides Alice and her brothers, King and Sir Kenelm Digby were to appear in the mask. The former was to play the Attendant Spirit; the latter, in accordance with his own offer, the god Comus. The part of the nymph Sabrina was assigned to a relative of Alice, because she possessed a beautiful voice, and her part consisted mostly of songs. Several guests had been prevailed upon to appear as dancers. The spacious hall of the castle was the scene of the rehearsals. All the performers manifested an earnest desire to acquit themselves creditably, and looked forward to the performance itself with unfeigned pleasure. The poet, in the first place, read the mask to them, and was rewarded with enthusiastic applause; even Sir Kenelm Digby could not refrain from clapping his hands at several passages.

Alice approached Milton to thank him. Filled with genuine enthusiasm, she seized his hand. A shudder ran through his frame when he felt this gentle contact.

"Instead of a mere occasional poem, you have created a masterpiece," she said, in a low voice. "Shakespeare himself would not be ashamed of this play; but you have committed a great wrong against me."

"I do not understand you," faltered out the poet.

"You have not been true to nature, but made of me an ideal which can nowhere be found in reality. I am far behind the picture you have drawn of me; but I will not expostulate with the poet; he uses his poetic license as he deems best. You should have spared me the blush that will suffuse my cheeks when I am to recite your verses in public."

"Every one will find that my prototype is worthy of even higher praise."

"Let us drop the subject," said Alice, coloring. "I thank you both for the magnificeut poem and your good opinion. I will desist from my charge, but only to prefer another. You avoid mixing with the company, and seem to shun us. Up to this time your labors have been a valid excuse, but from this day forward I count upon you. I long for more congenial conversation than I am able to find among the guests. I hope we shall resume, before and after the festival, the topics on which we formerly conversed."

Digby's approach rendered it unnecessary for the poet to make a painful reply to her. He withdrew with a stiff bow, and the rehearsal commenced. On the following day he sought likewise to avoid Alice. He was unable to conceal from her any longer the fact that he did so on purpose, and she vainly sought for the reason of his strange conduct. She examined carefully the course she had hitherto pursued toward him; she recalled every word, every glance, whereby she might have wounded the irritable and sensitive feelings of the poet; but she was unconscious of having done any thing of the kind. The more painful, therefore, was the impression which his manner toward her now made upon her. She was incessantly engrossed by the endeavor to discover the hidden cause of this strange change. She attributed it now to bodily suffering, misled by the sickly pallor of his face and the expression of pain stamped upon his features; now to domestic misfortunes. In the anxiety which the poet occasioned her, she applied to King for advice and information. King's replies were evasive, and by no means reassuring. He intimated to her that an unhappy affection for a lady of high rank was the cause of Milton's dejection. On hearing this statement, which was uttered in a very careless manner, Alice became greatly excited. More sagacious than King, she thought she knew the lady of whom Milton was enamoured. How much would she have given to learn her name, but her timidity prevented her from making further inquiries! Her heart trembled with delight, for now she understood it all—Milton's confusion, his endeavors to avoid her, his reserved conduct toward her. But at the same time she suddenly cast a glance into her own heart, and she knew then for certain that she loved the poet—an affection which had hitherto been a veiled secret to herself. This discovery filled her with unutterable transports; but already in the next moment doubts arose in her mind. Was it not, perhaps, another lady who was so happy as to have won Milton's love? Was it not, perhaps, a lady unknown to her? New hesitations, new doubts and fears.

Such being the frame of her mind, she avoided likewise being alone with Milton, although she longed to bring about an explanation. She felt greatly embarrassed whenever he approached her. He, however, interpreted her silence, her endeavors to avoid him, in an opposite sense, and felt the painful consciousness that the gulf which was to separate him from Alice for evermore was daily widening.

Meanwhile the rehearsals took their course, when suddenly an unexpected incident threatened to prevent the performance of the mask. The lady to whom the part of the nymph Sabrina had been assigned received quite unexpectedly a letter informing her that her mother had been taken dangerously sick. She resolved immediately to set out from Ludlow Castle, leaving the poet and the other performers in the greatest embarrassment. Lawes ran up and down like a madman, because he thought he had composed his fine music in vain. None of the ladies at Ludlow Castle possessed sufficient musical talents to fill the absentee's place.

"What are we to do now?" cried the excited musician. "Where shall we find at so short a notice an equally competent songstress?"

"I know one, and a better one," said Thomas, rashly.

"You?" asked his brother and Alice.

Thomas became somewhat embarrassed, and did not reply immediately. He thought of his beloved, whose beautiful voice he had often admired.

"For God's sake," interrupted Lawes, "tell me who and where she is. Why do you hesitate? You see that we have no time to lose."

All urged the youth in such a manner that he could not avoid making a candid reply.

"You know our former playmate Lucy Henderson," he said to his brother and sister, blushing. "She has a magnificent voice."

"That is true," said Alice, "but she has long since broken off all intercourse with us."

"Never mind," cried the excited musician; "that is of no consequence if she can sing well. She must be invited, sent for, and, if need be, forcibly abducted. Dearest Thomas, you must get us this treasure, this priceless jewel."

"I will try my best."

"Do so," said Alice, "and we shall all be glad to greet our friend again after so long an absence."

Under such circumstances Thomas was obliged to repair to Lucy Henderson and inform her of his sister's wishes. For some time past he had kept up a regular intercourse with the Puritan's daughter. Old Henderson's frequent absence from home facilitated the secret meetings of the lovers. At these interviews Thomas had depicted to the girl in glowing colors the interesting performance which was to be given on his father's birthday, and had thereby excited her curiosity. He offered her now an opportunity to be present at the mask, not only in the audience, as she herself had desired, but to take an active part in the play. The light-hearted girl was delighted with the invitation, and she uttered a cry of joy on hearing the message which Thomas brought to her. Her fears of her stern father, who considered such amusements sinful abomnations, vanished in the face of so alluring a prospect.

"I, I am to sing before all the noble lords and ladies, and before you?" she exclaimed, joyously. "Oh, Thomas, you are mocking me."

"I pledge you my word that I am in dead earnest. My sister requested me to invite you."

"And I shall meet again with Alice, my dear foster-sister? May I really venture to go with you?" she asked suddenly, dropping her eyes.

"Never fear," replied the youth, who understood very well what she meant. "No one at home suspects that we are lovers. I for one am only afraid of your father's anger, in case he should learn that you took part in a performance which he will of course regard as very sinful."

"He shall and must not learn any thing about it. I have made up my mind. I can no longer bear this thraldom. I shall flee with you so soon as you go to London. You pledged me your word that you would not leave me here."

"And I shall redeem my promise. I have already arranged every thing with Billy Green. He will accompany you to London."

"I will follow you to the end of the world, if need be. I do not ask for any thing else than to live with you. I am ready to be your slave, only permit me to breathe the air in which you live. Ah, how I long for the day when I may throw off these chains which are so burdensome to me! I count the minutes and the hours up to the moment when I may leave our gloomy house. With you and in London! My head swims when I think of it!"

"Try to be as calm as possible, lest you betray yourself. But how will you manage to play the part offered to you, appear at Ludlow Castle, and yet prevent your father from learning any thing about it?"

"He is absent from home, and will return only after five days. The housekeeper goes early to bed, and I will devise some plausible subterfuge. I have long since bribed the servant-girl; the man-servant alone would be dangerous, but he does not sleep in the house. It is true, the gate is locked, but Billy Green has furnished me with a rope-ladder, which I have concealed for some time past under my pillow."

"And the dog?" inquired Thomas, anxiously. "Will he not betray you by barking?"

"Father gave him, at my request, to an acquaintance of his. The dog did not like me, and growled at me ever since I once hurled a stone at him. I did not want him any longer about me; his eyes looked at me with so singular an expression. He seemed to rebuke me silently for what I had done, and I did not rest until he had been given away. Our new watch-dog knows me; I have made him quite tame by feeding him with cake. I need not fear him."

"So much the better," said Thomas, absently. "Then you can and will take the part upon yourself?"

"With the greatest pleasure," replied Lucy, "for what would I not do for you? Await me at the old place."

Lucy Henderson arrived on the following morning at Ludlow Castle to take part in the rehearsals of the mask. Alice received her former playmate and foster-sister with unfeigned cordiality, while she returned her caresses with some embarrassment. Her timidity, however, wore off very soon under the influence of the enthusiastic praise which all bestowed on her beauty, her fine voice, and musical talents. With great tact she managed to strike the key suitable to the company in whose midst she had been placed so suddenly. She moved in it as though it were her own sphere, for she possessed, in a remarkable degree, that talent of the fair sex to adapt herself to the most opposite conditions of life, and assume at least the outward bearing of aristocratic persons. Her eyes beamed and her lips smiled with delight at the sight of the splendor and luxury which she had missed so long. Her light-hearted spirit dispelled every fear of the possible consequences of her hazardous step. The flattery, homage, and kindness which were lavished upon her on all sides, filled her with intense delight, but amidst her triumph her eyes sought her lover. Thomas, however, deemed it prudent to approach her as little as possible, lest his *liaison* with her should be discovered. Lawes, the enthusiastic musician, indemnified her for her lover's involuntary absence. No sooner had he heard her first notes than he declared loudly and publicly that she was destined to eclipse all the *prime donne* in the world by her talents. He took it upon himself to teach her the songs he had composed, and already after a lesson of two or three hours she made the most gratifying progress.

"By the nine Muses!" exclaimed the delighted musician, "we have discovered a phœnix! It looks almost like a miracle. Dearest Thomas, how did you come to find this treasure?"

"You have heard already," replied Thomas, "that the young girl is Alice's foster-sister and the daughter of old Henderson."

"Don't tell me that! I should sooner believe that a thistle produces grapes and a blackthorn sweet tropical fruits. You mean to mock me. The surly, morose, canting Henderson, who has the voice of a hoarse bull-dog, the father of this lovely creature! Go, go! You talk nonsense. I will tell you who she is, and where she comes from."

"I am very curious to learn it."

"She is the nymph Sabrina in person, and dwells in the cool waters of the blue river. Have you not noticed that she is able to make herself suddenly invisible and disappear? The other day I saw her walking on the bank of the Teme; it was already after nightfall. I intended to follow her, when she disappeared all at once. I would almost swear that she plunged into the waters of the river."

"You are a dreamer," said the youth, smiling; "but I will give you a piece of well-meant advice: henceforth do not follow the lovely nymph, for you might get yourself into trouble."

"How so?"

"Old Henderson is a very rough sort of fellow, and Lucy does not want her father to find out that she is going to take part in our festival. Therefore, be cautious; otherwise he might prevent her yet from so doing."

"Never fear. I know how to be silent. I would bite off my tongue rather than lose such a songstress, who will do so much honor to my compositions. But I persist in it, she is the nymph Sabrina."

Notwithstanding this well-meant warning, the musician was already head over ears in love with the charming Lucy. This rapid conquest added to the mirth of the beautiful girl. She jested about it in an interview with Thomas, who advised her not to reject Lawes's homage, so that all suspicions might be diverted from himself. Thus the charming creature was flitting here and there in this intoxicating atmosphere, carelessly enjoying the pleasures of life, and displaying the amiable peculiarities of her light-hearted nature. Her delight was at its height, when Alice had her don one day, a short time previous to the performance of the mask, with the assistance of her maid, the costume which she was to wear as the nymph Sabrina. Her slender form was wrapped in a gold-embroidered white dress and a transparent veil. A wreath of bluish green reed-leaves, water-roses, and anemones crowned her dark hair, which flowed in long loose tresses down to her waist. A set of red coral jewelry adorned her beautiful neck and white arms.

Thus she stood, rapturously admiring her own image in the costly Venetian mirror, while Alice was feasting her eyes, without the least feeling of envy, on the beauty of her foster-sister, and arranging her costume with skilful hands.

"Do you know," said Alice, "that you have become one of the most beautiful girls I have ever seen? You have already conquered one heart here."

Lucy crimsoned, and her heart throbbed audibly.

"Well, you need not be ashamed of your triumph. Mr. Lawes is a very good young man and an excellent musician. How glad I would be if you should, in consequence of his affection for you, return to our house, for he is employed here as music-teacher! May I hope for this?"

"No, no," whispered Lucy, dropping her eyes.

"And why not? Do you not like him, then? He is young, amiable, a master of all instruments, and, what is most essential, head over ears in love. Nor do you seem to dislike him. You need not conceal any thing from me, for we have grown up like sisters. Tell me frankly if you like him."

"I—I do not know," faltered out Lucy, in great confusion.

"What, you do not know? And yet you accept his homage, and encourage him by your smiles and kind glances. Do you know, my child, that your conduct would be reprehensible and inexcusable, if Lawes really were indifferent to you? There is, in my opinion, no more contemptible being than a woman fooling an honorable man, playing with his most generous feelings, and then spurning the victim of her heartlessness. A highway robber is not as mean as she is, for he takes only what he has need of. Poverty and distress generally make a criminal of him, while such a woman commits a crime against the noblest boons God has vouchsafed to mankind, and robs her victim of his most precious possessions, his faith in woman and his love. No, no, you will not do so. I know my Lucy will not act so heartlessly. Perhaps you have not yet reflected upon it and examined your own heart. Young and inexperienced, you do not know life and the world. You are beautiful, but beauty is the most dangerous attraction which we poor girls possess. It diverts the mind only too often from higher things, and endangers our immortal soul. They resemble the foolish virgins whose lamp has gone out when the heavenly bridegroom makes his appearance."

Lucy heaved a deep sigh. Shame and repentance filled her heart, and she dared not raise her eyes to the innocent sister of her lover.

"Have confidence in me," added Alice. "If you love another young man already, let me know it. Our old friendship entitles me to your confidence. I have no sister except you, and you stand likewise solitary and alone in a world full of treachery and temptation. How easily is a young girl misled, and loses in an unguarded moment the happiness of her whole life! All the sufferings and joys of woman arise from the same source. Happy the girl that meets in her path with a noble and honorable man, who does not trifle with her love!"

Alice's words pierced the heart of her foster-sister like two-edged swords; for Lucy was not yet inaccessible to the force of such admonitions; but she thought of Thomas and kept silent. She had gone already so far, that she was unable to retrace her steps.

"No, no," she murmured, scarcely able to repress her tears; "I do not deserve your kindness, but I will be grateful to you all my life, for I know you will not condemn and despise me."

Before Alice was able to ask for an explanation of these strange words, Lucy, overcome by her feelings, embraced her with impetuous tenderness. Alice vainly tried to calm the excited girl. A stream of tears rolled down Lucy's blooming cheeks, and convulsive sobs indicated her profound agitation. But after a few minutes her former smile returned to her lips; it was forced at first, but soon again as natural as ever. Her light-hearted frivolity triumphed over this sudden outburst of the despair of a heart which contained a strange mixture of good and bad qualities.

Alice looked after her wonderingly and thoughtfully; her character was in striking contrast with Lucy's passionate and impressible nature.

CHAPTER XVI.

THE PERFORMANCE.

The earl's birthday came at last, and the performance of "Comus," by which it was to be celebrated, was about to commence. The stage had been erected in the large reception-hall. It consisted of a wooden platform, covered with beautiful carpets. The decorations and machinery were of very fine and ingenious workmanship, and by no means so simple as is generally believed nowadays. The so-called masks, a favorite amusement of the court and nobility, were always performed with an extraordinary and even lavish display of pomp and splendor. Such performances took place only on festive occasions of special importance, on coronation-days, at the weddings of the royal princes, on the birthdays of high dignitaries, etc. Their subjects were usually allegories, and more importance was attached to the expensive decorations and costumes displayed in them than to the poem itself.

The wealthy and munificent countess had spent a great deal of money for gorgeous scenery and dazzling costumes. The curtain which concealed the stage from the audience was profusely adorned with gold embroidery. A row of chairs was intended for the guests; in the middle of this row arose a sort of baldachin, under which the lord president and his wife were to be seated. The galleries were assigned to the servants and the inhabitants of the neighboring country. The wealthiest citizens of the town of Ludlow received permission to witness the performance, and they appeared now in the hall with their wives and daughters, dressed in their holiday attire.

The steward had enough to do to maintain order and decorum; and equally busy was Henry Lawes, who made his appearance at the head of his musicians, and took position with the band close in front of the stage. The orchestra consisted of several lutes, flutes, horns, and a harpsichord, which filled the place of our modern piano, and was played by Lawes himself. Six singers stood on both sides of the orchestra, to reënforce it by their voices. A lively commotion reigned behind the scenes. Actors and dancers, in fancy costumes, glanced once more over their parts, or performed their dances. Some stood in groups, conversing with great animation. The decorations offered to others cozy nooks, where they might talk with each other without being seen or heard by any one. In one of these recesses Thomas met with Lucy Henderson; a kiss and a few passionate words sufficed to dispel the doubts and fears which had arisen in the mind of the beautiful girl. Both spoke again of the flight of Lucy, which was to take place very soon, as the youth, in accordance with the wishes of his father, was to leave Ludlow Castle in the course of a few days, and accompany Sir Kenelm Digby to London, where a position in the household of her majesty had been procured for him.

Sir Kenelm Digby embraced this opportunity to approach Alice and do homage to her. In doing so he availed himself of the privilege which the place and his mask conferred upon him, and addressed her in the spirit of his part.

"Most beautiful of mortals!" he whispered in a low voice, "I lay my heart at your feet. I am called a powerful wizard by every one, and my fame fills this whole sea-girt island; but before you I feel my weakness. Who can behold with impunity so many accomplishments, coupled with such ravishing beauty, without being enthralled thereby?"

"You are not in keeping with your part," she replied, playfully. "Moreover, it is well known to every one that the god Comus is an arrant rogue, intent upon deceiving a poor girl."

"I swear to you that I never loved a woman as intensely as I love you."

"Not even Venetia Stanley, your first wife?"

The accomplished courtier was silent only for a moment. This reply had disconcerted him, but he soon recovered his wonted boldness, and overwhelmed Alice with impassioned protestations and insidious flatteries, which, however, produced the opposite effect on her. His dress, a doublet of red silk, covered with small bells, his bearing, and even the tone of his voice, reminded her only too painfully of her meeting with Billy Green, who appeared to her here a second time, though in a refined form, and with the manners of a well-bred courtier. Nay, she even secretly preferred the voluptuous bluntness of the shrewd vagabond to the refined sensuality of the courtier. The same brutal expression, only concealed under the mask of courtly politeness, deterred her distrustful heart from listening to the appeals of the unprincipled tempter. The approach of King, who was to perform the part of the Attendant Spirit, delivered her from the irksome presence of the dangerous courtier, who withdrew angrily, deferring his plans to a more favorable opportunity. Scarcely had her new admirer greeted her, when Milton gave the signal that the performance was to commence.

The first scene represented a wild wood. King as Attendant Spirit entered it and proclaimed his mission in the following well-sounding lines:

"Before the starry threshold of Jove's court
My mansion is, where those immortal shapes
Of bright aërial spirits live insphered
In regions mild of calm and serene air,
Above the smoke and stir of this dim spot,
Which men call earth; and, with low-thoughted care
Confined, and pestered in this pinfold here,
Strive to keep up a frail and feverish being,
Unmindful of the crown that Virtue gives,
After this mortal change, to her true servants,
Amongst the enthronèd gods on sainted seats.
Yet some there be, that by due steps aspire
To lay their just hands on that golden key,
That opes the palace of Eternity;
To such my errand is; and, but for such,
I would not soil these pure ambrosial weeds
With the rank vapors of this sin-worn mould."

After these introductory lines, the Spirit extolled the noble Earl of Bridgewater and his children. To protect those who had lost their way in the wood from the knavish devices of Comus, the most malicious of all gods, he said he would take the weeds and likeness of a swain that belonged to the service of the house, and caution the unsuspecting travellers against the baneful tricks of the wizard. So saying, the Spirit withdrew, and Sir Kenelm Digby entered the scene in the mask of Comus. In one hand he held an enchanting-rod, in the other his glass; with him a rout of monsters, with heads like various sorts of wild beasts, but otherwise like men and women, their apparel glistening. They came in, making a riotous and unruly noise, with torches in their hands. Comus addressed his companions quite in the spirit of his part:

" . . . . . Welcome joy and feast,
Midnight shout and revelry,
Tipsy dance and jollity!
Braid your locks with rosy twine,
Dropping odors, dropping wine.
Rigor now is gone to bed,
And Advice, with scrupulous head,

Strict Age and sour Severity,
With their grave saws, in slumber lie.
* * * * * *
The sounds and seas, with all their finny drove,
Now to the moon in wavering morrice move;
And, on the tawny sands and shelves,
Trip the pert fairies and the dapper elves.
By dimpled brook and fountain-brim,
The wood-nymphs, decked with daisies trim,
Their merry wakes and pastimes keep:
What hath night to do with sleep?
Night hath better sweets to prove;
Venus now wakes, and wakens Love.
Come, let us our rites begin;
'Tis only daylight that makes sin,
Which these dun shades will ne'er report.
Hail, goddess of nocturnal sport,
Dark-veiled Cotytto! to whom the secret flame
Of midnight torches burns.
* * * * * *
Come, knit hands, and beat the ground,
In a light fantastic round!"

The monsters now performed a characteristic dance, exhibiting their brutal peculiarities in the boldest and wildest leaps. The torches shed a lurid light on the dark scene and the wonderful groups. The goats made a fearful noise, and danced up and down the stage; the ass waltzed with a monkey, wolves and lions vied with each other in howling and roaring. The whole chorus expressed the brutal jollity of the attendants with great skill. Gradually, however, the noisy, bacchantic music assumed a gentler character, to indicate the approach of Alice, who had lost her way in the forest, and Comus shouted to the crazy dancers:

"Break off, break off, I feel the different pace
Of some chaste footing near about this ground.
Run to your shrouds, within these brakes and trees;
Our number may affright: some virgin sure
(For so I can distinguish by mine art),
Benighted in these woods. Now to my charms,
And to my wily trains!
* * * * * *
But here she comes: I fairly step aside,
And hearken, if I may, her business here."

Alice appeared now in the same dress which she had worn in Haywood Forest, and expressed fears as to the absence of her brothers, who had left her alone in the forest. Comus discovered the beautiful lady in her forlorn and unprotected state; and, to secure her as a prize for his unprincipled voluptuousness addresses her in the disguised character of a peasant, offering to conduct her to his own lowly but loyal cottage, which she trustfully accepts. Meanwhile, the brothers, unable to find their way back to their sister, become dreadfully uneasy lest some barm should befall her. John, the more prudent of the two, comforts his younger brother Thomas, and endeavors to quiet his fears:

Elder Brother.

"My sister is not so defenceless left
As you imagine; she has a hidden strength,
Which you remember not.

Second Brother.

. . . . . What hidden strength,
Unless the strength of Heaven, if you mean that?

Elder Brother..

I mean that, too, but yet a hidden strength,
Which, if Heaven gave it, may be termed her own:
'Tis Chastity, my brother, Chastity.
She that has that is clad in complete steel;
And, like a quivered nymph, with arrows keen,
May trace huge forests, and unharbored heaths,
Infamous hills, and sandy, perilous wilds,
Where, through the sacred rays of Chastity,
No savage fierce, bandit, or mountaineer,
Will dare to soil her virgin purity;
Yea, there, where very desolation dwells,
By grots and caverns, shagged with horrid shades,
She may pass on with unblenched majesty,
Be it not done in pride, or in presumption.
Some say, no evil thing that walks by night
In fog or fire, by lake or moorish fen,
Blue meagre hag, or stubborn unlaid ghost
That breaks his magic chains at curfew-time,
No goblin, or swart fairy of the mine,
Hath hurtful power o'er true virginity.
* * * * * *
So dear to Heaven is saintly Chastity,
That, when a soul is found sincerely so,
A thousand liveried angels lackey her,
Driving far off each thing of sin and guilt;
And in clear dream and solemn vision,
Tell her of things that no gross ear can hear;
Till oft converse with heavenly habitants
Begins to cast a beam on the outward shape,
The unpolluted temple of the mind,
And turns it by degrees to the soul's essence,
Till all be made immortal; but when lust,
By unchaste looks, loose gestures, and foul talk,
But most by lewd and lavish act of sin,
Lets in defilement to the inward parts,
The soul grows clotted by contagion,
Imbodies and imbrutes, till she quite lose
The divine property of her first being.
Such are those thick and gloomy shadows damp
Oft seen in charnal vaults and sepulchres

Lingering, and sitting by a new-made grave,
As loth to leave the body that it loved,
And linked itself by carnal sensuality
To a degenerate and degraded state."

The attentive audience greeted this beautiful passage with rapturous applause. The earl himself gave the signal for it, and all the others followed him. King, the Good Spirit, with whom the poem had opened, now entered again in the garb of a shepherd, and joined the anxious brothers. He informed them of the character of Comus, and his wicked designs upon their sister. At the same time he told them how to save her. He handed them a small unsightly root, but of divine effect, and of sovereign use against all enchantments. Armed with this amulet, he told them to assault boldly the necromancer's hall—

"Where if he be, with dauntless hardihood
And brandished blade, rush on him, break his glass,
And shed the luscious liquor on the ground,
But seize his wand; though he and his cursed crew
Fierce sign of battle make, and menace high,
Or, like the sons of Vulcan, vomit smoke,
Yet will they soon retire, if he but shrink."

The brothers promised to follow his advice, and departed, accompanied by the Good Spirit. In the mean time, the scene changed to a stately palace, gorgeously furnished, with soft music, and tables spread with all dainties.

Comus appeared with his rabble and the lady seated in an enchanted chair, to whom he offered his glass, which she put by, and attempted to rise; but the wizard waved his wand, and she sank back into her chair. The two leading persons played with great naturalness, for life and reality mingled with their artistic performance. Already behind the scene, Digby had renewed his efforts to gain Alice's favor by his flattery and homage; but she had, as heretofore, turned a deaf ear to him. He followed her even on the stage with his importunities, which she rejected with lively indignation. Thus the poet's words, which both emphasized in accordance with their real feelings, received a special significance. The mask passed into real life, and its fantastic words expressed, though in a manner concealed from the audience, the true state of their feelings toward each other. The most eminent actors could not have performed these parts better than Digby and Alice did. Both forgot that they were on the stage, and playing a mask; the impetuosity with which he urged her to yield to his propositions was no longer feigned, but interpreted truly his own desires. Voluptuousness and passionate longing were stamped on his countenance, and were betrayed by the tremulous tone of his voice, while Alice expressed to him most emphatically the horror and fear with which he inspired her. This was no longer an illusion; it was the whole, undisguised truth. The words which Milton had given them to speak corresponded in an almost incomprehensible manner to the singular position which they occupied toward each other. In writing these lines, the poet had perhaps borne in mind their individual characters and their striking contrast, and, in trying to portray general types and ideal events, had unconsciously, and with a prophetic spirit, reproduced the reality and life in his immediate surroundings. Digby-Comus attempted once more to prevail upon Alice to drink from the enchanted glass, and lavished the most hypocritical and false representations upon her, but she spurned him with virtuous indignation. She said to him:

"Hence with thy brewed enchantments, foul deceiver!
Hast thou betrayed my credulous innocence
With visored falsehood and base forgery;
And wouldst thou seek again to trap me here
With lickerish baits, fit to ensnare a brute?
Were it a draught for Juno when she banquets,
I would not taste thy treasonous offer.

Comus.

O foolishness of men! that lend their ears
To those budge doctors of the stoic fur,
And fetch their precepts from the cynic tub,
Praising the lean and sallow abstinence!
Wherefore did Nature pour her bounties forth
With such a full and unwithdrawing hand,
Covering the earth with odors, fruits, and flocks,

Thronging the seas with spawn innumerable,
But all to please and sate the curious taste?
And set to work millions of spinning-worms,
That in their green shops weave the smooth-haired silk,
To deck her sons; and, that no corner might
Be vacant of her plenty, in her own loins
She hutched the all-worshipped ore and precious gems,
To store her children with; if all the world
Should in a pet of temperance feed on pulse,
Drink the clear stream, and nothing wear but frieze
The All-Giver would be unthanked, would be unpraised,
Not half His riches known, and yet despised;
And we should serve Him as a grudging Master,
As a penurious niggard of His wealth;
And live like Nature's bastards, not her sons,
Who would be quite surcharged with her own weight,
And strangled with her waste fertility;
The earth cumbered, and the wingèd air darked with plumes,
The herds would over-multitude their lords,
The sea o'erfraught would swell, and the unsought diamonds
Would so imblaze the forehead of the deep,
And so bestud with stars, that they below
Would grow inured to light, and come at last
To gaze upon the sun with shameless brows.
List, lady; be not coy, and be not cozened
With that fame-vaunted name, virginity.
Beauty is Nature's coin, must not be hoarded,
But must be current; and the good thereof
Consists in mutual and partaken bliss,
Unsavory in the enjoyment of itself;
If you let slip time, like a neglected rose,
It withers on the stalk with languished head.
Beauty is Nature's brag, and must be shown
In courts, at feasts, and high solemnities,
Where most may wonder at the workmanship;
It is for homely features to keep home,
They had their name thence; coarse complèxions,
And cheeks of sorry grain, will serve to ply
The sampler, and to tease the housewife's wool.
What need a vermeil-tinctured lip for that,
Love-darting eyes, or tresses like the morn?
There was another meaning in these gifts;
Think what, and be advised; you are but young yet.

Alice.

I had not thought to have unlocked my lips
In this unhallowed air, but that this juggler
Would think to charm my judgment, as mine eyes,
Obtruding false rules, pranked in reason's garb.
I hate when Vice can bolt her arguments,
And Virtue has no tongue to check her pride.
Impostor! do not charge most innocent Nature,
As if she would her children should be riotous
With her abundance; she, good cateress,
Means her provision only to the good,
That live according to her sober laws,
And holy dictate of spare temperance;
If every just man, that now pines with want,
Had but a moderate and beseeming share
Of that which lewdly-pampered luxury
Now heaps upon some few with vast excess,
Nature's full blessings would be well dispensed
In unsuperfluous even proportion,
And she no whit encumbered with her store;
And then the Giver would be better thanked,
His praise due paid: for swinish gluttony
Ne'er looks to Heaven amidst his gorgeous feast,
But with besotted, base ingratitude
Crams, and blasphemes his feeders. Shall I go on,
Or have I said enow? To him that dares
Arm his profane tongue with contemptuous words
Against the sun-clad power of chastity,
Fain would I something say; yet to what end?
Thou hast nor ear nor soul to apprehend
The sublime notion and high mystery,
That must be uttered to unfold the sage
And serious doctrine of virginity;
And thou art worthy that thou shouldst not know
More happiness than this thy present lot.
Enjoy your dear wit and gay rhetoric,
That hath so well been taught her dazzling fence;
Thou art not fit to hear thyself convinced;
Yet should I try, the uncontrollèd work
Of this pure cause would kindle my rapt spirit
To such a flame of sacred vehemence
That dumb things would be moved to sympathize
And the brute Earth would lend her nerves, and shake,
Till all thy magic structures, reared so high,
Were shattered into heaps o'er thy false head.

Comus.

* * * * * *

. . . . Come, no more;
This is mere moral babble, and direct
Against the canon-laws of our foundation:
I must not suffer this; yet 'tis but the lees
And settlings of a melancholy blood;
But this will cure all straight; one sip of this
Will bathe the drooping spirits in delight,
Beyond the bliss of dreams. Be wise, and taste."

The Spirit made another attempt at inducing Alice to drink from his glass, but she refused, and pushed back his hand. Suddenly the brothers rushed in with swords drawn, wrested his glass out of his hand, and broke it against the ground. His rout made sign of resistance, but all were driven in. At the same time the Attendant Spirit came in again. He blamed the brothers for letting the false enchanter escape by not snatching his wand. He said:

" . . . . Without his rod reversed,
And backward mutters of dissevering power,
We cannot free the lady that sits here
In stony fetters fixed, and motionless;
Yet stay; be not disturbed; now I bethink me,
Some other means I have which may be used."

He told them that their sister could be freed

from the spell only by the nymph Sabrina. Upon his adjuration, there appeared the nymph herself, represented by Lucy Henderson. Fabulous sea-monsters drew the gilded car in which the girl was seated in the dress which we have already described. Her appearance drew a murmur of applause from the audience, which expressed its satisfaction even more emphatically when she rose and sang in a silvery voice:

"Shepherd, 'tis my office best
To help ensnared Chastity;
Brightest lady, look on me.
Thus I sprinkle on thy breast
Drops, that from my mountain pure
I have kept, of precious cure;
Thrice upon thy finger's tip,
Thrice upon thy rubied lip;
Next this marble venomed seat,
Smeared with gums of glutinous heat,
I touch with chaste palms moist and cold;
Now the spell hath lost his hold;
And I must haste, ere morning hour,
To wait in Amphitrite's bower."

Sabrina descended amid the sweet notes of gentle music, and Alice rose out of her seat. The scene changed, presenting Ludlow town and the president's castle. Then came in country dancers; after them the Attendant Spirit, with the two brothers. The Spirit presented them to their father and mother, saying:

"Noble lord and lady bright,
I have brought ye new delight;
Here behold so goodly grown,
Three fairy branches of your own;
Heaven hath timely tried their youth,
Their faith, their patience, and their truth;
And sent them here through hard assays,
With a crown of deathless praise,
To triumph in victorious dance
O'er sensual folly and intemperance."

Finally, King took leave of the audience in the following epilogue:

"But now my task is smoothly done,
I can fly, or I can run,
Quickly to the green earth's end,
Where the bowed welkin slow doth bend;
And from thence can soar as soon
To the corners of the moon.
Mortals, that would follow me,
Love Virtue; she alone is free;
She can teach ye how to climb
Higher than the sphery chime;
Or, if Virtue feeble were,
Heaven itself would stoop to her.'

CHAPTER XVII.

SIR KENELM DIGBY FOILED.

All concurred in praising the poem with great enthusiasm. Milton was surrounded by the whole audience, extolling the beauties of his creation. The lord president and his wife thanked him in the most flattering manner, and Alice approached him likewise to give vent to the delight with which the mask had filled her. His triumph was also her own, and the satisfaction which she felt lent new charms to the lovely girl. Flushed with the purest enthusiasm, she dropped her former reserve; she was carried away, and betrayed, in spite of herself, her most secret thoughts and feelings. Hence, the marked coolness with which the poet treated her, impressed her only the more painfully. He seemed to avoid being alone with her, and even conversing long with her. Alice could no longer bear this treatment, which bewildered and almost maddened her; she made up her mind to obtain an explanation from him at any cost, but neither the place nor the time favored her purpose. She was soon called away from his side and drawn into the whirl of the festival.

A sumptuous banquet took place after the mask was at an end, and a ball concluded the festivities of the day. The dancers moved around the brilliantly-illuminated hall, and Alice, the daughter of the house and leading belle of the occasion, could not absent herself from the ball. Notwithstanding her reluctance, she danced with Digby, who did not leave her a moment, and displayed all his seductive wiles. It was only for the purpose of escaping his importunities that she received much more readily than usual the homage which Edward

King rendered to her, and treated him with marked kindness. The happy youth allowed himself to be misled by her conduct, and rejoiced in what he was pleased to call his great triumph.

Milton stood leaning against a pillar, and gazing with a bleeding heart upon the gay scene. Whenever Alice flitted past him at the side of his friend, the most profound grief filled him anew, and he felt like crying out aloud in his agony. While rejoicing in the success of the happy King, he charged Alice with faithlessness, though he himself had wished that she should give him up. He accused the whole female sex of fickleness, levity, and want of principle. Instead of blaming himself, he blamed the purest of creatures, and transferred his own guilt to the beloved of his heart. He could no longer bear to look upon her; the air threatened to stifle him, the ceiling of the room menaced to fall down on him, and the dancers transformed themselves into infernal demons deriding him by their boisterous mirth. Scarcely knowing what he did, he rushed into the open air. The garden was bathed in silvery moonlight. Red and green lamps were burning on the balustrade in honor of the festival; flaming pitch-rings were blazing here and there amid the trees, and shedding a lurid light on the green foliage. Even here there was too much light for the poet, and the noise of the festival pursued him scornfully. He quickly descended the steps leading to the dark bowers and shady alleys, soon reached the solitude he longed for, and the notes of the music penetrated to him only as faintly as the dying echoes of lost happiness.

On the banks of the pond, where the waters seemed to utter low moans, and where he had once passed the most blissful hours at Alice's side, he gave way to his melancholy dreams. The stillness of nature calmed his wildly agitated heart, and the despair which had seized him in the ballroom passed into a gentle revery. The whispering breeze, the murmuring water, the dying notes of the music, lulled him to sleep. He slumbered on the stone bench, and forgot his grief, though only for a short time.

Was it a mere accident or mysterious sympathy? No sooner had Alice finished the last dance than she suddenly escaped from the host of her admirers and hastened from the hot ballroom into the garden. Some irresistible and mysterious force drew her toward the poet, whose absence she could scarcely have noticed. Like a white apparition she glided through the silent alleys, past the moonlit marble statues of pagan gods. She heard only the throbbing of her agitated heart, whose impetuous pulsations threatened to burst her airy dress. She dared not confess even to herself what had led her hither. She hoped and yet feared to meet the poet here. If she had known that she would find him, she would not have come; her virgin pride would have rebelled against it; she followed only the fascinating voice of a vague presentiment, without being fully conscious what she was about to do. Thus she strolled through the garden without a definite object, and yet pursuing one, deceiving herself and absorbed in melancholy dreams. Every noise caused her to start like a chased roe; the falling of a leaf, the rustling of a drowsy bird, the slightest note froze her blood. Her foot hesitated very often, but an inward longing, for which she was unable to account, urged her on with magic power. She felt as though she would meet Milton here and demand of him an avowal of the secret reasons which caused him to avoid her. He was to defend himself and break his mysterious silence. But even this purpose rose in her soul only like a distant dissolving view, and vanished almost immediately after it had appeared. Another will overcame her own and paralyzed her strength; she tottered like a somnambulist in her night-walk, until she reached her favorite place on the bank of the pond. Here she found Milton slumbering in the moonlight; his pale face beamed toward her, as if transfigured. She did not know whether she should stay or flee; with bated breath she gazed at the sleeper, fascinated in spite of herself by meeting him so suddenly. Thus she resembled the chaste goddess at the moment she found the sleeping Endymion for the first time in the silent forest. She shuddered with coy timidity, but her feet refused to move. She would have liked to bend over him and breathe a gentle kiss on his noble forehead. The happy poet might have been aroused by it, and have succumbed to this new temptation; he would then have lacked courage to sacrifice such a love to the demands of friendship.

Approaching footsteps aroused Alice from her contemplation; it was necessary that no one should see her here, and she disappeared quickly among the trees, after casting a parting glance on the sleeper. With a throbbing heart she hastened back toward the illuminated ballroom. The footsteps pursued her and came nearer and nearer to her; before she was able to reach the balustrade, she felt suddenly that two strong arms encircled her. She uttered a low cry of surprise, and tried to disengage herself from the stranger's embrace.

"Keep quiet," whispered a well-known voice to her. "I followed you."

"Sir Kenelm!" cried the frightened girl. "What do you want here?"

"To see you and speak with you. You must listen to me, for you are in my power now. Your efforts to escape from me will be in vain, I shall not let you go. I know full well that you hate and detest me at this moment; but this is better than your indifference. I love you, and therefore you will love me also."

"Never!" groaned Alice. "And if you do not take your hands from me, I will call for help."

"You are too sagacious," replied Digby, scornfully, "to do any thing of the kind. Even though your voice were heard, which I think is utterly impossible, your reputation would be lost. Therefore, you had better be reasonable and submit to your fate."

He pressed Alice with passionate impetuosity to his breast, and tried to cover her cheeks and neck with burning kisses.

"Let me go!" faltered out Alice, almost fainting with dismay.

"Do not attempt to disengage yourself from my arms. I am not afraid of your anger or your cries. Do you think I did not take the necessary steps beforehand in order not to be disturbed? Why do you resist me and display so much prudery now? I know what brought you here—I know that your lover is still concealed in the garden. You are in my power; your honor, your reputation, is in my hands."

"You lie!" cried Alice, indignantly.

"Not I, but you, my beautiful lady, say what is not true. If you are really innocent, why do you not shout for help? But I think you are too sensible to resort to so extreme a step. Do not be angry with me—forgive me. You shall soon become better acquainted with me, and it is my firm conviction that you will then do me full justice. Above all things, I pledge you my word of honor that no one shall learn any thing about this occurrence. I shall forget your little weakness and attach no special importance to the childish freak, which I believe it to be. I love you none the less for it, and do not care about this harmless error of a young heart. You see, I am a fair-minded man, and by no means such a were-wolf as you thought I was."

"Tell me, then, what you want of me?" asked Alice, in a milder tone, encouraged by his words, and anxious not to drive him to extremities.

"Your hand and your heart. You know

that I have sought for some time past to gain both. You have hitherto rejected my proposals, and any other man, perhaps, would have been deterred by your cold prudery. On me, hewever, it exerted an opposite effect; for difficulties stimulate my energy, and obstacles fire my courage. I do not care for enemies nor women whose resistance is easily overcome. I am a man of different mettle from common mortals, and do not like to walk the beaten track of others. I wrested my first wife from her relatives after a serious struggle, and I am going to win my second wife in spite of herself."

"And you believe you will succeed in so doing?"

"I have no doubt of it, for you will and must listen to me. I rely on your sagacity, which will enable you to see the folly of your conduct. An affection unworthy of your position has seized your heart; but on reflection you will admit that it would be preposterous for you to yield to it. Will you give your hand to an inexperienced young man, who is nothing and has nothing—a poet whose talents enable him at the best to write a little play for a birthday or a similar celebration, and who is tolerated in good society only on account of these talents?"

"You are mistaken," replied Alice, evasively.

"Believe me, I know life and the world. Never will such a union receive the consent of your parents. Will you rebel against their wishes, and take the consequences of such a step? Disowned by your family, you will then be the wife of a man who, notwithstanding his talents (for I do not deny that he is endowed with some), will have to work very hard in order to make a living. You are accustomed to splendor and luxury, and will then have to struggle every day with a thousand privations. Instead of the sumptuous apartments of a palace, the humble rooms of a cottage will be your dwelling-place. Your foot has hitherto trodden only soft carpets; a hard clay-floor will be painful to it. Will you go to market like the wives of other commoners, and quarrel about a farthing with the butcher and fishwoman? Go, go! You are not destined for such a lot. Your rank, your education, and your beauty, assign you a different position. Such a pearl must not perish in the filth of poverty; it is destined to adorn a royal diadem. I will give you my hand and conduct you to the right place. Become my wife, and you shall occupy a brilliant position at court, become one of the leading ladies of London society, and receive the homage due to you. A new life is in store for you there, a world full of splendor and pomp, intimate intercourse with the noblest and most refined men and women of the kingdom, the charms and perfumes of a more elevated and pure atmosphere, which is never obscured by the mists of want and the clouds of poverty. Why do you not reply to me? Will you accept my proposals?"

"Never!" replied Alice, resolutely.

"Then I must *compel* you to accept a lot that will redound to your happiness. Bear in mind that you have no other alternative than disgrace or my hand. Your absence must have been noticed already, and maybe they are looking for you everywhere at this moment. If they find you here, whether with me or with another man, your reputation will be gone forever. If I utter a loud word, you will be dishonored."

"I despise both your threats and your flatteries."

Alice tried to escape again, but Digby held her in his Herculean arms so that she was unable to stir. He relied on his strength, which, under similar circumstances, had often already made him victorious over feeble women. At the same time he counted upon Alice's confusion, upon her anxiety, her bashfulness, and her inexperience. He thought he would obtain his object by taking her by surprise, and the stubborn resistance with which he met, contrary to his expectation, only fanned the flame of his passions. He was one of those bold, reckless men who shrink from no violence. In contending with her, he tore from her the veil in which she was wrapped, and her dazzling shoulders and heaving bosom were exposed to his voluptuous glances. This sight inflamed his desires to the utmost. Instinct and calculation urged him to risk every thing in order to accomplish his purpose; he felt that he had already gone too far, that he must triumph or give up his plans forever, aside from the consequences in which this outrageous attack upon the daughter of a noble house would involve him.

Alice thought that she was lost, and feared lest she should faint. At this critical moment she uttered a loud cry. It was heard; a man emerged from the shrubbery. In the moonlight she recognized her friend Carbury. He was by her side at once, and drew his sword.

"Villain!" he shouted to Digby; "defend yourself, and show if you are as brave when you have to deal with men as you are against defenceless women."

But before Sir Kenelm Digby was able to reply, and accept the challenge, Alice threw herself between the two men.

"If you are my friend," she whispered, "sheathe your sword. No blood must be shed for my sake. I thank you for your kind intentions, Sir Robert Carbury; give me your arm, and conduct me back to the ballroom."

"And this man is not to be chastised for insulting you?" asked Carbury, indignantly.

"I will leave him to his conscience," she replied, in a dignified tone.

She cast a disdainful glance on Digby, who durst not follow her. He remained for a moment, gnashing his teeth, and absorbed in thoughts of revenge.

"Go, vain, foolish girl!" he murmured. "I shall know how to revenge myself. You shall not escape your fate. But am I not myself a greater fool? Instead of remaining calm, I allowed myself to be carried away by blind passion. It will be best for me to leave Ludlow Castle secretly; for I can no longer stay here, and further sojourn would be useless: my game is lost, and I must give it up. Bah! What does it all amount to? It is true, a hue and cry may be raised about it, and it may not; for, if the girl has any sense, and she seems to have, she will say nothing about it, and forbid that boorish fellow Carbury to mention the occurrence to any one. Fortune, I am afraid, has turned her back upon me here in England. Laud did not accept my offer either; and if the affair of the cardinal's hat leaks out, it will go hard with me, and I shall lose the remainder of my estates. I believe it will be best for me to make a tour abroad. I feel my old longing to see Italy. I will go, therefore, to Rome, and not take leave of the earl, whose farewell would probably not be very friendly."

Digby hastened immediately to his room, and awakened his sleeping footman. With his assistance he packed his trunks, and left Ludlow Castle as stealthily as a thief. He embarked already on the following evening on a ship bound for Italy, where he intended to live for some time, in order to escape the consequences of his unsuccessful intrigues.

CHAPTER XVIII.

LUCY'S ESCAPE AND FLIGHT.

As Digby had supposed, neither Alice nor her protector accused him, and the outrage which he had committed was not communicated to any one. The young lady had, in regard to it, a brief conversation with Carbury, which exerted an important effect upon their mutual fate. Carbury dropped his habitual bashfulness on this occasion, and showed that he could not only act bravely, but also think and feel in a delicate and high-minded manner. Not a doubt rose in his heart as to her innocence, and he looked up to her, as heretofore, as to a saint. In this manner he gained Alice's confidence and esteem, and when he left Ludlow Castle, after the festival, like the other guests, an inward voice told him that his love was not entirely hopeless. Milton and his friend departed, in gloomier spirits, from the castle. King had received a pressing letter from his father, who called him to Ireland. He was to set out immediately, and the separation from his friend and his beloved depressed his spirits. Never before had a separation saddened him so much; but nothing remained for him but to obey.

After the excitement of the festival was over, all who had taken part in it felt a certain weariness, which made upon no one a more painful impression than upon light-hearted Lucy Henderson. After the pomp and splendor which she had seen anew at the earl's castle, life at the Puritan's house had become more offensive and irksome to her than ever. Moreover, she was afraid lest Henderson should discover what she had done. How easily could her participation in the performance of the mask be betrayed to him! Her father had returned, and his gloomy features seemed to her guilty conscience more threatening and stern than ever before. Whenever she met his keen, piercing glance, a shudder ran through her frame. Formerly he had at least spoken to her, though in a rough, harsh manner; but, since his return, he did not break his ominous silence; he did not ask her a single question, and did not even inquire how she had passed her time during his absence, which he had hitherto never failed to do.

He sat all day at the table reading in his Bible, while Lucy was seated opposite him, with her needlework. When he did not read, he stared seemingly into vacancy; and yet Lucy felt that he did not avert his eyes from her, and penetrated into the innermost recesses of her soul. Wherever she turned, she met his eyes, and his piercing glance followed her all the time. By and by his presence became almost intolerable to her.

Thus passed the joyless day; when night came, she took her candle, said good-night to her father, and went to her chamber. She tried to sleep, but an inward anxiety prevented her from doing so, and she lay with eyes open in her bed. Whenever she endeavored to close them, she saw before her the threatening form of her father, and his piercing glance which froze her blood. Hour after hour went by; she could find no rest, and vain were her efforts to dispel the dreadful fancies of her imagination by fixing her thoughts upon more pleasant reminiscences. She recalled the events and scenes through which she had passed recently, the fairylike festival, the homage which had been rendered to her, the handsome dresses and trinkets which Alice had presented to her, and which she concealed now under her pillow; all was in vain, and her anxiety oppressed her breast like a nightmare.

The clock struck midnight, when the door of her chamber opened noiselessly. A shudder ran through her frame, and she closed her eyes involuntarily. Was it a dream or was it reality? Old Henderson stood on the threshold, and she distinctly recognized his slender, emaciated form in the moonlight. He held a flashing knife in his hand, and approached her bed on tiptoe.

Lucy made a violent effort to repress the cry which was about to burst from her lips, and scarcely dared to breathe. He bent cautiously over his daughter and touched her face softly, as if to satisfy himself whether she was asleep or not. Not a motion, not the slightest twitching of her features indicated that she was awake. The Puritan knelt down now and muttered a prayer. Terror had sharpened the senses of the girl, so that not a word escaped her.

"God of Israel!" prayed the fanatic, "Listen to Thy servant. As Abraham did not hesitate to sacrifice his beloved son, I will offer my child to Thee. It is better that my daughter should lose her life to-day than that her soul should go to hell for evermore. Thou knowest my heart and my anguish at this terrible hour of distress and sore trial, which Thou hast visited upon me. But Thou wilt lend me strength to bear it. My arm shall not falter on plunging the knife into the bosom of my daughter."

Lucy thought she was lost; she had heard her own dirge. Her father rose noiselessly and approached her bed again. However, before he carried out the bloody deed, another idea seemed to strike him.

"She shall not die without a prayer," he murmured to himself. "I will waken her."

The stern Puritan manifested profound emotion; a tear glistened in his eyes, when he gazed once more at his devoted daughter.

"How beautiful she is!" he murmured, admiring her unveiled charms. "So beautiful was also the first woman in paradise, who brought sin and crime into this world. Her cheeks bloom like roses, but venomous worms are concealed in the flowers. It is better that her body, and not her soul, should die."

Soon, however, the hard man overcame his emotion entirely, and his fanaticism resumed its sway. He stretched out his right hand, in which he held the flashing blade.

"Rise!" he said to Lucy, in a loud, imperious voice.

"For God's sake," she cried in dismay, "what do you want of me, father?"

"I have come to judge you."

"What have I done?" she cried.

"You have broken the commandments of the Lord, gone to the house of the unclean, and taken part in their abominations. Can you deny that you played a part in a sinful mask at Ludlow Castle contrary to my wishes, that you represented a heathen goddess, and sang infamous songs? You see I know all."

"And for this you intend to punish me so cruelly? I confess that I have done wrong, and will repent."

"Your repentance comes too late. You must die, but first you shall pray that your soul may be saved at least."

"Die! die!" cried the girl, despairingly. "I will not, cannot die. Oh, have mercy upon my youth, I am scarcely eighteen years old, and am already to leave the world and descend to the dark grave! No, no! it is impossible. Think of my mother; she would have defended me against you with her life. So long as she was standing by my side you were not allowed to speak a harsh word to me, nor to cast an angry glance on me. When a bee stung me she applied a healing plaster to the swelling; and when a thorn tore my hand, she wept and lamented with me. She sees and hears us at this moment. Do you not fear lest she should curse your cruelty in heaven?"

"Do not invoke your mother," replied the Puritan, gloomily. "She was a virtuous woman, such as is not to be met with again on earth. Had she suspected what would become of you, instead of the milk of her breast she would have given you poison. She will not curse me in paradise, where she is with the blessed, but will exult at my purpose to preserve her child from further corruption. Why do you tremble at the prospect of death? It is the fate that is sooner or later in store for us all. He who dies young is protected from sin, and eternal bliss awaits him. The Lord may as yet pardon your crime; but the longer you live the greater will be the guilt, until it will finally hurl you into hell. Do you believe that it affords me pleasure to shed your blood, and that your loss will not grieve my heart? But the father chastises his child because he loves it."

"Well, then, punish me; chastise me as severely as you please. Lock me up in the darkest cellar, deprive me of food and light, let me feel the full weight of your hand, or cast me off entirely; but do not take my life! Ah, it is so sweet to live, and death is so terrible that I dare not think of it."

Lucy had jumped from her bed and clasped the Puritan's knees. Despair lent her extraordinary strength, and she clung convulsively to her cruel father. With dishevelled hair and livid cheeks bathed in tears, sobbing and groaning, she implored him to spare her life. He vainly tried to shake her off; she allowed him to drag her on the floor.

"No, no," she screamed aloud, "you cannot kill me."

"I must," replied Henderson, inexorably. "I shrank a long time from the sore trial which the Lord imposed upon me. All day I tried to escape from the stern necessity of carrying out His will, but the Spirit pursued me incessantly. The voice of God ordered me to kill you as it once bade Abraham to sacrifice his only son. When the Lord orders me to do any thing, I obey Him."

"The all-merciful God does not demand such a sacrifice. He spared Isaac and took the ram in his place. God does not demand my blood. He forgives the sinner."

"And did He not sacrifice His own Son, our Redeemer, for the sake of mankind? Think of Him who died for our sins, and look up to the cross. Pray, pray!"

"I cannot!" groaned the unfortunate girl. "I cannot pray, and I cannot die."

"Then I will pray for you. Our father!"

"Our father!" she repeated in a dying voice.

"Who art in heaven."

"In heaven," gasped Lucy.

"Hallowed be Thy name. Thy kingdom come. Thy will be done on earth as it is in heaven.—Lucy, why do you not pray?" asked her father who had knelt down by the side of his daughter. "Will you give up your only hope of salvation, and descend to hell, loaded with all your sins?"

"Give us this day our daily bread," she said, mechanically.

"And forgive us our trespasses as we forgive those who trespass against us."

"Who—trespass—against—us," she faltered out.

"Lead us not into temptation, but deliver us from evil."

She prayed no longer, but jumped up from the floor. Every word was only a harbinger of death; how could she utter them any longer? The Puritan had risen likewise, and muttered the last words of the Lord's Prayer in an inaudible tone.

"Amen!" he said at last in a loud voice, brandishing the knife.

Lucy fled into the most distant corner of the chamber, ready to defend her life against her father.

"Submit to your fate!" shouted the fanatic to her. "You cannot escape it."

She uttered a piercing scream which shook the walls of the building. All was in vain. No one heard her, for old Henderson had removed the other inmates of the house, that no one might witness his bloody deed. He was alone with her, and she was in his power. She gathered once more her whole strength.

"Assassin!" she shouted to him. "You are not my father, for a father cannot kill his own child."

On hearing these words, which despair had put into her mouth, the Puritan started back in surprise, and the knife dropped from his hand. Instead of taking it up, he stood for

LUCY CLASPED THE PURITAN'S KNEES.

p. 114.

a few moments, absorbed in deep thought. He seemed to struggle with himself before making up his mind. Lucy watched the expression of his countenance, breathlessly.

There was a dreadful pause. The death-angel seemed to flit through the humble chamber, irresolute whether he should stay or flee.

"What she says is true," murmured old Henderson. "I have no right to kill her. One that has more power over her than I shall be her judge, and I will carry His decision into execution."

Without exchanging another word with Lucy, he left the room, which he locked carefully after him. Only the knife, lying on the floor, yet proved to her that she had not dreamed; otherwise she must have looked upon the whole occurrence as an illusion of her heated imagination. She was saved, but a prisoner. Gradually she recovered from the fearful anguish and terror she had endured; she regained her presence of mind, and took her singular situation into consideration. Her first idea was to escape and leave her father's house forever, as she had already agreed upon with her lover. This last scene with her father put an end to her hesitation; every bond that could attach her yet to her paternal home had been torn asunder. Means of escape were not wanting to her. She had a rope-ladder, by means of which she could easily leave her chamber and the house; she drew it now from under her pillow, packed up a few dresses and the best of her trinkets, and prepared to bid farewell forever to her home. She opened the window cautiously and listened; nothing was to be heard, and old Henderson seemed to have gone to bed. She fastened the frail rope-ladder with trembling fingers to the window-frame; it was strong enough, however, to bear her airy form. She descended quickly, and her foot soon touched the solid ground. It was not until she reached the open field that she breathed more freely. She had no time for reflection whither she should turn her steps. Her escape might have been discovered, and her father might already have started in pursuit of her; hence, she fled as fast as her feet would carry her in the direction of Ludlow Castle. There only, she thought, would she be safe, under her lover's protection.

Scarcely had she ran for fifteen minutes, a prey to incessant fears, when she met a number of horsemen. She made a movement to avoid them and hide in the neighboring shrubbery, but they had already seen her.

"Good heavens!" exclaimed a voice that was well known to her, "there is our little Puritan girl. Thunder and lightning! she has as nice a scent as the best pointer. So much the better; we need not go to her house now. Well, my little dove, what drove you from your warm nest at so early an hour?"

"God be praised that I meet you here!" replied Lucy, greatly encouraged; "is Mr. Thomas present?"

"Of course he is. Why, he stands before you now. Where have you got your eyes, my pretty child?"

"Indeed," said Thomas himself, "this is a wonderful coincidence. I am on my way to London, and was quite uneasy in regard to you. Billy Green was instructed to inform you of my departure, and, if possible, take you with him immediately. I intended to wait with my servants at the neighboring tavern, until he had brought me word; and now you come yourself, as though you had divined the impatience with which I was looking for you. But, tell me quick what has happened. You glance around with an air of terror, and look pale, as though you were afraid lest you should be pursued."

Lucy informed her lover hastily, and in a few words, of her dreadful adventure. He interrupted her narrative from time to time by loud exclamations of surprise and terror.

"The devil! I should never have thought

old Henderson capable of such villany. But wait, wait, you rascally Puritan! We shall meet again one day, and then beware of me! Poor child! How you must have suffered! Even a man would have trembled. I do, from merely hearing your account of the terrible scene. Weep no more. I will not forsake you. I will always be your faithful protector."

"I have no one now on earth save you," wailed the poor girl, throwing herself impetuously into her lover's arms. "Neither father nor mother—no place to lay down my head!"

"Never fear," said Thomas, consolingly. "I will be all to you. You will follow me immediately."

"Until death, wherever you wish me to go."

The youth signed to one of the servants, who dismounted, and arranged the saddle so that Lucy could sit very comfortably upon it. Thomas himself helped her to mount the horse, and then gave the signal to start. Before doing so, however, he called his confidant, Billy Green, to his side.

"Here," he said, handing him a few gold-pieces, "this is your pay. You may go now wherever you like."

"What, you intend to dismiss me?" asked Billy, in surprise. "No, sir, that will never do; since you have secured the little bird, you wish to repudiate the fowler, do you? I think that is very wrong."

"You see that servants are not wanting to me."

"You have awkward fools, but no servants. Do you believe, then, that any of these monkeys, in their gold-embroidered red coats, will be half as useful to you as Billy Green, who has more sense and grit in his little finger than all the lackeys in Old England? You wish to discharge me, but I refuse to be discharged. Never fear, I ask neither wages nor food of you; allow me only to accompany you. I will and must see London. I have made up my mind to do so, and no one shall prevent me. I do not like living in the country any longer; perhaps I may be more successful in the city. I am too good for the boors in the country; my place is at court, I am fully satisfied of it. Many a vagabond and rascal endowed with less sense than I has become a distinguished man there."

Thomas yielded at last to the importunities of the vagabond, who managed also to obtain Lucy's intercession in his behalf.

"Hurrah!" shouted Billy Green, jubilantly. "I shall go now to London, to court, and into the wide, wide world!"

CHAPTER XIX.

THE REAL FATHER—THE PURSUIT.

When the old Puritan awoke, on the morning after that terrible night, his first move was to go to the bedchamber of his daughter, but she was no longer there. The rope-ladder hanging from the open window told him how she had effected her escape. He set out at once in pursuit of Lucy. All his inquiries in the neighborhood were fruitless, for the girl had shrewdly exchanged her female dress for a suit belonging to her lover, and was thus riding in the handsome costume of a young cavalier by the side of Thomas. Being mounted on fast horses, both were soon beyond the range of pursuit, so that grim old Henderson had to go back to his home without accomplishing any thing.

He sat in his room, reading as usual in the Bible, when the door opened noisily, and a strange visitor entered. It was a man of forty, not very tall, but broad-shouldered and heavy set. At the first blush his face seemed coarse and rough, but a close observer could not but discover very soon that his broad, high forehead indicated an unusual understanding; that the firm, well-formed chin showed a high degree of energy and determination; and that a powerful soul was slumbering in the piercing bluish-gray eyes. As plain as his whole appearance was his dress, which was in no wise different from the common garb of a well-to-do English farmer. He wore a brown coat, round which was wrapped a cloak of the same color; a broad-brimmed felt hat covered his large head; his legs were encased in large cavalry-boots reaching up to his thighs. In the broad leathern belt encircling his waist a brace of pistols was gleaming, for at that time no one set out on a journey without being well armed.

The loud, almost majestic tone of these footsteps aroused the Puritan from his gloomy reflections. Twilight had already set in, so that he did not immediately recognize the new-comer, although he had been looking for his arrival. On hearing his greeting, old Henderson gave a start; the tone of this deep voice sounded like menacing thunder in his ears, and when he met the searching glance of the flashing eyes, all his doubts were dispelled. Only one man possessed this glance, whose magnetic charm was able to fascinate every one; and this man was the stranger who had arrived so suddenly. A wonderful expression animated old Henderson's rigid face, and a struggle between anxiety and joy was plainly visible in his features. He was scarcely able to rise from his easy-chair; his feet and the hands which he held out to the visitor trembled like aspen-leaves.

"Oliver!" he cried, almost in dismay.

"It is I," replied the visitor. "But why do you stare at me as though I were a ghost? Has old age confused your head and weakened your memory? You recognize your friend no more."

"Oh, how should I not recognize you? Welcome, whatever you may bring to me."

"Well, that is right. I greet you, then, once more in the name of Him who led me hither. I took a circuitous route for your sake, and have ridden to-day upward of thirty miles. The journey has whetted my appetite, and my body longs in the first place for earthly food."

"You shall be attended to immediately. Food and drink are not wanting in this house."

"I know that the Lord has endowed you here more richly than at the time when you lived in our own neighborhood. The soil is magnificent here; the waving cornfields present a splendid appearance, and you live now in very easy circumstances after formerly draining the bitter cup of poverty to the dregs."

"I should have perished had you not lent me the money I needed, and advised me to settle here. I owe to you all I am and have now."

"And you are so ungrateful," replied his visitor, with a tinge of humor, "as to starve me now. You would do better to get me some supper, instead of talking to me in this manner."

In a few minutes supper was ready, and the guest partook with great zest of the savory ham, which diminished rapidly under the inroads he made upon it, until nothing was left of it but the bone. At the same time he drank such large draughts from the jug which Henderson had placed before him, that it was soon empty and had to be filled again. In the mean time Henderson, who had not yet entirely recovered from his surprise, profited by this interval, during which little was said, to regain his presence of mind. The short but hearty meal ended almost too soon for him. The guest closed the lid of the empty jug noisily and wiped his mouth with an end of the table-cloth; he then clasped his bony hands and was about to say grace.

"Take some more food, or drink, at least, some of the beer which I have brewed myself," said Henderson, whom his confusion rendered quite polite.

"No, I have had enough," replied the guest, pushing back the food which Henderson offered to him. "You have refreshed me sufficiently and strengthened me with earthly manna. The more disagreeable it is for me to sadden you, but I cannot keep from you the news which you would sooner or later hear from other persons. The hand of the Lord rests heavily on His people."

"What has happened?" asked Henderson, eagerly.

"Nothing particularly new. The old burden which almost crushes us is heavy enough for us. Distress and suffering are the lot of true believers, and pious men are being persecuted and punished for the sake of their fidelity, because they do not bend their knees before the idols nor pass over to the Church of England, which is a sister of the Babylonian harlot, and holds adulterous intercourse with the Roman dragon. Our conscience is oppressed, our freedom is trampled upon. A Pharaoh is seated on the throne, and listens to the advice of his blind and infatuated priests instead of the voice of his people and Parliament. Our privileges are no longer respected, our liberties are violated, and the most barefaced despotism reigns instead of our sacred laws. The arrogance of our rulers knows no longer any bounds, and our native country, which was once envied by the nations of the world, has now become their butt. The best men in the country are mourning and averting their heads, for they are powerless against the encroachments of the government."

"What are you going to do about it?"

"The most pious and sagacious men, among whom I will mention my excellent uncle John Hampden, are going to turn their backs upon their ungrateful fatherland. I have consented to accompany them. We shall leave England in the course of a few weeks and embark for America, to recover there our lost liberties. We will intrust our lives and fortunes to the ocean rather than longer bear this grinding tyranny. It is better to live in the wilderness with a free conscience, than to be slaves in the midst of plenty and ease. The wild beasts will be more merciful and less cruel than these proud and insatiable bishops. We shall have to bear no other evils there than the inclemency of the climate, no arbitrary imposts, no other duties than the sweat with which we shall cultivate the virgin soil. There we shall find no coercion of faith, no arrogant and supercilious courtiers, no impudent and lustful priests. Among the mighty trees of the primeval forest we shall obtain an asylum for us and our children, and be allowed to worship the Lord freely and without fear of man in the churches which He built for Himself."

"Then you intend to emigrate and go to America?"

"Is there any other course left to us? We bid farewell to our native country with bleeding hearts; but man should attach a higher importance to the purity of faith and to liberty than to worldly considerations. I come to you as a man at the point of death, to take leave of you and settle my earthly affairs. You know that I intrusted you with something very precious to me."

"I am ready to pay you the last instalment of my debt," replied Henderson, evasively. "You can get the money immediately."

"I did not make this circuitous journey for the sake of the money coming to me, brother, although under these circumstances the sum cannot but be welcome, provided you are able to pay it without embarrassing yourself. I refer to something else that is much more precious to me. Where is the girl whom I intrusted to you? Call her, that I may see her once more and give her my blessing."

"What! you are really going to tell her that you are her father?" asked the Puritan, trying to recover his presence of mind, and merely intent on gaining time.

"No, I am not," replied the guest. "Never must Lucy learn who is her father. The secret of her birth shall be concealed from her forever; since her mother is dead, only you and I are aware of it. I have still the same reasons to hide the sins of my early years. Oh, would I had never committed this folly! But at that time I was not yet in a state of grace; I listened to the temptations of my sinful passions and tottered on the verge of hell. You know all, for Lucy's mother was the nearest relative of your wife; the poor girl atoned for her sin by death. She died in the hour that she gave birth to her daughter, and I intrusted you with the new-born child, the fruit of sin and shame. Years have gone by since then; the Lord has opened my eyes and shown me the true path; nay, I may justly claim that I have become another man; but I have been unable to blot out the remembrance of my fault, which stands all the time before my eyes as a dark spot. I will atone for the wrong I committed; I will repent to the best of my ability. The thought of it pursues me incessantly. Therefore, I came to you to humble myself once more at the sight of my daughter and recall my sins. Lord, Lord! I do not deserve that Thou shouldst look down and have mercy upon me. I violated Thy holy commandments, turned a deaf ear to Thy teachings, wallowed in sin and shame, and stained my immortal soul with all vices. Canst Thou forgive me and raise me up? Look at my repentance, at the tears which my early career wrings from me. I lie here in the dust before Thee and implore Thy forgiveness. Lord, my God, do not thrust me from the heavenly threshold which my foot is unworthy to cross."

The strange guest had knelt down with manifestations of the most profound contrition, and prayed fervently. His eyes beamed with wonderful enthusiasm, and his cheeks were flushed with feverish heat. He struck his breast repeatedly with his clinched fist. This fit, which seemed to border on insanity, lasted a short time; the stranger then rose, calm and composed, without exhibiting the slightest trace of so profound an emotion. He resumed the conversation in as measured a tone as though nothing remarkable had happened.

"Well, then, I came to you to see the girl once more previous to my departure. Besides, I wished to make all necessary arrangements with you, brother, and provide for Lucy's future. Let us first settle our earthly affairs. You may keep the hundred pounds and fifteen shillings which you owe me yet, and spend them for her. I have also brought with me another sum of about the same amount. It is to be her dower when she finds a suitable husband and enters the holy state of matrimony. Keep the money in a secure place; I have saved it by undergoing a great many privations. I have not taken a farthing of it from the property of my present wife and my legitimate children, who must not suffer any detriment in consequence of my sins. Above all things, do not lose sight of Lucy's salvation; she is the daughter of a frivolous mother, and the vices and weaknesses of the parents are entailed upon the children. Therefore, watch her carefully, and do not treat her with undue lenity. You have taken an arduous duty upon yourself, for you are responsible for this child not only to me, but to God Himself."

"Oliver," cried the Puritan, "I cannot call your daughter, for she is no longer in my house."

"What do you say?" replied the stranger, frowning. "You have sent her out of your house and lost sight of her?"

"I did not send her away; she left it of her own accord. She has escaped."

"And you sit still here? You do not pursue her?"

"I started at once in pursuit, and followed her for many miles, but was unable to discover her track."

"You are responsible for all consequences. Henderson, you must restore my child to me, even though you have to go to the ends of the earth. But tell me first what has happened, and why she has left your house. Oh, I know you; your severity has driven her to despair; you have maltreated her and punished her too harshly. Give me back my child, my child!"

"Be a man, Oliver! Listen to me calmly; you shall judge between me and her. I will not conceal any thing from you."

The stranger allowed himself to be calmed by and by, and the Puritan gave him a truthful account of the events of the night.

"Your child was in the snares of hell; you yourself had conferred on me paternal power over Lucy. Can you deny it?"

"Certainly not," murmured the guest, gloomily; "but I feel that a father would have acted otherwise."

"For this reason I did not carry my resolve into execution, though the spirit prompted me to do so. I determined to leave her punishment to you."

"You frightened her, and she fled in consequence of it. It is a terrible misfortune. It is not only that she is exposed to all the temptations of the world, but that you have burdened my heart with heavy solicitude. We must discover her whereabouts. Avail yourself of all your sagacity; make even more minute inquiries in regard to her; do not overlook the slightest hints, for they may help us to discover where she has gone. Above all things, inquire at Ludlow Castle, for I must be greatly mistaken if she has not friends and confidants there, and perhaps a lover, who assisted her in escaping."

The Puritan set out at once to comply with the instructions of his friend. The stranger displayed on this occasion, despite his religious fanaticism, a wonderful clearness of thought and a surprising knowledge of human nature. A few hints were sufficient for his keen mind to fathom the true state of affairs. The news which Henderson brought with him on his return from Ludlow Castle, were apparently insignificant; he informed him merely that the earl's younger son had gone to London.

"Do you know the lad?" asked the stranger.

"I know him well; he is a rash and overbearing fellow."

"And he came to see Lucy repeatedly?"

"My man-servant told me he saw him often prowling round my house."

"Call your man-servant."

The servant came, and Oliver examined him very carefully. The servant asserted that he had seen Lucy and Thomas one evening at the lonely three pines, and added that he had been so much afraid of the ghosts haunting that gloomy spot, that he did not venture to approach them.

"Enough said," replied the guest. "I am greatly mistaken if Lucy did not escape with the young man to London. We must look for her there."

"You will sooner find a needle in a haystack than your daughter in London."

"That is my lookout. You know me; you know that I can always do what I *will* do."

This time, however, the stranger's self-confidence was to be disappointed. On the same day, after a short rest, he left the Puritan's house, accompanied by Henderson, to go to London and ferret out the whereabouts of his lost daughter. However, all his efforts were in vain, as Thomas took good care to conceal Lucy for the time being. Billy Green displayed his talents again on this occasion. The vagabond had rented a house in an out-of-the-way part of the city, where the girl lived safely under his vigilant care. After a great many fruitless efforts, Henderson, at the stranger's suggestion, called upon Thomas himself to make inquiries in regard to Lucy. He found him in a sumptuous suite of apartments in the neighborhood of Whitehall. On hearing the Puritan's accusation, the youth burst into a peal of laughter.

"What! you charge me with abducting a girl, and that your own daughter, friend Henderson? What do you take me for? If we were not old acquaintances, I should have responded to your charge with the horsewhip. This time I will overlook the offence and forgive you."

"But Lucy was seen in your company."

"In my company, and in that of many others. What does that prove? But I have no time to spare for arguing with you; I have business at court. Go, and beware henceforth of charging a nobleman with a crime, without being able to prove it. You might easily incur a heavy penalty for libel. Well, why do you stand still? You had better leave me as quickly as possible." And the overbearing youth brandished his flexible riding-whip playfully around the ears of the old Puritan, who gnashed his teeth and returned to his friend. He found him sitting at the door of the tavern and looking for his return.

"Well, what do you bring?" he said eagerly to Henderson.

"Nothing but the impertinent reply of an arrogant cavalier. Oh, I would I could have chastised him as I longed to do!"

"The time will come when we shall call them to account for every thing, for every thing," murmured Oliver in a prophetic voice. "The present state of affairs cannot last for any length of time. The people will not bear this thraldom much longer; they will arise in their might. Woe unto those who have incurred their wrath! These haughty prelates, these overbearing nobles will repent when it is too late. Their sins will be brought home to them. Another deluge will then set in; but blood, and not water, will drown the impious sinners. As for ourselves, brother, let us watch and pray, that we may be prepared on the day of judgment, when the Lord calls us. For the time being we must submit to His will. I can no longer stay in London; my family is waiting for me at Huntingdon. I must, therefore, desist from further steps, by which we should, moreover, hardly attain our object. The Lord has visited me in wrath and heaped bitter woe on my head. I am afraid lest this child of sin should cause me yet a great deal of grief and solicitude, but I have done all I could to recover her. You may likewise go back to your home and await there the events which will surely come to pass."

"And the seducer of your daughter—shall he not be punished?"

"Who says he should! I know him now, and that is sufficient; I shall not forget him; his name is in my ledger, and I warrant you that he shall pay me one day every penny he owes me."

The friends then parted, and each returned to his home.

CHAPTER XX.

DEATH OF EDWARD KING.

Milton had led a very lonely and retired life, and been engrossed in profound studies since the festival at Ludlow Castle. He had not seen Alice again, and declined all invitations of the Bridgewater family. He had to do even without the intercourse of his friend and his long daily walks with him, as King had set out for Ireland. His beloved books, with which he was occupied night and day, were his only solace and enjoyment. These incessant studies, by which he sought to drown his grief and divert his thoughts from his unhappy love, were injurious to his health. His face became very pallid, his bright eyes were dimmed, and his gait was weary and languid. These changes did not escape the eyes of his tender mother, who had herself been an invalid for some time past. She called the attention of Milton's father to his sickly appearance, and he persuaded his son to make a trip to the sea-shore, and strengthen himself by breathing the bracing sea-air and contemplating the sublime ocean. The poet accepted this suggestion reluctantly and with secret misgivings. He was profoundly moved on bidding farewell to his sick mother.

He reached his destination after a short journey, during which he had met with no adventures. He found the whole population in a state of great excitement, owing to a terrible disaster which had just taken place near the shore. The dreadful storm which had raged all night long had driven several vessels into the breakers, where they had been wrecked before the eyes of the inhabitants. Many lives were lost, and the waves threw the corpses of the drowned sailors upon the beach. Milton learned all this from the talkative daughter of the landlord at whose tavern he had stopped.

"Oh, see," exclaimed the loquacious girl, "they are just bringing another drowned man this way. O, my God, what a handsome young man! He looks as though he were the Prince of Wales himself. He must belong to a noble family."

Milton stepped mechanically to the window which opened upon the sea. He could distinctly hear the roar of the waves, whose fury had not yet subsided. A mournful procession moved along the beach. Several fishermen were carrying the corpse of a youth who seemed to sleep. Only the matted golden ringlets, soiled with sand and sea-grass, and the closed eyes, showed that he was dead. His travelling-dress, which was that of a wealthy and aristocratic man, was saturated with water, and indicated the manner in which he had lost his life. A crowd of sorrowing persons followed the fishermen and lamented the melancholy fate of the unhappy young man. The procession came nearer and nearer to the tavern, and Milton was able now to recognize the features of the drowned man.

Uttering a piercing cry, he rushed from the house and hastened to the corpse.

"King, my Edward, my Lycidas!" he cried, and sank to the ground, overwhelmed with grief.

The crowd had stepped aside on beholding him, and the fishermen had gently put down their load. All honored this outburst of profound grief.

"Can he not be saved?" asked Milton, after a long pause.

"He is dead," replied a kind-hearted sailor. "All is in vain; you see he has been several hours in the water. Poor young man!"

"Where did you find him?"

"The waves threw him on the beach near those rocks yonder. There are several other corpses yet, all belonging to the same ship. But as the young gentleman seemed to be of noble birth, we thought we would give him a Christian burial first of all."

"God bless you for it!"

"You seem to be his brother, or some near relation of his. I suppose, therefore, you will take charge of his funeral. Where do you want us to carry the corpse?"

"To the tavern. I shall not leave him until he is buried."

At Milton's request, the carriers took up the corpse again, and conveyed it to the tavern, where it was laid on a bed. After paying the fishermen for their trouble, the poet remained alone with the corpse and with his grief.

"My friend, my brother, my Lycidas!" he cried, despairingly. "Thus you had to perish—at the threshold of youth, in the midst of all the promises and joys of life! Oh, I would cruel death had taken me in your stead!

With you, I bury my friendship and love. Woe to me! The sacrifice I made to you was in vain. A cruel fate has decreed otherwise."

Such were Milton's lamentations by the side of his friend's remains. It was not until the next day that he recovered sufficient presence of mind to send a messenger with the mournful intelligence to King's father in Ireland, and make the necessary preparations for the temporary burial of the corpse. The poet was the only mourner that followed the coffin to the grave.

"Farewell, farewell!" he cried, as the earth covered his friend's remains.

The grave-digger had long since gone away, but he still sat on the freshly-raised mound. Dusk was already setting in; a gale was blowing from the sea, the waves roared furiously, and upon the sky scudded dark, ragged clouds, from which the moon burst pale and weird. In his despair, Milton did not notice that many hours passed by. Unutterable woe weighed him down; he had lost all: his friend, his beloved, his youth, all were buried in this grave. When he rose at last, he had become a man, ripe, sober, and grave; his ideals were destroyed; his purest and holiest feelings had left him. He became afterward acquainted with other men and women; his poetical heart throbbed for them too, but no longer so warmly and enthusiastically as it had once done for King and Alice. Ah, man rises only once on the wings of youth to heaven; paralyzed by the thunderbolts of fate, or by the hand of time, he is no longer able to soar to those divine heights.

Milton returned mournfully to his father's house, where another blow was in store for him. His mother's disease had become so aggravated that she was at the point of death. The faithful son did not leave her bedside until she breathed her last in his arms. This new loss was too much for him; it undermined his health. His favorite occupations became distasteful to him, and there was every prospect of his becoming a confirmed hypochondriac. His physician advised a foreign tour. At first Milton refused to leave his father, but he yielded at last to his entreaties, and consented to go to Italy.

Before taking leave of England for so long a time, he visited once more the graves of his mother and his beloved friend. Their remembrance accompanied him, and he wrote the sweetest verse in honor of the lamented Edward King. "Lycidas" was the name he gave to the most touching monody ever dedicated by a poet to the memory of his friend:

" . . We were nursed upon the self-same hill:
Fed the same flock by fountain, shade, and rill.
Together both, ere the high lawns appeared
Under the opening eyelids of the morn,
We drove afield; and both together heard
What time the gray-fly winds her sultry horn,
Battening our flocks with the fresh dews of night;
Oft till the star, that rose at evening bright,
Toward Heaven's descent had sloped his westering wheel.
Meanwhile the rural ditties were not mute,
Tempered to the oaten flute.

* * * * * *

But, oh, the heavy change, now thou art gone,
Now thou art gone, and never must return!
Thee, shepherd, thee, the woods and desert caves,
With wild thyme and the gadding vine o'ergrown,
And all their echoes, mourn:
The willows, and the hazel-copses green,
Shall now no more be seen
Fanning their joyous leaves to thy soft lays.
As killing as the canker to the rose,
Or taint-worm to the weanling herds that graze,
Or frost to flowers, that their gay wardrobe wear,
When first the white-thorn blows;
Such, Lycidas, thy loss to shepherd's ear.

* * * * * *

Weep no more, woeful shepherds, weep no more;
For Lycidas your sorrow is not dead,
Sunk though he be beneath the watery floor:
So sinks the day-star in the ocean bed,
And yet anon repairs his drooping head
And tricks his beams, and with new-spangled ore
Flames in the forehead of the morning sky;
So Lycidas sunk low, but mounted high,
Through the dear might of Him that walked the waves;
Where other groves, and other streams along,
With nectar pure his oozy locks he laves,
And hears the unexpressive nuptial song,
In the blest kingdoms meek of joy and love.

There entertain him all the saints above,
In solemn troops and sweet societies,
That sing, and singing, in their glory move,
And wipe the tears forever from his eyes.
Now, Lycidas, the shepherds weep no more;
Henceforth thou art the Genius of the shore,
In thy large recompense, and shalt be good
To all that wander in that perilous flood.
Thus sang the uncouth swain to the oaks and rills,
While the still morn went out with sandals gray.
And now the sun had stretched out all the hills,
And now was dropped into the western bay;
At last he rose, and twitched his mantle blue:
To-morrow to fresh woods and pastures new."

BOOK II.

CHAPTER I.

PARIS—HUGO GROTIUS.

ITALY is a Circe, a sweet enchantress, who, with seductive smiles, presents the cup of forgetfulness to the Northern wanderer. Her soft breezes caress and fondle him, until they smooth his ruffled brow and drive his grief from his heart. Despair cannot dwell long under that ever-clear, azure sky, and the golden sunlight dispels the gloom of the soul; even night is there not the time for melancholy and contemplation, but for mirth and enjoyment. The light-hearted people prrform the tarantella over ruins and tombs; the guitar and tambourine fill the air with their gay notes, and the merry youths move in the graceful mazes of the dance. Love—not the cold and sober affection of the North, but the glowing, devouring passion of the South—dwells amid green myrtles and the flaming red blossoms of the pomegranate. The orange-tree bends under the load of its golden fruit, and the vine spreads its luxuriant leaves, in whose shade the happy reveller quaffs his fiery mnst. Every thing breathes pleasure and enjoyment, and temptation smiles in every nook. Beautiful women, with dark ringlets and burning eyes, weave their charming nets around the Northern barbarian; they are the daughters of those sirens who sang with such sweetness that they who sailed by forgot their country, and died in an ecstasy of delight; the language of the country still sounds as sweet as music, and retains its ancient charm. The voluptuousness of Italy is not coarse and repulsive, but clad in the garb of beauty and art; religion itself is in its service. The Madonna is only a lovely woman, a happy mother with her charming boy in her arms; she smiles at sinners, and forgives the guilty with feminine mildness. These saints and martyrs, notwithstanding their torments, are splendid men and women, whose beautiful forms delight the eyes of the educated beholder. The churches are radiant with variegated colors, golden ornaments, and mosaics; the choir sings in strains of surpassing beauty; and faith is not angry with love entering its sanctuary. With fervent prayers mingle the ardent sighs of earthly passion, and on beholding the heavenly virgin, the worshipper thinks also of the lovely girl kneeling so close by his side that the hem of her garment touches him. Their eyes meet, their glances speak an eloquent language, even though their lips must be silent; signs of a secret understanding are exchanged, and the clasped hands often indicate, in a manner understood only by the initiated, the hour when they shall meet again. The penitent sinner kneels in the confessional, and the indulgent priest grants absolution to the contrite girl. The treasures of art and science, amassed in the museums and libraries, give the mind unequalled opportunities to familiarize itself with the wonders of the past, and forget, in contemplating them, the sufferings and humiliations of the present time. The scholar becomes absorbed in old manuscripts and faded parchments, and a new world rises from the mysterious characters which he deciphers. The sages and great men of all times surround him, and he derives comfort and calmness from their consolation. Remains of ancient art abound, and he is allowed to hold undisturbed intercourse with the immortal gods.

Milton likewise experienced the soothing charms of life in Italy. He had left England, and passed through France. A teacher and patron of the poet, Sir Henry Wotton, had given him the most cordial and flattering letters of introduction to foreign *savans* and statesmen, and added to them the adage, *Il viso sciolto e i pensieri stretti.* ("The countenance open and the thoughts close.") Urged on by longing impatience, Milton hastened in the first place to Paris, where he stayed only a short time. He liked neither the country nor Richelieu, the all-powerful minister, who then ruled over France. He joyfully embraced the opportunity offered him by the English ambassador to make the acquaintance of the celebrated Hugo Grotius, who represented Sweden at the court of France, after being exiled by his ungrateful country. The illustrious scholar and statesman received with the most gratifying kindness the poet who had been so warmly recommended to him. He saw very soon that the young man was highly gifted, and already, after a brief conversation, Milton was no longer a stranger to him.

"I am glad," said Grotius, "that you are going to Italy, and it would be better yet if you should extend your trip to Greece. Oh, how envious I am of your being permitted to pass your time in sweet leisure on that sacred classical soil, while I am unfortunately detained here by the pressing affairs of my embassy!"

"Who could lament this more sincerely than I?" replied Milton; "for in your company only would my eyes open fully to all those sublime wonders which my good fortune will allow me to behold. What new and grand impressions should I, and the world with me, receive through you, who have penetrated the spirit of classical antiquity more profoundly than any other scholar of our times! The learned world justly regrets that politics should withdraw you from science; but, then, Europe and diplomacy would regret it still more if the learned world should claim you as its exclusive property. Your labors and position show me, in a very striking manner, that science and poetry may go hand in hand with practical life, and that one may be at the same time a poet and a politician; for in your person are united the two elements which seem to exclude each other. You are a citizen of two worlds, of heaven and earth."

"You do me too much honor, and but for your frank face and manly bearing, I should feel tempted to take you for a common flatterer. Fate familiarized me with life at an early age. I was almost a boy yet when the degree of Doctor of Laws was conferred upon me. This honor was bestowed upon me in my fifteenth year, and to it was added the even greater one which my paternal friend and patron, the noble Barneveldt, conferred upon me, by taking me with him to Paris and the court of Henry IV., to whom he was accredited as minister plenipotentiary of the Dutch Republic. My precocity delighted the great king, and I am indebted to him for many kind and flattering distinctions. But I attach a much higher importance to the influence which that august person could not but exert upon all those who, like me, were fortunate enough to be on intimate terms with him. Every one extols him, and his memory will live as long as the French people. Now, the most glorious quality of great men is, that they resemble the sun, whose light kindles many thousands of small stars; these stars continue to beam long after the sun has set, and they illuminate the gloom that set in after the sun's disappearance. By my intercourse with the illustrious king I became acquainted with a different system of politics from that established by Machiavelli, which has, nowadays, unfortunately been adopted by most of the European sovereigns. I then learned that a ruler has no other task but that of securing the welfare and tranquillity, first of his own people, and then of mankind generally. Fate put a premature end to the life of this extraordinary prince, and buried his mighty plans, some of which he communicated to me, a wondering youth, or made me divine, at least. After his death I returned to the Netherlands, where I strove to live and act in his spirit. In the violent struggle which the two hostile parties there were waging with each other, I espoused the cause of that of my friend Barneveldt, because I was convinced that right and liberty were on its side. The old man sealed his noble efforts on behalf of his party with his death. He was beheaded, amid the cheers of the infatuated populace. I was sentenced to imprisonment for life, at Castle Löwenstein. You have doubtless heard of the heroic deed of my noble wife. By means of a box, in which she sent me some books, she managed to deliver me, at the risk of her own life. I went in the first place to France, where Louis XIII., mindful, perhaps, of the friendship with which his great father had once treated me, or for the sake of my own insignificant merits, granted me a pension of three thousand livres; but I did not enjoy it long. Cardinal Richelieu, the all-powerful minister, whom I would not flatter, deprived me of the pension, and I was once more exposed to poverty, and even want. Exiled from my native country, I travelled with my poor family from one place to another, until I finally came to the wealthy commercial city of Hamburg. Here I became acquainted with the influential and wise Chancellor Oxenstiern, who promised me protection, and took me into the service of his sovereign."

"In truth, notwithstanding your sufferings and privations, you have been very prosperous. You have had the rare good fortune to be on intimate terms with the greatest men and women of our times. You were allowed to sit at the feet of a great king, who communicated his vast and far-reaching plans to you, and to call friend a man like Oxenstiern, who is universally acknowledged to be the greatest statesman of Europe."

"Nevertheless," said Grotius, in a grave tone, "I should like to change situations with you, my young friend, and to devote myself, as you are allowed to do, exclusively to the study of science, and to intercourse with the sweet Muses. Believe me, only true poets and scholars, who live in an ideal world of dreams and thoughts, are perfectly happy. They preserve that innocence of the heart and soul, of which contact with the real world must deprive the politician. We are like actors behind the scenes, who are familiar with the lamp-black, the rouge, and the coarse paintings, by which the spectators are deceived. The beautiful faces lose their charms there, the magnificent robes become miserable rags, and the splendid landscapes coarse canvas daubed with a sign-painter's brush. When thinking of this, I always remember what the great Oxenstiern wrote to his son: 'Thou dost not yet know, my son, with how little wisdom mankind is governed.' But I will not make your heart prematurely heavy. Take my advice, enjoy your youth, and, above all things, go to Greece."

"I shall follow your advice, particularly as I have for several years longed to visit the country to which we owe our modern civilization, to tread the soil on which Miltiades ventured upon the gigantic struggle with Asiatic despotism, Leonidas gloriously sacrificed himself, Socrates lived and died like the best Christian, Plato taught, and Pindar sang. All I am I owe solely to the sublime examples and teachings which this extraordinary people has left to us. Oh, had I inherited the wonderful eloquence of Demosthenes, I should now raise my voice and call upon all Europe, and first of all upon my native country, to deliver Greece, the cradle of art and poetry, the original seat of eloquence, from the yoke of the cruel Turks. Is it not a disgrace to the whole civilized world that the sons of those heroes should be the slaves of a barbarous people, and that Christians should drag the chains of unbelievers ?"

"I share your wishes in this respect," replied the learned statesman, "although I think that the fate of the modern Greeks is that of most of the heirs of a great name. They resemble their ancestors as the cat resembles the lion. To judge from what I have seen and read of them, I feel inclined to consider them not less barbarous and uncivilized than their tyrants. They have, moreover, acquired all the vices of a people living in slavery and oppression: they are stubborn, insidious, and cowardly."

"I cannot believe that every divine spark can be extinct in them. I myself know some excellent representatives of this nation, and they prevent me from despairing of the regeneration of Greece."

"May your hopes be fulfilled! I comprehend fully that a poet may look with rapturous enthusiasm upon the fatherland of poetry even in its present decay. But the dead past must not cause you to forget the living present. Our own time is not destitute of great men in the realm of science. I should like to introduce you to one of its heroes, who, moreover, wears the martyr's crown. You will, of course, go to Florence; do not fail to visit the neighboring Arcetri and call upon the celebrated Galileo, who so gloriously maintained the laws of Nature in the face of a preposterous system, and whom the Inquisition in consequence persecuted in the most outrageous manner. Go and see him, particularly as the old man, to whom science is so greatly indebted, is so much weakened by disease, care, and grief, that he will probably die at an early day. Hence, we should carefully profit by the little time during which we may still enjoy the instruction of so great a teacher. I am sure the celebrated man will receive you very kindly, if you bring him greetings from me; for he knows that I am one of his most ardent admirers."

Milton thanked him for this new recommendation, and promised to profit by the opportunity to make the acquaintance of one of the most eminent men of the century. Grotius, who was beginning to take the liveliest interest in the promising young man, requested him to visit him as often as possible during his brief sojourn in Paris. By this intercourse with one of the greatest statesmen of his time, the poet not only became familiar with the political situation of Europe, but he also obtained an inside view of the different parties and interests which were in conflict with each other. His conversations with Grotius exerted a powerful effect upon his political principles, and caused him to adopt the views which he advocated afterward with so much ability. In their long interviews they expatiated often on the most important questions of political and social science. The critical spirit with which religious matters were treated at that time, extended also to political discussions. Once aroused from the dreamy torpor of the Middle Ages, the human mind shook with youthful vigor all the barriers impeding its progress. Resuscitated science, after surmounting the ramparts of religious thraldom, attacked the bulwark of political tyranny, and opened its critical batteries upon all existing institutions. The Reformation had thrown a universal ferment into the world, which was struggling for a transformation and new organization. The authority of the pope and the belief in his infallibility having been attacked and much shaken, royal absolutism was likewise endangered. The princes themselves were infatuated enough to open to the enemy the gate by which the torrent of revolution would overwhelm them sooner or later. They had, mostly for selfish reasons, seconded the Reformation to the best of their power, and loosened the ties binding the nations to Rome, in order to appropriate the treasures and estates of the clergy, or to unite the spiritual authority of the pope to their own temporal power. In France especially, royalty waged a desperate war against the feudal nobility and the magnates of the kingdom. Its object was absolute sovereignty, but, by overthrowing the natural pillars of its throne, the clergy and the nobles, and degrading them to the position of mere servants of the crown, it exposed itself afterward, bound hand and foot, to the attacks of its enemies.

Grotius explained all this to his attentive pupil with wonderful clearness and sagacity.

"We have arrived," he said, "at the dawn of a new and great era of history. The ancient world is dead and in a state of corruption; but we can distinctly see that a new life is developing itself out of its remains. This cannot take place without a terrible struggle; birth is always preceded by the pains of labor. But the spirit which is now stirring everywhere must, in the long run, achieve a brilliant victory. This spirit is the spirit of liberty, the breath of God, whose invigorating influence pervades the whole world. It is true, all the black clouds of tyranny, the mists of superstition, and the shades of night impede its progress; but it will overpower and dispel them. The daylight which has once dawned upon the nations cannot be extinguished any more. This boon we owe solely to science and its creations. In truth, it is wonderful what mankind have achieved during the last centuries, and we need no longer shrink from comparing ourselves with the nations of antiquity. The art of printing, above all things, lent wings to the mind, and enabled it to fly from one end of the globe to the other. It gave to the word a thousand-fold echo, penetrating into every heart. The works of the Greek and Roman classics, and above all the Bible, rose from the dust and mould in which they had lain for long centuries, and became the common property of all. Knowledge and civilization, and not brute force, rule now over the world. There are no longer laymen and priests; we have all become a people of priests, as the Bible predicted we should. Thus delivered from its chains, Science becomes a sacred spirit destined to enlighten and save the nations. If I am not mistaken, my young friend, you are likewise chosen to fill this holy office. Receive, therefore, from me the fraternal kiss which will initiate you into the great republic of letters, which unites the enlightened minds of the whole world in a holy and powerful league."

CHAPTER II.

FLORENCE—GALILEO.

Thus prepared for his future career, Milton took leave of the illustrious statesman, and set out for Italy. He had soon crossed the Alps, and arrived safely at Florence. The impressions he received here were almost overwhelming. It is true, the glorious era of the first Medicis was already at an end, but there was still a lingering echo of that period which had exerted so powerful an effect upon the development of art and literature. With eyes radiant with delight, the poet hastened through the streets of the beautiful city. Leaning against the bridge of the Arno, he followed the course of the river, which darts like a silver arrow through the city, crowned on both sides with magnificent palaces, built in the best and chastest style of architecture. These palaces, resembling fortresses, notwithstanding their beautiful appearance, creations of a bold republican spirit, monuments of terrible party struggles, saw their proud pinnacles and rampart-like walls reflected in the waters of the swift-flowing river. The manly and independent spirit of republicanism seemed to be still on guard as a mail-clad sentinel in front of the closed portals, and to wait for the signal of the bloody combat. But Milton's attention was riveted still more by the countless treasures of art and science amassed here, than by these historical reminiscences. He passed many hours every day in the galleries and libraries, now turning over the leaves of an ancient manuscript, now admiring an antique statue, or a painting created by Titian's master-hand. A new world, the world of art, was revealed to him, and the poet's susceptible mind received here the first indelible impressions of a beauty, of which he had not had an idea up to this time. His sick heart gradually began to recover, and his gloomy melancholy yielded to the now gay, now lofty feelings with which the monuments and charming environs of Florence inspired him.

Nor was social intercourse to be wanting to him. At Geneva he had become acquainted with a young *savant*, named Diodati, who lived there, and who had given him letters of introduction to his friends and relatives in Florence. Milton met with an exceedingly kind reception at their hands, and was introduced by them to the most distinguished families of the city. The educated classes of Florence took the liveliest interest in the development of art and science, and the native city of Dante, Boccaccio, and Machiavelli, contained yet a great many eminent men. The noblest and wealthiest families took pride in protecting artists and scholars, and entertaining them with munificent hospitality. Their palaces, villas, and gardens were the rendezvous of foreign and native talents; musicians performed their compositions here, critics expatiated on art and literature, philosophers read their essays, poets recited their epics and lyrics, and even a handsome theatre was built, in which amateurs performed the comedies of Terence, or modern dramas, such as *Pastor fido*, by Guarino, or Machiavelli's sprightly *Madragora*. The ladies took part in these amusements, and their learning proved in many instances by no means inferior to that of the men.

The centres of this intellectual life were the academies, which were established and named after Plato's model. No large Italian city would do without them, and they exerted a most powerful influence upon the education of the nation, and the course of public opinion. The poetical and scientific contests were held in these academies; poets and scholars read their works to a select audience, which criticised them with profound sagacity and crowned the victor with a laurel-wreath. In this manner science and literature were subject to peculiar influences, such as are unknown to our times, when the dead letter has long since taken the place of the living word. It is true, these academies were not free from a certain theatrical ostentation, and they were also frequently affected with an almost childish imitation of antique forms, coupled with stiff pedantry; but their advantages outweighed most decidedly these objectionable features.

Milton was introduced into such an academy by his Italian friends, and requested to recite some of his Latin poems. The specimens of his poetical works, which he read on this occasion, met with an applause which far exceeded his expectations; he received even a number of laudatory letters, which Italians do not address very often to transalpine writers.

This unexpected success, however, did not make our poet vainglorious. It only incited him to renewed efforts and higher aspirations, for he judged his works with greater rigor than his delighted audience did. Above all things, he acquired the conviction that a true poet should not use a foreign language, but his mother tongue. He resolved to write one day a grand work in English, and to relinquish forever the stiff Latin forms which he had mostly used up to this time.

In this manner the poet passed his time at Florence under the most agreeable circumstances, honored and courted by the best circles, which opened to him with charming hospitality. He enjoyed the pleasures of life once more, and the melancholy reminiscences of the past months faded gradually from his memory. He took the liveliest interest in the social intercourse with refined and accomplished persons, who lavished proofs of their esteem and friendship upon him. At times he made excursions into the environs of the city, and their surpassing beauties completed his cure. On one of these occasions he visited the small town of Arcetri, where the celebrated Galilei lived in a sort of compulsory exile. Amidst vineyards and fruitful olive-trees Milton ascended the hill on which the humble house of the greatest and most unfortunate of natural philosophers was situated. Upon reaching the summit, the poet rested a little and gazed upon the magnificent valley at his feet. There lay the city, with its spires, palaces, and bridges, in the golden sunshine, so clear and distinct, that it seemed to him as though his hands could seize it; the Arno meandered like a silver ribbon through the fertile fields and meadows, a picture of prosperity and amply rewarded industry, undulating knolls covered with vines and olive-trees, and dotted with white villas, lined the banks of the beautiful river. The whole country resembled a vast garden spread out before the beholder in indescribable beauty and grandeur, until the ragged mountains of Carrara arrested his transported eyes.

Absorbed in the contemplation of the magnificent landscape, Milton perceived an old man who had seated himself on a marble bench close by, and by whose side a nun with a large flowing veil was standing. Their forms riveted his whole attention immediately. The countenance of the old man seemed to the poet the most venerable he had ever seen; the expansive forehead, which indicated him to be a profound thinker, was adorned with long silver hair; a beard of the same color surrounded the pale wan cheeks, and flowed nearly down to the breast. But the most touching impression was produced by the dark eyes, whose light was extinct. They stared lustreless and dull into the endless night of incurable blindness. The slender nun bent over the unfortunate old man; her delicate, sickly face was illuminated with the rays of piety and filial love.

"Let us go," said the old man, rising and leaning upon his daughter's arm. "You will return to your cloister, for if I am not mistaken, evening is drawing nigh. The cool breeze ascending from the valley tells me so. This has been a very fine day, and night will set in with all the glorious beauties of the star-spangled sky. Oh, I miss the stars much more than the sun. I would I could just once rejoice in their glorious aspect, and admire them from my observatory!"

"Poor father!" murmured the nun, compassionately.

"Do not pity me. The decline of my strength tells me that the day cannot be far off when I shall be permittèd to walk in the midst of my stars. Then I shall know all about the eternal laws regulating their course, which I have hitherto divined only in an imperfect manner. In my dreams, which give me a foretaste of future bliss, I see the vast golden worlds revolving round the radiant sun. Lovely Venus, glowing Mars, and august Jupiter gather like children round the mother that gave them birth, and our globe is revolving with them in harmonious rhythms. No, I was not mistaken; Science does not lie. God Himself wrote the truth in flaming star-letters upon His firmament, and He will be to me in His mercy a wiser and milder judge than the Inquisition, which compelled me to assert on my knees that the sun moved round the earth."

"Calm yourself, father," said his pious daughter, beseechingly; "we must obey the Church and submit to its commandments."

"The Church, yes; but not the Inquisition. I am as good a Catholic as any one in Italy; and I believe that God has revealed Himself to us both in the Bible and in Nature. The world, therefore, is the work, and the Bible the word, of the same God; but the word, rendered in human language, is susceptible of many interpretations; and hundreds of passages, if literally understood, would not only be heresies, but downright blasphemies, by representing God Himself as capable of anger, repentance, forgetfulness, and revenge. Nature, on the other hand, the servant of God, is eternally immutable, and human wishes and opinions have no influence over it; in regard to the motion, shape, and system of its component parts, the universe is always the same. The moon will and must always be a spherical body, although the common people long believed her to be a flat disk. Nature is not subject to manifold interpretations like the word; and human opinions are powerless in the face of eternal truth. Hence, I have adopted it as my guide, and taken infinite pains to discover its holy teachings and laws. Nature was my Bible; I read in it night and day without becoming tired of it. And could my efforts to recognize the Creator in His works be heresy? Oh, such a charge was most painful, but still more painful to me was my solemn recantation, which was a crime against truth."

"You consented to it in obedience to the supplications of your children and friends, and to the advice of the prince who protected you as long as he was able to do so."

"And yet I ought not to have yielded, for truth must be more sacred and precious to us than wife and children, than the whole world. Did the holy martyrs ever deny their faith and bow to the idols of their tormentors? They rather suffered the most excruciating tortures and death. Oh! I ought to have imitated their example; and I grieve bitterly at having lacked courage and strength to do so. Nature, to which I turned recreant, wreaked a terrible vengeance on me. It deprived me of my eyesight, that I might no longer behold and admire its sublime beauties. This is a just retribution for my recreancy."

The pious daughter made no reply, but dropped a scalding tear upon her father's hand.

"Do not weep," said the venerable man, in a voice tremulous with emotion. "This earthly blindness cannot last much longer; I shall soon see what no earthly eye ever beheld. Already the rays of a higher sun penetrate the gloom of my existence, and a reflex of the eternal light fills my soul. I often feel as though I were seated on a lofty tower, fanned by purer air, holding in my hand a telescope by far more perfect and powerful than my own instruments; the galaxy passes my eyes; on looking at it without a telescope, we think it is a fine silvery mist; but to me it appears as an ocean of light, filled with an enormous number of new suns, round which move planets and moons larger and more beautiful than those which have hitherto been discovered. These celestial suns and planets follow in endless succession up to the throne of the Almighty, who is hidden behind this dazzling ocean of light, and whose face none but the blessed are allowed to behold. I hope I shall likewise see Him amidst the glorious world of His stars."

Concealed behind a tree, Milton had listened to this conversation, which he did not venture to interrupt. He could no longer doubt that the unfortunate old man was the illustrious Galileo, to whom Grotius had recommended him. As the blind sufferer was about to re-enter his house, the poet hastened after him and overtook him at the threshold.

"If I am not mistaken, I greet in you the illustrious Galileo, to whom one of his many friends and admirers, Hugo Grotius, has requested me to bring greetings and this letter."

"Come in," said the old man, "that my daughter may read to me my excellent friend's letter."

Milton complied with this invitation, and was conducted into an humble room filled with books and dusty instruments. The nun, who had immediately veiled herself when the stranger joined them, now removed her veil, and read, in a timid voice, the recommendation and the praise which Grotius had bestowed in the letter upon the talented youth. A sweet blush suffused her delicate ethereal face, and, despite her piety, she looked up from the letter and fixed her gentle eyes upon the slender, fine-looking form of the visitor. When their glances happened to meet, she was scarcely able to conceal her confusion, and she went out for a short time under the pretext of looking after the supper.

The distrust with which the blind Galileo, surrounded as he was by spies, could not but look upon every stranger, gave way to a more cordial understanding so soon as they had exchanged a few words. There were many points of contact between the two men, for the great naturalist was also a lover of poetry and music.

The longer Milton was with him, the more unreserved and trustful became the amiable old man. It was only in regard to the persecutions he had suffered at the hands of the Inquisition that he kept silence, although his guest in the course of the conversation alluded repeatedly to this subject; but he became eloquent when Milton referred to the progress of the physical sciences.

"In your country, too," said Galileo, "there has risen a man who combated, like me, the errors of scholastic philosophy, and entered the only true path of observation and experiment; I refer to the great Chancellor Bacon, the father and restorer of modern science. Thus the spirit of truth bursts everywhere the chains with which Aristotle, or rather his blind adherents, fettered it. For centuries mankind, like the Israelites, wandered about in the wilderness of falsehood and delusion, and only a vigorous generation finds the land of promise. But I feel like the dying Moses, who is not allowed to tread the sacred soil, but only to overlook the land of Canaan from the top of a high mountain. What a glorious sight! The seed scattered by the mind bears fruit a hundredfold. Temples and altars are erected everywhere to science, new inventions of the most wonderful description bring earth nearer to heaven, and all virtues go hand in hand with growing civilization. Milder manners supplant the old barbarism, superstition disappears, war and discord must flee, and the blessings of peace and harmony render the world happy and prosperous."

"Then the truth will be able to raise its voice fearlessly, and its adherents need not be afraid of executioners and tormentors," added the poet, significantly.

There was a solemn pause. Galileo, whose face beamed with the enthusiastic expression of a prophet, seemed to be absorbed in the dream which the best men of all times have cherished in the innermost recesses of their souls, and which reminds us of our higher origin. A gentle smile played over the pale, emaciated features of the sufferer. The sun was setting, and its last fiery rays penetrated through the open window into the small room, filling it with golden light and surrounding Galileo's venerable head with a halo. Milton thought of the first martyrs of Christianity, whom those of science were to follow. A foreboding of his own future fate stole upon the young poet at the sight of the blind Galileo. The features of the great Italian stamped themselves indelibly on his soul.

The nun opened the door softly, and, assisted by an old servant, put the dishes noiselessly on the table. She then waved her hand to the guest and invited him to sit down. Galileo partook likewise of the simple meal, which consisted mostly of fruits. During the repast Milton addressed a few words to the pious girl, and her answers indicated a rare understanding and excellent education. He expressed his regrets to the father that he had to do without the company of such a daughter, as the rules of her cloister permitted but rarely such a visit as she had paid him to-day.

"My child did right," said Galileo, "in seeking refuge with God from the temptations of the world and all troubles and sufferings. I myself am too old and infirm to give her the necessary protection. She is a good daughter, and does not forget her old father. Whenever the prioress grants her permission, she comes to Arcetri and stays with me. From her earliest youth her heart turned toward heaven, and it was well that it did. She has escaped many a trial thereby, for faith is the safest guide in this world. One day, when I close my eyes, she will stand at my death-bed, and an angel will implore God to have mercy upon me."

A tear glistened in the eye of the nun, and Milton also was profoundly moved. Their emotion was enhanced by the *Ave Maria* which penetrated to them from the churches of the city and proclaimed the departure of day. No sooner did the nun hear the sacred notes, than she knelt down and prayed, holding the rosary in her delicate white hands. Galileo, who, notwithstanding his scientific investigations, had remained a pious Catholic, followed her example. But the prayers which ascended from their lips to heaven were probably very different from each other. During this devout ceremony, the poet remained standing and contemplated in silence the old man and the lovely girl, who seemed to him embodiments of science and faith.

When the prayer was over, the nun rose and cast a searching and almost reproachful glance on the stranger, who did not share her devotion.

"You do not pray?" she asked wonderingly.

"Pardon me, signora," replied the poet, in a firm voice, "I do not belong to your Church."

"I hope you are not a heretic?" she cried, in dismay. "That is impossible."

"The gentleman," said Galileo to his pious daughter, "is an Englishman, and his nation adopted the doctrines of John Calvin."

"Then he is a heretic after all," murmured the pale nun. "Santa Maria! You do not pray, you do not believe in God and the Redeemer?" she added, in a loud, mournful voice.

"You are mistaken, signora," replied Milton, with a gentle smile. "We believe likewise in God and the Redeemer who died for us on the cross, although we worship Him in a different manner."

"I hope the Lord will lead you back to the fold of His holy Church, you and your people. For this purpose I will pray every day to the Madonna in your behalf. Pray accept this consecrated rosary; it will shield you from all the dangers of a long journey, and remind you also of this hour and our interview."

Milton was unable to sneer at the pious delusion, which seemed to him so touching, and took the rosary with heartfelt thanks. When his outstretched hand touched that of the nun, he felt that it trembled.

"May the Madonna protect you," she whispered in a tremulous voice. "I must go, for my time is up."

She bent over her blind father, who imprinted a tender kiss upon her forehead, and then turned once more to the guest.

"Farewell," she said, deeply moved. "I shall never fail to remember you in my prayers."

Wrapped in her veil, she left the room to return to her cloister. Leaning against the window, the poet gazed after her, holding the rosary thoughtfully in his hand, until the growing darkness and the distance concealed her slender form from his eyes. After a short while he likewise took leave of his host, deeply moved by the manifold impressions of this visit.

Galileo's daughter knelt in her cell and prayed fervently to the Madonna for the salvation of the young heretic.

CHAPTER III.

ROME—LEONORA BARONI.

After a two months' sojourn, abounding alike in enjoyment and solid instruction, Milton proceeded on his journey to Rome. Here, too, his reputation and the letters of introduction which he brought with him secured him a friendly reception; he was admitted to the best society, and the most distinguished houses opened to him. During the first days after his arrival he visited the learned Holstenius, the celebrated librarian of the Vatican. Holstenius introduced him to his patron, the accomplished and influential Cardinal Barberini, who received the poet with surprising kindness and courtesy, and overwhelmed him with friendly attentions. It was still at that time customary for strangers in Rome, according to their nationality, to receive protection and hospitality at the palaces of the high dignitaries of the Church. The sumptuous apartments of the Barberini palace were opened to the sons of Albion. The cardinal, who was not yet very old, combined in his person the dignity of a distinguished prelate with the gay philosophy of an epicure, and was a most amiable host to his numerous guests.

At night the gorgeous halls and apartments were almost always filled with a select circle of eminent and distinguished persons; foreigners and natives, priests and laymen, scholars and poets, surged up and down in a motley crowd, and engaged in the most animated conversation. Here walked a venerable bishop by the side of an artist, there a bearded monk by the side of a smooth-shaved dandy; in the midst of the fiery, black-haired Italians moved blond Englishmen, with a measured step, and stiff as tapers. Nor were the ladies excluded, for, despite his clerical position, the lively cardinal did not seem to be a woman-hater.

Milton was delighted with the easy, unaffected tone reigning in this circle, and he was almost always to be found there on the regular reception-nights. But, in addition, he was often invited to special festivals, and treated, generally, with a distinction which could not but surprise him.

"You are very fortunate," said the learned librarian to him, playfully; "and, if you wish, you can attain all your objects here. Cardinal Barberini, the pope's cousin, is your friend."

"I am indebted to your recommendation for the kindness with which he treats me."

"No, my friend: you seem to have still other secret protectors; for when I mentioned your name to his eminency for the first time, he seemed to have heard it before, and acted as though he knew you already."

"Possibly one of the numerous Englishmen who have visited the cardinal may have mentioned my name."

"That must be it," replied Holstenius, cautiously breaking off the conversation.

Milton was rendered quite thoughtful by what he had just heard, but his rising apprehensions soon subsided, and he looked upon the extraordinary kindness of the cardinal only as the condescension of an aristocratic patron. Other secret intentions, he thought, the distinguished prelate could not entertain in regard to an almost unknown young man. Hence he did not hesitate to accept his invitations as heretofore. One evening, on entering the crowded hall at a later hour than usual, he heard wondrous singing; a female voice, of a compass and beauty such as he had never heard before, was performing one of Palestrina's hymns with rare perfection. The poet hastened involuntarily forward to see the singer.

She stood on a gilded dais as a queen on her throne. Her slender form was wrapped in a dark-red dress; her magnificent arms and the classical neck, for which the Roman women are noted, were bare; only two precious cameos fastened the dress on her shoulders and voluptuous bust. A wreath of flaming pomegranate-blossoms surrounded the beautiful temples and raven hair, which was tied in a knot, after the fashion of the ancients; but countless little ringlets mocked the ribbon, and protruded, like small seductive serpents, in natural exuberance. The proud neck was surmounted by a magnificent head, combining Junonian dignity with the graces of Venus. A golden tinge colored her slightly-flushed cheeks, whose soft roundness reminded the beholder of the swelling forms of the peach; her slightly-curved nose and well-shaped chin indicated unusual firmness, while the clear, smooth forehead seemed to be the throne of an extraordinary understanding. Dark eyebrows and silky lashes shaded two stars, than which the nocturnal sky contained none more radiant. They were beaming now with the glow both of enthusiasm and innate fire. From her swelling crimson lips flowed the charming notes of the glorious hymn. Her whole form on the dais resembled a statue of the goddess of art.

The audience stood or sat around her, deeply moved by her divine voice; a breathless stillness reigned, and the easily-transported Italians gave vent to their delight and enthusiasm only in almost inaudible, stifled sighs. It was not until the singer had finished the hymn that the general enthusiasm burst forth like a raging tempest.

"*E viva Leonora! brava! brava!*" shouted the enthusiastic countrymen of the artiste.

"St. Cecilia!" said a gray-headed bishop who was standing by Milton's side. "My ears never heard such singing before."

The applauded lady thanked her admirers with an imperceptible nod of her head, like a princess receiving the due homage and tribute of her subjects.

"*Ancora bis!*" cried those who were standing close to her, and the whole audience echoed their shouts.

An imperceptible smile of satisfaction played around her beautiful lips, and her beaming eyes cast proud glances on the crowd of her admirers. She whispered a few words to the cardinal, who was seated near her; Barberina nodded kindly, and the artiste disappeared behind the green curtain leading to the inner apartments of the palace. The audience was breathless with suspense; it felt that another surprise was in store for it.

A few moments afterward a very prepossessing youth made his appearance. His beautiful form was wrapped in a short Greek tunic, white as snow, and trimmed with gold lace; an ivy-wreath crowned his dark, flowing ringlets; in his hands he held a golden lyre.

His noble face expressed profound grief and depair.

"Orfeo!" murmured the audience.

The artiste, indeed, represented the unfortunate Orpheus. His complaints for his lost consort flowed with touching power from her lips. It was not alone the singing that produced an almost indescribable effect, and carried away the audience, but the wonderful perfection of the execution, blended with the striking and most appropriate expression of her countenance. This voice, expressive of the most profound feeling, wept and sobbed, hoped and feared, rose to the acme of grief and sank to the lowest depths of despair. Not an eye was tearless, and the artiste achieved the grandest triumph.

A profound stillness reigned in the hall even long after she had concluded. No one dared to break the silence, for all felt as though something tremendous had happened, and as though they themselves had witnessed an extraordinary event. They seemed not to have heard a fable, a myth, but to have seen it all with their own eyes, and taken part in it. It was only after a long pause that they recovered their full presence of mind. The cardinal himself gave the signal of applause, which, if possible, surpassed the previous outburst of enthusiasm. The Southern vivacity and transports of the Italians were no longer confined to the usual manifestations of applause. Ladies and gentlemen rose from their seats and threw flowers, rings, bracelets, and diadems—in short, whatever ornaments and trinkets they had—at the feet of the great artiste. She scarcely, however, vouchsafing a glance to these rich offerings, bowed, and disappeared, to change her dress. But a little boy in the guise of an angel, who had stood by her side, carefully gathered in a neat basket the tribute paid to the artiste.

Milton, too, was deeply moved. He leaned against a pillar and gazed after the charming creature. Indescribable feelings filled his breast; it seemed to him that he had now learned, for the first time, the true meaning and power of art, and that all he had hitherto heard and seen had been insignificant and scarcely worthy of being remembered. The truly feminine delicacy and modesty of Alice Egerton, the touching piety of Galileo's pale daughter, faded by the side of this radiant sun which had now risen before him. He had never seen a woman endowed with such surpassing talents, nay, with such genius and irresistible, majestic power. He stood now before a being of a higher order, an inspired priestess of divine art. And with his enthusiasm and delight blended still another emotion: the appearance and even the name of the artiste awakened old, long-forgotten reminiscences in his mind. A picture which had slumbered in his soul for many years past emerged from his memory, and he recalled involuntarily his singular meeting with the beautiful stranger in the college garden at Cambridge.

While he was thus absorbed in his reverie, the cantatrice had returned. She had exchanged her male attire for her former female garb. A host of admirers thronged around her as she walked, with a proud step, by the side of the cardinal through the hall. She approached nearer and nearer, until she stood in front of the poet. She conversed in the most animated manner with her companions, and the sweet sound of her silver voice, which is peculiar to the Roman women, struck Milton's ear; he lifted his eyes to her, their glances met, and a deep blush suffused his delicate and almost feminine countenance; even the pale cheeks of the cantatrice colored slightly.

"Who is the stranger?" she said in a low voice to the cardinal, on whose arm she was leaning.

"Permit me, signora," replied Barberini,

with a smile, "to introduce to you a votary of the Muses, Signor Milton, from England, distinguished alike as a poet and scholar."

Before the poet was able to utter a word, and express his admiration to the artiste, she said to him:

"You are an Englishman. I know your country, for I lived there with my father for a short time. I believe I have seen you somewhere; your features seem to me quite familiar, and remind me of a prank I played in my youth."

"You were in Cambridge?"

"I was, indeed," replied the cantatrice, wonderingly. "How do you come to know that?"

"You visited the college garden, which ladies enter but very rarely. If I am not mistaken, you were accompanied by an older lady."

"My poor mother; she is dead—a saint in paradise! But proceed, proceed!" exclaimed the cantatrice, impatiently.

"A boy lay there asleep under a tree. He had a wonderful dream; he fancied he saw an angel bending over him and dropping a rose."

"The boy was as handsome as Endymion, but I thought he was slumbering," added the cantatrice, smiling.

"He did not sleep; only his eyes were closed."

"Ah, the rogue deceived me, and I allowed myself to be carried away by my exuberant spirits, and added to the rose a few lines which I wrote hurriedly. Did the boy read and remember the lines?"

"He engraved them, as well as the lovely apparition, forever on his memory."

"Signor Milton can, perhaps, recite the doubtless charming lines," interposed the cardinal, with a good-natured smile.

"I do not know if I am allowed to do so," replied the poet, casting an inquiring glance on the cantatrice.

"I grant you permission to recite the lines, and shall be glad if you have not forgotten my first poetical effort."

Milton blushed again, and so great was his emotion, that he could falter out only the first line:

"Oh, fairest eyes, ye orbs of blissful light—"

"I see," said the artiste, "that I must come to the assistance of your memory; the lines were as follows:

'Oh, fairest eyes, ye orbs of blissful light,
If closed, ye such power wield,
What could my heart, if ye were open, shield?'"

"*Brava, brava!*" exclaimed the cardinal, gallantly. "You were born to be not only a cantatrice, but also a poetess; Leonora Baroni is and remains in every respect the most gifted and accomplished lady in the world. Do you not think so, too, Signor Inglese?"

Milton was unable to join in his playful tone; his heart was too deeply moved by this strange meeting. He had not dreamed, then; the ideal of his youth was not a vain creation of his imagination, and the sweet reality was before him in its most beautiful embodiment. How should or could he find words for the emotions filling his heart at this moment? Language seemed too tame and feeble for the delight which he felt all at once. Leonora divined, doubtless, what was going on in the young man's heart, and his silence pleased her better than the trivial praise which was lavished on her from all sides, and with which she was already surfeited. She delighted in his confusion, though not with her wonted pride and haughtiness, but with a quiet smile and a gentle glance from her sparkling eyes. But the cardinal laughed at the mute poet.

"What, sir poet," he asked, "you do not say a word to the most beautiful lady and foremost cantatrice of Italy? Forsooth, if I were a poet like you, I should write a poem on her."

"The signora has no need of my poems,"

replied Milton, gravely. "The whole Parnassus of Italy renders homage to her, and she will not miss the awkward foreigner."

"Do you not know that that which is foreign is particularly attractive for our sex?" said Leonora.

"You are above the average of your sex."

"Are you a flatterer, too? I shall punish you for this, by compelling you to write a sonnet on me; and you shall do so, not in your rough language, but in my own."

"And you call that a punishment for him?" asked the cardinal.

"I shall await you with your poem to-morrow at my house. *A rivederci!*"

Milton bowed to the cantatrice, who left the hall soon afterward. He also withdrew soon after the disappearance of the beautiful magnet that had attracted him so powerfully. He wandered dreamily through the nocturnal streets of the Eternal City. It was a magnificent summer-night; the golden stars twinkled in the azure heavens with a radiance such as is known only to the happy South. The moon shed her silver rays on the countless cupolas, towers, and ruins. His way had led him from Barberini's palace to the Monte Pincio. On its summit he enjoyed the magnificent prospect of this chaos of palaces, splendid churches, pillars, and obelisks, which, in that magic illumination, looked like a scene from fairyland. At his feet lay the Piazza Spagnuola, with its bustling crowds, whose noise was scarcely to be heard at this distance, but blended harmoniously with the murmurs of the numerous fountains. From time to time the silence was broken by the sweet notes of a guitar or mandolin, to which a lover sang ritornelles in a sonorous voice. The warm breeze caressed the tops of the green sweet-pines lovingly, and only the dark cypress did not move its branches and foliage. The poet's soul sank into that sweet reverie which nowhere more readily steals over the wanderer than in the Eternal City, where the past and present, life and death are so wonderfully blended in an incessant contact. Forgotten were all his former sufferings and struggles; only here and there a reminiscence emerged like a lone pillar or a ruin amidst the chaos of new impressions and feelings. As luxuriant ivy and exuberant vines clad the ruins and rubbish all around him, so, in the poet's heart, the hope of future happiness blossomed on the ruins of the past. What were his sufferings compared with the fate of Rome, his grief compared with that of this Niobe among the cities of the earth? She had seen her best sons die, she had wept over Cæsar's corpse, and survived the downfall of the republic; she had been hurled from her proud position; the old mistress of the world had been subjugated and devastated by barbarians; her children were degenerate, and bowed their proud necks to the yoke; and still a serene smile played round her lips, and her eyes beamed with ardent desires.

Is man alone to yield always to his grief and never to forget his sufferings? Life offers a thousand compensations, and when one flower fades, another blooms only the more beautifully. The world is so rich and magnificent, and the very fact that it is subject to decay and destruction lends additional charms to it. Ancient Rome has fallen; another Rome has taken its place. Instead of heroic deeds we admire now the surpassing beauty of its art; the air resounds no longer with battle-cries, but with love-songs, and strength and valor have given way to poverty and want. The human heart longs at all times to live, love, enjoy, and be happy.

The warm, voluptuous breeze whispered such thoughts to the poet; they rustled in the gently-moving foliage; the graceful waters of the fountain muttered them, and they flitted in the pale weird moonlight.

"To live and love!" he repeated in a low voice, on leaving the hill, and descending the magnificent staircase, whose arched windings led him to the Piazza Spagnuola, where the people were yet enjoying themselves despite the lateness of the night.

CHAPTER IV.

THE POET AND HIS MUSE.

On the following day Milton repaired to the house of the celebrated cantatrice. She came to meet him with the kindest greetings, and conducted him to a swelling divan, on which she invited him to seat himself by her side. Her whole surroundings wore a gay artistic aspect. The high, cool walls of the room were covered with beautiful frescoes representing the power of music. Here stood Apollo among the shepherds of Admetus, and played on the lyre, while the shepherds listened with unfeigned delight to his divine strains. There Orpheus tamed the wild beasts of the forest by his music, so that they followed him willingly. The frieze was formed by a chain of Cupids and children performing on all sorts of instruments, blowing trombones with swelling cheeks, or striking cymbals together with their tiny hands, or wielding the bow. On the ceiling was to be seen St. Cecilia with transfigured face, surrounded by kneeling angels who held the music-book before her or flitted round the open organ. On examining her a little more closely the beholder perceived that the saint bore Leonora's features, a great though sincere flattery on the part of the painter, who was one of her most ardent friends and admirers. All around stood or lay in picturesque confusion all sorts of vessels and precious gifts, vases and statues of exquisite workmanship, either real antiques of high value, or excellent imitations. On the outstretched arm of a Venus hung the Greek tunic which the cantatrice had worn yesterday, and a lute leaned against the feet of a winged Mercury. Laurel-wreaths and similar offerings, which her admirers had bestowed upon her, lay on the table amidst music-books and poems written in honor of the celebrated artiste. She herself wore a white dress, transparent enough to show her magnificent form; and the usual veil of the Roman ladies she had wound picturesquely round her head. This strange head-dress, from which a mass of dark ringlets flowed down on her shoulders, reminded the poet of one of Raphael's Sibyls, to whom the cantatrice bore a striking resemblance at this moment.

"I was looking for you," she said, in a soft, sonorous voice. "You keep your word promptly, like all Englishmen; but let me see what you have brought to me."

The poet handed her with an embarrassed air the sonnet, which she read aloud. It was written in Italian, and read as follows:

"Giovane piano, e semplicetto amante
Poi che fuggir me stesso in dubbio sono,
Madonna a voi del mio cuor l'humil dono
Faro divoto; io certo a prove tante
L'hebbi fedele, intrepido, constante,
De pensieri, leggiadri accorto, e buono;
Quando rugge il gran mondo, e scocca il tuono,
S'arma di se, e d'intero diamante;
Tanto del forse, e d'individia sicuro,
Di timori, e speranze, al popol use,
Quanto d'igegno, e d'alto valor vago,
Edi cetra sonora, e delle muse;
Sol troverete in tal parte menduro,
Ove' amor mise l'insanabil ago."

A pleasant and gratified smile played round the lips of the cantatrice when she had read the poem, and she held out her beautiful hand to the poet.

"Indeed," she said, "your poem is beautiful, almost too beautiful to be true."

"What, signora, you doubt my sincerity?"

"I will believe you, for I do not like to treat you like my common admirers. Besides, I have been told that love in the North is not a fugitive blossom, but as firm and durable as its oaks."

"That is true. Put me to the test."

"I may soon have an opportunity to convince myself whether or not I have mistaken your character. Your poem breathes a manly spirit, such as I look for in vain among my countrymen. The ancient Romans are gone, and their descendants bear but a slight resemblance to them. Once we were masters of the world."

"And so you are now, though in a different manner. Rome formerly conquered the world by her valor; she does so now by art and beauty."

"You are right. Divine art has remained to us. The heavenly fire is not yet extinct; it burns in the lyrics of our poets, in the colors of Raphael, in the sublime figures of Michael Angelo."

"And in the performances of Leonora Baroni."

"Hush, hush! You must not flatter me," replied the artiste, striking his arm gently with her fan.

Milton hastened to kiss the hand which chastised him so charmingly.

"You are a stranger here," added the signora; "therefore, I will be your guide in Rome."

"You are too kind."

"I know of no greater pleasure than to communicate to others the grand and sublime things which delight me. Therefore, if you accept my offer, we will commence this very day our walks through the Eternal City."

"I shall always be obliged to you, and am desirous of no better guide—for a lifetime."

"Who knows if you would not soon regret that?"

"The Muse should always go by the side of the poet."

"But I am afraid he would soon get tired of the company of the Muse. After a while he would see in her a woman like all others."

"Your divine origin protects you from such a fate."

"Permit the Muse now to withdraw for a few moments, that she may go to the kitchen. You are my guest to-day, and if you do not want to starve to death, I must give the necessary orders to my servants."

Milton remained alone, and yielded entirely to the impression which Leonora's beauty and understanding had made upon him. He confessed to himself that he had never met in his life-path a woman like her. Her whole bearing and appearance breathed a certain artistic enthusiasm, grandeur, and a gracefulness which helped the bashful poet to surmount the barriers of conventionality, without wounding his delicacy in any manner. The atmosphere surrounding him here seemed more suitable to his peculiarities than any other. He was likewise an ardent lover of music, and upon poesy he always looked as the most sublime vocation. He had now met with a lady who seemed to him an embodiment of his own ideal longings and aspirations. She shared his inclinations, she comprehended him and his most secret thoughts, she sympathized most ardently with his aspirations. To all this was to be added the fascination of her manners and her radiant beauty, which was only a most suitable garb of a highly-cultivated mind and talents bordering on genius. No wonder that she had taken the poet's heart by storm, and kindled the most passionate love in it. Even the grievous loss which he had sustained previous to his departure from England, rendered him only the more susceptible of a new affection.

Youth never ceases to hope and love. If vernal frosts nip many a bud, they do not kill the healthy fruitful sap; new buds spring up in place of those which were blighted, and new blossoms take the places of those which fell off. Spring is rich enough to repair all injuries.

Meanwhile Leonora had returned with a servant-girl, who brought in a table and covered it with choice dishes. Even on this occasion the cantatrice had an opportunity to display her refined and poetical spirit; she arranged every thing herself, and in doing so evinced the most exquisite taste. The costly Majorca plates, painted by skilful artists, lay on the gorgeous silken table-cloth; numerous gold and silver vessels, wrought and finished perhaps by Benvenuto Cellini himself, stood among magnificent vases filled with flowers and laurel-branches. Wine flashed and sparkled, like liquid gold, in Venetian crystal decanters.

"You shall have a classical meal," she said, inviting the poet to seat himself. "There is genuine Falernian wine; Horace himself never drank better. Fill your glass and touch mine. Long live poesy!"

"The Muse!"

"Life!"

"Love!"

"Life and love," added Leonora, thoughtfully. "That exhausts every thing. I still remember enough of your mother-tongue to know that live and love sound almost alike. There is a deep meaning in that."

"To live is to love, and only he who loves lives," affirmed the poet, flushed with the generous wine.

"I should hardly have deemed your language, which sounds barbarous to my Italian ears, capable of moulding such beautiful words."

"You treat it unjustly. It is true, the English language is not as pleasing to the ear as Italian, but, on the other hand, it possesses a manly strength and tenderness which I believe it owes to its Germanic origin. I should not like henceforth to write poetry in any other language."

"Nor I to sing in any other than my mother-tongue."

"Do so, pray do so! Yesterday I had to share my admiration with the crowded audience; oh, let me enjoy to-day what such a crowd is unable to appreciate."

"You are more of an egotist than I thought you were; however, I will not imitate the bad example of so many sisters of mine, who cause themselves to be entreated and urged in order to enhance thereby the value and charm of their performances. I am very fond of singing. Already when a little child, I sang all day, whether I walked or sat, whether I worked or was idle. It was a kind of inward necessity for me to do so, and I sang even before I was able to talk plainly and rationally. My dear mother, who is now in paradise, called me only 'her little bird;' the whole neighborhood called me by that name, and I kept it a long time. One day I heard at church the celebrated Antonio Liberti, the greatest singer in Italy. He made so powerful an impression upon me that I was taken sick and had to be carried home. A violent fever and delirium were the consequences of my youthful enthusiasm. Mother told me afterward that I sung during my delirium, in a wondrously beautiful voice, passages from the requiem which I had heard at church. She said I did not omit a note or commit a single mistake. Everybody said it was a miracle, and persons came from the most distant parts of the city to listen to my singing while I was delirious. I remember only a dream which I had every night at that time. St. Cecilia sat at my bedside and sang to me in a heavenly voice the most beautiful hymns, which I endeavored to repeat. Possibly I may not have dreamed, but the saint may have really descended to me."

"You do not believe that in earnest, do you?" asked Milton, with a slight, wondering smile.

"You do not understand it," replied the cantatrice, half seriously, half jestingly. "You are unfortunately a heretic, but I hope to convert you yet."

"You will hardly succeed in doing that."

"Well, I will make an effort. It is worth while to convert men like you; and no matter how earnestly you may resist me, I shall not give up all hope of gaining you over."

The tone in which Leonora alluded to this subject seemed to make an unpleasant impression upon the poet; she, therefore, deemed it imprudent to recur to it, and continued her narrative.

"Whether St. Cecilia appeared to me in a dream or in reality, certain it is that my talent developed from that time in a surprising manner. I was looked upon as a prodigy, and even many eminent and aristocratic men came to our house, to convince themselves with their own eyes and ears. Among them was my present friend and protector, Cardinal Barberini; as my parents were poor, he generously took charge of my education. He took me to Antonio Liberti, whose pupil I became. Already a year afterward I was the cantatrice who stands before you now."

"Who is admired by all Italy, and to whom a northern barbarian is permitted to listen in an ecstasy of delight. You promised to sing a song to me alone, and I remind you now of your promise."

"Well, then, you alone shall hear this song. I have never sung it to any other person. It has hitherto been, as it were, locked as a secret in my bosom. But I cannot conceal any thing from you, sir barbarian."

She looked at him with flaming, devouring eyes, promising him so much delight and happiness, that a shudder of ecstasy ran through Milton's frame. What a charm there was in her voice, what a fire gleamed in her eyes, while she was singing! All the joys and pains of existence trembled in those divine notes; they were jubilant, and revealed the innermost secret of a loving female heart to the transported poet. He sat breathless, and listened in a trance of delight to her glorious strains. When she ceased to sing, he knelt down before her; she bent over him, and he felt the warm touch of her swelling lips on his forehead.

"Leonora!" he sighed in the ecstasy of his bliss. "My goddess, my Muse!"

"I belong to thee," she said, gently disengaging herself from his embrace. "With this kiss I give thee my soul, my whole heart. And now come with me. These stone walls are too narrow for me; I long for the open air."

Hand in hand they left the house of the cantatrice and wandered through the Eternal City.

CHAPTER V.

THE STRUGGLE OF LOVE AND FAITH.

Guided by the beautiful Leonora Baroni, Milton became only now fully familiar with the precious treasures of the Eternal City, its churches and palaces, its ruins and relics of antiquity. She showed him the statues of the gods, the creations of the modern poets, and, being herself deeply initiated into and an ardent lover of art, she revealed to him the significance and leading ideas of the highest achievements of mankind. He stood admiringly with her before the Apollo-Belvedere, the dying Gladiator, and the Faun; with enraptured eyes he contemplated Raphael's Madonnas and Michael Angelo's "Last Judgment," on the walls of the Vatican. His own imagination was particularly attracted by the noble works of this sublime master. He felt that he possessed a kindred genius, and in his soul dawned in vague outlines the plan of a poem which was to vie in boldness and grandeur of conception with the immortal frescoes of Michael Angelo. Leonora did not share his predilection for this majestic painter, but inclined more toward the divine Sanzio, who in his sublime creations never overstepped the rules of æsthetics and beauty.

"Your predilection for old Angelo," she said, with charming gayety, "proves to me again that, despite your accomplishments, you still remain half a barbarian. I admit that he is grand and gigantic, but the Graces did not stand at his cradle. I do not know how it comes, but, whenever I stand before his works, I also see the stern, sullen master before me, with his gloomy features and angry zeal. I always feel as though he did violence to Art, as though he struggled with her, and compelled her to serve him. She never loved him; she only feared and obeyed him. It is true, his strong arm overpowered the marble, and the stone succumbed to the irresistible strokes of his chisel; but the sweet world of colors mocked his tyranny. It revealed itself to its favorite; it disclosed to him, without trouble or toil, the secret of its eternal beauty. Divine Raphael, how dearly I love thee!"

"I am almost glad that he is dead. I should have been jealous of him, and, it seems, not without cause."

"He is dead," said Leonora, mournfully, "and the dead can no longer be dangerous to the living. I should have loved him, perhaps, more than his Fornarina, who was unable to appreciate his genius. Do not be angry at my sincerity, my Giovanni. You live, and I love you; what else do you want?"

She held out to him, with a winning smile, her white hand, which he covered with kisses. However, a slight cloud remained on his forehead all day. The longer Milton was on intimate terms with Leonora, and the better he became acquainted with her, the deeper was the insight he acquired into her peculiar nature. This nature was more artistic than feminine, and, even in Milton, she seemed to love the poet rather than the man. Notwithstanding this observation, which often forced itself upon him, to his great regret, he was unable to break with her. Love is not blind, but only generous. It excuses weaknesses, it overlooks faults, and disregards even bitter mortifications. It believes in its power, and, therefore, it always hopes for a change for the better, and is exceedingly indulgent until the cup is full to overflowing, and further faith is out of the question; even then it still clings to the shadow, and lives on illusions, on a dream, until it vanishes too, and leaves it in the gloom of eternal night.

This inward antagonism returned very often, but, so far from leading to a rupture, always terminated in reconciliations which attached the poet only more tenderly to Leonora. He met her enthusiastic religious zeal with delicate reserve; she was an ardent Catholic, and betrayed more than once her earnest desire to convert Milton. Numerous opportunities for making efforts in this direction were not wanting. He often visited the principal churches of the city with her, and sometimes when high mass was chanted. She managed, under all sorts of pretexts, to take him there on such occasions; now she told him there were celebrated paintings and statues which he had not yet admired; now she invited him to attend a solemn church-festival. He yielded willingly and unsuspectingly to her wishes, though the impressions which he received were not such as she had expected. He admitted, in his conversations with her, that the Roman service was more pompous and gratifying to the senses than the sober worship of the Protestants; but he refused to make further concessions, although Leonora did not despair of converting him by and by entirely. With the shrewdness of her sex, she waited for a favorable moment, and counted upon the power of habit and the triumph of her love.

One day, after a prolonged interval, she resumed her efforts to convert him with redoubled zeal. She went with Milton to St. Peter's, where a high church-festival was celebrated. The gigantic building was crowded with worshippers, and Catholicism displayed all its pomp. At the head of his cardinals appeared the Holy Father himself, wearing the golden tiara on his head. The highest dignitaries of the city surrounded the throne on which he was carried to the church, and a retinue worthy of the first prelate of Christendom accompanied him. At his appearance the worshippers knelt, and the choir of the Sistine Chapel intoned the Ambrosian Chant to the majestic notes of the organ. It was a scene such as the traveller can see nowhere but in Rome. The sublime dome, with its gigantic cupola and unrivalled colonnades, resembled a picture of heaven itself. Countless wax-lights shed a most dazzling glare into all parts of the vast structure. The walls were radiant with their magnificent frescoes and mosaics; the numerous altars blazed with gold and precious stones. Blue clouds of fragrant incense rose from silver censers up to the lofty ceiling. Through these clouds flashed from time to time the splendor of the church, like a flood of sunshine. Gorgeous paintings and richly-embroidered banners surged over the heads of the worshippers, and the statues of the saints and martyrs stretched out their hands as if to bless them.

The Holy Father himself now stepped up to the principal altar, and knelt before the picture of the Redeemer, attired in his golden vestments, whose heavy burden almost weighed him down. A reverential silence reigned throughout the vast church; one might have heard the falling of a leaf. It was as though the spirit of the Lord were passing through the immense building. The pope prayed.

When he rose again, the trombones rang out their jubilant notes, the kettle-drums rolled, the organ poured forth its majestic strains, a flood of tones swept down from the choir, and the acoustic vault of the gigantic dome echoed the melodious waves. This was no earthly chant, but the gates of heaven had opened, and the angels sang their triumphal hymns.

Milton left the church with Leonora in silence, and deeply moved despite his convictions. On the way to her house they were joined by Sir Kenelm Digby, who had just returned from a trip to Naples, and whom Milton had not yet seen during his sojourn in Rome. He greeted with kind words the poet and his companion, with whom he was likewise acquainted.

"How glad I am to meet you!" he said to them. "Apollo and his muse! You have followed my advice, then, and come to Rome. I see that you have no reason to regret my advice."

So saying, he cast a searching, significant glance on the signora. Milton, however, did not seem overjoyed at this meeting. In his heart rose again the old aversion to the accomplished courtier, whose whole character was at variance with his own nature; but Sir Kenelm was treated very kindly and politely by the signora, who shook hands with him, and invited him to follow her. On the way to her house, Sir Kenelm Digby informed the wondering poet that he had now openly adopted the Catholic faith, to which he had already secretly belonged in England.

"I hope," he added, "you will soon follow my example. It will be best for you to do so at the earliest moment, for our native country will sooner or later return to the bosom of the Catholic Church."

"What leads you to believe this?"

"My faith in the irresistible power of Catholicism, and my knowledge of the views and wishes of the English court. It is true, King Charles is as yet a member of the Church of England, and is profuse in his protestations of devotion to it; but his convictions must bring him gradually nearer and nearer to us. The queen is a devout Catholic, and exerts the greatest influence over her husband. Even Archbishop Laud is favorable to our cause, and promotes its interests to the best of his power. Several of the most influential and distinguished members of the king's suite have already returned to the ancient faith, and you know the reply a lady made to a bishop who reproved her for her defection. 'My lord,' she said, 'I do not like to go with the crowd.'"

"You speak only of the court and its adherents, but the people cling firmly to their faith."

"The people," replied Sir Kenelm Digby, shrugging his shoulders, "the people are of no consequence in this respect. The same blind populace which allowed Henry VIII. to force the Reformation upon it, will not resist the efforts of Charles I. to lead it back to the bosom of the Catholic Church. The king commands, the people obey."

"You are greatly mistaken. When Henry VIII. established the Reformation, as I will admit, actuated by selfish motives, he himself was but an instrument in the hands of Providence, and was impelled unwittingly by the spirit of his time to take this momentous step. The ground had been sufficiently broken and prepared by Wycliffe, Luther, and Calvin. It was only necessary for the sower to scatter the seeds, that the plant might spring up and bear fruit. It was not the imperious command of a king, but the solemn and profound conviction of the people, that brought forth the Reformation. Since then its roots have grown more tenacious, and it showed the hold it has upon the minds of the people amidst the persecutions during the reign of Bloody Mary. Its roots spread in the blood-stained soil, fertilized by the ashes of the martyrs who had died at the stake for the sake of their religion. Queen Elizabeth fostered the young shoot, which became a majestic tree under her protection. She became great with and by the Reformation, seconded and upheld by the people and their new-born strength. Then it was that our country rose to an unheard-of greatness and power, because it placed itself at the head of the spiritual movement which shook the world to its foundations. Deprive England of her Reformation, and you cut her great artery."

Leonora, who had hitherto listened in silence, said now smilingly:

"Giovanni, I do not understand any thing about your politics, and the fate of your native country does not concern me; but your eternal welfare does, and the interests of art also. You really are a barbarian, as I have often called you playfully, if you do not see that the Catholic Church is the only mother and protectress of the fine arts. What has your vaunted Reformation brought forth up to this time? Nothing but bloody civil wars, domestic dissensions, havoc, and devastation. Can the Muses live and prosper there? Look around, and you must admit that I am right. Rome is the first city of the world; her churches and palaces are filled with the masterpieces of the greatest painters and sculptors; poetry and music have taken up their abode here. And all this splendor and glory proceed solely from the eternal source of the Catholic faith. It inspires the artist, and fills his soul with those heavenly forms which we behold everywhere. Look, Raphael's divine Madonna, the portraits of the sainted martyrs, are but embodied reflexes of the Catholic Church. Now, what does your Reformation offer us for all this? Bare walls, cold repulsive structures, and a service devoid of ardor and enthusiasm."

"But it gives us truth instead of a deception of the senses, freedom instead of religious coercion, sublime science instead of enticing art. If we owed the Reformation only the general circulation of the Bible, this alone would suffice to entitle it to the everlasting respect and gratitude of mankind."

"The Bible will always be a two-edged sword in the hands of laymen," replied Sir Kenelm Digby. "The populace should not know the whole truth. It will abuse its freedom, and the healing medicine becomes only too easily a fatal poison in the hands of the inexperienced. Only physicians have the right and duty to apportion the dose which the patient needs."

"The Bible is no medicine, but health itself, our most vital element. He who withholds it from us, deprives us of the air we breathe, and of the conditions of our existence. The Sacred Scriptures must not be the property of a separate class; they belong to the whole world. See, how impetuously the people throng toward the eternal source from which they derive comfort, faith, and salvation! God reveals Himself in it, and you would chain the Holy Ghost, but it braves and mocks your power. You can no longer subjugate it; it bursts its fetters violently. It pervades the whole world, and sheds its divine light on all men. It is freedom, and Rome can exist only by the spiritual servitude of the nations and individuals. Free investigation and its truths are abominations in her eyes, and Science is her mortal enemy. Still smokes the stake at which she burned Giordano Bruno, and I have myself seen the unfortunate blind Galileo. His fate alone is sufficient to fill me with everlasting aversion to Catholicism."

"Has the father no right to punish his disobedient children? Whither is this spiritual licentiousness to lead us unless bounds be set to it in time? Have not these fatal innovations brought Germany and our own country to the verge of ruin? The false doctrines of the Anabaptists, Brownists, and other dissenters threaten to shake the foundations of society. In their wild fanaticism they preach the annihilation of all established institutions, and war against the government, law, and order. All of them appeal to the Bible; they pretend to derive their tenets from the gospel, which they interpret and distort in the most arbitrary manner. In this wild and impious uproar, the Church of Rome stands as firm and immovable as a rock in the tempest-tossed sea; it rests on the promises of the Redeemer, on the merits of its saints and martyrs, on the teachings of the apostolic fathers, and on the temporal and spiritual power which the Lord has conferred upon it forever. Here are grandeur and simplicity, power and wisdom, severity and lenity. You cannot contemplate its gigantic structure without awe and admiration; mankind never saw any thing more sublime. It has already stood for upward of a thousand years, and will also triumphantly weather this storm of the Reformation."

"In truth," added the signora, "Signor Kenelm himself has spoken like one of the apostolic fathers. Giovanni! do not shut your ears to the words of our friend, but follow his glorious example. But a short while ago he was likewise a heretic, but he listened to the voice of the mother he had forsaken, and returned penitently into her arms. The Blessed Virgin will lead you too back to the true path and forgive you. Oh, you do not know how good she is, how mildly and sweetly she bends over the believer; for she is a loving, tender-hearted woman. Therefore, I pray her every day to touch and illuminate your heart. I will not belong to you entirely until you return to the bosom of the Catholic Church; then the last barrier that separates us will fall immediately."

With her soft arms she drew the reluctant poet with her, and he was unable to resist the sweet temptation, although he had made up his mind never to sacrifice his convictions and religious freedom to his love.

CHAPTER VI.

THE HERMIT.

Such scenes recurred now very frequently, and Milton justly ascribed this increased zeal of his mistress to convert him to the presence of Sir Kenelm Digby. The courtier remained in Rome, and pursued from thence with great circumspection and prudence the schemes whose object was the restoration of the Catholic faith in England, either by wily intrigues or high-handed measures. He was a welcome ally to the Society of Jesus, which was then at the height of its prosperity, displayed the most indefatigable activity, and shrank from no means calculated to promote its ends. The young poet, whose eminent talents were acknowledged every day more willingly and universally, received due attention at the hands of the Jesuits; they thought they would be able to make of him a most effectual instrument for their vast and far-reaching schemes. Hence, they left no stone unturned to gain him over to their side. Cardinal Baberini encouraged these efforts, and continued to treat him with the greatest kindness and distinction; he held out to him prospects well calculated to entice an ambitious young man, and intimated to him that it would be easy for him to gain a distinguished and influential position. Love was likewise in the service of the powerful order; the ardent passion which Leonora Baroni had kindled in the poet's heart did not escape its keen-scented glance, and was used only to bait the victim with greater certainty. Thus surrounded by snares and nets of every description, Milton would have succumbed but for his love of freedom, and his unfaltering devotion to his principles and convictions. However, a violent struggle was yet in store for him; the attacks and scenes recurred every day; the cantatrice availed herself of all the seductive power of her charms and talents to bring about his defection. Now she frowned at him, now she lavished upon him the sweetest blandishments and caresses; and, to attain her object, she set the whole arsenal of her seductive wiles in motion, tears and smiles, prayers and threats. Milton felt the danger becoming every day more imminent; his strength was exhausted, and to escape further temptations, he resolved to leave Rome, even though but for a short time; he hoped the separation would exert the most salutary effect upon Leonora and himself.

It cost him a violent effort to tear himself from the arms of his beloved, who insisted on accompanying him; but by the solemn promise to return at as early a day as possible, he prevailed upon her to desist from her purpose. He had long wished to visit Naples, and, if possible, Greece; he now carried his plan into execution. Accompanied by a faithful servant, he set out on this journey, by which he hoped to divert and calm his mind. He left Rome and his mistress on a fine day in spring, and was soon in the midst of the desolate Campagna. The sterile brown wilderness extended in endless desolation before his eyes, dotted only here and there with a decayed aqueduct or a pile of ruins. He rode for hours without meeting anybody but the wild shepherds of the Campagna, clad in rough sheepskins, their feet encased in goatskin shoes, and their sunburnt heads covered with pointed felt hats; and thus he was able to brood undisturbed over his Roman adventures. At times his love for Leonora seized him again with all its former power, almost impelling him to turn his horse, return to the city he had just left, and hasten back into the arms of his beloved. On the first evening he arrived at Albano, but neither the classical reminiscences attached to the name of Alba Longa, nor the far-famed beauties of the women of that place, were able to dispel his mournful longings. On the following morning, when he awoke refreshed and reinvigorated, and continued his journey, the beautiful scenery exerted its wonted charm upon him. He had scarcely been a quarter of an hour on the road when he arrived at the Lake of Albano, with water clear as crystal, surrounded by steep and richly-wooded banks, and adorned by the noble edifice of Castel Gandolfo. The monuments and relics of antiquity scattered everywhere riveted his whole attention; at a most idyllic spot he sought and found the tomb of the great Pompey, and the poet recalled the gigantic contests which had preceded the downfall of the republic. Farther on was a solemn scene, the Lake of Nemi, anciently Nemus Dianæ, from the grove sacred to that goddess; it was small, seated in a deep hollow of the mountain, which it partly fills, and surrounded with wooded and highly-cultivated banks. In the centre of this lake, Trajan had moored a floating palace, in the form of a ship, of which some fragments were dug up in the sixteenth century. At the beautifully situated Ariccia, Milton recalled the time when Horace resided here, and, far from the noise and bustle of the capital, enjoyed the quiet pleasures of rural life. At every step as he advanced, Milton met great historical reminiscences, before which his own petty adventures faded from view, and by which his mind was strengthened and purified. The blue sea soon arose before his eyes at a distance, and its aspect filled his soul with unutterable delight.

Milton had also found a fellow-traveller. In the vicinity of Terracina, in the shade of one of its mighty trees, he met with a hermit who held his siesta there during the noonday heat; an humble donkey, loaded with provisions, the gifts of devout believers, was grazing by his side. The perpendicular and scorching sunbeams led the languishing poet to profit with his companion and the weary horses by the cool and pleasant shade. He therefore alighted from the horse and greeted the hermit, who invited him kindly to seat himself by his side. The hermit was a good-natured old man with prepossessing features. His silver beard flowed down to his breast, and imparted to him, notwithstanding his simplicity, a most venerable appearance.

"Welcome in the green shade!" he gayly shouted to Milton already from afar. "If you wish to share my palace, you will be a very welcome guest; for though I am a hermit, I like company and a pleasant chat."

"You have a beautiful house, indeed," jested the poet. "Your palace here surpasses all that I saw in Rome."

"To be sure it does, for human hands did not build it. The green roof is more airy and cool than any architect on earth could make it, and the view is surpassingly beautiful. Just look around, and you will say so too."

Milton glanced around, and could not but assent to what his kind host had said. Yonder lay the blue sea in the golden sunshine; here rose the picturesque summits of the mountains. A special attraction was added to the wild romantic landscape by the small gardens hanging like colored carpets on the rock among the houses, and clothing the bare slopes in the most charming manner. Orange and lemon trees were suspended on the verge of the ravine, and bent under the weight of their golden fruit; among them were to be seen peach and almond trees in the full beauty of their gentle colors. The lonely palm rose as straight as a pillar to heaven, and displayed its fantastic crown, reminding the beholder of Oriental fairylands. The dark foliage of the black cypress was in picturesque contrast with the tender leaves of the poplar and silver willow. Countless shrubs, covered with blossoms, among them the fragrant myrtle, protruded from every cleft, while the naked fig-tree with its tortuous arms, seemed to climb from one terrace to another. The whole landscape, bathed in the sunshine of a southern sky, produced a truly magic effect.

"Oh, how beautiful your fatherland is!" said Milton to his companion, in an ecstasy of delight.

"Well, was I not right?" replied the hermit, with a pleasant smile. "Is there on earth a more beautiful palace, with a finer view? And wherever I go, I find one like it."

"You are a rich man," said the poet, "and I almost envy you."

"To be sure, I am a rich man. As I do not own any thing on earth, the whole world belongs to me. Can you solve this riddle?"

"I understand you, and I see, moreover, that you are also a great philosopher."

"For God's sake, do not speak so loud, for philosophy has a bad reputation in this country. Let us rather speak of something else. You seem to have come from a remote country to Italy."

"I come from England."

"I suppose, then, that you are a heretic."

"I should be sorry if that should render my company less agreeable to you."

"On the contrary, it gives me an excellent opportunity to lead an erring lamb back to the true path."

"Good father, I am afraid all your efforts in this direction will be in vain."

"Well, I will not trouble you, then. For the rest, what does it concern me? If you are intent on not going to heaven, it is your own fault. For all that, we may journey yet a while together, and if you have no other place where you would prefer to stay overnight, my humble hermitage is at your disposal."

So saying, the hermit rose from the ground and saddled his donkey; Milton likewise prepared to set out. Both continued their journey together, and the longer their intercourse lasted, the more they delighted in each other's company. The hermit displayed in his conversation a clear, keen understanding, coupled with a gay, mild view of life. He knew the world, and his opinions were generally very sagacious, and withal gentle and forbearing. He kept silence as to his former life, and his words and whole bearing showed only that he had once belonged to the aristocracy, and filled a distinguished position in the world. It was obvious that he had enjoyed an excellent education, and in the course of the conversation he quoted classical passages frequently from the authors of antiquity and the best poets of his native country.

When Milton told him that he was a poet, and recited to him some of his Latin verses, the hermit manifested the liveliest interest.

"You are a genuine poet," he said, "and therefore, as you are going to Naples, I will give you a letter of introduction to an excellent nobleman, who was the most intimate friend of the immortal Tasso, with whose glorious poems you are doubtless familiar. Poor Tasso!"

Contrary to his habit, the hermit seemed to be filled with melancholy on alluding to the author of "Jerusalem Delivered."

"You yourself seem to have been acquainted with Tasso?" said Milton to his companion, who became every moment more interesting to him.

"Pardon me for not referring to the most mournful recollection of my whole life. His history is that of genius devouring itself to illuminate the earth with its light. I made his acquaintance in Rome, when he lay, broken in body and spirit, on his sick-bed at the convent of St. Onofrio. But even in that decayed form he still appeared to me like one of those temples of antiquity, whose ruins and broken columns bear witness to their former beauty and magnificence. But I will introduce you to his best friend, Battista Manso, Marquis di Villa, and I am convinced that you will always be grateful to me for it."

Thus the travellers, conversing pleasantly on

all kinds of topics, reached a charming valley; here stood the hermit's cottage, surrounded by evergreen oaks and birches. In front of the door, a crystal spring bubbled from the volcanic soil, and a picture of the Redeemer greeted the wanderer at the threshold. The kind hermit invited the poet to follow him, and as a hospitable host he hastened to prepare a plain supper for him. After partaking of it, both took seats on the turf-bench, and enjoyed the delightful coolness of the night. The stars twinkled with golden lustre in the azure sky, and the moon shed her silver rays on an earthly paradise. The conversation gradually took a more serious turn, and the two men expatiated on the important questions which riveted public attention at that time. Italy had likewise taken part in the religious struggles of the Reformation, and produced philosophers and thinkers who, like Giordano Bruno, had to expiate the boldness of their opinions at the stake. In the inaccessible valleys of Piedmont lived the descendants of those Waldenses, who had rebelled against Rome already in the Middle Ages and adopted the Scriptures as the sole rule of their faith. The hermit alluded to all this in a spirit of mildness and toleration; he was likewise imbued with the conviction that the abuses of the Church should be corrected, as he was more familiar with the ills of Catholicism than Milton. He denounced with especial bitterness the Jesuits, whom he called the principal obstacle to the most pressing requirements of progress. However, he was as sincerely opposed to the Reformation, which he considered a most lamentable schism.

When Milton argued against this view from his own stand-point, and attacked the tenets of Rome with unsparing severity, his host cautioned him with well-meant words.

"Beware, my friend, of giving the reins to your tongue. I myself can bear contradiction, and forgive many an imprudent word on account of your youth. But the holy Inquisition is very sensitive and any thing but indulgent, and the Society of Jesus has the sharpest ears and longest arms. You are in Italy, that is, surrounded by spies. The prisons in which heretics are confined are deep, and their walls are so thick that your complaints would not be heard by anybody. I am not angry with you, for I share your opinions in many respects, but I love and long for peace. I do not yet give up the hope that these accursed dissensions will come to a peaceful end. *Peccatur intra et extra muros*; both sides have committed errors and sins. Rome refused to listen to the just wishes of the nations, and they broke with it in an arbitrary and unjustifiable manner. This unfortunate schism will be most injurious to both sides. I hope, therefore, that a reconciliation will take place sooner or later. For the time being we will set a good example, and shake hands in peace and harmony."

Such were the words of the amiable hermit, and his actions harmonized with them. He shared his couch willingly with the poet, and the heretic slept by the side of the pious Catholic. The next morning Milton continued his journey to Naples. The kind hermit insisted on accompanying his young friend for a mile or two; and, on taking leave of him handed him the letter to the Marquis di Villa, Tasso's intimate friend.

CHAPTER VII.

NAPLES—TASSO.

MILTON reached Naples without further adventures. He repaired immediately to the palace of the marquis, to whom he delivered his letter of introduction. He found an amiable old man, who had formerly filled an important public position, and who, since he had retired from active life, devoted himself exclusively to the study of science and to poetry.

"An old friend of mine," said the marquis, "recommends you to me in this letter in the most urgent and flattering manner. I bid you twice welcome, as I see from the letter that you are a young poet."

"Pardon me for troubling you already by my curiosity; but I presume you will deem it but natural if I inquire the name and history of that kind hermit, to whom I am indebted for your acquaintance."

"He was an old fellow-soldier of mine, and life has used him harshly. After burying his wife and two children, he retired from the world. I feel almost like envying him for his lonely hermitage and the cheerful spirit he has preserved. I cannot tell you his name, for he does not want it to be divulged."

Milton was obliged to content himself with this scanty information, and the conversation soon took another turn, which seemed not less interesting to the poet. The marquis told him, without being requested to do so, of his intercourse with Tasso.

"It was my good fortune," said the venerable man, "to grant the poet, who was persecuted by external and internal foes, an asylum in one of my villas on the sea-shore. There he finished his 'Jerusalem Delivered' in blessed retirement, after leaving the house of Prince Conca. A dreadful suspicion haunted him, and he was incessantly afraid lest his manuscripts should be seized and used to his disadvantage. He had full and implicit confidence in no one but myself. I profited by it to restore his greatly affected health, to enliven his languishing imagination, and incite his Muse to renewed sublime creations."

"Happy the poet who meets with such a friend and protector in his life-path. Your merit almost equals his own, for to you we are indebted for these last immortal works of his genius, the glorious farewell of the setting sun."

"You attach too great importance to my merit; and how amply was I rewarded for it! Aside from his friendship, which I consider the greatest boon vouchsafed to me, he dedicated to me his celebrated dialogue on friendship, which will hand down my name from age to age. At the request of my mother he also wrote his poem, 'The Seven Days of Creation.' Thus I still remained in his debt. Unfortunately I was unable to discharge this debt during his lifetime, and I will erect to him now, after his death, a monument worthy of his fame. I intend to write his biography, which abounds in wonderful events."

"I have heard a great deal about his unfortunate love-affair with the Princess Leonora d'Este. This *liaison* is said to have been the cause of all his sufferings."

"So far as he himself told me the particulars of this love-affair, it never overstepped the limits of virtuous and chivalrous affection. I was myself acquainted with the august princess; she was an ornament of her sex, one of those great characters which are but rarely met with. Noble and generous, she took the liveliest interest in the intellectual progress and literature of our country. She spoke the Latin language with the fluency of a learned professor, and read the immortal Homer and most of the Greek poets in the original. No wonder that she held much intercourse with Tasso, and befriended the poet. She was passionately fond of the conversation of great men, and in her eyes talents, not birth, entitled men to esteem and admiration. As she was much older than he, her friendship seemed to be that of a devoted sister. Oh, Tasso passed at that time glorious days at the court of Ferrara. The noblest men and most amiable ladies had met there and formed an intellectual court headed by the duke himself. All these eminent persons esteemed and befriended the poet. Especially was he a favorite of the ladies whom he immortalized in his lyrics. There was a sort of tender jealousy among them in regard to him, and each of them tried to gain his exclusive love. At first, the charming young Lucretia Venadidio was victorious, and conquered his heart. She became the subject of his poetical effusions; but she really deserved the homage he rendered her, for spring cannot be more beautiful than this lovely lady was. But the lofty mind of Leonora and her equally-gifted sister deprived her of her admirer, and the poet walked between the two princesses, absorbed in Platonic conversations, through the blooming gardens and shady avenues of Bellriguardo. Afterward came the charming Countess Leonora Sanvitale, consort of the Count di Scandiano; she likewise courted the friendship of the poet, and took part in the rivalry of the lovely ladies. Before long she was the sovereign queen of his heart. So much favor and distinction bestowed upon him on all sides could not but arouse enmity and jealousy against him. His worst enemy, however, was his constantly-growing melancholy, which could not but terminate sooner or later in insanity. This calamity was not brought about by the meanness of the courtiers, by the quarrel which he had at the palace with a footman of the Duchess of Urbino, or, least of all, by the duke's conduct toward him. The noble Alfonso bore the whimsical freaks of the poet at first with the greatest patience and forbearance, and took the utmost pains to calm and cure him. At Tasso's own request he had him conveyed to the monastery of the Franciscans, in order to await his recovery there. Notwithstanding the most careful nursing, his condition grew worse and worse; he believed himself surrounded by dangers and persecuted by imaginary enemies, and overwhelmed himself with the most groundless reproaches. His derangement became such that in an unguarded moment he escaped from the monastery, destitute of every thing, and leaving behind him even those papers and manuscripts to which he had hitherto attached the highest importance. He hastened to his sister Cornelia, a widow, who lived at Sorrento. By her tenderness and solicitude she succeeded in calming him, and restoring his reason to him. The unfortunate poet took heart once more, and the most magnificent flashes of his genius burst radiantly through the gloom veiling his mind, and changing only too soon into the everlasting night of insanity. He longed to return to Ferrara, and thought the wedding of the duke with Margaret Gonzaga the most favorable time for this purpose. However, his expectations were bitterly disappointed. Instead of giving him a kind and honorable reception, the court treated him with coldness and indifference, and his adversaries sneered and laughed at him. Both the duke and the princesses refused to see him. His patience was soon exhausted, and he denounced Alfonso and his court so bitterly that the prince was obliged to have him conveyed to St. Anna's Hospital, and keep him there in close confinement."

"Poor Tasso!" interrupted Milton. "Are poets, then, born only to suffer?"

"One should think almost," replied the venerable marquis, "that a crown of thorns is the only endowment of genius. For seven years the greatest poet of Italy was immured in his cell, surrounded by idiots and maniacs, whose ravings and shrieks would have sufficed to deprive even the healthiest man of his reason. In the mean time, his numerous friends were not inactive. His works had created the greatest enthusiasm throughout his native country, and Alfonso was urged on all sides to release Tasso. Princes and cities, above all Bergamo, the poet's birthplace, sent ambassadors to him to demand his release. At last the duke was unable to resist these pressing representations any longer; he set him at liberty, but the great, sublime genius emerged crushed and broken from the jail, and the light of his reason was nearly extinct. Too late came an invitation from the pope for the poet to go to Rome and be solemnly crowned at the capital as prince of Italian poesy. His strength was exhausted, and while the most gorgeous arrangements were being made for his coronation, the great man breathed his last at the convent of St. Onofrio."

The marquis paused in profound emotion, and a tear trembled on his gray eyelashes. Milton was likewise deeply impressed by what he had heard of Tassò's sufferings. Common grief attached the youth to the old man, and from their sorrow for the departed poet arose the new league of their friendship. The venerable marquis treated with paternal kindness the foreign poet, who rewarded his affection with filial love and reverence. The marquis made Milton thoroughly familiar with Naples and its beautiful environs. Besides, his frequent conversations with the amiable old man on literature, and the most noteworthy productions of the Italian poets, exercised an extraordinary influence over him. It was owing to the marquis's suggestions that Milton conceived the first plan of writing in his mother-tongue a great epic, such as those by which Tasso had immortalized himself. He communicated his ideas to the marquis, who encouraged him, gave him many excellent hints, and generally exercised the most salutary influence over the poet.

In one of their conversations he said smilingly: "I am destined to be the friend and patron of talented men, and I am glad and proud of it; for, next to the joy which men of genius derive from their creations, I know none that could be compared with that which intimate intercourse with them gives us. I would not be willing to exchange this humble position for any other, and I am content if a ray of the sun, whose light fills the whole world, falls to my own share."

"You really deserve," replied Milton, "that every poet should praise your name, for few men possess the noble quality of delighting in the productions of talented men without envying them and of assisting them in their thorny path, as you did in the case of the immortal Tasso. Your name will never be forgotten, but it will be handed down from age to age jointly with his own."

Only one thing disturbed from time to time the tender relations between the two friends, who were so widely separated by age, rank, and nationality, and yet so closely united by their intellectual aspirations. This was the difference of their creeds. Although the marquis manifested a great deal of toleration, Milton was carried away by his zeal and youthful impetuosity to utter many an imprudent word in Naples, which caused trouble and even danger to his noble host. The marquis cautioned the rash young man vainly against the dangers in which he himself might be involved in consequence. It is true, Milton abstained as much as possible from expatiating on religious questions and the tenets of the different Churches; but, after the conversation had once turned to such topics, he could not forbear uttering his opinion freely and openly, and in doing so he frequently overstepped the bounds of prudence. Of course, the gentle reproaches of the marquis touched him; but when the amiable old man, filled with serious solicitude for the salvation of the young heretic, made a gentle attempt to convert him, he met with the most serious resistance. Thus Milton remained under all circumstances true to his religious convictions, and both love and friendship were unable to shake his faith. He deemed the Reformation the only road to intellectual progress, and he considered Protestantism equivalent to liberty.

Notwithstanding these slight dissensions, his relations with the marquis continued to be of the most cordial and friendly character.

The old man invited him often to make excursions with him into the environs of Naples. He visited with him one day the charming little port of Sorrento, where some of Tasso's relatives were yet living. The town lies at the extremity of the bay, on the precipitous slope of high mountains, which, descending almost perpendicularly to the sea-shore, form a gigantic terrace covered everywhere with orange-trees. The small white houses with their flat roofs, on which the inhabitants pass most of their time in order to enjoy the coolness of the sea-breeze, emerge from a perfect sea of fragrant blossoms. One of these houses belonged to Tasso's sister, and her sick, weary brother had found here a welcome asylum for a short time. Milton, conducted by the marquis, crossed the hospitable threshold with profound emotion and reverence. At the door stood a young matron with a rosy babe in her arms, the image of the Madonna and child. An elder boy was playing at her feet. On beholding the marquis, the young mother uttered a cry of joy, and hastened to meet him.

"How glad mother will be!" she shouted to him already from afar. "She is in the garden, and I will inform her immediately of the honor conferred on our house."

"I will go to her myself," replied the marquis. "Lead the way, we will follow you. Notwithstanding my advanced age, I am yet hale and strong enough to treat ladies with the consideration due to their sex."

So saying, the marquis hastened to follow the young matron who was leading the way, and to climb the stairs hewn into the rock, which led to the garden. Here Tasso's sister Cornelia, a venerable lady of eighty, awaited them. It was a touching scene when she held out her hand to the faithful friend of her brother. Her face still bore distinct traces of former beauty, and especially were her dark eyes yet wonderfully radiant. She would have risen from the chair on which she was seated in the open vine-clad bower, but the marquis prevented her.

"Sit still, Cornelia," said the kind-hearted old man. "I intended long since to visit you, but old age often prevents me from following my inclinations. But why do I speak of old age? You look as young and fresh as in your best years."

"Oh, do not mock me," replied the old lady. "I feel the decrease of my strength more and more every day, and I shall doubtless soon follow my poor brother. How glad I am that it was vouchsafed to me to see the day when all Italy acknowledges and praises him as her greatest poet. Since full justice has been done to him, and even his enemies and enviers have been compelled to admit his greatness, I can calmly bid farewell to the world. I should not have thought that so many persons would flock one day, as to a sanctuary, to this humble house where he lived with me. Hardly a day passes that distinguished persons do not call on me and inquire of me about the most insignificant events of his life. Thus, in the evening of my days, I enjoy yet the happiness of witnessing and participating in his triumph."

"And you have amply deserved this happiness by the devotion with which you nursed and comforted him. It is not only Italy that honors her great poet, but even the most remote nations now render him homage. This young man, my friend, is an Englishman, who desires to see the place and make the acquaintance of Tasso's sister. He himself is already renowned as a poet in his native country."

"You are welcome," said the old lady, in a dignified tone. "May the Holy Virgin grant you the fame of my poor brother, and preserve you from his sufferings!"

At a beck from Cornelia the young matron, who was her daughter, Tasso's niece, hastened to offer some refreshments to the guests.

Meanwhile her husband, an intelligent shipmaster, had come home and took part in the conversation. In the circle of this happy and contented family Milton felt that the hours were passing with the speed of moments. The setting sun, which plunged with southern splendor into the blue sea and turned it into flaming purple, reminded the guests that it was time for them to depart. The shipmaster offered to convey the two friends in his boat to Naples, and they accepted his kind proposition. It was a magnificent evening, and the breeze swelling the sails was impregnated with sweet odors. Milton left Tasso's house profoundly moved, accompanied by the greetings and blessings of the noble Cornelia.

"Farewell!" she said to him, "and become to your native country what my brother was to Italy. He is indemnified by everlasting glory and immortality for his sufferings on earth."

Her noble face seemed transfigured by the rays of the setting sun, when she uttered these words in a solemn voice.

The waves through which the boat sailed in its rapid course murmured and moaned gently. The moon had risen and illuminated the sea and the cliffs whose fantastic outlines disappeared in the mist. The two oarsmen had but little to do, as a fresh breeze swelled the sails of the boat. One of them, a stout lad with dark, curly hair and full whiskers, his head covered with a red sailor's cap, raised his voice all at once in gentle, plaintive strains. What the listeners heard was a song and recitative, strangely impressive and in beautiful harmony with the sweet murmur of the waves. The words grew more and more distinct, and Milton and the marquis soon recognized lines from Tasso's "Jerusalem Delivered." The other oarsman, who was older than his companion, sang in a deeper voice when the first singer paused; his companion soon joined in his song, and the poet was delighted with their melodious strains.

"If I am not mistaken," said the marquis, turning to the shipmaster, "your men are singing from Tasso's 'Jerusalem Delivered.'"

"You are right," replied Cornelia's son-in-law. "Most of our sailors know the poem by heart, and while away their time on the sea by singing passages from it. They love the poet, and the heroic deeds of Rinaldo, the enchanted palace of Armida, and Clotilda's love, live in the mouths of these simple-hearted men."

"Indeed!" exclaimed Milton, enthusiastically. "Now I can no longer deplore Tasso's fate. He has achieved the most glorious triumph of the poet: his works live in the mouths of the people!"

CHAPTER VIII.

RECALL TO ENGLAND—ESCAPE FROM ASSASSINATION.

After a sojourn of several weeks, which had passed in the most rapid and agreeable manner, Milton was about to carry his former plan into execution and visit Greece. He had already made the necessary preparations and taken an affectionate farewell of the noble marquis, when he received a letter from his father which caused him to give up his plan. He learned from this letter that important events had occurred during his absence. Civil war seemed imminent in England, and a terrible revolution was about to break out. The infatuated king, who did not lack many excellent qualities of the head and heart, allowed himself to be carried away by his advisers, and still more by the high idea which he entertained of his royal dignity, and committed high-handed violations of the ancient institutions and laws of the country. Thrice he had summoned Parliament, and as many times dissolved it. For ten years past he had governed without consulting the representatives of the people. As the necessary funds were lacking, he resorted, in order to extricate himself from his embarrassments, to all sorts of arbitrary extortions and reprehensible devices. Old taxes which had not been levied for centuries, were declared in full force again, and imposed upon the people; he who refused to pay them was subjected to heavy fines and imprisonment. One of these arbitrary impositions was the so-called ship-money, which former princes had raised only in time of war, and which was then charged on the ports, cities, boroughs, and counties of England, for providing and furnishing certain ships for the king's service. Even the royalists could not deny that this imposition was not exacted for this purpose, but was destined merely to provide the king with money, and that he could exact it to any amount and use it in the most arbitrary manner. The whole nation protested most vehemently against this measure, which was pronounced the most dangerous blow yet levelled at the liberties of the country. Especially were the people afraid lest the king should use the money thus obtained for the organization and maintenance of a standing army, by which a despotic ruler might destroy the institutions of the country and the bulwarks of popular liberty. At this juncture John Hampden, a wealthy landed proprietor of Buckinghamshire, of honorable descent, and highly esteemed in his neighborhood, but until then little known throughout the country, opposed the arbitrary measures of the king in the most courageous and determined manner. He refused emphatically to pay the illegal imposition; and in a lawsuit which he instituted against the government, he asserted that it had no right whatever to raise ship-money. Although the venal judges, who were mostly dependent on the court, decided against him, his courageous conduct gave the signal of general resistance. The extreme hostility to the king and the court, which had prevailed until then, was now raised to such a pitch that the slightest spark would suffice to kindle the flames of revolution and civil war.

Even more dangerous religious troubles were added to the political discontent of the people. At once both spiritual and temporal ruler of his country, the king deemed it incumbent upon him to make the Episcopal Church the only lawful Church both in England and Scotland. In accordance with the deplorable advice of the bigoted and fanatical Laud, Charles had issued new, and, if possible, more stringent and rigorous laws against the Presbyterians and other dissenters. Excommunication and all its dire consequences were to be inflicted on whosoever dared to question the divine right of the execrated bishops. All meetings and conventicles held by private persons and preachers for the purpose of explaining the Bible were prohibited under severe penalties. But the most dangerous innovation (most dangerous because it was most obvious to the common people) concerned the form of divine worship. Divine service was thenceforth to be held only in strict accordance with the precepts of the Church of England, and the rites reminding the people of the Catholic service were to be restored. Already the mere news that the king had resolved upon such measures created the most intense excitement throughout Scotland; especially were the people of the northern capital extremely indignant at the proposed innovation. On the day when the service was to be held for the first time in accordance with the new rites, the churches were crowded with men and women determined to resort to extremities in order to prevent the introduction of ceremonies reminding them of Roman Catholicism. No sooner had the bishop, dressed in his white surplice, and accompanied by the other prelates and the magistrates, entered the church, than a storm of imprecations and invectives burst forth against him. The dean, who read the service, was interrupted by the loud sobs and sighs of the aristocratic ladies, while the women of the lower classes received him with wild cries, and flung the backs and legs of broken chairs at him. When the bishop entered the pulpit, the noise grew more deafening. He was unable to utter a word. Amidst shouts of "A pope! a pope! Antichrist! Stone him!—knock him down!" he had to withdraw and flee from the church in order to save his life. The furious populace smashed the windows of the cathedral and all the chapels. The riot soon became general. The men incited each other to offer the most unflinching resistance to all religious innovations; the women likewise took part in the movement, and, as is always the case, with fanatical zeal and ardor. The Presbyterian clergy thundered furiously against popery and the liturgy, which they said were the same thing. The pulpits resounded with imprecations against Antichrist; and the people who had first declared against the liturgy were compared in a not very flattering manner to Balaam's ass speaking "with a man's voice." The general fanaticism was enhanced by the passions of the political parties; private interests stimulated the spirit of liberty, and on all sides were to be seen the most menacing symptoms of the speedy outbreak of a terrible revolution. Had the king issued an amnesty under these circumstances, and acted only with some degree of forbearance in regard to the liturgy, the danger might have been averted. But instead of adopting so prudent a course, he proceeded with the utmost rigor, and accelerated the outbreak of the crisis by the most unyielding obstinacy. Before long the most distinguished men were drawn into the whirlpool of the movement, which had originated among the lowest classes, and a real and important revolution grew out of a street riot. The heads of the Scottish nobility and the foremost commoners concluded the famous league of the Scottish Covenanters, by which they bound themselves to resist all interference in their religious services. Charles attempted to put down the Covenanters with the sword, but ineffectually. As he was destitute of money and soldiers, nothing remained for him but to summon a Parliament. This was done in the spring of 1640.

Such was the intelligence which Milton received from his father. He did not hesitate a moment, but made his choice immediately as a friend of liberty and of his country. He resolved to return at once to England; for he deemed it disgraceful to roam idly in foreign lands, while his fellow-citizens were arming for the great struggle for liberty. A short time previous to his departure from Naples some English friends in Rome cautioned him against returning to the Eternal City. They were merchants who did business in Rome, and wrote him, that his bold utterances in regard to Catholicism, and especially the visit he had paid to Galileo, had aroused the hostility of certain persons, and chiefly that of the Jesuits. Nevertheless, he returned to Rome. The Eternal City embraced him once more with her siren arms, and it seemed to him as though he could never bid farewell to her. Love contributed not a little to the prolongation of his sojourn in Rome. So long as he had been separated from Leonora Baroni and diverted his mind by his familiar intercourse with the distinguished marquis, his passion had slumbered; but at the sight of the beautiful cantatrice it awoke again with redoubled ardor. She received him with a cry of joy, and fascinated him more than ever by her caresses. It is true, he remembered the sorceress Armida in Tasso's "Jerusalem Delivered," but he lacked the courage to liberate himself from his voluptuous bondage. Whenever he alluded to his departure, she closed his lips with burning kisses. But despite the happiness which he felt in her company, a profound melancholy stole over him amidst all his pleasures. He felt a secret foreboding of the struggles and troubles which were in store for him in his native country. He seemed to hear a voice calling upon him to hasten to the assistance of his distressed fatherland. He often started up from her arms and gazed gloomily into vacancy.

"What ails you, Giovanni?" asked Leonora, in dismay.

"I can no longer stay with you; I must set out for England. My country is in danger."

"You naughty man! What does your country concern you? My heart, my bosom, shall be your home for evermore."

"Leonora, follow me; I can no longer withhold my assistance from my fellow-citizens."

"I must follow you, and whither? To a remote country whose gray, leaden sky threatened to crush me, and whose language I do not understand. Stay with me in Rome, in our magnificent Italy, where the sun shines so radiantly, and where the sweetest pleasures of life may be enjoyed. Do not leave me, for it would kill me to lose you."

She burst into tears, and Milton was too weak to resist so touching an appeal. Similar conversations recurred almost every day. It was in vain that his reason struggled against this powerful passion. At times he attempted to liberate himself from this voluptuous bondage, and he then wandered alone in the silent night, amidst the monuments and ruins of the Eternal City. During these lonely walks he noticed that a stranger, whose features were concealed by his hat and cloak, often dogged his steps, but he paid no particular attention to him. One day, when he visited the Coliseum after dusk had set in, and was admiring the sublime edifice on which the moon was shedding her pale weird light, a man wrapped in a cloak, and concealing his features under a broad-brimmed hat, rushed toward Milton. In his uplifted hand he held a flashing dagger; but before the assassin was able to carry his fell purpose into effect, a strong arm had wrenched his weapon from him. The villain succeeded in escaping, owing to the darkness, without being recognized. Milton thanked his liberator, a young man who introduced himself to him as a countryman of his, named Marvell. The amiable young man impressed Milton very favorably, and they were soon on intimate terms.

"I am greatly obliged to you," said the poet.

"Not to me, but to the accident which led me this way. My name is Marvell."

"And mine is Milton."

"I have already heard of you, and am therefore doubly glad of having rendered you a slight service. But, above all things, permit me to caution you. Friends have told me that attempts would be made here in Rome to assassinate you."

"I do not see why such attempts should be made."

"The frankness with which you have uttered your principles on all occasions has excited attention. You have enemies here that will not shrink from the most infamous outrages. You have just seen that people in Rome attempt to settle a religious dispute by the stab of an assassin, and to cut off not only the words of an eloquent speaker, but also the thread of his life."

"I did not think that they attached so much importance to my humble person."

"You are too modest, and do not appreciate your own worth. Your poems, which were publicly recited in the academies of Florence and Rome, have met with extraordinary favor and applause. Besides, I understand that our talented yet unprincipled countryman, Sir Kenelm Digby, intended to use you as an instrument to promote his dark schemes and intrigues. Thank God, you did not lend yourself to such vile purposes! Many of your countrymen, who took the liveliest interest in your welfare, feared the worst, and rumors were rife everywhere that you had been converted to the Catholic Church."

"What an infamous slander!"

"Your manly conduct was the best refutation of these absurd rumors, which nevertheless had an air of great probability, as you were received in so exceedingly kind a manner at Cardinal Barberini's palace. But what seemed to confirm those rumors more than any thing else was your intimate intercourse with Signora Baroni. Pardon me for speaking so unreservedly, but I deem myself in duty bound not to conceal any thing from you."

"What do you know about Leonora Baroni?" asked Milton, hastily.

"I know that the celebrated singer was used by the Jesuits and by Sir Kenelm Digby, half wittingly and half unwittingly, as a tool to convert you. I am sorry to tell you so, but it is not the first time that the signora has been used for similar purposes. Last year a young French nobleman, a distinguished Huguenot, languished in her nets precisely like you. After he had forsworn his faith, Leonora turned her back upon him. The poor fellow did not survive this double loss, and the thought of having sacrificed his convictions to a chimera. He threw himself into the Tiber, and reposes now in an unconsecrated grave. If you like it, we may visit his grave. It might be a wholesome warning to you, Mr. Milton."

"But who is this Leonora Baroni?" asked the poet, mournfully.

"Some assert that she is the daughter, others the mistress of the cardinal; perhaps she is both. Since the time of Lucretia Borgia, such things are by no means rare in Rome. But, however that may be, follow my advice and leave the siren, the sooner the better. Escape from the danger, for the eyes of the Italian women are even worse than the daggers of the Italian men."

Marvell's words seemed to make a powerful impression on the poet. He had already heard similar rumors, but had refused to believe them. Now he resolved to examine them carefully, and, if they should prove well-grounded, to break with Leonora forever. Accompanied by his new friend, he returned to his rooms. On the way they conversed a great deal on the precarious state of affairs in their native country, and exchanged views on this interesting subject. Milton found that Marvell shared his political and religious opinions, and was an enthusiastic lover of liberty.

"We are on the eve of important events," said Marvell, "and no man is allowed to lag behind now that we are called upon to defend our most sacred boons. For this reason I shall return immediately to England. The time of idleness and enjoyment is past for me; duty calls me, and I shall obey it."

"And I will follow you."

"Let us shake hands," replied the young man, holding out his right hand enthusiastically to Milton. "We will both dedicate our strength to our oppressed country. War against tyranny! war for freedom of conscience!"

"War against tyranny, war for freedom of conscience!" repeated Milton, solemnly.

CHAPTER IX.

FAREWELL TO LEONORA—"ADAMO CADUTO."

Milton ascertained that Marvell's statements in regard to Leonora's character were partly true, although she was not as guilty as he had hinted. She was only half wittingly a tool of the wily Society of Jesus. No sooner had Milton acquired this conviction, than he resolved to leave her. He met her with entire frankness, but brought about the rupture with becoming delicacy. He felt sincere pity for this magnificent creature, who had succumbed to the force of circumstances. When he mentioned the young French nobleman, she gave a start, and her pallor proved that she was guilty.

"Luigi!" she sighed. "Poor Luigi!"

"You were the cause of his death," said Milton, in a mild tone. "Do you feel no repentance?"

"Why should I repent of having saved his soul, and led it to the Madonna? I only lament the poor young man, or rather I lament myself. I could not love him, and now fate has overtaken me. I love you, and you will forsake me!"

"I cannot help it. I should have to despise myself if I were to act otherwise."

"Cruel man! I will follow you and be your slave. Abuse me, kill me, but do not forsake me. If you are bent on leaving me, I must die."

A flood of tears accompanied these words.

"Leonora!" replied the poet "you will not die. You mistake your attachment to me. Your whole nature prevents you from feeling so profound a passion. You are, above all, an artiste, and art alone affords you full satisfaction. I have observed you too well. Pride and gratified vanity will and must indemnify you for the joys of love. You are first an artiste, and then a woman. When your singing carries away the souls of your audience, every other feeling gives way before the triumph achieved by the singer. Accustomed to rule over so many hearts, a single one can no longer satisfy you, and least of all for a lifetime. We should have parted sooner or later in any event, even though faith, nationality, and language had not separated us."

"Barbarian! you do not know my heart, nor the ardent love I feel for you."

"And when art no longer satisfies you, you will have recourse to religion."

"Yes, you are right," she said. "I will retire from the world and take the veil. In a cloister I shall atone for the grievous sin of having loved a heretic so intensely."

She uttered a wild cry, embraced Milton once more, and imprinted a glowing kiss on his lips.

"Accursed be the lips," she exclaimed with southern vivacity, "that dare to kiss yours after me; accursed yourself, if you dare to love another woman! And now go, go; the Madonna will give me strength to forget you, sweet, faithless heretic!"

She disengaged herself impetuously from his arms and pushed him back; she then disappeared, and left the poet stunned and bewildered by this strange farewell.

Milton left Rome on the following morning with a heavy heart. He had passed the night sleepless and reading in the Bible, for he greatly needed strength and comfort. The deepest gloom filled his heart. In taking leave of Rome he had likewise bidden farewell to love and art. He felt that he was going to meet a grave and stormy future, and that he had arrived at the great turning-point of his fate.

In such moments the mind plunges once more into the past, that great graveyard of our thoughts and feelings. It walks there amid the graves and shades of years long gone by. It sheds tears on the faded wreaths and withered flowers, and laments the loss of youth and happiness.

Such was the frame of mind in which Milton set out from Rome. Notwithstanding his longing for his home, he did not accelerate his journey. He tarried at Florence and Venice as though he were unable to bid farewell to the beautiful scenery and azure sky of Italy. His heart, a part of his life and love, remained here. To dispel his melancholy thoughts, he visited at Florence the theatre, where he happened to witness the representation of a singular drama which was to exercise a decisive influence over his whole poetical life. The play was entitled "Adamo Caduto," by Andreini, and reminded him of the so-called mysteries of the Middle Ages. The subject, which was taken from the Bible, was the fall of man.

When the curtain rose, the audience beheld a chorus of angels singing praise to the Lord. After their hymn was at an end, God the Father appeared with the Spirit of Darkness; the former a venerable old man with a long silver beard and clad in a blue star-spangled dress; the latter wrapped in a costume of fire-colored taffeta, with fine though diabolical features. In a brief dialogue God commanded Lucifer to contemplate the beauty of His creation and listen to the gratitude of Adam and Eve, who uttered their joy and adoration in loud words. This aroused the ire of the Evil Spirit, and he swore everlasting hatred to the good angels and destruction to the mortals. At his bidding, the seven Deadly Sins, which he summoned, arose from hell. Their names in the drama were: Melecano, or Pride; Lurcone, or Envy; Ruspicano, or Anger; Arfarat, or Covetousness; Maltea, or Idleness; Dulciato, or Lust; and Guliar, or Gluttony. Unseen by Adam and Eve, Lurcone and Guliar watched them; but the prayer of Adam and Eve, who turned to God with fervent piety and child-like reverence, drove away the Evil Spirits, who hastened back to the infernal regions. In their place appeared the Serpent, accompanied by Ambition and other demons. It approached Eve, and seduced her to pluck the forbidden fruit. After a tender dialogue with Adam, she produced the fruit; her husband expressed first intense horror at this violation of God's commandment, but finally yielded also to the temptation. They immediately knew that what they had done was not good, but evil. Their souls were filled with shame, and fear and repentance. They sought, as sinners, to conceal themselves from God, and hid among thick bushes. Satan announced his triumph to hell, and called upon his demons to rejoice and render homage to him. A chorus of evil spirits celebrated the event by demoniacal songs and wild dances, which presently passed into exclamations of dismay at the approach of God and His heavenly host. He came to judge the two sinners, Adam and Eve. He cursed them, and told them they should not dwell any longer in Paradise; whereupon the Archangel Michael drove them out of it amid thunder and lightning. The angels closed the act with a chorus exhorting the sinners to repentance and hope. In the next act Lucifer appeared again, surrounded by the princes of hell, profoundly grieved because he had become aware of the predestined incarnation of Christ and the redemption of the world, which would frustrate his evil designs. The evil spirits tried to comfort him, and he devised new snares into which Adam and Eve were to fall. He called to his assistance three demons, having the characteristic names of Death, the Flesh, and the World. Meanwhile, Adam was bewailing his fate, and even more piteously the sufferings of his wife. Wild beasts pursued them; they were compelled to flee, and felt the full extent of their misery. Hunger, thirst, fatigue, and despair appeared in the shapes of horrible demons, and tormented the unfortunate creatures to the utmost, so that Eve begged Adam to kill her and himself. Death, armed with a sharp scythe, a frightful skeleton, upbraided Eve with her terrible guilt, and prophesied to her the fate of all her children. Seized with horror, Adam and Eve fled into the mountains. Here the Flesh, in the shape of a lovely girl, approached Adam and sought to seduce him; but he withstood the new temptation courageously. Lucifer appeared to him, and told him he was a man, an elder brother of Adam; but a cherub, sent from heaven, rescued the victim from the hands of the evil one, and struggled with him. A fine-looking man, called the World, approached Eve, and promised her splendor, ease, and luxury. At his bidding there emerged from the ground a magnificent palace, filled with sumptuous things of every description. Wanton nymphs thronged around Eve, and invited her to enjoy herself, but Adam warned her of her peril. The exasperated World called the demons of hell, who chained the two. Eve begged for mercy, but Adam exhorted her to be firm and put her trust in God. Lucifer and Death rushed upon the sufferers, when suddenly the Archangel Michael, clad in a radiant coat-of-mail, sword in hand, and accompanied by the other angels, descended from heaven. After a violent struggle, Lucifer succumbed to him. Adam and Eve rejoiced at Michael's victory, and thanked him, and he comforted them by promising them that God would take compassion on them. Angels closed the drama with hymns of praise, in which they announced the coming of the Redeemer.

Although this drama, by its turgid language and all sorts of fantastic additions, materially impaired the sublime simplicity and grandeur of the Biblical account of the fall of man, it did not fail to make a powerful impression on the susceptible mind of the young poet. For the first time he conceived the idea of writing an epic on this grand subject, which he afterward carried out in his immortal "Paradise Lost." Engrossed with the scenes he had just witnessed, and with the plan of his future epic, Milton left the theatre, accompanied by an eminent Florentine gentleman to whom he had been recommended. Signor Diodati, noted for his learning and accomplishments, broke the poet's silence by commenting, in a most sagacious manner, on the subject and the performance of the drama.

"Of all the revelations of the Holy Scriptures," he said, "the account of the creation and the fall of man has always made a particularly profound impression on me. How childlike and yet how sublime, how simple and yet how grand, is the manner in which it treats the most profound philosophy, the most difficult and important question in regard to the nature of man and the origin of sin! In the form of a parable, which all can understand, it reveals the highest wisdom, and the narrative solves the mysterious problem of human life and nature, so that even children are able to comprehend it."

"You have given utterance to my own ideas on the subject," replied Milton. "No book in the world, not even the works of the Greeks, which I esteem so very highly, equal the Bible in this respect. Whenever I open it, a feeling of awe seizes me; I feel the presence of God, who reveals Himself in it to the world. All that human wisdom and genius have conceived or devised is unable to cope with the truths which it teaches. Its words are like 'apples of gold in pictures of silver,' and combine the simplicity of childhood with the wisdom of mature age. Heaven and earth, flowers and stars, the wonders of creation and human life, are to be found in glowing beauty on every page. To the happy, as well as to the afflicted, it gives food, solace, and comfort. It is indeed the *word* of God, as the world created by Him is His *deed*. Each is the complement of the other, and both reveal the greatness, omnipotence, and wisdom of the Lord. The better we become acquainted with the Bible, the more enchanting beauties we discover in it. Thus a new star has risen upon me also to-day, and the profound philosophy of the creation and the fall of man has produced an extraordinary impression on me. Adam and Eve are the representatives of mankind, and Paradise is the state of human innocence. The voice of God, forbidding Adam to eat of the fruit, is the voice of reason. So long as it retains its sway over the passions, man is happy and contented; the world is then a paradise for him. But the serpent does not sleep; it beguiles him to gratify his sinful desires. He loses his innocence, and with it paradise. Grief and misery then befall him, and repentance fills his heart; from this arise the knowledge of the good and salutary contrition. He turns once more toward God, struggles manfully with sin, and triumphs by the mercy of the Lord, who raises up the fallen sinner. Salvation is granted to him, and he recovers the lost paradise. Such is the history of Adam, or rather man. Eve is destined to show us the peculiarities of woman and female nature. She is first beguiled by the serpent, because her heart is more accessible to temptation, and because her husband is made of sterner stuff. Her senses and passions dominate her, and hence she is punished more harshly. God says to her, 'Now shalt thou bear children with pain, and in sorrow shalt thou bring them up.' This simple narrative abounds in profound wisdom and sublime truths."

"I share your admiration entirely, but it always looks to me like a desecration to see such sacred traditions performed on the stage, and God Himself and His angels represented by actors whose private life is generally at variance with the parts they play. In my opinion, they are entirely unfit for dramatic representation, which cannot but impair their dignity and the reverence with which the people look upon them."

"I think you are right, and will confess to you that the drama has suggested to me the idea of treating this profound mystery in a more becoming form. Like Tasso, I would like to create a Christian epic which should, if possible, do full justice to the sublime subject. I have already long sought for such a task, on which I might try my strength. Hitherto, I thought of writing a poem on the exploits of King Arthur, but the drama to-night has caused me to change my mind, and pointed out to me a nobler and loftier task. Can the poet do any thing better than to make man in general the hero of his poem, celebrate the wonders of the creation, and praise the greatness and mercy of God? Heaven and hell, with their mysteries, shall be the theme of my epic, and my imagination revels already in the depths of everlasting darkness and in the land of the blessed. I see the Lord seated on His glorious throne, surrounded by His angels and cherubim; while Lucifer, with his demons, rules over the infernal regions, clad in the lurid glare of diabolical majesty. As Homer depicted the war of the Trojans and Greeks with surpassing truth and beauty, so I will portray the far more sacred and grand struggle between good and evil, virtue and sin, heaven and hell. I have not vainly seen the works of the great Italian artists, the painted and sculptured poems of Raphael and Michael Angelo; they shall be my models, and I will strive to equal them."

"And you will succeed in your efforts," said Diodati, deeply moved by the poet's enthusiasm. "I see in my mind already your poem combining the grace of our Raphael with the power and energy of Michael Angelo, for you possess that of which the poet has need above all things, faith in God and love of country."

CHAPTER X.

THOMAS EGERTON AT COURT.

WHILE Milton thus found the subject of his great poem, the affairs of his native country were constantly assuming a more threatening aspect. The parties were more at variance than ever before: on one side, the newly-summoned Parliament was instigated by religious and political fanatics to take extreme measures; on the other side, the infatuated king, with his court and his reckless and overbearing adherents, became every day more obstinate and defiant. One of the most ardent royalists was the rash Thomas Egerton, who had received an appointment in the queen's household, and, as one of her majesty's favorites, soon took a prominent position in his new sphere. The bold youth had plunged recklessly into the whirl of intrigues and pleasures which the court offered to him at that period. There was a continuous round of festivals, although the times were any thing but favorable to such diversions; the court and its adherents were literally dancing on a terrible volcano.

The indignation of the people was at its height. By all sorts of illegal and despotic measures the crown had forfeited the confidence and love of the nation, which sided enthusiastically with the courageous adversaries of the king, and with the members of Parliament who attacked the government in the most vehement manner. Such men as Pym and Hampden were the heroes of the day, and enjoyed the greatest popularity. They alone were regarded as true patriots, friends of the people, and, above all, genuine and sincere Christians. Even an entirely pure and unobjectionable attachment to the court was considered and derided as slavish servility, and confidence in the king's promises was looked upon as shameless venality and corruption. This current of public opinion was irresistible, and the sudden dissolution of the Parliament had added to its strength.

Notwithstanding these threatening symptoms of an impending revolution, the court, and particularly the queen, were engrossed with the most brilliant amusements and entertainments. Charles was too grave, and almost pedantic, to take a leading part in the gay life of the court; but the queen was extremely partial to festivities, dancing, and theatrical representation. An amiable companion and a good dancer, wit and humor were always welcome to the sprightly Frenchwoman; and hence Thomas, who combined all these qualities in his person, had at once found favor in her eyes. Treated with extraordinary distinction by her majesty, he excited already the attention and jealousy of the other courtiers. The polished Jermyn, the fine-looking Percy, and he were publicly called the queen's pets. He was very proud of this, and fanatically devoted to his august mistress. The kindness and condescension of the royal lady awakened in the favorite's heart a feeling of boundless gratitude, which soon passed into the most ardent love. It is true, Henrietta never acted in a manner derogatory to her royal dignity, but she was too much of a Frenchwoman not to be pleased with the homage rendered her by the handsome and agreeable youth. She did not deem illicit a kind smile, a winning glance from her fiery hazel eyes, and added thereby to the flame devouring his heart. He would willingly have given up his life in order to obtain such favors. His attachment to poor Lucy Henderson, who had accompanied him so trustingly to London, had to give way to this new love; for the humble country girl, of course, could not vie with the Queen of England. She felt indeed that he did not treat her with the same tenderness as formerly, but in her innocence she did not suspect the true reason, and ascribed his coldness to the change in his circumstances, his new position, and the occupations connected with it. She loved him nevertheless as tenderly as ever, and contented herself with the crumbs falling from the table of his love. When he told her in the most enthusiastic manner of the beauty and amiability of the queen, she did not feel a particle of jealousy; for how could she envy a princess? On the contrary, she shared his feelings, and, although she had never seen Henrietta, she worshipped her as a saint, and was, like her lover, ready to sacrifice her life for her.

Quite different were the sentiments animating our friend Billy Green. The impudent fellow was exceedingly well pleased with life in the streets of London, and still better with what he saw at court, where he appeared as the footman of his young master. He was soon generally known there, and well liked on account of his merry jests and tricks. He was always to be found among the idle servants of the courtiers, and feasted with them at the expense of the royal exchequer. A great change had taken place in his appearance; he took pains to imitate the tone of the great city, and particularly of his surroundings, and was very successful in his efforts. Dressed in the cast-off clothes of his master, he played the distinguished cavalier in a somewhat exaggerated manner. The plumed round hat sat obliquely on his head. A broad lace collar covered the upper part of the variegated doublet, and very large trousers encased his plump thighs, while his white stockings exhibited a pair of fine calves. He always strolled about the halls and passages of the palace, and tried to assume the bearing and air of an influential and polished courtier. He really succeeded in deceiving a few short-sighted petitioners, whom he promised to intercede in their behalf, of course only in consideration of a suitable reward, with the king and other distinguished persons of the court. Billy Green was also a greater favorite of the fair sex in his new garb than heretofore, and he entered into many a tender *liaison* with chambermaids and the daughters of commoners, on which occasions his modesty generally caused him to deny that he was only a footman, and to play the *rôle* of a real cavalier. In short, the merry fellow was exceedingly well pleased with his new position, and blessed the moment when he had exchanged the fields of his native county for the pavement of the capital. He remained faithful to his young master, save in one point. His nature inclined more to the independent spirit of the cat than the affectionate attachment of the dog. Like the former, he moused on his own account, and preserved a certain freedom of action. He possessed far more than feline cunning, and whenever a wily trick was to be played, Billy Green assisted his master in the most effective manner. To-day he was engaged in dressing his master for the festival, which was to be given at night in the apartments of the queen, and for which Davenant, the laureate, had written a mask. Henrietta liked to divert and surprise her husband on such occasions by witty and pleasant plays and representations. To the great indignation of her Puritan subjects, she herself frequently took part in these performances, particularly in the dances. Thomas Egerton had been invited to take part in a quadrille, in which the queen intended to appear, and of course he paid a great deal of attention to his dress, as he was well aware of the importance which his august protectress attached to a tasteful costume and fine personal appearance. With the assistance of his footman, he donned a coat of white silk, richly embroidered with gold, and adorned with the costliest Brussels lace and waving ribbons. While dressing his master, Billy Green diverted him by all sorts of droll stories and witticisms, indicative of his low cunning and shrewdness.

"You will have a fine time to-night," he said to Thomas. "I have already been in the kitchen. Good Lord, what an amount of cooking and roasting was going on there! My mouth waters at the mere recollection. And what generous wines will be set before the guests! The chief-butler had to tap his best casks. Ah! I should like to feast just once in my life at the royal table! The clerical black-coats will rave and thunder again when the odors of the roasts in the royal kitchen reach their pious noses. Believe me, Sir Thomas, all the dissatisfaction of the clergymen arises from their empty stomachs."

"You may be right," replied the youth,

absently, buttoning his coat, and putting on his scented gloves.

"The other day," added Billy, "I went for fun to one of their churches, and listened to the sermon. If I was king, I would have the rascally preacher hung. You ought to have heard him rave. He compared the king with Saul, who perished because he refused to listen to Samuel's voice. Samuel, of course, was no other than the roundhead preacher himself. He inveighed even worse against the queen, whom he called the scarlet woman, another Jezebel, the ruin of England, and the plague of the world."

"If he were here, I would shut his foul mouth with my sword, and give him a taste of cold iron," said Thomas.

"I could not stand it any longer, and commenced groaning aloud. But this only added to his fury. 'Out with the son of Baal!' cried the preacher; and the whole congregation rushed upon me, and thrust and kicked me until I got out of the church—I hardly know how. I got a bump on my head as big as a melon, all in honor of our gracious queen, whom may God protect!"

"There, take this doubloon as smart-money," said the youth, opening his heavy purse and handing a gold-piece to his footman.

"Long live the queen!" exclaimed Billy, waving his hat, and well pleased with the success of his feigned loyalty.

Thomas left his room and repaired to the gorgeous apartments of Whitehall. Large numbers of the invited guests were already assembled there. Courtiers, statesmen, and beautiful ladies thronged the halls and galleries, which were adorned with the masterpieces of the most celebrated Dutch painters. Charles I. was a lover of art, and lavished riches and honors on painters such as Rubens and Van Dyke. The court presented a most dazzling spectacle at this moment. Like the setting sun, court-life shed once more its most lustrous rays. The pomp, splendor, and beauty of the whole kingdom seemed to be concentrated here. The luxury and magnificance displayed on this occasion have never been equalled since. Especially charming was the spectacle exhibited by the decorations of the royal palace, and the rich costumes of that period. The absence of simplicity was amply compensated by its gorgeous magnificence. The halls and apartments where the guests assembled were filled with gilded ornaments, costly hangings, and gobelins. Gigantic mirrors of Venetian glass leaned against the pillars. In the corners stood large tables groaning under a load of silver vessels, decanters, goblets, and massive bowls of beautiful workmanship. The ceilings were adorned with frescoes, representing scenes from Greek mythology in the most glowing colors. Numerous candelabra and lustres with thousands of wax-candles illuminated the apartments in the most brilliant manner. The style of the *Renaissance*, which was then at its height, achieved here its greatest triumph. In entire consonance with the gay and luxurious character of the court, it was blended with the manners and costumes of the period into a harmonious whole. The court, in accordance with the times, was extravagant, dashing, brilliant, and passionately fond of pleasure.

The richly-attired guests surged in these magnificent halls and apartments, and awaited the arrival of their majesties. The costumes of the gentlemen, which were made of velvet, and frequently so thickly studded with pearls and precious stones, that the original stuff was scarcely to be seen; the heavy dresses of the ladies, made of gold-embroidered silks, and sparkling in all the colors of the rainbow, were in perfect harmony with their gorgeous surroundings. A number of separate groups had formed; friends and acquaintances met, greeted each other, and conversed on the events of the day and on politics. There were several parties among the adherents of the king. Some of his friends, who were strongly supported by Henrietta, were animated with a blind hatred of the Parliament and the existing laws, which were checks upon the arbitrary aspirations of the government; they advised high-handed, bold, and decisive measures. Most of them were dissipated young men, fond of women and play, courtiers rather than politicians, soldiers rather than statesmen, reckless lovers of pleasure, to whom restraints of any kind were repugnant, and who derided the religious zeal, the stern simplicity, and the austerity of the Puritans. They did not lack courage and impetuous valor, but were destitute of earnestness, perseverance, and sagacity. They were called cavaliers, and the people detested them on account of their arrogance and immorality. Another party embraced a number of honorable and distinguished friends of the king, headed by Lord Falkland; they were not blind to the impending crisis, but they were still in hopes that they could succeed in averting the danger. Occupying a mediatorial position between the crown and the Parliament, between the government and the people, they resisted all efforts either to impair the royal authority or to encroach upon the rights of the country. They incurred the usual fate of such a position, and were denounced by both sides. The cavaliers considered them traitors in disguise, and the popular party regarded them as enemies of liberty. The king himself failed to do them justice, and mostly sided with the extremists. Nor were secret and open enemies of the court wanting in the assembly. Where so many easily-injured interests crossed each other, a conflict was altogether unavoidable. Ambition and vanity, thirst for intrigues, and the whole host of evil spirits, found ample scope here for their pernicious activity.

Thomas moved with his innate grace and ease among these various groups, and soon met with a circle which he joined. A number of young men distinguished by their elegant attire, and arrogant and almost noisy tone, bade him welcome.

"This way, Thomas!" said one of them to him. "Where were you yesterday, my friend? We greatly regretted your absence from our merry circle. We were at the Anchor, and played until daybreak. Percy was finely fleeced. Just look at the wry face he makes!"

"I was on duty at her majesty's apartments," replied Thomas.

"I do not believe a word of it. I know your tricks, my fine fellow. You have a sweetheart with whom you pass your evenings. Everybody knows that. As soon as you are tired of the fair one, give me a hint, and I will willingly take care of the deserted Dido."

"Of course!" sneered another. "Villiers buys his clothes and sweethearts at second hand. He gets them cheaper in that way."

"By the way," interposed a third, "what about the Scottish army? I have been told that the Earl of Strafford will arrive here to-night, and then undertake to chastise the villanous rebels."

"That will gladden Lady Carlisle's heart; she will certainly accompany him. She is such a faithful friend of his, she will never leave his side," said the first speaker, sneeringly.

His words elicited a burst of laughter. A new-comer added to the frivolous turn which the conversation had taken. It was Davenant, the poet laureate, who was as witty and talented as he was unprincipled and dissipated. His expressive countenance exhibited the traces of a vicious life. A contagious disease had deprived him of his nose, but his dark eyes sparkled with intelligence and mischievousness. According to his own assertion, he was

Shakespeare's illegitimate son, and his mother was the landlady of a popular tavern.

"Well, son of Apollo," said Lord Wilmot, one of the most reckless young men, "how is your poetic soul?"

"Very well, thank your lordship. Permit me to express my satisfaction at your having escaped the gallows up to this time."

"Davenant is not Apollo's son, but a bastard of William Shakespeare," remarked the handsome Percy.

"There you are right," replied the poet. "My mother did more for me than yours did for you; she gave me a father who was a man of genius; and I would rather be the bastard of a genius than the legitimate son of a blockhead. We may both be content, as we have inherited the qualities of our fathers."

The handsome Percy deemed it prudent to break off this duel of words with the malicious and sarcastic poet, who had all the laughter on his side. He, therefore, turned his back on him and nodded to a young man who entered the hall at this moment. He was the model of a perfect courtier, the greatest favorite of the queen, and her equerry, Lord Jermyn. Although he was not as handsome as Percy, his whole appearance was distinguished by the highest elegance and refinement. His dress of brown velvet, richly embroidered with gold, relieved his slender form to the greatest advantage. His features bore the genuine aristocratic type; carefully-arranged blond ringlets fell down on his shoulders; his eyes were blue and radiant, but as cold as steel; and an arrogant and perfidious smile played round his finely-chiselled lips. Not only the queen, but almost all the ladies of the court were enthusiastic admirers of the polished courtier, and the more hearts he broke the more ladies longed for a similar fate. It had become fashionable to be deceived and rendered unhappy by Lord Jermyn.

He was greeted by the young men in an almost reverential manner, so far as such a circle was capable of feeling reverence for any one. He enjoyed here, at least, a degree of respect which men of greater wealth refused to him; for he was, as it were, the leader and model of these young men, and treated his satellites with affected condescension.

"Good-evening, Goring, Percy, Wilmot, Egerton," he said to them, nodding his head. "Ah, you are there too, Davenant! Her majesty just now spoke to me of your mask, and expressed herself well pleased with the subject and the manner in which you handled it.—Well, gentlemen, have you heard the great news of the day?"

"That all women are virtuous and all men are sensible," sneered the poet laureate; "that Percy no longer gambles, that Villiers has ceased lying, that Egerton is no longer a hot-headed enthusiast, and that Jermyn is no longer a lady-killer."

"You are utterly mistaken, my noble poet. I will tell you something that is a great deal better. The Lord Lieutenant of Ireland, the Earl of Strafford, has just arrived in London, and is at this moment with the king in his majesty's cabinet. So far as I have learned, he advises the government to adopt the most energetic measures, and he is the man to carry them into execution. He is opposed to a policy of conciliation and concessions, and proposes to subdue by main force both the rebellious Scots and the seditious people of England. He brings from Ireland money enough to fill the exhausted exchequer, and, what is even better, ten thousand well-drilled soldiers, who, under a commander like him, are not afraid of the devil himself. So soon as he is through with the Covenanters, he will attend to London and put an end to this parliamentary nuisance. By the Eternal, I myself should like to take part in a short campaign under Strafford; for the whole affair will not last longer than two weeks. Well, gentlemen, what do you think of such an excursion to the frontier? It would be a pleasant change in our life."

"It would be a mere breakfast-party, at which each of us would devour ten Scotchmen," boasted the handsome Percy.

"The only trouble is, that the fellows are too tough and indigestible," remarked Goring.

"Then we will pummel them until they grow soft enough," jested Egerton.

"Do so," replied Jermyn, sneeringly; "you will thereby gain the special favor of his majesty, and you would have a splendid opportunity to distinguish yourself."

"That is to say," replied Thomas, smilingly, "dear Egerton, do me the favor of allowing a barelegged Scotchman to break your neck, that you may no longer be in my way."

A disdainful smile curled the lips of the haughty favorite, and he cast a proud glance on his rival. "I am not afraid of any *man*, much less of a beardless boy!" he replied.

"Beware of the beardless boy!" threatened Thomas, angrily; "he might tear a hole in your magnificent costume and your milky face."

Another insulting remark was already on the courtier's lips, when the folding-doors opened, and the usher announced the arrival of their majesties in a loud voice. The adversaries had only time to cast furious glances on each other, as their position required them to go to meet their majesties. The other guests ranged themselves in the order of their rank and birth, and awaited thus the approach of Charles and Henrietta.

CHAPTER XI.

CHARLES I. AND HIS QUEEN AND COUNCILLORS.

Charles I. was not a man of imposing appearance: his form was of a middle stature, and his bearing was timid and embarrassed. Being a younger son, he had originally been destined for the Church, and it was not until after his elder brother had died that he became heir to the throne of his father. The peculiarities of his early education still clung to him, and his whole bearing was that of a learned theologian rather than the son of a King of England. It is true, long-continued military and equestrian exercise had gradually imparted considerable strength to his body, but nevertheless a certain awkwardness, such as is often peculiar to scholars, stuck to him. His face was regular, handsome, and well-complexioned, and a singular expression of melancholy, a foreboding as it were of his terrible fate, was stamped on his features. Physiognomists assert that this peculiarity is often noticed in persons destined to die by violence. His slightly-defective utterance added to his timidity and reserve.

The character of this prince was a strange mixture of good and bad qualities. Weakness was the leading feature of his whole nature, the key of all his actions; he displayed stubbornness and obstinacy when energy and manly dignity were indispensable; and, when he was unable to resist the force of circumstances, he resorted to low cunning and the most reprehensible deception. His beneficent disposition was clouded by a manner not very gracious; his piety was tinctured with superstition; his good sense was disfigured by a deference to persons of a capacity much inferior to his own; and his moderate temper exempted him not from hasty and precipitate resolutions. Many of his good qualities were offset by some latent frailty, which, though seemingly inconsiderable, was able, when seconded by the extreme malevolence of his fortune, to disappoint them of all their influence. His strong inclination to promote the interests of his friends misled him into blind devotion to unworthy favorites; his attachment to the queen and his family rendered him their abject slave. He loved art and literature, but fostered them without exercising a salutary and vivifying influence over them, because he did not give them as much freedom as they needed, but caused them to pine away in the unhealthy atmosphere of the court. Like most men of weak character, he often had fits of sullen stubbornness, which he believed to be strength and energy; on such occasions his despotism was tinctured with a spirit of cruelty which was foreign to his original and better nature. In his contests with his adversaries he did not shrink from the most unscrupulous measures; and the honesty and straightforwardness which always go hand in hand with manly strength, were entirely wanting to him. He knew neither how to yield nor to be firm in time; he allowed himself to be compelled to make concessions which he might have easily granted of his own accord; and while tendering liberty with his right hand to his people, he already held out the left to take back his gift. As he lacked strength and courage to refuse openly, he resorted to all sorts of subterfuges and prevarications, by which he utterly forfeited the respect of his subjects. Estimable in his private life, and adorned with many domestic and human virtues, fate had put on his head a crown which his weak shoulders were unable to bear. Nevertheless, he might have become an excellent ruler if he had lived in quiet times. Unhappily, his fate threw him into a period when the genius of the people ran violently toward liberty, and the tempest of revolution shook the foundations of the British empire.

The king was accompanied at this moment by a man made of sterner stuff than himself. It was Thomas Wentworth, Earl of Strafford, the all-powerful minister, who at once became the cynosure of all eyes. His firmly-knit frame, with its powerful chest and shoulders, seemed chiselled out of granite; his muscles and sinews forged out of steel, such was their strength and elasticity. The powerful neck, which was not accustomed to bend, was surmounted by a magnificent head crowned with a dense mass of ringlets. His high, expansive forehead, and his clear, piercing eyes, indicated the mind of a great statesman and diplomatist; while his bushy eyebrows, his arched temples, his defiant mouth, and firm chin, which was fringed with a black beard, told the beholder that he was an intrepid soldier and experienced captain. His decided bearing, and his firm, noisy gait, betokened a spirit of defiant energy shrinking from no difficulty whatever. Formerly an enthusiastic adherent of Parliament, an advocate of popular rights, the most eminent orator and statesman of his party, he had succumbed to the flatteries of the court and to the craving of his ambition, and turned his back upon the cause which he had defended with so much eloquence and ability. Like all apostates, Strafford now persecuted his former political friends with wild fanaticism. Never at a loss for resources, and inexorable in his hatred, he was at this juncture the most dangerous adversary of Parliament and of popular liberty. He constantly advised the most energetic measures and determined resistance, and cautioned the king against the dangers in which, he asserted, a conciliatory course would involve him. He devised a plan to place the king in a perfectly independent position by organizing a standing army and making large reductions in the public expenditure, and afterward boldly repealing the constitution. For this purpose he had already taken all necessary steps, levied troops, collected taxes in Ireland, and secured the coöperation of the most ardent royalists. He was now only waiting for a favorable moment, and especially for the termination of the Scottish war, to carry out this plan, which was fully approved by his sovereign. The people, who justly considered him the author of all oppressions and persecutions, of all violent and illegal measures of the government, detested him instinctively.

He was execrated all over the country, but he laughed the threats of his enemies to scorn, and persecuted with relentless perseverance his former friends, who were now his mortal enemies. But the great man had even at court many opponents whose enmity he had aroused by his implacable severity, his boundless pride, and his rude bearing. Even the queen and her adherents were jealous of the influence and friendship which Charles granted to his minister. Two persons only were strongly attached to Strafford, the beautiful and accomplished Countess of Carlisle, who was generally believed to be his mistress, and the bigoted Archbishop Laud, the spiritual adviser of the king. By means of the countess, who was an intimate friend of Queen Henrietta, he influenced her majesty, and the fanatical prelate helped him to retain his power over Charles himself. With their assistance Strafford deemed his position perfectly safe and impregnable.

With his proud consciousness he accompanied his sovereign through the magnificent apartments of Whitehall; and so great was the impression produced by his appearance, that he eclipsed the less distinguished figure of his royal master and riveted the attention of all guests. Charles perceived this with a slight tinge of envy, to which his suspicious mind, which was so fully impressed with the dignity of his position, was always very prone. Meanwhile the queen had seated herself on her throne, surrounded by a bevy of her beautiful ladies of honor. Maria Henrietta, according to the portraits which have been handed down to us, was a lovely and sprightly princess, deficient neither in charms nor understanding. It is true her features were not entirely regular, but her elegant form, her dark hair, her shapely mouth with dazzling white teeth, the arch dimples of her cheeks and chin, and above all her brilliant eyes, rendered her very piquant and interesting. Educated by her ambitious mother, and instructed by Richelieu as to the best use she might make of her position, she went to England with the firm determination to render important services to the Catholic religion and the members of her church. She pursued her course with less prudence than was necessary in a Protestant country, and placed herself at the very outset in a false position toward her subjects. Though her husband was very fond of her, she did not succeed in obtaining much influence over him until after the death of Buckingham, the king's favorite adviser. So long as the duke was alive, the king always followed his counsels. After his death, Henrietta took his position, and exercised soon a decisive influence over the government and its political measures. Ignorant of the customs and peculiarities of the people, hostile to the laws which set bounds to the king's authority, she contributed not a little to the dissensions and difficulties prevailing between the king and his subjects. As a Catholic, she was already from the start an object of suspicion in the eyes of the people, who soon began to hate her, as she did not know how to humor their prejudices. Her worldliness and thirst for enjoyment were also highly distasteful to the austere Puritans. The pulpits resounded with scathing attacks upon the queen, whom the fanatical preachers called a Canaanite, a daughter of Heth, and an idolatress. On her part, she repaid hatred with hatred, and persecutions with even more relentless persecutions. It was principally at her instigation that several popular orators were prosecuted, and that a heavy fine was imposed upon the celebrated Pym. Although no definite charges could be preferred against her morals, her frivolity often gave rise to the most injurious reports.

At to-night's festival, Henrietta acted again in a very imprudent manner. To the regret of all sagacious adherents of the court, she played a part in Davenant's mask, and recited some verses in it, an innovation upon which no Queen of England had ventured up to this time, and which even many old courtiers deemed utterly incompatible with royal dignity. Henrietta, however, derided such scruples, and gave rein to her merry and vivacious temper in the most unconcerned manner. She danced alternately with Jermyn and Thomas, whom she delighted by her condescension.

"Sir Thomas Egerton," she whispered, smilingly, "you have made considerable progress; in a very short time you have become the best dancer of our court."

"How could it be otherwise, when I had so august a model before my eyes?"

"To-morrow all the preachers of London will denounce again my harmless pleasures."

"Command me, and I will shut the mouths of these miserable preachers with my sword."

"The time for that has not come yet; but you may, perhaps, in the course of a few weeks have an opportunity to draw the sword for your queen."

"And you accept me for your knight?"

"If you are faithful and discreet."

"Put me to the test, your majesty. Demand my life, my blood, and I will joyfully give them up."

Henrietta rewarded the youth's enthusiasm with her most winning smile, so that Thomas forgot all around him. He was very near kneeling down before his adored mistress in the presence of the whole court. Jermyn, who was standing at a distance, observed with secret rage the progress which his rival made in the queen's favor. While he looked entirely unconcerned and smiled sweetly, he brooded over a scheme for removing his dangerous adversary as soon as possible.

The king had, shortly after his arrival, withdrawn again with the Earl of Strafford, to confer with him and some other advisers of the crown as to the measures necessitated by the impending war with the Scottish rebels. Most of them counselled the king to pursue a conciliatory course, and enter into negotiations with the Scots; but the proud minister urged Charles to carry on the war with the utmost energy.

"I hope," he said, in the consciousness of his strength, "to put down this Scottish rabble in a very short time; and then I intend to carry into execution the plan which I have long since laid before his majesty, and to quell these disorders at a blow. Believe me, my lords and gentlemen, the populace is like a barking dog; if you betray timidity, it will only bark the louder and show its teeth; but give it a kick, and it will run away with a whine. For God's sake, do not suffer yourselves to be cowed, and do not yield an inch in the face of its demands! Above all things, we must shut the mouths of some noisy leaders, and silence them either by force or by bribery. The blind multitude has always one or several leaders; deprive it of these leaders and it will be utterly helpless and disperse. Remove the props, and the whole edifice of revolution sinks in ruins. In the first place, I shall subdue the Scots with a well-disciplined army, loyal and devoted to his majesty, and then teach the people of England that disobedience to the king's orders is a grievous crime."

"But a standing army is contrary to the laws of our country," remarked the noble Falkland, faithful to the ancient constitution.

"He who has the power need not trouble himself about the laws," replied the Earl of Strafford. "Tell me a better means, if you are aware of any."

"A new Parliament will, perhaps, prove less obstinate, and vote the necessary troops and supplies."

"You are utterly mistaken. A new Parliament will be even more arrogant than its predecessors. The people will elect only men of whose hostility to the government they are firmly convinced. Under the present circumstances it would be the height of imprudence for us to summon a Parliament. Oh, I am familiar with those men and their evil designs; I know the insidious Pym, and the wily Hampden, who conceals the most boundless ambition under the mask of straightforwardness. Summon them, and they will shake the throne so frantically that it will soon totter to the earth. The king will have to purchase every shilling that they vote with a sacrifice of some of his prerogatives, until nothing remains to him save the empty title, the vain shadow of his dignity, provided the Parliament is gracious enough to leave him so much."

"And religion will also thereby incur the greatest perils," remarked Archbishop Laud, who took part in the conference. "The enemies of the Episcopal Church are waiting only for an opportunity to carry their pernicious purposes into effect; they demand freedom for their accursed teachings, and toleration of their sectarianism. What is to become of the state if the Church loses its dignity, and is mocked and derided by the people?"

"I do not want to summon a Parliament," cried the king, resolutely; "I will not tolerate any other masters by my side! Strafford and Laud are right. The throne and the altar would be exposed once more to the furious assaults of their enemies. God Himself placed the crown on my anointed head, and intrusted me with my power; and I shall know how to maintain them. The Lord will grant me His protection and chastise my adversaries."

"Amen!" said the archbishop, clasping his hands.

The other advisers of the crown, and especially Lord Falkland, ventured once more to offer a feeble resistance; but the king adhered to his resolve to comply with Strafford's counsels.

"I do not want to summon a Parliament," repeated Charles incessantly, with petulant obstinacy, until he had completely intimidated and silenced his faithful adherents. He thereupon instructed Sir Henry Vane, the secretary, to note down what the Earl of Strafford had proposed, and add the paper to the documents preserved in the secret archives.

The festival was drawing to a close. The queen, tired by the dance, retired to her rooms. On taking leave of the overjoyed Thomas she once more smiled graciously upon him, and he left Whitehall in an ecstasy of delight, and dreamed of the love of a princess.

CHAPTER XII.

PARLIAMENT—TRIAL OF STRAFFORD.

The success of the war with the Scottish rebels was by no means such as Strafford had expected. The noble earl had under-estimated the strength of his adversaries; their religious fanaticism made up for what they lacked in numbers and discipline. The soldiers of the king were demoralized, and dissatisfied with a contest with a kindred people, for whose opinions and principles the people of England felt the liveliest sympathy. Notwithstanding the efforts and surpassing ability of the commander-in-chief, the army made no progress, and even sustained some serious defeats. The king was again in want of money and troops, and, to extricate himself from his embarrassments, he applied to the Lords, where he expected to meet with a more submissive spirit than in the House of Commons. Contrary to his expectations, the Lords likewise demanded that he should speedily summon a Parliament, and declared themselves incompetent to afford the requested relief to the government. Thus urged on all sides, the king was obliged, against his will, to comply with the wishes of his subjects.

When the nation was so generally discontented, no wonder that almost all elections ran in favor of those who had espoused the cause of the opposition. Old and new opponents of the king filled the benches of the House of Commons, and, firmly supported by public opinion, they soon obtained almost absolute sway. This was the time when genius and capacity of all kinds, freed from the restraint of authority, and nourished by unbounded hopes and projects, began to exert themselves and be distinguished by the public. Then was celebrated the astuteness of Pym, more fitted for use than ornament; matured, not chilled, by his advanced age and long experience. Then was displayed the mighty ambition of Hampden, supported by courage, conducted by prudence, embellished by modesty. Then, too, were known the dark and ardent character of St. John; the impetuous spirit of Hollis, violent and sincere, open and entire in his enmities and in his friendships; the enthusiastic genius of young Vane, extravagant in the ends which he pursued, sagacious and profound in the means which he employed, incited by the externals of religion, negligent of the duties of morality.

By the daily harangues and invectives against illegal usurpations, not only did the House of Commons inflame themselves with the highest animosity against the court, but the nation caught new fire from the popular leaders, and took the liveliest interest in the proceedings of Parliament. Meetings were daily held; and every man, neglecting his own business, was wholly intent on the defence of liberty and religion. By stronger contagion, the popular feelings were communicated from breast to breast in this place of general rendezvous and society. The preachers discussed the public questions and most important events of the day with a fanatical zeal, raising the excitement of their audiences to the highest pitch. The press, delivered from its former restraints, began to stir, and was used on either side with more exasperation than prudence and ability. Innumerable pamphlets and treatises were printed, and offered for sale in the streets of London under all sorts of strange titles calculated to allure purchasers. Even Parliament and the government did not disdain this means of influencing the people on all important occasions.

A political club named "Rota," a society of the most prominent and active leaders of the opposition, was formed at this time. Speeches were made there, and political and religious topics were discussed by its members. The poet Harrington developed there in his "Oceana" the plan of a social republic, nearly two centuries before Cabet, the Communist, published his "Icarie."

Frightened by these forerunners of the impending crisis, Charles I. in his distress looked around for a savior. He thought no one could serve him better than the Earl of Strafford, whom he deemed strong enough to guide the leaking ship of the government with a firm hand through the tumultuous waves of the revolution. Strafford, sensible of the load of popular prejudices under which he labored, would gladly have declined attendance in Parliament; but Charles, who relied entirely on the earl's capacity, thought that his counsels could not be dispensed with during the critical session which approached; and when Strafford still insisted on the danger of his appearing amidst so many enraged enemies, the king, little apprehensive that his own authority was so suddenly to expire, promised him protection, and assured him that not a hair of his head should be touched by Parliament.

No sooner was Strafford's arrival known, than a concerted attack was made upon him in the House of Commons. At the head of his sworn enemies was now the all-powerful

Pym. They had been friends in former years, and had shared the same political opinions, before Strafford passed over to the government side. This only served to sharpen their mutual exasperation, and Pym, in a long-studied discourse, divided into many heads, enumerated all the grievances under which the nation labored; and, from a complication of such oppressions, inferred that a deliberate plan had been formed of changing entirely the frame of government, and subverting the ancient laws and liberties of the kingdom.

"We must inquire," said the speaker, "from what fountain these waters of bitterness flow; and though doubtless many evil counsellors will be found to have contributed their endeavors, yet there is one who challenges the infamous preëminence, and who, by his courage, enterprise, and capacity, is entitled to the first place among these betrayers of their country. He is the Earl of Strafford, Lieutenant of Ireland, and President of the Council of York, who, in both places, and in all other provinces where he has been intrusted with authority, has raised ample monuments of tyranny, and will appear, from a survey of his actions, to be the chief promoter of every arbitrary counsel."

Pym afterward entered into a more personal attack on the earl, and dwelt even upon his love-affairs with the Countess of Carlisle and other ladies. And in conclusion he called upon Parliament not to spare the criminal because he was invested with an exalted dignity, but to proceed against him regardless of his position, and impeach the Earl of Strafford of high-treason. Pym sat down amid loud applause, and the impeachment was immediately voted in secret session. The doorkeeper of the Commons, James Maxwell, was sent to the House of Lords, which Strafford had just entered, to summon him to the House of Commons. He appeared there with his wonted haughtiness, and would have seated himself, but loud shouts arose, ordering him to wait at the door until he should be called. After a short consultation, he was summoned to the bar; he was ordered to fall on his knees and listen to the resolution passed against him. He was thereupon delivered into the hands of the doorkeeper of the House, who was instructed to keep him in custody until he had purged himself of all the charges preferred against him. The proud earl once more gathered his whole energy and attempted to address the assembly, but his voice was drowned by the general clamor, and he was ordered to withdraw in silence. At the door, Maxwell took his sword from him, and conducted him through the gaping crowd to his carriage. No one greeted him; no one took off his hat before the all-powerful man, to whom the wealthiest and proudest lords had bowed that very morning. The people received him in silence; yet few ventured to deride him, for even after his downfall he maintained so dignified a bearing that the populace could not refuse him respect. On arriving at the place where he had left his carriage, it could not be immediately found. He had therefore to retrace his steps through the same curious crowd. It was not until some time afterward that the carriage arrived and conveyed him to his prison. Laud also was immediately, upon the same general charges, sequestered from Parliament, and committed to custody.

The king, who in the former part of his reign had offered the most obstinate resistance to the as yet moderate encroachments of the Commons, seemed as if struck by lightning, and completely paralyzed by these events. He looked on quietly while his foremost advisers and best friends were arrested, and made no attempt to deliver them. Perhaps he hoped to regain the confidence of his people by pliableness, by concessions, and by a total conformity to their wishes and inclinations; perhaps he was all at once overcome by the

STAFFORD TOOK THE FLOOR.

p. 177.

feeling of his impotence in the face of public opinion. Perhaps he thought too he would in due time retrace his steps and recover all he had lost. For the time being, however, he kept perfectly quiet, resented none of the attacks made upon him, and did not interfere with the proceedings instituted against Strafford.

To bestow the greater solemnity on this important trial, platforms covered with red cloth were erected in Westminster Hall, where both houses sat, the one as accusers, the other as judges. Besides the chair of state, a close gallery was prepared for the king and queen, where they could witness the proceedings unseen. An accusation carried on by the united effort of three kingdoms against one man, unprotected by power, discountenanced by authority, was likely to prove a very unequal contest; yet such were the capacity, genius, and presence of mind displayed by this eminent statesman, that, so long as argument, reason, and law, had any place, he obtained an undisputed victory. And he perished at last, overwhelmed, but still unsubdued, and his death cannot but make us forget the faults and errors of his life.

On the 21st of May the prisoner was conveyed under a strong escort from the Tower to Westminster Hall. Besides the Parliament, there were present the king, the queen, and the whole court; the most distinguished ladies, and, above all, the Countess of Carlisle, took the liveliest interest in the trial, and sympathized almost without exception with the prisoner. Strafford wore a simple but costly velvet dress. He firmly glanced over the brilliant assembly, and many a beautiful eye met his own with heart-felt sympathy. After the articles of impeachment had been read, Strafford took the floor. Never did an arraigned prisoner reply with greater majesty than did Strafford in his last defence before his accusers and his king. Athens and Rome present no incident of more tragic sublimity in their united annals.

"Unable to find in my conduct," said Strafford, in the course of his admirable defence, "any thing to which might be applied the name or punishment of treason, my enemies have invented, in defiance of all law, a chain of constructive and accumulative evidence, by which my actions, although innocent and laudable when taken separately, viewed in this collected light, become treasonable. It is hard to be questioned on a law which cannot be shown.

"Where hath this fire lain hid so many hundreds of years without smoke to discover it till it thus bursts forth to consume me and my children? It is better to be without laws altogether than to persuade ourselves that we have laws by which to regulate our conduct, and to find that they consist only in the enmity and arbitrary will of our accusers. If a man sails upon the Thames in a boat, and splits himself upon an anchor, and no buoy be floating to discover it, he who owneth the anchor shall make satisfaction; but if a buoy be set there, every one passeth it at his own peril. Now where is the mark, where the tokens upon this crime, to declare it to be high-treason? It has remained hidden under the water; no human prudence or innocence could preserve me from the ruin with which it menaces me. For two hundred and forty years every species of treason has been defined, and during that long space of time, I am the first, I am the only exception, for whom the definition has been enlarged, that I may be enveloped in its meshes. My lords, we have lived happily within the limits of our own land; we have lived gloriously beyond them, in the eyes of the whole world. Let us be satisfied with what our fathers have left us; let not ambition tempt us to desire that we may become more acquainted than they were with these destructive and perfidious arts of incriminating innocence. In this manner, my lords, you will act wisely, you will provide for your own safety and the safety of your descendants, while you secure that of the whole kingdom. If you throw into the fire these sanguinary and mysterious selections of constructive treason, as the first Christians consumed their books of dangerous art, and confine yourselves to the simple meaning of the statute in its vigor, who shall say that you have done wrong? Where will be your crime, and how, in abstaining from error, can you incur punishment? Beware of awakening these sleeping lions of your own destruction. Add not to my other afflictions that which I shall esteem the heaviest of all—that for my sins as a man, and not for my offences as a minister, I should be the unfortunate means of introducing such a precedent, such an example of a proceeding so opposed to the laws and liberties of my country.

"My lords, I have troubled you longer than I should have done were it not for the interest of these dear pledges a saint in heaven hath left me." Here he stopped, letting fall some tears, and then resumed: "What I forfeit myself is nothing; but that my indiscretion should extend to my posterity, woundeth me to the very soul. You will pardon my infirmity. Something I should have added, but am not able; therefore let it pass. And now, my lords, for myself, I have been, by the blessing of Almighty God, taught that the afflictions of this present life are not to be compared to the eternal weight of glory which shall be revealed hereafter. And so, my lords, even so, with all tranquillity of mind, I freely submit myself to your judgment; and whether that judgment be for life or death, 'Te Deum laudamus.'"

So powerful was the impression of this speech that the judges, filled with compassion, wavered, and Strafford's enemies feared lest he should be acquitted. He had refuted every charge preferred against him, and his conviction seemed impossible. If he had been acquitted, his adversaries would have been pursued with relentless vindictiveness by the inexorable and indefatigable minister. It was a mortal combat. The lion had shown his former strength; his voice had resounded as of old, and its tremendous notes had struck terror into the hearts of the leaders of the opposition. The king himself, seated in his grated gallery, had followed the proceedings with the closest attention and suspense. Now he rejoiced at the triumph of the earl, whose acquittal seemed no longer doubtful. At this moment rose the gloomy St. John, who conducted the prosecution. A sinister smile played round his lips. After expatiating on the nature of political trials, and arguing that the judgment should rest on the moral conviction of the judges rather than the strength of the proofs, he drew forth a paper which he read in a loud voice. It contained the advice which Strafford had given to the king a short time ago, and of which Sir Henry Vane, secretary, had taken notes. A few days ago he had sent the keys of his cabinet to his son, Sir Henry, in order to search for some papers which were necessary for completing a marriage settlement. Young Vane, falling upon this paper of notes, deemed the matter of the utmost importance, and immediately communicated it to Pym and St. John, who now read the paper to the assembly. "The question before the council was, 'offensive or defensive war with the Scots.' The king proposes this difficulty: 'But how can I undertake offensive war, if I have no more money?' The Earl of Strafford then made the following proposition: 'Borrow of the city a hundred thousand; go on vigorously to levy ship-money. Your majesty having tried the affections of your people, you are absolved and loosed from all rules of government, and may do what power will admit. Your majesty, having tried all ways, shall be acquitted before God and man. And you have an army in Ireland, which you may employ to reduce *this* kingdom to obedience; for I am confident the Scots cannot hold out five months.'"

During the reading of this decisive document, a stifled cry burst from the royal gallery. Charles had bent forward and clutched the wooden trellis, concealing him from the eyes of the assembly, so violently with both hands, that it broke in pieces. He himself now remained exposed to the eyes of all. The courageous Strafford turned pale, but he soon regained his former composure, and, with great ingenuity, called the attention of his judges to the vagueness of the words, which might be understood of the Scottish rebels rather than the people of England; and, besides, he denied ever having made the proposition imputed to him. Nevertheless, the evidence of Secretary Vane caused the judges to convict the prisoner.

They found the Earl of Strafford guilty of high-treason, and passed sentence of death upon him.

CHAPTER XIII.

THE QUEEN'S CONSPIRACY—EXECUTION OF STRAFFORD.

The king left Westminster Hall, profoundly moved, and firmly resolved to strain every nerve in order to save his minister. He immediately summoned his privy council to take the necessary steps into consideration. Contrary to his expectation, with the exception of the venerable Bishop Juxon, no one spoke in favor of the condemned earl. All pointed more or less emphatically to the necessity of sacrificing the prisoner to public opinion. Yet the king would not allow himself to be convinced, and was still in hopes of being able to save Strafford's life.

The people of London received the sentence passed upon Strafford with bloodthirsty exultation, and demanded the execution of the prisoner with the utmost impetuosity. The populace flocked about Whitehall, and accompanied their demand for justice with the loudest clamors and most open menaces in order to force the king's assent to the sentence. Sinister rumors were circulated, and the popular passions were lashed into a ferment which threatened some great and imminent convulsion. On whichever side the king cast his eyes, he saw no resource or security. All his servants, consulting their own safety rather than their master's honor, declined to interpose with their advice between him and his Parliament. Strafford himself, hearing of Charles's irresolution and anxiety, took a very extraordinary step; he wrote a letter, in which he entreated the king, for the sake of public peace and his own safety, to put an end to his unfortunate life, and to quiet the tumultuous people by granting them the request for which they were so importunate. "In this," he added, "my consent will more acquit you to God than all the world can do besides. To a willing man there is no injury. And as, by God's grace, I forgive all the world, with a calmness and meekness of infinite contentment to my dislodging soul, so, sire, to you I can resign the life of this world with all imaginable cheerfulness, in the just acknowledgment of your exceeding favors."

Perhaps Strafford hoped that this unusual instance of generosity would engage the king still more strenuously to protect him; perhaps he gave up his life for lost, and this conviction armed him with that courage and constancy which thenceforth never left him. The king, who had repeatedly assured him that he would protect him, was a prey to the most violent anxiety and doubt, and he was not courageous enough either to defend or desert his minister. He sat, brooding over his misfortunes, in his cabinet at Whitehall, when the queen came in and very gently encircled him with her arms.

"What ails you?" said Henrietta to her mournful husband.

"I am required to sacrifice my best friend, my most faithful servant, to the fury of the populace. Henrietta, do you comprehend the grief with which this idea fills me?"

"Charles, it must be done. Think of me, of your children."

"You advise me to break my royal word. Who will henceforth repose confidence in me? I shall stand, a dishonored sovereign, before myself, before my servants, before the whole country. No, no; never, never will I do it!"

"It is better that one man should perish than all of us. He is your servant, and his life belongs to you. Strafford himself has offered his head to you."

"But I am not at liberty to accept his offer. The whole world would despise me if I should sign the death-warrant of my best and dearest friend."

"The signature would not be so important, inasmuch as the execution of the sentence might be deferred. Yield to the will of Parliament, and submit seemingly to the importunate demands of the populace. Leave it to me to devise a plan for saving the earl. Charles, my lord, my beloved! submit to stern necessity, and preserve the menaced throne to yourself and your children. What we lose to-day, we may regain to-morrow. There will be better times, when you will recover your authority and your royal power. You know the fickleness of the people; although they are now rebelling against you, they may in a few weeks prostrate themselves at your feet. Prudent concessions accomplish frequently a great deal more than obstinate stubbornness. It was not Achilles, with his savage strength, but the wily Ulysses with his ingenuity, that vanquished the Trojans. Imitate the example set by Ulysses, who, after sustaining many misfortunes, triumphed over his enemies, and killed the impudent suitors."

The lovely queen in this manner overwhelmed him with supplications and blandishments, and when they proved insufficient, resorted to tears, until Charles was weak enough to yield to her importunities. He signed the death-warrant in her presence. No sooner had he taken the fatal step, than he buried his face in his hands as if to conceal his shame and repentance even from his consort. Her smile encouraged him again.

"Rely on me," she said, comforting him. "Strafford shall not suffer death, for all that."

"What are you going to do to avert the doom from his head?"

"That is my secret for the time being. It is better for you not to know anything about it, as I know your timidity. I will tell you only that I have friends who will not hesitate a moment to sacrifice their lives for me."

"You are more fortunate, then, than I," said the unhappy monarch.

No sooner had Henrietta left her husband, than she called her devoted lady of honor, Madame de Motteville, a Frenchwoman, who had accompanied her to England, and in whom she could repose implicit confidence.

"Motteville," she said, "take this note, and deliver it secretly to Sir Thomas Egerton. I shall await him toward dusk. You will conduct him to my cabinet by the private staircase."

The wily Frenchwoman, who suspected, perhaps, an illicit *liaison*, looked inquiringly at her mistress.

"Go!" said the queen, impatiently; "lose no time, and be as silent as the grave."

The elegant, musk-scented note of the queen, which contained an invitation to a *tête-à-tête* at an unusual time, filled the passionate youth with no little excitement. Hopes and fears agitated his heart, and, a prey to the most intense impatience, he counted the slowly-passing hours of the day until the moment came which promised him so much happiness. He cautiously approached the indicated door, which, according to his agreement with Madame de Motteville, opened to him after he had softly knocked at it three times. Madame de Motteville received him at the door, and conducted him to the private cabinet of the queen. Henrietta was languidly reclining on a crimson divan. A lamp filled with perfumed oil shed a magic lustre upon her lovely and interesting face. She held out, with a winning smile to the dazzled youth, her delicate hand, which Thomas, kneeling before her, pressed to his burning lips.

"Sir Thomas," said the queen, "I sent for you in order to ask you to render me an important service."

"Ask my life, and I will give it up for you with the utmost willingness!" exclaimed Thomas, in an ecstasy of delight.

"I was not mistaken in counting upon you. Be seated, and listen calmly to me; but we must have no witnesses."

The queen made a sign to Madame de Motteville, who locked the door carefully, lowered the crimson curtains, and left the room. Nevertheless, we cannot doubt that Madame de Motteville overheard the following conversation by applying her ear to the thin partition, and glancing from time to time through the key-hole. She was, however, disappointed in her expectations, as neither the queen nor her adorer overstepped in any manner the bounds of propriety, or of the tone prevailing in court circles. Keeping at a respectful distance, Thomas contented himself with silently admiring the charms of his august mistress. After a short pause the queen said to him:

"I have need of a resolute and discreet man who shrinks from no danger whatever; such a one I believe I have found in you. I have conceived a plan, destined to save not only the Earl of Strafford, but also the threatened throne. He who takes its execution upon himself may imperil his head in case the plan should miscarry."

"I should lay it unmurmuringly on the block for my queen. Command me; what am I to do?"

"You must set out for the camp this very night, and try to gain over the army to our side. I know that you are intimately acquainted with most of the officers; besides, you will meet there several friends of mine. O'Neale, Pollard, Ashburnham, are devoted to me and to the king. Jermyn, Percy, Wilmot, and Goring shall assist you. In the first place, try to win over the commanders, and, next, the soldiers; I shall furnish you with the necessary funds for this purpose."

"And what is to be done in case my mission should succeed?"

"The first object to be attained is to intimidate the Parliament. For this purpose, have a strong petition to the king and Parliament drawn up, and get it subscribed by the army. This petition must be written very carefully. The petitioners must represent the great and unexampled concessions made by the king for the security of public peace and liberty; the endless demands of certain insatiable and turbulent spirits, whom nothing less will content than a total subversion of the ancient constitution; the frequent tumults which these factious malcontents have excited, and which endanger the liberty of Parliament. To prevent these mischiefs, let the army offer to come up and guard that assembly."

"But would it not be better for us to lead the army at once to London, and disperse the Parliament by its aid?"

"Certainly it would, but I am afraid of the lukewarmness of many officers, and of the soldiers who are still imbued with attachment to the constitution; besides, the people would immediately take up arms and resist such high-handed measures. For the present, we must try to retain the semblance of law, and fight Parliament with its own weapons. As it is menacing and intimidating the government by means of petitions and seditious tumults, so we will now pursue the same course toward it. If the House of Commons sees the army siding with us, it will become more pliable, and comply with our wishes. We may then demand of it Strafford's release, and still other concessions. You see, therefore, how much depends on a rapid and careful execution of this plan."

"I will set out this very hour."

"Count upon my unbounded gratitude. Deliver these letters to Jermyn and Percy; they are to be your credentials. Tell them, however, to burn them immediately in your presence."

Thomas took the letters from the queen's hands, although he would have much preferred to bear the dangers and reap the honor of the enterprise all alone. At the same time Henrietta handed him a large sum of money, which she had realized by the sale of some of her jewels. She took the most gracious farewell of the youth, who left her cabinet fully determined, if need be, to sacrifice his life for his adored mistress. He ordered Billy Green in hot haste to saddle his horse, and, attended by his shrewd footman, set out immediately for the camp. On his arrival there, he fulfilled without delay the commission intrusted to him. Most of the officers assured him that they would energetically second her majesty's plan, and by means of the money which he had brought with him, and scattered with lavish hands, he hoped to gain over a majority of the soldiers, who were displeased at some marks of preference given by the Commons to the Scots.

The insidious Jermyn feigned the greatest devotion towards Thomas, and seemed to have entirely forgotten the quarrel which he had had with him some time before. The officers met at his tent, and bound themselves by a solemn oath to keep the utmost secrecy, and second the queen's plan to the best of their ability. A banquet of the reckless cavaliers closed the consultation. They drank a great deal of wine, and, in their defiant mood, quaffed many a cup in honor of the queen, coupling with the toast the most imprudent threats against Parliament. Billy Green, who was standing behind his master's chair, carefully treasured up every word he heard. On the following morning Thomas hastened back to London, to inform the queen of the results of his mission. Jermyn had promised him to get the petition subscribed immediately, and to deliver it himself, at the head of all the officers, to the Parliament. However, no sooner had Thomas, relying on this promise, left the camp, than the insidious courtier summoned his friends, Wilmot, O'Neale, Pollard, and Goring to his tent. He told them he did not disapprove at all of the plan of her majesty the queen, but was utterly dissatisfied with the choice of the confidant of whose services she had availed herself on this occasion.

"I believe," he said, "there are other men who might conduct such an enterprise far better than a beardless stripling, who has passed only a few months at court. We must not suffer such a spirit of favoritism. Moreover, his imprudence may involve us in fearful dangers. If Parliament should hear of the conspiracy, we should be hopelessly lost."

"What are we to do?" asked Goring, who began to tremble for his head. "Already too many men know of the secret. Therefore, it will be best for us to take the matter into our own hands, and drop Egerton entirely. We will draw up the petition, and, instead of subscribing it, submit it to the king to sign it. When his name heads those of the other signers, we have nothing to fear. Under his sanction, we may present the petition with perfect impunity to the House of Commons."

This proposition met with unanimous applause. The same cavaliers who, a few months afterward, fought with the greatest valor and intrepidity for the king, and in courage yielded to none of their adversaries, were now filled with cowardly fear of the authority of Parliament, and cautiously retired behind the ægis of the royal name. However, their prudence was in vain. Billy Green had lived at court, and became acquainted with the demoralization, perfidy, and venality reigning there. The result of Strafford's trial had greatly shaken his confidence in the power of the king, and shown him both the authority of Parliament and the sentiments of the people. He possessed a certain political instinct, and under different circumstances he might have become a successful politician. He was satisfied that he could no longer derive much benefit from his connection with the royal cause; and although at bottom he was filled with aversion to the ruling party, owing to its Puritanic austerity, he felt attracted toward it, like all mean men who follow the tide and join the victorious side. He knew, besides, that a rogue and hypocrite might do just as he pleased under the mask of virtue, and that at bottom even the sternest Puritans were men, secretly drank their wine, and kissed their sweethearts. These ideas had long filled the mind of the shrewd vagabond, and he only waited for an opportunity to leave his master and turn his political and religious coat. His sympathies for his young master had never been strong enough to induce him to sacrifice for them his self-interest, and the prospect of obtaining a large reward.

Such thoughts engrossed the attention of Billy Green during the journey from the camp to London. He had accidentally discovered a secret which he resolved to turn to account, and sell as dearly as possible to the enemies of the government. This was the time of mutual espionage and treachery; both the court and Parliament availed themselves of the lowest tools to watch each other. The conscience of parties is never very scrupulous in the choice of means, provided they are calculated to lead to the desired ends. Billy Green counted already in anticipation the gold-pieces which he hoped to receive for his treachery.

No sooner had he reached London, than he went to Pym, the well-known leader of the opposition.

"What will you give me," asked the impudent fellow, "if I betray to you a secret on which the safety of Parliament depends?"

Pym fixed his cold, piercing eyes on the vagabond.

"You do not look like one to whom anybody would intrust an important secret; but let me hear what you know."

"Not before I have secured my reward."

"If your information is really important, you will be liberally rewarded."

"All right, sir. Let me tell you, then, that my master and the most distinguished officers have agreed to disperse Parliament by the aid of the army, under the pretext of protecting the Commons."

"Have you any proofs?"

"I knew you would not trust my word, and took my steps accordingly. Read these letters which the queen herself has written."

"And how did you obtain them?"

"In a very simple manner. I was instructed to throw them into the fire, but preferred to keep them."

"You were right in so doing, and are entitled to a liberal reward. Take this purse on account. Parliament will take care of you. For the present you may return to your master, and when you have additional news of importance for me, you know where to find me."

Billy Green withdrew, overjoyed and well satisfied with the reward, and with the prospect of a lucrative position which Pym had held out to him. On the way back to his master's rooms, however, he felt some remorse, and resolved to caution Thomas.

"Every one," argued Billy to himself, "is in duty bound to take care of himself. It is not until he is through with his own affairs that he can think of others. My master, who, on the whole, has treated me tolerably well, shall see that I am grateful. I fulfil my duty to myself and to my fellow-men. At bottom Sir Thomas must thank me for preventing him from committing such an act of extreme folly. A change of air will do him good, and the sooner he gets away from here the better for him. I will write him a letter, and tell him that it will be best for him to leave London."

So saying, Billy Green went to the next tavern, where he refreshed himself with a glass of wine; he then requested one of the waiters to convey to Sir Thomas Egerton a letter which he had written to him in a disguised hand, and in which he informed him that every thing was betrayed, and that he could save his life only by speedy flight.

On the same day Pym opened the matter in the House. The disclosure concerning the conspiracy of the officers was received with general indignation, and the House resolved at once that the guilty parties should be prosecuted with inexorable rigor. Constables were sent out to take them into custody. Thomas had received Billy Green's letter and made his escape in time. He took the road to Wales, where his sister Alice was living with her husband. He hoped his place of concealment there would not be discovered. Percy succeeded likewise in finding a safe hiding-place, and Jermyn deemed it prudent to go to France and wait there for the storm to blow over. Goring, however, was arrested and examined by a committee of the House of Commons. A prey to the most abject terror, he made a full confession, and betrayed his friends as well as the queen, whose complicity, moreover, was clearly established by the autograph letters delivered to Pym.

The failure of this project damaged the royal cause far more than its success would have benefited it. The charges heretofore preferred against Charles and his consort were reiterated with redoubled vehemence. But the immediate consequence was, that the unfortunate Strafford's execution became inevitable. The people demanded his head with the utmost impetuosity, and all the pulpits resounded with violent denunciations of his adherents. Execrated by the populace, urged by the entreaties of his advisers and the tears of the queen to raise no further obstacles to the execution of the prisoner, Charles nevertheless made a last effort in Strafford's behalf. He sent by the hands of his little son, the Prince of Wales, a letter addressed to the peers, in which he requested them to confer with the Commons about a mitigation of Strafford's sentence, and begged at least for some delay. But all remained deaf to the voice of the father and the intercession of the child.

Strafford was prepared for every extremity after being abandoned by those whom he had most loved and served on earth. Nevertheless, when it was announced to him that the king had signed the death-warrant, nature triumphed over resignation, and a reproach escaped him in his grief. "*Nolite fidere principibus et filiis hominum*," he cried, raising his hands in astonishment toward the vaulted ceiling of his prison, "*quia non est salus in illis.*" "Put not your trust in princes, nor in the sons of men, for in them there is no help."

He requested to be allowed a short interview with Archbishop Laud, imprisoned in the Tower on a similar charge with himself. This interview, in which the two royalists hoped to fortify each other for life or death, was refused. "Well," said Strafford to the governor of the Tower, "at least tell the archbishop to place himself to-morrow at his window at the hour when I pass to the scaffold, that I may bid him a last farewell."

The next day it was pressed upon Strafford to ask for a carriage to convey him to the place of execution, for fear the fury of the people should anticipate the executioner, and tear from his hands the victim denounced by Pym and the orators of the House of Commons as the public enemy. "No," replied Strafford; "I know how to look death and the people in the face; whether I die by the hand of the executioner or by the fury of the populace, if it should so please them, matters little to me."

In passing under the archbishop's window in the prison-yard, Strafford recollected his request of the previous night, and raised his eyes toward the iron bars, which prevented him from seeing Laud distinctly. He could only perceive the thin and trembling hands of the old man stretched out between the bars, trying to bless him as he passed on to death.

Strafford knelt in the dust and bent his head. "My lord," he said to the archbishop, "let me have your prayers and benediction."

The heart of the old prelate sank at the sound of his voice and emotion, and he fainted in the arms of his jailers while uttering a parting prayer.

"Farewell, my lord," cried Strafford; "may God protect your innocence!"

He then walked forward with a firm step, although suffering from the effects of illness and debility, at the head of the soldiers, who appeared to follow rather than to escort him.

Strafford's brother accompanied him weeping. "Brother," he said, "why do you grieve thus? Do you see any thing in my life or death which can cause you to feel any shame? Do I tremble like a criminal, or boast like an atheist? Come, be firm, and think only that this is my third marriage, and that you are my bridesman. This block," pointing to that upon which he was about to lay his head, "will be my pillow, and I shall repose there well, without pain, grief, or fear."

Having ascended the scaffold with his brother and friends, he knelt for a moment as if to salute the place of sacrifice; he soon arose, and looking around upon the innumerable and silent multitude which covered the hill and Tower of London, the place of execution, he raised his voice in the same audible and firm tone which he was accustomed to use in the House of Commons, that theatre of his majestic eloquence.

"People," he said, "who are assembled here to see me die, bear witness that I desire for this kingdom all the prosperity that God can bestow. Living, I have done my utmost to secure the happiness of England; dying, it is still my most ardent wish; but I beseech each one of those who now hear me, to lay his hand upon his heart, and examine seriously if the commencement of a salutary reform ought to be written in characters of blood. Ponder this well upon your return home. God grant that not a drop of mine may be required at your hands! I fear, however, that you cannot advance by such a fatal path."

After Strafford had spoken these words of anxious warning to his country, he again knelt, and prayed with all the signs of humble fervor for upward of a quarter of an hour. Then, hearing a low murmur either of pity or impatience in the crowd, he arose, and addressing those who immediately surrounded him, said, "All will soon be over. One blow will render my wife a widow, my children orphans, and deprive my servants of their master. God be with them and you!

"Thanks to the internal strength that God has given me," he added, while removing his upper garment, and tucking up his hair, that nothing might interfere with the stroke of the axe upon his neck, "I take this off with as tranquil a spirit as I have ever felt when taking it off at night upon retiring to rest."

He then made a sign to the executioner to approach, pardoned him for the blood he was about to shed, and laid his head upon the block, looking up, and praying to Heaven. His head rolled at the feet of his friends. "God save the king!" cried the executioner, holding it up to exhibit it to the people.

CHAPTER XIV.

MILTON'S MARRIAGE—RUPTURE BETWEEN THE KING AND PARLIAMENT.

During these tragic scenes Milton had returned from Italy. His sojourn in foreign lands, his intercourse with the most distinguished and illustrious men, had ripened his understanding; the youth had become a man. The time of idle reveries and poetical enthusiasm was past for him; he longed for a serious and useful field of action, a permanent and well-regulated occupation. In the first place, he resolved to carry into effect the plan he had conceived long since, and become a teacher of youth. The profession of a teacher was at that time neither very honorable nor lucrative; yet Milton did not hesitate a moment to devote himself to the service of mankind. He moved into an humble house in the neighborhood of St. Bride's churchyard, and instructed there his two nephews, John and Edward Phillips, the sons of his sister, as well as several boys who were confided to him. He devoted himself to his task with the most disinterested zeal, and followed out his own system, the result of mature reflection. In his opinion, a complete course of education should enable the pupils to discharge all the duties of public and domestic life, of war and peace, in a skilful, able, and thorough manner. He afterward expressed the principles guiding him in this respect, in a passage of "Paradise Lost," as follows:

> "But apt the mind or fancy is to rove
> Unchecked, and of her roving is no end:
> Till warned, or by experience taught, she learn,
> That not to know at large of things remote
> From use, obscure and subtle, but to know
> That which before us lies in daily life,
> Is the prime wisdom: what is more, is fume."

It was in this manner that he developed the minds of his pupils by strengthening their morality, arousing their latent energy, and familiarizing them with the duties and tasks of practical life, without neglecting their scientific studies. Notwithstanding the scrupulous conscientiousness with which Milton discharged his duties as a teacher, he found leisure to take part in the great events of the times, and in the discussion of the questions agitating the public mind. He did not possess that objective calmness, or rather indifference, which would have led him to be an idle looker-on of the struggle, keeping aloof from the contests of parties, and secluding himself anxiously from the world. The time for writing poetry was past for him at present, and life imposed graver duties on him. Well prepared by thorough theological and political studies, he felt called upon to break his silence and espouse the cause of liberty in the most energetic manner. Since Strafford's death and Laud's arrest, Parliament had devoted a great deal of attention to the affairs of the Episcopal Church. The bishops were chiefly to blame for the oppressive measures adopted against the dissenters. Milton attacked their pretensions in a short treatise, which exposed the disastrous consequences of their system, and urgently demanded a thorough reform in matters of faith. Written in an enthusiastic and dignified style, his treatise created the greatest sensation both among friends and foes. The author was admired, applauded, and attacked. Several replies were published, and Milton noticed them in a becoming manner. Before long the poet was also famous as a political essayist. The most distinguished members of Parliament, and especially the younger Vane, visited him in his retirement and became his friends. He was requested to come to the Rota, that political club which was the model of all subsequent societies of the same description. On appearing there, he saw himself surrounded by numbers of young and old men who ardently longed to enter into relations of intimate friendship with him. Especially was he soon on terms of great cordiality with the brave and liberal Overton, whom we have met already in Haywood Forest, where he attended the secret service of the Puritans, and chastised with his sword the arrogant Thomas Egerton. He felt attracted to Milton, and the stern, austere republican became the life-long friend of the poet.

Milton, however, did not suffer himself to be unduly involved in the whirlpool of politics, but maintained even here a certain independence. The party whose cause he espoused was neither that of Parliament nor that of the extreme republicans and religious fanatics, but that of liberty, common-sense, and justice. Amidst these manifold labors and occupations he was one day surprised by his father, who visited him at his house. After their first greetings were over, the venerable old man, who was filled with tender solicitude for the welfare of his son, spoke of a subject to which he had already frequently alluded in his letters to Milton.

"I think," said his father, after a few introductory remarks, "it is time for you to marry. You can no longer remain a bachelor. If you have not yet made a choice, I should like to point out to you a young girl who lives in my neighborhood, and would certainly be a good partner for you."

"I cannot make up my mind so easily," replied the poet, who thought of Leonora Baroni at this moment.

"And yet I am very anxious that you should marry and settle before your old father dies. You have already reached an age when 'it is not good for man to be alone.' The enthusiastic dreams of youth are behind you, and your judgment must have told you that wedded life only is the source of true happiness. Follow my advice, and hesitate no longer to gladden your old father's heart by complying with his wishes. I shall not leave London until you consent to accompany me, and, at least, make the acquaintance of the girl whom I have selected for you. If you do not like her, you will, at least, have complied with my wishes, and may follow your own inclinations."

Milton yielded to his father's entreaties, and accompanied him to his country-seat in order to see his young intended. Close to his father's house there lived a wealthy country gentleman, Richard Powell, whose daughter Mary, a blooming girl of nineteen, made a very favorable impression upon the poet. She was of slender form, and her rosy face, surrounded with a mass of blond ringlets, combined many a sweet charm with youthful freshness. She was not destitute of accomplishments, and seemed to possess a serene and pleasant temper. In her eyes, too, the delicate and intellectual beauty of the poet's face found favor, the more readily as she longed to marry as soon as possible, and exchange her rural surroundings for the noisy and brilliant life of the capital. Like a true daughter of Eve, she was exceedingly fond of fine attire, diversions, and amusements, all of which she hoped to obtain by her marriage to a gentleman from the city. Her wit and good-humor caused Milton to overlook many a fault of her education, and her voluptuous gracefulness prevented him from perceiving that she lacked depth of the heart and mind.

A kind of resignation which had seized his soul facilitated the conclusion of this union. His female ideals had escaped him, partly by his own fault, partly by that of others. Alice

Egerton had become Carbury's wife, and lived with him in Wales; since his return to England he had not had any news from her. She was lost to him, and, as he was obliged to admit to himself, owing to his foolish self-abnegation. In Leonora Baroni he had met with a truly artistic nature, but as a woman she had been unable to satisfy the longings of his ardent heart. He was downcast now, and had obtained the conviction that weakness was the inheritance of woman, and that no woman was entirely faultless.

The cheerful life which the inmates of Forest Hill were leading, and the cordial reception with which he met at their hands, prevented these thoughts from fully maturing in his mind. A gay spirit reigned at Richard Powell's house. The tables were loaded down with good cheer, and there was no lack of wine and old ale. The hospitality of the house was well known all over the county, and there were not wanting to it guests old and young, who gave zest to the repast by their jests and witticisms. Red-nosed squires from the vicinity, with their sons, and broken-down cavaliers, who liked to feast at the expense of other people, flocked to the house in large numbers. In the spacious hall the merry company was seated round the large fireplace, in which a whole forest seemed to burn. Apples were roasted at the fire and thrown hissing into the foaming beer. Amid loud laughter, the young folks amused themselves with the game of forfeits, during which many a kiss was half snatched from rosy lips, half given by them, while the old folks, seated in their large easy-chairs, were conversing about days long gone by, and telling stories of the past.

Here was still to be met merry old England, full of exuberant mirth and good-natured humor; the noise and quarrels of parties had not yet penetrated into this hospitable house. All drank the health of the king, and paid little or no attention to politics. The merry, harmless life at Powell's house afforded a pleasant diversion to the poet, and after the bustle and excitement reigning at the capital the tranquillity of the country-seat made a most agreeable impression upon him. Originally he intended to stay only a few days at Forest Hill; but he passed several weeks in the company of fair Mary, who received his proposals most favorably, and, after the lapse of a month, accompanied him as his wife to London. There, however, she was grievously disappointed; instead of the brilliant life to which she had looked forward so longingly, she saw herself confined to the house of a young scholar, and to the intercourse with him and his few friends and pupils.

Immediately after his marriage, Milton resumed his former studies and occupations, leaving the management of the household affairs to his young wife. Mary, however, did not like this at all; neither wedded life nor her position in London was in accordance with the expectations she had entertained in regard to them. She had dreamed of festivals, dances, amusements, and parties, but the capital was utterly averse to such pleasures. The playhouses were empty or closed; flutes and violins were silent; the most popular amusements had gone out of fashion. Neither bear-baiting nor cock-fights attracted any spectators, and the circus and arena were lonely and deserted. On the other hand, the churches were filled with vast crowds, listening attentively to the popular pulpit orators. The more vehemently they inveighed against the former amusements of the people, the more eagerly they were listened to. Men and women laid aside their silken garments, and all their ornaments and trinkets, and dressed in plain black or brown. In obedience to their enthusiastic convictions, or to hypocrisy—as the power of the Puritans was constantly on the increase—they put on very sanctimonious airs, and renounced all the joys of the world. Public banquets and balls were abominations in the eyes of the pious, and even a harmless jest was considered a grievous sin. The streets of London mostly exhibited a gloomy aspect, and the daily tumults and alarms filled the mind with terror and anxiety. The leaders of the opposition, for reasons easy to divine, favored these disorders; they constantly feigned fears of the treacherous schemes of their adversaries, whom they charged with all sorts of well-grounded or utterly fictitious projects to disperse Parliament and subvert the constitution.

Billy Green had a great deal to do now. The shrewd vagabond was employed as a hired spy and informer, and made daily reports to his patron Pym. To inspire more confidence, he had assumed the bearing and garb of a devout Puritan. He had his hair cropped, wore a pointed hat, exchanged his embroidered doublet for a brown woollen coat, and his white collar was of exaggerated breadth. Hanging his head, with eyes downcast and hands clasped in prayer, he was always prowling in the neighborhood of Parliament, so as to be always on hand when he was needed. He was highly successful in imitating his patterns; he assumed a most sanctimonious air, and took care to interlard his conversation with pious phrases and Biblical quotations. In this new guise he appeared every day with fresh information, partly true, partly false, for which he received a round price. Whenever matter was lacking, he did not shrink from inventing stories, in which his lively imagination rendered him valuable service. He had formed a regular society of fellows like himself, in order, if need be, to have with him witnesses who might confirm his statements, and who had acquired great fluency in perjuring themselves.

By the aid of a boon companion, a broken-down tailor, named Beale, Billy Green had discovered another conspiracy, the plot of the officers having proved so lucrative for him. The two honorable men informed the Commons that, walking in the fields, they had hearkened to the discourse of certain persons unknown to them. A hundred and eight ruffians, they learned, had been appointed to murder a hundred and eight lords and commoners, and were promised rewards for these assassinations at the rate of ten pounds for each lord, and forty shillings for each commoner. Billy and his friend did not hesitate to swear to their statements. New arrests, mostly of innocent persons, were the natural consequence of such false information, which, in a time of general excitement, was only too readily credited.

At last Charles seemed to awake from his apathy. Frightened by the progress which Parliament made every day, tired of the concessions he had already made, and irritated at the resistance with which he met nevertheless, he suffered himself to be led on to a high-handed step which added fresh fuel to the flames of the revolution, and involved him in the most disastrous consequences. He resolved to seize the leaders of the opposition at a blow. For this purpose, he sent Herbert, the attorney-general, to the House of Lords to enter an accusation of high-treason against Lord Kimbolton and five commoners, Hollis, Sir Arthur Hazlerig, Hampden, Pym, and Strode. The articles were to the effect that they had traitorously endeavored to subvert the fundamental laws and government of the kingdom, to deprive the king of his regal power, and to impose on his subjects an arbitrary and tyrannical authority; that they had invited and encouraged the Scots to invade England, and had actually raised and countenanced tumults against the king and Parliament. Great was the astonishment and indignation of the assembly, whose liberty and existence were threatened by this step; but the members had not leisure to wonder at the indiscretion of the king. A sergeant-at-arms followed the attorney-general, and, in the king's name, demanded of the House the five members; he was sent back without any positive answer. The king employed messengers to search for them and arrest them. Their trunks, chambers, and studies were sealed and locked. The House voted all these acts of violence to be breaches of privilege, and commanded every one to defend the liberty of the members. The king, irritated by all this opposition, resolved to come in person to the House, with the intention of demanding, perhaps of seizing in their presence, the persons whom he had accused.

This revolution was betrayed before it was carried into execution, and intelligence was privately sent to the five members. The Countess of Carlisle, Strafford's former mistress, since the death of the earl, whose ruin she not unjustly attributed to the king's weakness, had entered into a secret understanding with the leaders of the opposition. The beautiful countess was a lady of spirit, wit, and intrigue. So long as Strafford was the foremost statesman in England, she was faithfully attached to him, and her ambition felt flattered by his love and homage. After his death she cast out her nets for Pym, the most influential leader of the opposition. Like Dame Fortune, she always followed the victor, and turned her back without shame or remorse upon the vanquished. As lady of honor to the queen, she was informed of all the plans of the court, and did not hesitate to warn her new favorites of the danger menacing them.

The king, accompanied by a numerous retinue, and by two hundred soldiers armed with halberts, repaired to the House. He left the latter at the door, and advanced alone through the hall, while all the members rose to receive him. The speaker withdrew from his chair, and the king took possession of it. After having been seated, he made the following speech:

"Gentlemen, I am sorry for this occasion of coming to you. Yesterday I sent a sergeant-at-arms to demand some who, by my order, were accused of high-treason. Instead of obedience, I received a message. I must here declare to you, that though no king that ever was in England could be more careful of your privileges than I shall be, yet in cases of treason no person has privilege. Therefore am I come to tell you, that I must have these men wheresoever I can find them. Well, since I see all the birds are flown, I do expect that you will send them to me as soon as they return. But I assure you, on the word of a king, I never did intend any force, but shall proceed against them in a fair and legal way; for I never meant any other. And now, since I see I cannot do what I came for, I think this no unfit occasion to repeat what I have said formerly, that whatever I have done in favor and to the good of my subjects, I do intend to maintain it."

When the king was looking around for the accused members, he asked the speaker, who stood below, whether any of these persons were in the House. The speaker, falling on his knee, prudently replied: "I have, sire, neither eyes to see nor tongue to speak in this place, but as the House is pleased to direct me, whose servant I am. And I humbly ask pardon that I cannot give any other answer to what your majesty is pleased to demand of me."

The Commons were in the utmost disorder; and when the king was departing, some members cried aloud, "Privilege! privilege!"

That evening the accused members, to show the greater apprehension, removed into the city, which was their fortress. The citizens were in arms the whole night. Some people, who were appointed for that purpose, or perhaps actuated by their own terrors, ran from gate to gate, crying out that the cavaliers were coming to burn the city, and that the king himself was at their head. Billy Green, accompanied by a crowd of armed apprentices and idlers, moved from one quarter of the city to another, and added to the tumult. He met several officers and partisans of the king, and he entered into a violent altercation.

"Down with the cavaliers, with the bloodhounds!" he cried out in a thundering voice.

"Down with the roundheads, with the villanous Puritans!" was the furious reply.

From words they passed to blows; the apprentices brandished their bludgeons mounted with iron; the cavaliers drew their swords, and soon there was a general *mêlée.* But, while the populace and the courtiers were breaking each other's heads, the wily vagabond deemed it prudent to sneak away, and let others fight out the quarrel which he had stirred up.

Next morning Charles resolved to make some concessions, in order to allay the general excitement. He sent to the mayor, and ordered him to call the Common Council immediately. About ten o'clock, he himself, attended only by three or four lords, went to Guildhall. He told the Common Council that he was sorry to hear of the apprehensions entertained of him; that he was come to them without any guard, in order to show how much he relied on their affections; and that he had accused certain men of high-treason, against whom he would proceed in a legal way, and therefore presumed that they would not meet with protection in the city.

After many other gracious expressions, he told one of the two sheriffs, who was thought the least inclined to his service, that he would dine with him. Yet he departed from the hall without receiving the applause which he expected. In passing through the streets, he heard the cry, "Privilege of Parliament!—privilege of Parliament!" resounding from all quarters.

On a corner sat an old man; it was the austere Henderson. When the king drew nigh, the zealous Puritan rose and called out with a loud voice, "To your tents, O Israel!" the words employed by the mutinous Israelites when they abandoned Rehoboam, their rash and ill-counselled sovereign. Charles was frightened by the fanatical fury which Henderson's wild glances flashed at him.

"Who are you?" he said to the Puritan.

"A servant of the Lord," replied the gloomy fanatic, "who has come to warn thee. 'Mene, mene, tekel!'"

The king ordered his coachman to drive faster, in order to escape from the crowd, but Henderson's cry of "Mene, mene, tekel!" pursued him incessantly. He arrived at his palace in utter exhaustion, and sank into gloomy reflections.

Meanwhile Parliament had resolved that the accused members should, with a triumphant and military procession, take their seats in the House. The river was covered with boats and other vessels, laden with small pieces of ordnance, and prepared for fight. Skippon, whom Parliament had appointed major-general of the city militia, conducted the members, at the head of this tumultuary army, to Westminster Hall. The more to intimidate the king, Parliament renewed the expedient of petitioning. Billy Green displayed the most astonishing activity on this occasion, and showed great skill in collecting and forging signatures. At the head of his apprentices, he presented to the House a petition signed by six thousand persons, who promised to live and die in defence of the privileges of Parliament. It is true, many did not know what they had subscribed, and were by no means willing to be taken at their word. The very women were seized with the same rage, owing to Billy's persuasive eloquence. One day he appeared with several thousand women, headed by a corpulent brewer's wife, with whom he was well acquainted. The latter, who, with her little black mustache and bloated face, looked like a man rather than a woman, demanded, in her own name and in that of her sisters, to be admitted to the House in order to present a petition, in which the petitioners expressed their terror of the papists and prelates. They had been necessitated, they said, to imitate the example of the women of Tekoah; and they claimed equal rights with the men, because Christ had purchased them at as dear a rate, and in the free enjoyment of Christ consists equally the happiness of both sexes. Pym came to the door of the House. A sarcastic smile played round his lips when he thanked the brewer's wife for her zeal.

"My fair friends," he said, with a hypocritical air of cordiality, "cook and wash for your husbands, and, if you have any time to spare, pray for the success of the Commons."

The women retired with loud shouts of "Long live Pym! Long live Parliament!"

Under such circumstances Charles's last hope was the House of Lords, a great many of whom were faithfully devoted to him, and opposed the encroachments of the Commons upon the authority of the king. Hence, the leaders of the opposition endeavored to turn public opinion against the Peers and shake their authority. Every act of opposition to the Commons was regarded as a crime. The populace out of doors were ready to execute, from the least hint, the will of their leaders; nor was it safe for any member to approach either House who pretended to control or oppose the general torrent. Both Pym and Hollis declared loudly that the people must not be restrained in the expression of their just desires. Especially was the queen an object of their hatred. The rage of the people was, on account of her religion as well as her spirit and activity, levelled against her. She was vehemently denounced, and, in part not unjustly, charged with being at the bottom of the sore troubles of the kingdom. Under these circumstances she resolved to leave England and escape to Holland. In order to facilitate her escape, she advised the king to make further concessions. However, the more he yielded, the more exorbitant became the demands of the opposition, whose leaders introduced a bill, which was passed, transferring the control of the armed force of the kingdom from the king to Parliament, or rather to its partisans among the officers of the army. Charles refused to sanction this bill, and as his position at the capital became daily more precarious, he resolved to remove farther from London, and went to York, where he issued a public manifesto against the encroachments of Parliament, and prepared likewise for war.

Civil war, then, was declared, and the sword was to decide the great question of the times.

CHAPTER XV.

MILTON AND HIS WIFE—WAR DECLARED.

On a bleak evening in March, Milton's young wife was seated in her humble room. The wild equinoctial storms howled around the house; snow and rain pelted noisily the closed window-shutters, and the wind rushed down into the fireplace and threatened to extinguish its flames. A small lamp was burning on the table, and all around lay books in picturesque disorder. A feeling of profound loneliness stole over the young wife; she had dropped her needlework on her knees, and stared into the glare of the coal-fire. Her eyes filled with tears when she thought of the fine days she had passed at the house of her parents, where merry conversation and pleasant society had never been wanting. Now she had to do without both, much as she longed for them. Her husband passed most of his time in his school-room with his pupils, and even late at night he occupied himself more with his books than his wife. The gulf between these two entirely different characters widened every day. The light-hearted wife was unable to appreciate the lofty aspirations and sublime genius of her husband; she thought he neglected her shamefully, and overwhelmed him with reproaches. Nevertheless, she was passionately fond of her husband, but her affection was entirely egotistical; she was intent on possessing him exclusively, and was jealous even of the books, which, in her opinion, engrossed him by far too much.

After brooding for some time over her supposed grievances, she suddenly sprang to her feet and by her quick movement threw a few folio volumes from the table. Instead of taking them up, she disdainfully pushed them aside with her small foot, and wreaked in this manner a childish revenge upon her supposed enemies.

"You may lie there," she said angrily, kicking the innocent books once more. With a quick step she then hastened to the door leading to her husband's study. She rapped twice without receiving a reply; at last her patience was entirely exhausted, and she rushed into the calm asylum of the poet. He seemed not to notice her, and continued writing until she stood before him, her face flushed with anger, and seized his arm.

"What is the matter?" he asked, irritated at being interrupted in his labors.

"What is the matter?" cried the young wife, greatly excited. "The matter is, that I can no longer bear the life I am compelled to lead here. Do you think I married you for the purpose of pining away? All day long I am confined to my lonely room, and hardly know how to kill my time, while you are buried amidst your books, or repeating Latin words with your school-boys. I cannot stand it any longer."

"Oh, do not get excited," replied Milton, who had calmly listened to her reproaches. "I shall soon finish the work on which I am now engaged, and we will then pass the evening together. My friend Overton will take supper with us."

"I do not care much about his company. A fine companion, indeed, is this melancholy Puritan, whom I have never heard laugh yet. In truth, I would rather be alone than have this mournful fellow about me."

"You would do well to speak in more respectful terms of your husband's friends," said Milton. "Mr. Overton is a gentleman distinguished alike by his mind and character."

"Of course, you prefer his company to that of your wife. You will sit together again, talk of the wretched Parliament, and inveigh against the poor bishops, who are a thousand times better than your Overton, no matter how pious he may feign to be."

"Mary!" said the poet, beseechingly, "do not use such language. You allude to a subject which, owing to your education, you do not understand at all. Let us drop this unpleasant subject, and go to your kitchen in order to prepare our supper."

"Of course, I am always good enough for that. The poor wife is to cook, bake, wash, and sew, and that is all. You treat me as a slave."

"Your reproaches are utterly unjustified, as I treat you on all occasions, as I do to-day, with a forbearance bordering on weakness."

"And I repeat that I am only a slave, a servant-girl, in your house. I must work all day, and at night, when all other husbands are with their wives, making visits or going to parties with them, you pore over your books or talk politics with your friends. You converse eagerly with them, but do not address a word to your poor wife. I am too stupid for you; I am not able to appreciate your learning; I am only a poor ignorant woman, for whom you do not care at all."

So saying, Mary burst into tears and loud sobs. Although this scene was by no means the first of the same description, Milton allowed himself to be touched anew; he pushed his books aside, and tried to pacify his excited wife by his kisses and gentle remonstrances. Mary soon passed from one extreme to the other. The most playful mirth succeeded to the outburst of her despair, and while the tears were yet glistening on her rosy cheeks, her crimson lips smiled already, and her eyes beamed with arch gayety. She was a true daughter of Eve, whimsical as the sky in April, and fickle as the sea. Amid laughter and jests she hastened to the kitchen to prepare their supper.

At the wonted hour appeared the expected guest, whom Mary received more cordially than usual. Milton and Overton were soon engaged in an animated conversation concerning the desperate condition of the country.

"I believe war is inevitable," said Overton. "Parliament is already levying troops and calling out volunteers for the impending struggle. I have likewise enlisted, and received an officer's commission."

"I intend to take the same step," replied Milton.

"You?" asked Overton, wonderingly. "That would be downright folly on your part."

"And why should I not, just as well as you, devote my life to my country, now that it is in danger?"

"Because you can be more useful to it with your head than we with our hands. Every one after his own fashion. The scholar is a soldier too; his weapon is the pen; it is even sharper than the sword, and more pointed than the lance. It requires more courage to declare and defend one's opinion than to rush into the thickest of the fight on the field of battle. The mind has achieved more victories than brute force. Therefore, stay quietly with your books, and leave it to us soldiers to fight out this struggle."

"Then you do not believe in the possibility of a reconciliation between the king and Parliament?"

"If the contest were confined to those two, peace might not be impossible; but the struggle is greater, it is much more important and extensive. It is the old war between liberty and tyranny, between despotism and republicanism, between intolerance and freedom of conscience. No mediation is possible between these two sides. Men no longer oppose men, but truth combats falsehood, liberty oppression, and despotism law and order. Mortal enemies may be reconciled, but immortal principles, eternal contrasts, do not admit of a reconciliation: their war will continue to the day of judgment."

"Yes," exclaimed Milton, enthusiastically, "it is thus that I imagined the struggle of the fallen angels with the host of the Lord, of light with darkness. I see my dreams embodied, and the creations of my imagination realized. It is not Charles and Parliament, but the great and mighty contrasts of the world, that are at war, and light will and must triumph."

The entrance of Mary, who brought in the supper, turned the conversation in another direction, and, for his wife's sake, Milton avoided further allusions to political affairs.

Unfortunately their domestic peace was disturbed again a few days afterward by the arrival of Mary's parents. Richard Powell, Milton's worthy father-in-law, and his wife paid their long-promised visit to London. On his journey he had passed through York and seen the king. His loyal heart was overflowing with devotion and fidelity to Charles and his cause. The honest country squire of Forest Hill did not conceal his political sentiments.

"How long will it be," said the loyal old gentleman, "until the king recovers his full authority and returns to London? I was at

York and saw him in person; he was so affable and condescending that I should have at once drawn my sword for him but for my advanced years. The whole country, with the exception of the accursed capital, shares my sentiments; but London will certainly submit as soon as war breaks out in earnest. Hitherto the king has been by far too gracious and indulgent. If I were in his place, I should know what to do. I should summon all my loyal subjects and march directly upon the accursed city. I would catch a few of the ringleaders, have them strung up, and the whole fuss would be at an end."

Milton contented himself with quietly listening to the narrow-minded opinions of the excellent squire; but when Mr. Powell rebuked his son-in-law for his political course, and particularly for his treatise against the authority of the bishops, he broke his silence, and replied to his father-in-law with manly dignity. The discussion terminated in a violent altercation, which led to the speedy departure of the old gentleman. Mary's mother, however, allowed herself to be persuaded by her daughter to stay yet a few days at Milton's house. Mrs. Powell improved this opportunity, like a genuine mother-in-law, to sow the seeds of as many weeds as possible in the young household; she encouraged Mary in her resistance, and in all sorts of whims. Never did she fail to disparage Milton in the eyes of his wife, to blame his retired life, and to deride his political views. Mary was unfortunately a most impressionable creature, and her mother exercised unlimited influence over her. The teachings of the old lady fell into a fertile soil and grew with amazing rapidity. On her departure, Mrs. Powell invited her daughter urgently to pass the summer at Forest Hill.

"You will be able," said the worthy matron, "to recreate and divert yourself there. If you do not like to live in London, and with your husband, you will always find an asylum in your parental home. It is true, you will not meet there with any books, nor with learned conversations, but with a good piece of roast-beef, foaming ale, and merry friends and acquaintances, who will be very glad to see you again."

So saying, the mother-in-law took leave of Milton's house. Mary soon followed her advice, and begged leave of her husband to pass a few weeks at the house of her parents. He willingly complied with her request, and permitted her to stay there till Michaelmas, although her absence inconvenienced him not a little. He hoped that this brief separation would exercise a favorable effect upon himself and his wife. A few days after her departure, his father suddenly arrived at his house. The old gentleman had removed to the residence of his younger son, a lawyer and royalist at Reading; but at the outbreak of hostilities between Charles and Parliament he deemed it prudent to take up his abode at Milton's house in London. He met with the most tender and reverential reception at the hands of his distinguished son. On account of his arrival, Milton desired his wife to return at an early day; but Mary did not seem disposed to comply with his wishes; she was too well pleased with the numerous amusements which she enjoyed at her father's house. Her brothers and relatives had sided with the king, whose prospects seemed far more hopeful at this juncture than heretofore.

In compliance with the king's proclamation, the nobility of York and the adjoining counties flocked to the royal headquarters. Before long he was surrounded by a numerous retinue and army; his ministers, Falkland, Hyde, and Colepeper, had arrived from London; over forty peers followed them, and so did many of the commoners. From all quarters came country gentlemen, veteran officers, and cavaliers, with squads of men; it is true, these soldiers lacked arms, uniforms, ammunition, and, above all things, discipline; but in return they were animated with ardent zeal and courage. The streets of York exhibited a most lively spectacle. They were crowded with courtiers and soldiers; the taverns were filled with jovial guests, who never tired of drinking the king's health. The cavaliers dragged their long swords noisily over the pavement, and the courtiers raised their heads again with their former haughtiness. The air resounded with derisive songs about Parliament, the Scots, and the Puritans, and they were never mentioned but in terms of boastful arrogance. The cavaliers were in the highest spirits, and vented their insolence in all sorts of defiant expressions and jests. Although the queen was still in Holland, where, disposing of the crown jewels, she had been enabled to purchase a cargo of arms and ammunition, most of her former courtiers and adherents had repaired to York. The handsome Percy, the dissipated Wilmot, Ashburnham, and O'Neale, had left their hiding-places; Jermyn had returned from France, and Thomas Egerton had hastened up from Wales as soon as he heard that hostilities were about to break out. All these young men joyfully looked forward to the campaign, which they considered an agreeable change in their mode of life. Nor were ladies wanting to the new court, and the cavaliers promised to perform the most valiant exploits under the eyes of their mistresses. The ladies were by no means idle; besides the usual court and love intrigues, they entered into communication with the most influential men in London, in order to win them over to the royal cause.

No sooner had Lucy Henderson heard of Thomas Egerton's arrival at York, than she hastened thither. Uttering a cry of joy, she rushed into the arms of her lover, who was not a little surprised at her arrival. She did not notice the confusion and coolness with which he received her, as the image of the absent queen still engrossed his heart. After the first outburst of her joy was over, he tried to prevail on her to leave York again, representing to her that she could not possibly stay there, so near the court, and in the midst of the camp. But she never tired of overwhelming him with tearful supplications.

"I am willing," she said, clinging to him, "to conceal myself from all the world, as I know that my presence might involve you in unpleasant consequences. Since Billy Green left you, you have no footman; let me be your servant."

"That will not do."

"Oh, let me see to that, I have already thought of it before now, and procured a boy's suit, which I will don immediately."

She took an elegant doublet and a hat from the small bundle which she had brought with her. In a few moments she was disguised and appeared in the garb of a page. The close-fitting costume sat very well on her charming form, and Thomas could not refrain from admiring her appearance.

"And now," she added, smilingly, "you will not send me away any more. No one will recognize me, and I will be a more faithful footman to you than Billy Green ever was."

"I am afraid you will be unable to bear the fatigues of military life. We shall set out in a few days, and attack the enemy."

"Have no fears on that head. I can bear any fatigue if I am allowed to share it with you. Henceforth I shall no longer leave your side. I shall accompany you, even though you go to the ends of the world; I shall nurse you, undergo all dangers with you, fight by your side, and, if you should be wounded, not leave your bedside. I will gladly do all, all; only do not drive away your poor Lucy, who for your sake sacrificed every thing, and has no one but you in the whole world."

Touched by her self-sacrificing love and generous devotion, Thomas was no longer able to withstand her entreaties, and kept Lucy with him. No one recognized her in this new garb, and all believed her to be her master's page.

In the mean time events assumed a more menacing aspect. The king had so far completed his preparations that he caused his standard to be unfurled on the 29th of August. It was a stormy evening. The sun set in blood-red clouds. Charles appeared, attended by his most faithful adherents, on the castle-hill at York, where a large crowd had assembled to witness the scene. Marshal Verney bore the colors containing the royal coat-of-arms, and a hand pointing to the crown, which was surmounted by the inscription, "Render unto Cæsar the things which are Cæsar's." The ground was so stony that they were hardly able to dig a hole for the flag-staff. The crowd was profoundly impressed with the ceremony, and the king looked even gloomier than usual. Even the arrogant cavaliers abstained from jesting; they foresaw the sufferings which awaited them. The profound silence was broken only by the flourishes of the bugles and the deep roll of the drums. A herald read in a loud voice the declaration of war against the rebellious Parliament. All then took off their hats and shouted, "God save the king!"

The same night the storm redoubled in violence and upset the ill-fastened flag-staff. This occurrence was considered a bad omen by Charles's partisans.

CHAPTER XVI.

SEPARATION OF MILTON AND HIS WIFE.

The summer was drawing to a close, and Mary had not yet returned to her husband's house. She did not answer his repeated requests and letters. However, her parents were most to blame for this unpardonable conduct. Since the king had planted his standard at York, fickle Dame Fortune seemed to smile on him again. Surrounded by experienced officers, who assisted him in reorganizing his army, he had obtained important victories over his less-disciplined adversaries. His adherents, with whom Richard Powell openly sympathized, now raised their heads proudly, and passed from the deepest dejection to the most overbearing arrogance. The family of Milton's young wife began to repent of having bestowed their daughter upon a man who sided with the opposition, and had incurred the displeasure of the court by his work against the bishops. They feared lest this union should discredit their loyal sentiments, and stain the honor of their escutcheon. Self-interest, too, influenced their course on this occasion, inasmuch as they expected that the king, in case he should recover his power, as seemed more than probable now, would reward their fidelity in the most liberal manner.

Mary was weak enough to listen to their insinuations, although she still loved her husband. Her mother intentionally withheld Milton's letters from her, so that in this respect she was much less guilty than she seemed to be. At times she felt remorse, and made up her mind to return to London and to her husband; but these better resolves were always nipped in the bud by her own frivolity and the bad advice of her parents. Milton's pride was wounded in the most painful manner; he resolved to make another attempt to lead his disobedient wife back to the path of duty. For this purpose he requested his friend Overton to go to Forest Hill and bring Mary back to London. This choice was not a happy one; the young wife had always felt a great aversion to the grave and almost gloomy friend of her husband. If Milton himself had gone to her, she would surely have yielded and followed him; but she received his messenger with a coldness bordering on disdain.

"My friend Milton has sent me to you,"

said Overton to her, as soon as he was alone with her. "Your husband is profoundly grieved at your conduct, and insists on your immediate return."

"I shall go to him when it suits me," replied Mary, sullenly.

"Consider well what you are doing. You owe obedience to your husband, according to divine as well as human law."

"You had better preach your sermons at your conventicles; we have no need of them here."

"For the sake of my friend, I will not take umbrage at your insulting remarks. But, above all things, I demand a definite reply, whether you will accompany me or not."

Mary reflected and hesitated; she would probably have followed her better nature and gone with him, but for her mother, who rushed impetuously into the room and interrupted their conversation.

"My daughter," cried Mrs. Powell, in the imperious tone which had become habitual to her, "will stay here; she will not return to the bookworm, the hypocrite, who feels neither respect for his majesty nor regard for the venerable bishops. Tell him that he has no use for a young wife, because he prefers his musty parchments and his miserable friends to her society. Neither does Mary long for the dry old curmudgeon. My poor daughter revived only after she had returned to us, for she did not even get enough to eat in London."

"But, mother—" interposed Mary, timidly.

"Let me speak out; I will make a fitting reply to this gentleman. My child is too good for a schoolmaster, who makes a precarious living by giving lessons to naughty boys. Our family is highly respected all over the country, and even his majesty (God save him!) knows us well. Instead of appreciating the honor we conferred upon him by this union, Mr. Milton disgraces us and ruins our reputation in the whole neighborhood. My excellent husband tears out his gray hair, and his loyal heart bleeds at the conduct of his son-in-law; wherever he goes, people talk of the accursed scribbler and his contemptible writings. I curse the hour that he set foot in our house, and that Mary gave her hand to this beggar!"

"And yet," replied Overton, angrily, "this beggar took your daughter without the dower of one thousand pounds into his house, and never demanded nor received the money."

"A thousand pounds!" cried Mrs. Powell, enraged at hearing him mention this fact, which she could not deny. "A thousand pounds! A thousand stripes he should get from us for the ill-treatment which our daughter received at his hands. Indeed, a thousand pounds for such a vagabond!"

Mary sought in vain to pacify her angry mother; the furious woman was perfectly beside herself, and gave the reins to her violent and sordid nature.

"I will curse you," she shouted, "if you only think of returning to Milton. And now, sir, you have heard our answer; repeat it to your friend, and the sooner you do so the more agreeable it will be to me. At all events, you have no business here."

Notwithstanding this insulting hint, Overton deemed himself in duty bound to hear Mary's own reply; but she was so completely under her mother's sway, that she did not dare to contradict her.

"Tell my husband," she replied to him, evasively, "that I intend to stay yet a while with my parents."

Without vouchsafing to her another glance or word, Overton left Powell's house. No sooner, however, had he gone, than she felt the keenest remorse, and was near hastening after him. It was too late, and only a flood of tears bore witness to her repentance and weakness. However, she soon dried her tears, and her rosy face beamed with childish joy when her mother, to console her, presented her with some trinkets, for which her daughter had long wished.

Milton awaited his friend's return with the utmost impatience. When Overton had given him a detailed account of his unsuccessful mission, and of Mary's conduct, he was seized with poignant grief, which soon gave way to violent anger.

"Very well," he said, after a short inward struggle. "Nothing remains for me then but to obtain a divorce."

"You can hardly hope to accomplish your purpose, as our church regulations and civil laws render it almost impossible for any one to get a divorce."

Milton admitted this, and said:

"If it were seriously asked (and this is the very question now) who, of all teachers and masters that have ever taught, has drawn the most disciples after him, both in religion and in manners, it might be not untruly answered, Custom. Though virtue be commended for the most persuasive in her theory, and conscience in the plain demonstration of the spirit finds most evincing, yet, whether it be the secret of divine will, or the original blindness we are born in, so it happens, for the most part, that Custom still is silently received for the best instructor, although it fills each estate of life and profession with abject and servile principles, and depresses the high and heaven-born spirit of man far beneath the condition wherein either God created him, or sin has sunk him. Custom is but a mere face, as Echo is a mere voice, and she rests not in her unaccomplishment, until, by secret inclination, she accorporates herself with Error, who, being a blind and serpentine body, without a head, willingly accepts what he wants, and supplies what her incompleteness went seeking. Hence it is, that Error supports Custom, Custom countenances Error; and he who opposes them must submit to slander and enmity. For truth is as impossible to be reached by any outward touch as the sunbeam; though this ill hap wait on her nativity, that she never comes into the world, but, like a bastard, to the ignominy of him that brought her forth; till Time, the midwife rather than the mother of truth, have washed and salted the infant, declared her legitimate."

"I am afraid you will not only be strenuously opposed, but those men, to whom no liberty is pleasing but unbridled and vagabond lust, without pale or partition, will laugh broadly to see you arguing, as they suppose, in favor of their debaucheries."

"Bad men, like spiders, draw venom from the most innocent flowers. But this cannot prevent us from telling the truth, to wit, that honest liberty is the greatest foe to dishonest license. I deem the question of divorce of the highest importance to society, although it is not treated yet by any means with the attention which it deserves. Indeed, man's disposition, though prone to search after vain curiosities, yet, when points of difficulty are to be discussed, appertaining to the removal of unreasonable wrong and burden from the perplexed life of our brother, it is incredible how cold, how dull, and far from all fellow-feeling we are, without the spur of self-concernment. Now, what thing is more instituted to the solace and delight of man than marriage? And yet the misinterpreting of some Scripture, directed mainly against the abusers of the law for divorce, given by Moses, has changed the blessing of matrimony not seldom into a familiar and coinhabiting mischief; at least into a drooping and disconsolate household captivity, without refuge or redemption. No place in heaven or earth, no place except hell, where charity may not enter; yet marriage, the ordinance of our solace and contentment, the remedy of our loneliness, will not admit now either of charity or mercy to come in and mediate, or pacify the fierceness of this gentle ordinance, the unremedied loneliness of this remedy. He who marries, intends as little to conspire his own ruin as he that swears allegiance; and as a whole people is in proportion to an ill government, so is one man to an ill marriage. If they, against any unworthy authority, covenant, or statute, may, by the sovereign edict of charity, save not only their lives but honest liberties from unworthy bondage, as well may he against any private covenant, which he never entered to his mischief, redeem himself from unsupportable disturbances to honest peace and just contentment. For no effect of tyranny can sit more heavy on the commonwealth than this household unhappiness on the family. And farewell all hope of true reformation in the state while such an evil as this lies undiscerned or unregarded in the house, on the redress whereof depends, not only the spiritual and orderly life of our own grown men, but the willing and careful education of our children."

"I have no doubt of the correctness of your views; however, they are not in accordance with the teachings and principles of the Church, which acknowledges only adultery as a cause of divorce."

"And yet all sense and equity reclaims, that any law or covenant, how solemn or strait soever, either between God and man, or man and man, should bind against a prime and principal scope of its own institution. And what God's chief end was of creating woman to be joined with man, His own instituting words declare, and are infallible to inform us what is marriage, and what is no marriage. 'It is not good,' saith He, 'that man should be alone; I will make him a help meet for him.' From which words, so plain, less cannot be concluded, nor is by any learned interpreter, than that in God's intention a meet and happy conversation is the chiefest and the noblest end of marriage; for we find here no expression so necessarily implying carnal knowledge, as this prevention of loneliness to the mind and spirit of man. And with all generous persons married thus it is, that where the mind and person pleases aptly, there some unaccomplishment of the body's delight may be better borne with, than when the mind hangs off in an unclosing disproportion, though the body be as it ought; for there all corporal delight will soon become unsavory and contemptible. And the solitariness of man, which God had namely and principally ordered to prevent by marriage, has no remedy, but lies under a worse condition than the loneliest single life; for, in single life, the absence and remoteness of a helper might inure him to expect his own comforts out of himself, or to seek with hope; but here the continual sight of his deluded thoughts, without cure, must needs be to him, if especially his complexion inclines him to melancholy, a daily trouble and pain of loss, in some degree like that which reprobates feel."

"For this reason the most careful examination ought to precede the choice of a consort, and he who resolves to marry should proceed with the utmost deliberation."

"The utmost deliberation and care do not exclude mistakes in all human matters. The most deliberate and calm men are generally those who have the least practical experience in this regard. But it does not follow from this that any one, by committing so pardonable a mistake, should forfeit his happiness for all his lifetime. Marriage is a covenant, the very being whereof consists not in a forced cohabitation, and counterfeit performance of duties, but in unfeigned love and peace. I do not know if you are familiar with the parable of the ancient sages, which, it seems to me, might be aptly quoted on this occasion."

"I am not, and would like to hear it from your lips."

"Eros, the god of love, if he be not twin-born, yet has a brother wondrous like him, called Anteros; whom while he seeks all about, his chance is to meet with many false and feigning desires, that wander singly up and down in his likeness; by them in their borrowed garb, Eros, though not wholly blind, as poets wrong him, yet having but one eye, as being born an archer aiming, and that eye not the quickest in this dark region here below, which is not love's proper sphere, partly out of the simplicity and credulity which is native to him, often deceived, embraces and consorts him with these obvious and suborned striplings, as if they were his mother's own sons; for so he thinks them, while they subtilly keep themselves most on his blind side. But after a while, as his manner is when soaring up into the high tower of his Apogæum, above the shadow of the earth, he darts out the direct rays of his then most piercing eyesight upon the impostures and trim disguises that were used with him, and discerns that this is not his genuine brother as he imagined; he has no longer the power to hold fellowship with such a personated mate: for straight his arrows lose their golden heads and shed their purple feathers, his silken braids untwine and slip their knots, and that original and fiery virtue given him by fate all on a sudden goes out, and leaves him undeified and despoiled of all his force; till finding Anteros at last, he kindles and repairs the almost faded ammunition of his deity by the reflection of a coequal and homogeneous fire. Thus mine author sung it to me; and by the leave of those who would be counted the only grave ones, this is no mere amatorious novel, but a deep and serious verity showing us that love in marriage cannot live nor subsist unless it be mutual; and where love cannot be, there can be left of wedlock nothing but the empty husk of an outside matrimony, as undelightful and unpleasing to God as any other kind of hypocrisy."

Overton had listened approvingly to the parable; nevertheless, he renewed again and again his objections to Milton's resolution to obtain a divorce from Mary. Milton, however, persisted in it, and continued to present additional arguments to his friend.

"What can be a fouler incongruity," he said in the course of the conversation, "a greater violence to the reverend secret of nature, than to force a mixture of minds that cannot unite, and to sow the sorrow of man's nativity with seed of two incoherent and uncombining dispositions? Generally daily experience shows that there is a hidden efficacy of love and hatred in man as well as in other kinds, not moral but natural, which, though not always in the choice, yet in the success of marriage, will ever be most predominant. But what might be the cause, whether each one's allotted genius or proper star, or whether the supernal influence of schemes and angular aspects, or this elemental crasis here below; whether all these jointly or singly meeting friendly or unfriendly in either party, I dare not appear so much a philosopher as to conjecture. Seeing, then, there is a twofold seminary, or stock in nature, from whence are derived the issues of love and hatred, distinctly flowing through the whole mass of created things, and that God's doing ever is to bring the due likenesses and harmonies together, except when out of two contraries met to their own destruction He moulds a third existence; and that it is error or some evil angel which either blindly or maliciously has drawn together, in two persons ill embarked in wedlock, the sleeping discords and enmities of nature, lulled on purpose with some false bait, that they may wake to agony and strife, later than prevention could have wished, if from the bent of just and honest intentions beginning what was begun and so continuing, all that is equal, all that is fair and possible has been tried, and no accommodation likely to succeed; what folly is it still to stand combating and battering against invincible causes and effects, with evil upon evil, till either the best of our days be lingered out, or ended with some speeding sorrow! If the noisomeness or disfigurement of body can soon destroy the sympathy of mind to wedlock duties, much more will the annoyance and trouble of mind infuse itself into all the faculties and acts of the body, to render them invalid, unkindly, and even unholy against the law of nature. What is life without the vigor and spiritual exercise of life? How can it be useful either to private or public employment? Shall it therefore be quite dejected, though never so valuable, and left to moulder away in heaviness, for the superstitious and impossible performance of an ill-driven bargain? It is not when two unfortunately met are by the canon forced to draw in that yoke an unmerciful day's work of sorrow till death unharnesses them, that then the law keeps marriage most unviolated and unbroken; but when the law takes order, that marriage be accountant and responsible to perform that society, whether it be religious, civil, or corporal, which may be conscionably required and claimed therein, or else to be dissolved if it cannot be undergone. This is to make marriage most indissoluble, by making it a just and equal dealer, a performer of those due helps which instituted the covenant; being otherwise a most unjust contract, and no more to be maintained under tuition of law, than the vilest fraud, or cheat, or theft, that may be committed. Let not, therefore, the frailty of man go on thus inventing needless troubles to itself, to groan under the false imagination of a strictness never imposed from above. Let us not be thus over-curious to strain at atoms, and yet to stop every vent and cranny of permissive liberty, lest nature, wanting those needful pores and breathing-places, which God has not debarred our weakness, either suddenly break out into some wide rupture of open vice and frantic heresy, or else inwardly fester with useless repinings and blasphemous thoughts, under an unreasonable and fruitless rigor of the most unwarranted law."

CHAPTER XVII.

ANNA DAVIES—REUNION OF HUSBAND AND WIFE.

The longer Mary delayed returning to him, the more fixed became Milton's purpose to repudiate her forever. But, in reflecting on the nature of matrimony and divorce, he had in view not so much his own individual case as the general welfare of his country. He longed to abate the evils which he believed exerted the most injurious effects, and he really intended to benefit his fellow-citizens far more than himself. His own case seemed less important to him than the pernicious consequences of that legislation which made the institution of wedlock an indissoluble bond, an intolerable tyrant for all. He did not wish to deliver himself alone, but the whole world was to enjoy the liberty for which he strove. Thus he rose above his own grief, and sought to free himself from the sufferings weighing him down, in a less egotistical manner, and to the benefit of all men. For this reason he wrote out in an elaborate manner the ideas to which his conversation with Overton had given rise, and dedicated his "Doctrine and Discipline of Divorce" to the British Parliament.

Milton was not a little surprised at the unexpected attacks which were made upon this work from a side whence he had expected them least. The Presbyterian clergy, which he had defended so courageously and ably in his pamphlet against the Episcopal prelates, took umbrage at this essay, and preferred charges against the author on account of his liberal sentiments. The same party, which had but a short time ago groaned under the persecutions of the bishops, and fought for freedom of conscience and faith, persecuted truth now that it had achieved a victory. Fortunately, Parliament did not listen to its intolerant charges, and dropped the whole matter.

Deserted by his wife, Milton sought to comfort and divert himself at the house of a noble lady. Lady Margaret Ley was the daughter of the Earl of Marlborough, and endowed with rare qualities of the heart and mind. At her house met the most eminent men and women, who, amidst the troubles and disorder of a bloody civil war, preserved a refined taste for art and science, and worshipped the Muses and Graces in this peaceful asylum. Here Milton was a welcome and much-courted guest. His domestic sorrows added to the interest which the ladies took in the poet, while his genius and learning captivated the men. He passed his evenings there in pleasant and instructive conversation. Eminent members of all parties met there, as it were, on neutral ground, and it was at this house that Milton made the acquaintance of the accomplished Lady Ranelagh and her distinguished brother, the Honorable Robert Boyle, the celebrated naturalist. Natural philosophy was cultivated with especial predilection in those days, and it had become fashionable even for ladies to speak of phlogiston, observe an eclipse of the moon through the telescope, and admire magnified infusoria by means of the yet imperfect microscope.

One evening Robert Boyle brought with him the air-pump which Otto Guericke had invented, and the construction of which he had materially improved, and astonished the spectators by his ingenious experiments. Removing from two hollow balls the air contained therein, he pressed them together in such a manner that they could not be torn asunder, and demonstrated thus the pressure of the atmosphere around us on all bodies.

"The air around us," said Milton, on this occasion, "resembles our ideas. Both exercise an invisible power over man. We are accustomed to acknowledge as forces only such as influence us in a palpable manner, while we are only too much inclined to consider as non-existent those mysterious powers which escape our coarser senses. And yet they are the rulers of the world and the principal wheels of the creation."

"You are right," replied Lady Ley; "above all, it seems to me, love is one of those mysterious forces of Nature which are revealed to man only by their effects. Unfortunately, we have no natural philosopher who demonstrates its peculiarities to us as clearly as our friend Boyle did in regard to air."

"Love would only lose thereby," said a timid young lady. "Its nature requires secrecy, in which it hides itself from the world. Take from it the veil in which it is chastely wrapped, and it is no longer love. The poet, and not the naturalist, has alone the right of revealing the purest and most sacred feelings of the human heart."

Milton applauded the words of the youthful speaker, who was graceful and interesting rather than beautiful. He had long since noticed the charming creature. A sweet expression of melancholy was stamped on the slender form, which was slightly bent forward, and on the noble features of the girl, who was a daughter of Dr. Davies. From her blue eyes beamed a glorious soul; they resembled a mountain lake, and were, like it, clear, deep, and mysterious. Generally she was taciturn and reserved, and she was one of those women who know even better how to listen than to speak, and who, therefore, are so agreeable to talented men. Her manners indicated true womanly grace, and a modesty equally remote from unbecoming bashfulness and secret pride. When Milton approached her now, a sweet blush suffused the pale cheeks of the amiable Anna, and her charming confusion made her almost look beautiful. The poet soon entered into an animated conversation with her, in which she displayed profound knowledge and learning. In the course of the conversation she expressed her sympathy for the misfortunes of the poet, and the delicate manner in which she uttered her compassion added to its value.

On his next visit to Lady Ley, the kind-hearted lady bantered him for the attention he had devoted to Anna on the previous evening.

"If you were divorced," she said, "Anna would be an excellent wife for you. I believe she is quite fond of you. She is a dear friend of mine, and will surely render happy the man upon whom she bestows her hand. Her accomplishments and the excellent education which her father gave her qualify her especially to become the wife of a learned man like you."

Milton made no reply; he was absorbed in deep thought. The lady, however, with feminine persistency, would not so easily drop the plan which she had suggested. She praised Anna's virtues and accomplishments until she had excited in him the liveliest desire to become more intimately acquainted with the excellent girl. It was not difficult for Milton to gain access to Dr. Davies's house. Here Anna made an even more favorable impression upon him than in the brilliant circle where he had met her hitherto. The deep but not chilling gravity with which she always received him, and her dignified but cordial kindness, attached him to her, and gradually there arose between them an affectionate friendship, which, however, never threatened to overstep its bounds and pass into a more tender feeling. Milton was not yet divorced from his wife, and hence he could not enter into a new union; and Anna was too conscientious and sensible to encroach upon the rights of another woman, however much she had deserved her fate. With seeming tranquillity she saw the poet come and go; but in the innermost recesses of her heart she bore a more tender affection, which she carefully concealed both from him and the world. She possessed extraordinary self-command, and would have died rather than betray the secret of her heart. To her natural timidity were added all sorts of religious scruples on account of her attachment to a married man, for such she considered Milton so long as he was not divorced from his first wife. The incessant struggle with herself threatened to kill her; she became even paler than before, and her father, a skilful and sagacious physician, feared lest she should fall a victim to consumption, of which Anna's mother had died.

Although Milton's wife lived apart from him at the house of her parents, her love for him was not yet entirely extinct. She never lost sight of him, and frequently inquired of her London acquaintances concerning his life and all that happened at his house. Thus she was also informed of the frequent visits which he paid to Anna. This news filled her with profound grief. Fear and repentance seized her soul, and what neither Milton's remonstrances nor her own reason had been able to accomplish was brought about by jealousy, and by the thought that another woman might obtain her place. Hitherto Mary had allowed her parents, and particularly her mother, to guide her in her conduct toward her husband; now she suddenly recovered her independence, and instead of her usual weakness, she displayed now an almost unfilial harshness. Mrs. Powell was not a little surprised at this change, and still more at the reproaches with which her daughter overwhelmed her. They had exchanged parts: the weak daughter showed an unusual vehemence, and the imperious mother the most extraordinary forbearance, as she feared lest a harsher course on her part should drive Mary to extremities. For days the latter locked herself in her room, bathed her face with scalding tears, and refused to take food. She was near cursing her mother, as the latter had threatened to do in regard to her if she returned to her husband. As usual, she had not been able to appreciate what she possessed until she had lost it. Possession does not make us half as happy as the loss of the thing possessed renders us unhappy.

It was not until a rival threatened to rob her of Milton's love that she felt the full extent of her guilt, and the whole worth of the man whom she had mortified so grievously only a short time since. Swayed by her passions, and not by reason, and going from one extreme to another, she gave way to unbounded despair. As formerly her sojourn in London, so now her abode under the parental roof, had become an intolerable burden to her. The ground, as it were, was burning under her feet, and she was desirous only of returning as soon as possible to her husband.

Meanwhile Milton was a daily visitor at the doctor's house. He had likewise perceived Anna's pallor and feebleness.

"You seem to be unwell," he said compassionately, taking her hand.

A slight shudder ran through her frame, and he felt the tremor of her hands.

"What ails you, dear Anna?" he asked, still retaining her hand. "If you grieve, communicate your sorrow to me, for assuredly you have no better friend in this world than me."

"It is only a slight indisposition," she replied, evasively.

"Your father is quite anxious and afraid lest you should be taken sick. Pray take good care of yourself for his and my sake."

"Why should I?" she replied, with a suspicious cough. "The world will not lose much by the death of a poor girl like me. Since I saw my mother die, I am no longer afraid of death. She fell asleep so gently and blissfully, with a sweet smile on her pale lips, that I almost envied her fate. Blessed are the dead!"

"You commit a grievous sin if you yield to such gloomy feelings, I myself was formerly a prey to these sombre spirits of melancholy; they are in our blood, and in the air, but we must keep them down. Life is so beautiful if we only know how to take it; and even our sufferings are only the passing shadows accompanying and enhancing the light."

"You are right, and I will enjoy yet the brief span vouchsafed to me."

A mournful smile played round her pale lips, and she endeavored at least to seem serene. Nevertheless, their conversation remained grave, owing in part to their peculiar surroundings. They were seated in the small garden, which bore already an autumnal aspect. The breeze stirred the foliage, and sear yellow leaves flitted softly at their feet. The whole scene breathed gentle melancholy; it was as though it were preparing for its departure. Anna gazed thoughtfully on the withered foliage, and felt as if she herself were about to bid farewell to earth. Contrary to her habit, she gave way to her emotion, and tears trembled in her eyes.

"Winter is close at hand," she said, after a pause, in a tremulous voice, in order to break the dangerous, oppressive silence.

"And spring will succeed to winter," replied Milton, with an encouraging smile.

"Death and resurrection!" murmured Anna, in a low voice.

"Nature confirms thus the faith which keeps up our hope. Every tree, every flower preaches in autumn that immortality which only fools can question. We shall meet again one day."

"Certainly, we shall meet again," repeated Anna, her face transfigured with heavenly joy.

"And what we have lost we shall recover purified and ennobled," added Milton.

"I wish *you* would recover as soon as possible what you have lost. You have a wife—"

On hearing Mary alluded to, the poet gave a start, and looked at Anna beseechingly.

"No, no," she said; "you shall and must listen to me. I have hitherto avoided alluding to an affair which cannot but stir sorrowful recollections in your bosom; but the time has come when I must speak to you frankly, and as your true friend. I have attentively read your essay on divorce, and, despite my religious scruples, I must admit that you are right on the whole. You have convinced my mind, but not my heart; and you are aware that women reason with the heart rather than the head. I am sure your wife is far more to blame than you, but are *you* entirely free from guilt? Should you not accuse yourself also, instead of blaming only your weak wife?"

"No man is devoid of faults."

"Therefore, judge not that ye be not judged."

"Another motive guided me. The longer I lived with my wife, the more I was impressed with the fact that the sympathy necessary for wedlock was wanting to us, and that our characters were incompatible."

"It was because you neglected to devote the necessary time and attention to bringing about this harmony. We women resemble delicately-stringed instruments which must be played by artistic hands to utter their true sound. A breath of air, to say nothing of a rude contact, untunes us at once. We must be treated tenderly and affectionately. If you fail to do so at the outset, there remains a dissonance, which it is difficult afterward to remove. I am afraid this happened in your wedded life. You did not know how to play the instrument intrusted to you, and as it did not at once emit sweet sounds, you cast it disdainfully aside. Give it another trial, take it up again tenderly, familiarize yourself with its innermost nature, devote yourself fondly to studying its peculiarities, and you will discover every day new and beautiful harmonies, such as slumber in every female heart, and such as true men and artists are almost always able to elicit from it."

"My wife is not a euphonic instrument. Education and habit have spoiled her better nature."

"In accusing her, you excuse her. What her parental education spoiled should be repaired by her matrimonial education. For matrimony is a continuous mutual school, in which husband and wife are both pupils and teachers. The sternness of the husband is to be lessened and ennobled by the mildness of the wife; the weakness of the wife by the strength of the husband. And as some claim to have noticed that married persons, after a long wedded life, begin to bear a strong physical resemblance to each other, so by and by that intellectual and moral sympathy, which your essay on divorce declares the essential condition of matrimonial happiness, will not be wanting to them. Therefore, do not turn a deaf ear to my request, but reconcile yourself with your wife. I can neither conceive nor approve the idea of your being divorced from her."

"What! You ask me to take her back?" said Milton, mournfully.

"I earnestly call upon you to take this step," replied Anna, with dignified resignation. "I demand it as a proof of your friendship and esteem."

He was about to make a reply, but Anna, who was afraid lest he should make a declaration of love to her, interrupted him quickly.

"Pledge me your word that you will reconcile yourself with your wife as soon as she feels repentance and returns to you."

Milton hesitated, but he was unable longer to withstand her pressing entreaties. Finally, to indicate his consent, he held out to her his hand, which she grasped in thoughtful melancholy. She then averted her face, and signed to him to leave her. No sooner had he done so, than she pressed her white handkerchief to her feverish lips: when she removed it, the fine cambric was reddened with the blood flowing from her lungs. She leaned her head in utter exhaustion on her arm.

"It will soon be over," she murmured, in a low voice.

Her father came into the garden. She perceived him, and hastened to conceal the traces of her heart-struggle and her disease from his searching eyes.

"How are you?" he asked, anxiously.

"I am better, much better," she replied, although her pale cheeks refuted her cheerful words.

Milton was unable to banish Anna's image from his heart; he was thinking all day long of the excellent girl with whom he had become acquainted too late. He was vividly impressed with the sentiment which he expressed afterward in the following lines of his "Paradise Lost:"

". . . This mischief had not then befallen,
And more that shall befall; innumerable
Disturbances on earth through female snares,
And strait conjunction with this sex: for either
He never shall find out fit mate, but such
As some misfortune brings him, or mistake;
Or whom he wishes most, shall seldom gain,
Through her perverseness, but shall see her gained
By a far worse; or, if she love, withheld
By parents; or his happiest choice too late
Shall meet, already linked and wedlock-bound
To a fell adversary, his hate or shame:
Which infinite calamity shall cause
To human life, and household peace confound."

A few weeks afterward, Milton paid a visit to a near relative in St. Martin's Lane. He was, as he had always been, received by the family with great kindness, but not without a certain embarrassment. While he was engaged with the husband in an animated conversation on various topics, the wife was walking up and down in great uneasiness. From time to time she added a remark to the conversation, which she took pains to turn toward Milton's wife.

"Have you heard any thing of Mary?" she inquired.

"For months past I have not had any news whatever from Forest Hill," he replied, evidently unwilling to speak of this subject.

"You do not know, then, that she has left her parents secretly?"

"I do not. What may have induced her to take such a step, and whither has she gone?"

"I believe she acknowledges the fault which she committed, and that it was repentance that drove her from the house of her parents. The poor woman is at a loss whither to turn, and is now wandering about among strangers—without parents, without her husband."

"If she really were repentant, she would not hesitate to approach him."

At these words, the door leading to the adjoining room opened suddenly. A sobbing woman approached Milton and threw herself at his feet.

"Mary!" exclaimed her husband, in surprise.

"Yes, it is I," she sighed; "it is your guilty wife, who implores your forgiveness on her knees. Oh, have mercy on me!"

He averted his head irresolutely. Pride and just sensibility struggled in his heart with his innate kindness and the pity with which her humble condition filled him. She had clasped his knees and moistened his hands with her scalding tears. Her dishevelled hair fell upon her heaving bosom, and her rosy face betrayed the most profound grief of which she was capable.

"Do not disown me!" she wailed, with uplifted hands. "I willingly admit that I alone am to blame for every thing, but I can no longer live without you. I left the house of my parents secretly to return to you. If you do not take me back, I do not know where to go; nothing remains for me then but to die."

His relatives added their prayers to Mary's supplications. His anger began to give way, and he cast a milder glance upon his guilty wife. His eyes beamed with forgiveness, and, deeply moved, he bent over the penitent woman, and raised her up. She encircled him with her soft arms, and folded him to her heart.

"Oh, you are so good, much better than I!" she exclaimed, smiling amid her tears. "Henceforth I will obey you, and comply with your wishes as though I were your servant."

"You shall not be my servant, you shall be my wife," he said, soothing her violent agitation. "I am not blameless either."

"No, no," she cried, vehemently. "You displayed more forbearance than I deserved. Oh, repeat to me that I may stay with you, and need not leave you again."

"You shall stay with me forever," he replied, imprinting a kiss on her crimson lips.

Perfectly reconciled, Milton and his wife left the house of their relatives. A few months afterward, Anna Davies was buried; her father said she had died of hereditary consumption. She herself knew and concealed the cause of her sufferings. A short time previous to her death, Milton received from her a letter, the characters of which indicated extreme debility. The last words were: "Be happy, and forget your unfortunate friend."

A withered linden-leaf was enclosed in the letter. Milton moistened both with his tears. Never in his whole life did he forget the virtuous and lovely Anna.

CHAPTER XVIII.

CIVIL WAR—FREEDOM OF THE PRESS.

Peace had been restored to the poet's house, but civil war was raging with terrific violence throughout the country. Every town was transformed into a camp, every castle into a fortress. The citizen relinquished his trade, the peasant laid down the plough, and both took the sword. The whole nation was in a state of intense excitement, and the parties were more at variance than ever before; on one side, the king with his cavaliers; on the other, the Parliament with its adherents. It is true, many eminent men raised their voices in favor of peace, but their appeals were not heeded by either party. Charles had transferred his headquarters to Oxford in the course of the summer. The fortune of war had favored him hitherto, and Parliament deemed it prudent to enter into negotiations. However, they failed, owing both to the obstinacy of the king, which increased with every victory, and to the distrust and the unabated demands of Parliament. After various fruitless attempts, the decision was left again to the sword and the fortune of war.

But, the more furious the struggle grew, the higher the tide of revolution rose, the more marked became the dissensions which had hitherto slumbered in the bosom of the Parliament. Presbyterians and Independents, or Brownists, who, up to this time had been striving harmoniously to attain the same ends, namely, to overthrow the absolutism of the government and the tyranny of the Episcopal Church, separated from and made war upon each other. The Presbyterians had accomplished their purpose, and were ready to make peace with the king. They had striven for the correction of abuses and the introduction of reforms, but not for the overthrow of all existing institutions. But the zealous Independents, with whom the republicans united, did not content themselves with this. They were intent on bringing about, if possible, the downfall of royalty and of all church institutions. What they lacked in numerical strength and influence they made up by their courage, activity, and indefatigable energy. These were the very qualities which could not but secure their triumph over their adversaries, the Presbyterians, whom their previous successes had rendered careless and lukewarm. In a revolution, victory will always perch, at least for a time, on the banners of that party which acts with the utmost consistency, and shrinks from no measures, how hazardous soever they may be.

Milton himself, who naturally was not an extremist, was forced, almost against his will, by the course the Presbyterians pursued toward him, to side with the Independents. One of the first acts of the Parliament had been the deliverance of the press from the restrictions with which it had been fettered by the government of the king, particularly by the hateful Star-Chamber. All the laws interfering with the freedom of the press were repealed. London and the whole country were at once flooded with countless pamphlets conveying from one end of England to the other the hopes and grievances of the Presbyterians, who were in the ascendant in Parliament. Some of these passionate satirical papers created a great sensation, and became exceedingly popular. King Charles, who read them all, and often replied to them, once paid ten pounds for a copy of a scurrilous pamphlet which he was anxious to read. At this time the press, and especially the newspapers, acquired great importance, and became a formidable weapon in the hands of the parties. The *Mercurius Pragmaticus* long defended the cause of the Presbyterians, while the *Mercurius Aulicus*, edited by Sir John Birkenhead, was the organ of the court. None of these journals were slow in deriding, and even slandering their opponents. After a while, this freedom of the press displeased the Presbyterians, and, having availed themselves sufficiently of this auxiliary, they strove to destroy it when they had no longer need of it, and when it threatened to become dangerous to themselves. They had intended only to wrench a powerful weapon from the hands of the government and the Episcopal Church; and, although they themselves had established freedom of the press, they indulged in secret threats against the writers who openly espoused the cause of the king. They dreaded even more the Independents, who could not be silenced so easily. The Presbyterians trembled before the spirit which they had called up, and resolved to chain it again. They were not bold enough, however, to take this step backward in an open and high-handed manner. Under all sorts of vain pretexts they tried to reëstablish the old restrictions imposed on the press, and to walk in the steps of the Star-Chamber, which they had so furiously assailed.

Great was the sensation and indignation which this oppressive measure created. Milton was profoundly grieved at this blow levelled at the press, which he justly regarded as the bulwark of civil liberty in England. He was resolved to reconquer this natural right, so highly important to the people, and spare no efforts to overthrow this new tyranny. He was obliged to assail the same Presbyterians with whom he had united to overthrow the Episcopal Church, and establish liberty and the longed-for Parliament, from which England had expected so many blessings. He did so, with as much courage as sagacity.

Milton went again to the Rota, the celebrated political club, where he had not been for a long time past. His presence was noticed immediately, and his friends and acquaintances thronged about him. He denounced the restrictions recently imposed on the press; and even some of the members of this club, which was noted for its revolutionary spirit, were opposed to the freedom of the press. One of the latter, the gloomy St. John, a distinguished lawyer, said to Milton: "It is not possible that you can advocate entire and unlimited freedom of the press."

"Certainly not," replied Milton. "I deny not but that it is of greatest concernment in the Church and commonwealth, to have a vigilant eye how books demean themselves as well as men; and thereafter to confine, imprison, and do sharpest justice on them as malefactors; for books are not absolutely dead things, but do contain a progeny of life in them to be as active as that soul was whose progeny they are: nay, they do preserve as in a vial the purest efficacy and extraction of that living intellect that bred them. I know they are as lively, and as vigorously productive, as those fabulous dragons' teeth; and being sown up and down, may chance to spring up armed men. And yet on the other hand, unless wariness be good, as good almost kill a man as kill a good book: who kills a man kills a reasonable creature, God's image; but he who destroys a good book, kills reason itself, kills the image of God, as it were in the eye. Many a man lives a burden to the earth; but a good book is the precious life-blood of a master-spirit, embalmed and treasured up on purpose to a life beyond life."

"But license," objected St. John, "is as old as literary production. So long as any books have been written, the state has had the right of watching and suppressing them, when they do more harm than good."

"I must deny the correctness of this assertion. Neither the Greeks nor the Romans knew the licensing of books. Even during the first centuries after Christianity had been established, the Church condemned only such books as were directly immoral and attacked the fundamental truths of religion. After the Nicene Council in the eighth century, the popes introduced a formal censorship, which is not only a disgrace to humanity, but an utterly useless invention which never yet attained its object. Good and evil, we know, in the field of this world grow up together almost inseparably; and the knowledge of good is so involved and interwoven with the knowledge of evil, and in so many cunning resemblances hardly to be discerned, that those confused seeds which were imposed upon Psyche as an incessant labor to cull out, and sort asunder, were not more intermixed. It was from out the rind of one apple tasted, that the knowledge of good and evil, as two twins cleaving together, leaped forth into the world. And perhaps this is that doom which Adam fell into of knowing good and evil. As therefore the state of man now is, what wisdom can there be to choose, what continence to forbear, without the knowledge of evil? He that can apprehend and consider Vice with all his baits and seeming pleasures, and yet abstain, and yet distinguish, and yet prefer that which is truly better, he is the true warfaring Christian. I cannot praise a fugitive and cloistered Virtue unexercised and unbreathed, that never sallies out and sees her adversary, but slinks out of the race, where that immortal garland is to be run for, not without dust and heat."

"You forget that all men are not strong enough to withstand temptation. Do you not fear the infection that may spread?"

"If you fear the infection that may spread, all human learning and controversy in religious points must remove out of the world; yea, the Bible itself; for that ofttimes relates blasphemy not nicely: it describes the carnal sense of wicked men not elegantly. The ancientest fathers must next be removed, as Clement of Alexandria, and that Eusebian book of evangelic preparation, transmitting our ears through a hoard of heathenish obscenities to receive the gospel. If you shut and fortify one gate against corruption, you will be necessitated to leave others round about wide open. If you think to regulate printing, and thereby to rectify manners, you must regulate all recreations and pastimes, all that is delightful to man. No music must be heard, no song be set or sung, but what is grave and Doric. There must be licensing dancers, that no gesture, motion, or deportment be taught our youth, but what by their allowance shall be thought honest. It will ask more than the work of twenty licensers to examine all the lutes, the violins, and the guitars in every house; they must not be suffered to prattle as they do, but must be licensed what they may say. And who shall silence all the airs and madrigals that whisper softness in chambers? The windows also, and the balconies, must be thought on. The villages also must have their visitors to inquire what lectures the bagpipe and the rebec read, even to the ballatry and the gamut of every municipal fiddler. And even though you should succeed in shutting all these gates against the mind, what would you gain thereby? Truth is compared in Scripture to a streaming fountain; if her waters flow not in a perpetual progression, they sicken into a muddy pool of conformity and tradition."

"To preserve the purity of truth is the duty of its servants, the ministers of the Church, and Parliament."

"I reply that a man may be a heretic in the truth; and if he believe things only because his pastor says so, or the assembly so determines, without knowing other reason, though his belief be true, yet the very truth he holds becomes his heresy. A wealthy man, addicted to his pleasure and to his profits, finds religion to be a traffic so entangled, and of so many piddling accounts, that of all mysteries he cannot skill to keep a stock going upon that trade. What should he do? Fain he would have the name to be religious, fain he would bear up with his neighbors in that. What does he therefore, but resolves to give over toiling, and to find himself out some factor, to whose care and credit he may commit the whole managing of his religious affairs; some divine of note and estimation that must be. To him he adheres, he resigns the whole warehouse of his religion, with all the locks and keys, into his custody; and indeed makes the very person of that man his religion; esteems his associating with him a sufficient evidence and commendatory of his own piety. So that a man may say his religion is now no more within himself, but is become a dividual movable, and goes and comes near him, according as that good man frequents the house. He entertains him, gives him gifts, feasts him, lodges him; his religion comes home at night, prays, is liberally supped, and sumptuously laid to sleep; rises, is saluted, and after the malmsey, or some well-spiced brewage, and better breakfasted than He whose morning appetite would have gladly fed on green figs between Bethany and Jerusalem, his religion walks abroad at eight, and leaves his kind entertainer in the shop trading all day without his religion. These are the fruits which a dull ease and cessation of our knowledge will bring forth among the people. No, no, we must not suffer this. The time demands freedom of thinking and writing for all. Whether all the storms of opinion will sweep at once through the world or not, Truth is in the field and well able to cope with Error. Truth indeed came once into the world with her divine Master, and was a perfect shape most glorious to look on; but when He ascended, and His apostles after Him were laid asleep, then straight arose a wicked race of deceivers, who, as that story goes of the Egyptian Typhon with his conspirators, how they dealt with the good Osiris, took the virgin Truth, hewed her lovely form into a thousand pieces, and scattered them to the four winds. From that time ever since, the sad friends of Truth, such as durst appear, imitating the careful search that Isis made for the mangled body of Osiris, went up and down gathering up limb by limb still as they could find them. We have not yet found them all, nor ever shall do, till her Master's second coming; He shall bring together every joint and member, and shall mould them into an immortal feature of loveliness and perfection. Suffer not these licensing prohibitions to stand at every place of opportunity forbidding and disturbing them that continue seeking, that continue to do our obsequies to the torn body of our martyred saint."

Milton's speech was warmly applauded by all the members, and even the gloomy St. John admitted that he had refuted his argument. The noble defender of freedom of the press was requested to write a pamphlet on the subject and publish it. He promised to do so, and issued shortly after his "Areopagitica, a Speech for the Liberty of Unlicensed Printing," which he likewise dedicated to Parliament. The poet thus defended with manly courage one of the noblest boons of mankind, and up to the present time hardly any thing equal to this noble essay has been written on the same subject. It met, however, with vehement opposition. The learned Baxter, perhaps the most eminent of the nonconformist divines of this period, published a violent attack on the freedom of the press, alleging that it led to the publication of countless books by bad and incompetent authors, and was decidedly injurious to the dissemination of truth.

"Better books must be written, then, and you may be sure that, like the staff of Moses, they will swallow the works of the impious," replied Milton to him.

Baxter went so far in his blind zeal, that he wished to die previous to the triumph of the detested liberty of unlicensed printing. While the Presbyterians were at the helm of government, the press was fettered as heretofore. During Cromwell's protectorate, it is true, the system of licensed printing was abolished, but prosecutions of authors and printers were not unknown. Manuscripts were frequently taken from authors while they were being printed. Such was the fate of Harrington's "Oceana," for even the republic did not protect the republicans. Milton's pamphlet, however, produced one effect which bore witness to its sterling value: one of the censors of the press, named Gilbert Mabbot, resigned his office after reading the "Areopagitica," stating that his office seemed to him illegal, dangerous, and injurious rather than useful. At the same time he proposed that all authors who signed their writings should be allowed to print them, on condition of being called to account by the courts in case their books contained any thing contrary to law and morality.

CHAPTER XIX.

THE REBELLION IN IRELAND—CROMWELL AT MARSTON MOOR.

On a stormy day in February, Sir Kenelm Digby, attended by a man who, notwithstanding his concealed tonsure and careful disguise, was evidently a Catholic priest, rode across one of those numerous bogs which extend for many miles in the interior of Ireland. The ground had been softened by long-continued rain, and transformed into black mire. The saturated soil trembled at every step of the horses, and the strong animals were in constant danger of sinking into it. An icy breeze, which dashed the large rain-drops mixed with snow-flakes into the faces of the travellers, added to the uncomfortable frame of their minds.

"By the saints!" growled Sir Kenelm, "I would we were already under shelter. Night will soon set in, and then it will be impossible for us to advance another step. Nothing would remain for us but to encamp in the accursed bog, if we do not prefer perishing in it."

At these by no means encouraging words

his pious companion heaved a deep sigh and crossed himself.

"Perhaps there is a cabin near by," he said, "where we might find shelter for the night. Exert your eyes, dear friend. The snow-storm has almost blinded mine."

"I am afraid I shall not be able to see any more than you, reverend father. Beautiful Erin does not abound with habitable dwellings, and what few of them were left have been destroyed by our dear friends, the Irish rebels."

"*In majorem Dei gloriam*," said the priest, clasping his hands.

"I would our hot-headed friends had done their work less thoroughly. Moreover, they should have deferred their insurrection for a time; but such are the Irish, always rash and imprudent. Every thing was arranged in the most judicious manner, all necessary dispositions were made, and Dublin would have fallen into their hands without their striking a blow; but these men cannot wait, and want to pluck the fruit from the tree before it is ripe."

"You forget entirely that the conspiracy was prematurely betrayed. That was not their fault."

"And then the unnecessary massacre of the Protestants, the cruelties committed against innocent women and children! I am entirely opposed to bloodshed, and do not want our just cause to be stained by such abominable outrages. As a matter of course, the king had to repudiate and attack them. He would have forfeited the last remnant of respect felt for him by the people of England, if he had not treated the rebels as enemies and traitors. Policy itself compelled him to adopt this course."

"But he is secretly negotiating with the Irish. You know this better than any other man, for what other object can your journey to Ireland have, and why did you come to me and persuade me to take part in this journey, which I have cursed already more than once on account of the fatigues and privations to which it subjects us? I am afraid it will involve us in serious trouble."

"You are mistaken on that head. What I am doing, I do on my own responsibility. I am first of all a good Catholic, and afterward a subject of his majesty. The Irish have risen in the name of the Catholic religion; their other motives do not concern me. Hence, I deem myself in duty bound to assist them with my advice. The men who are at the head of the rebels need it, for Phelim O'Neale has no more sense in his thick skull than the horse I am riding."

"And what do you purpose doing?"

"Above all things, I am going to obtain a clear insight into the whole situation. When I know the strength of the rebels, and the means at their disposal, every thing else will follow of itself."

"And in what capacity are you going to introduce yourself to the leaders?"

"As Sir Kenelm Digby, as a zealous Catholic, as a true friend of our oppressed Church."

"They would certainly bid you welcome, if you came as envoy of the king to negotiate with the Irish."

Sir Kenelm made no reply to the further questions of his fellow-traveller, but accelerated the step of his horse so far as the mire permitted him to do so. The day was drawing to a close, and twilight had set in. The situation of the two travellers became more and more disagreeable. There was no house far and near; not even a wretched hovel was to be seen anywhere; only the black bog extended as far as the horizon, where it seemed to blend with the clouded sky. The road was almost invisible, and withal impassable. There were places where the horses stuck in the mire, and could be extricated only after almost superhuman efforts. Moreover, they feared lest they should be attacked in this dismal region, which had become more unsafe than formerly, owing to the civil war. Sir Kenelm, therefore, deemed it prudent to cock his pistols and keep them in readiness for an emergency. They had continued their way through the darkness for about half an hour, when the road became entirely invisible. Night had set in, and they could not see a step before them. Already they were preparing to pass the night in the open air, when the loud bark of a dog stirred new hopes and fears in their bosoms.

"There must be men close by," said Sir Kenelm, cautiously drawing his pistol.

"Holy Ignatius!" prayed the Jesuit, "protect us, and send us an angel to lead us back to the right path!"

A few minutes elapsed in anxious suspense; the dog then barked once more, and louder than at first. The roar of the storm, and the darkness, prevented them from perceiving the approach of some persons who soon surrounded the travellers.

"Who are you?" asked a rough voice with a strong Irish brogue.

"Poor travellers who have lost their way," was the reply.

"Whence do you come, and where are you going?"

"We have come across the channel, and are going to the camp. My friend," added the priest, "can you not give us shelter? We shall be very grateful to you."

"Follow me."

So saying, the stranger seized the bridle of the priest's horse, while his companion did the same with Sir Kenelm's animal. Both seemed to be perfectly familiar with the peculiarities of the road. Despite the utter darkness, the travellers advanced more rapidly than before, and soon was to be seen a light, indicating the proximity of a human dwelling. The guide uttered a shrill whistle, whereupon several men rushed out of the door of a house and conducted the travellers into a spacious room where a comfortable fire was burning. Around the fireplace sat or lay several armed men, whose appearance and manners were not exactly calculated to inspire them with confidence. Their costume consisted of a few rags, and their shaggy unkempt hair hung down on their shoulders. Their language and lively gestures indicated that they were natives of the soil. On the entrance of the strangers, they rose with flashing eyes and threatening gestures.

"They are Englishmen!" cried a Herculean man, raising the hatchet which he held in his hands.

"In that case they must die," added another, casting a covetous glance on the golden chain and costly weapons of Sir Kenelm Digby.

The priest trembled with terror, while Digby was calm and collected.

"You are mistaken, my friends," he said, with a quiet smile. "It is true, we are Englishmen, but we are good Catholics and friends of Ireland. We wish to go to the camp and see your leader Phelim O'Neale, as we are the bearers of important news for him."

His words seemed to make some impression on the men; at least they held a brief consultation, the result of which was favorable to the travellers. The guide, whose dress was not less ragged than those of the others, but who seemed to exercise considerable influence over them, took part in the consultation, and announced to Sir Kenelm Digby and his companion that their lives were not in danger, but that they would have to accompany him immediately to the camp. The priest heaved a deep sigh on being told to bid farewell to the uncomfortable, but at least warm room, and ride again through the dark night, God knew whither. However, nothing remained for him but to comply with the bidding of the guide and follow the example of Sir Kenelm Digby. It was past midnight when the travellers arrived at the camp. Already from afar they saw numerous camp-fires glistening in the darkness; but on coming up closer to them, they seemed to be in the abode of demons rather than a camp of soldiers. Groups of half-naked persons squatted round the fires in various positions; and even women and children were warming themselves, while others were dancing in wild intoxication round the fires of burning wood and straw, and uttering screams and roars reminding the hearers of the cries of the doomed. The guide conducted the travellers through these groups, awakening here and there with a kick a sleeper stretched out across the road, or pushing him quickly aside. At last they reached the tent of the chief, where they had to wait a long time before they were admitted. Phelim O'Neale, surrounded by his officers and several Catholic priests who were staying in the camp, met them in the proud consciousness of his dignity. The coarse features of his countenance indicated energy rather than understanding or shrewdness.

"Who are you?" he asked the travellers, imperiously.

"My name is Sir Kenelm Digby," replied the courtier, "and I believe you are acquainted with my companion."

At these words the Jesuit advanced a few steps toward the chief.

"Reverend father!" exclaimed Phelim, in surprise. "What! you yourself have come to me, and in so bleak a night?"

"At the request of Sir Kenelm Digby I left my safe asylum, and shrank from no danger to second his plans. If I am not mistaken, he is the bearer of important news, and he comes with the firm determination to serve you and the good cause."

"Both you and he are a thousand times welcome!" said the chief, holding out his hands to them.

While Phelim O'Neale was conversing with them, a squad of soldiers approached with two prisoners. The officer in command of the squad spoke a few words to the chief, who nodded assent.

"Hang them at sunrise," he said, laconically.

The doomed prisoners were about to defend themselves, but Phelim ordered them to be silent.

"You are convicted spies," he added, "for what else brought you so close to the camp? Besides, you are natives of England, and therefore our enemies. Prepare for death."

"Pardon me," replied one of the prisoners, fearlessly, "I have a secret message for you. This is the reason why I approached the camp."

"From whom is the message?"

"I can only tell you that alone, and not in the presence of witnesses."

On hearing the first words of the prisoner, Sir Kenelm had cast a glance on him, and recognized him immediately.

"Sir Thomas Egerton!" he exclaimed, in surprise.

"You know the man?" asked the chief of the rebels.

"I know him, and warrant the truth of what he says. He cannot be an enemy, a traitor, since he is in the service of her majesty the queen."

At a beck from the chief, Thomas and his companion, who was no other than Lucy Henderson, in male disguise, were delivered from their fetters. Thomas, in the first place, thanked Digby with much feeling and warmth for the service he had rendered him.

"How do you happen to be here?"

"The queen sent me hither," replied Thomas, in a low voice. "Her majesty commissioned me to repair to the camp of the rebels."

A significant smile played round Digby's lips when he received this reply.

"In that case I am doubly glad of having rendered you this insignificant service. I believe we have both come hither for the same purpose, and may, therefore, speak without reserve."

As the night was already too far advanced for them to speak of business matters, the chief dismissed his guests, to whom he assigned a common tent. Exhausted by the fatigues of the journey and the dangers they had incurred, Lucy and the priest soon fell asleep, while Thomas and Sir Kenelm Digby conversed yet for a time. Digby had soon ascertained the object of the mission intrusted to Thomas. He was instructed by the queen to offer her support secretly to the Irish rebels, and assure them that Charles was disposed to conclude an armistice with them. This communication filled Sir Kenelm Digby with glowing hopes for the Catholic party, whose triumph he fondly wished to bring about.

On the following morning Thomas had the wished-for interview with the chief of the rebels, and received from him an autograph letter to the queen, whereupon he left the camp, while Sir Kenelm Digby remained there for some time longer. On taking leave of his young friend, the courtier offered of his own accord to conduct the negotiations between Charles and the Irish rebels under the seal of profound secrecy. The king, after some hesitation, accepted the offer, and while he was seemingly waging war with the rebels, Sir Kenelm Digby managed secretly the threads of an intrigue, the object of which was, in the first place, only an armistice, to which was then to succeed the conclusion of a formal alliance, so that Irish troops might help the king to put down the Parliament, and subvert the liberties of England. It was by such steps, which could not be entirely concealed from the people, that Charles forfeited the sympathies of even those of his subjects who were still attached to him, but whose fidelity to the Protestant religion and horror of popery far surpassed their devotion and loyalty to the king. His worst enemy was his duplicity, which, like all his failings, proceeded from his innate weakness.

The fortune of war, which had hitherto smiled on Charles, seemed to desert him. The Scottish Covenanters had formed a junction with the army of the Parliament, and the united forces had given battle to the Royalists on Marston Moor, and inflicted a disastrous defeat on them. Prince Rupert, son of the king's sister, commanded the royal cavalry, and suffered himself to be carried away too far in the ardor of the battle. He was opposed to a general alike brave and sagacious, Oliver Cromwell, a man whose name had only recently become generally known. In Parliament, of which he was a member, he had hitherto achieved very little distinction. He was a poor speaker, but a great captain and party leader. In the course of a few months he had secured a commanding position by his valor and skill in organizing troops. On Marston Moor his boldness, coupled with extraordinary presence of mind, decided the battle in favor of Parliament.

The setting sun shed his rays on the bloody field of battle, and on the corpses of the slain. Here and there severely wounded soldiers uttered groans and craved relief. Horses without riders sped spectre-like through the darkness. The loud booming of artillery had died away, and been succeeded by profound stillness. Cromwell rode across the gory moor, attended by old Henderson, who had not left his side during the battle. A broad wound on his forehead, which was but slightly dressed, bore witness to the gloomy Puritan's intrepidity. Both were grave and taciturn. It was not until the moon rose and shed her pale light over the battle-field that Cromwell opened his lips, round which a triumphant smile was playing.

"The Lord has delivered His enemies into our hands. In truth, England and the Church of God have been greatly blessed by Him. No more brilliant victory has been gained since war broke out."

"The country is chiefly indebted for this triumph to your valor and wisdom."

"The praise and honor are due to the Almighty. His is the glory. I am only His and the Parliament's servant."

"If you chose, you might be the Parliament's master."

"What do you say, Henderson! I must not listen to such suggestions."

"Will you shut your ears to the truth? You are not blind, Oliver. You know as well as I that the Spirit of God no longer illumines the assembly at Westminster Hall. Many of its members resemble Korah and his company, and rebel against the Lord and His saints."

"Alas! what you say is but too true," sighed Cromwell.

"Nor are all the generals like you, Oliver, the elect of the Lord. Essex, Fairfax, and Waller adhere to the Presbyterians, who refuse to carry on the war against Charles. Their arms have become weak, and their hearts are intimidated."

"You inveigh against men who are braver and worthier than we are; and yet there is in your words a grain of truth, which I will sift out. I likewise look in vain for the necessary harmony and zeal that should animate the warriors of the Lord. I will reflect on the best way of remedying this evil, confer with our friends, and particularly seek for the necessary light in prayer. The war should be continued with greater zeal and energy, if it is to be brought to a successful termination. I am afraid all of our men are not possessed of such purity of heart as you and I. There are among them ambitious persons, who, for the sake of their exalted position and of other worldly advantages, would like to protract the war. That must not be tolerated."

"You may count upon the support of the pious, whenever you bring the matter before Parliament."

"God forbid," exclaimed Cromwell, feigning dismay, "that I should oppose those worthy men, who, moreover, are friends of mine!"

"Others, then, will do it. I shall see Sir Harry Vane, St. John, and Nathaniel Fines about it. The command-in-chief should be intrusted to more deserving hands, and I know of no one worthier of our confidence than you."

"What the Lord resolves in regard to me will be done, and I shall submit to His will. Do what the Spirit prompts you to do, and act according to God's will. But, above all things, go now and have your wound carefully dressed, lest the cool night-air prove injurious to it."

"Have no fears on my account. This wound gives me no more pain than the bite of a gnat; it shall always remind me of him who struck the blow, and whom, by God's help, I hope to hit better one day than he did me."

"Who was it?"

"Your enemy, as well as mine—the impious youth who abducted your Lucy."

"Woe to him, if I ever should meet him!"

"I perceived him in the thickest of the fight, and singled him out. Our blades crossed each other, and I believed already that the Lord had delivered him into my hands, when suddenly a beardless boy, who seemed to be his servant, attacked me from behind. While facing about to defend myself against this new assailant, I received this wound across the forehead. The streaming blood blinded my eyes and prevented me from seeing. The next moment both my adversaries had disappeared, and I did not see them any more."

"He will not escape us, and a fearful retribution will then be wreaked upon him. Have you heard nothing of Lucy?"

"My researches were in vain. I only learned that she left London secretly, but no one knows where she went."

"Her death cannot grieve me more bitterly

than her sinful life. She is lost to me, lost forevermore."

Cromwell urged Henderson again to leave the field, that his wound might be attended to, and that he might enjoy the necessary repose. He himself remained, absorbed in deep reflections. His past life appeared before his eyes. Only a few years since entirely unknown, and, for the sake of his faith, intent on leaving his native country and emigrating to the wilds of America, he had now, in consequence of the revolution, become a famous general, and one of the most influential leaders of the most powerful party. His ambition, which had hitherto slumbered unknown to him in his bosom, began to stir impetuously. He was one of those great and peculiar men whom Providence calls forth in revolutionary times to fulfil a special mission. Cromwell combined in his extraordinary nature the most opposite qualities. His sincere piety by no means excluded a certain worldly shrewdness and great power of dissimulation. Endowed with a keen understanding, he was an ardent fanatic, and his nice penetration and keen judgment were frequently blended with a somewhat scurrilous humor. He was a hero with the manners of a clown, a sagacious politician in the awkward shape of an English grazier; the genius of his age with all its faults. There could be no greater contrast than that between Cromwell and his royal adversary. Weakness was the leading trait of the one, strength of will that of the other. Charles was descended from a long line of august ancestors, and combined in his person all the good and bad qualities of the English aristocracy, while Cromwell embodied the peculiarities of the commoners of his age; he was, as it were, an incarnation of religious zeal, coupled with the keenest intellect—the revolutionary spirit of the period, opposed to the despotic obstinacy of the king. In obedience to a higher necessity, the two principles met in mortal combat.

The higher Cromwell rose, the clearer and more far-sighted became his judgment. He grew with events, and, on reaching the summit, he stood a mortal of colossal size. Not only his understanding, but a certain demoniacal instinct, urged him onward in the path which he had entered. It is true, the necessities of the moment dominated him, but he always knew how to profit by circumstances in the most judicious manner, and thus he was simultaneously their master and their servant. His power of dissimulation, and the hypocrisy with which he has so often been reproached, did not arise from his innermost nature, but were imposed on him by his peculiar position—his auxiliaries, as it were, but which he disbanded after gaining a victory. His purposes were always great, but his actions were often necessarily little; yet he never lost sight of his chief aim, namely, to render England powerful and respected.

At this moment, he was gazing into vacancy. White mist arose from the moor and veiled the dead; they united and assumed all sorts of fantastic shapes in the pale moonlight. A long weird procession, as it were, composed of the ghosts of the slain, passed him. Fear did not seize him, for he was insensible to it; but a slight shudder ran through his frame. He thought of the immediate future and the menacing events to which this fratricidal war would lead.

"No, no," he murmured to himself; "this war must not be continued; a speedy end must be put to it, or it will involve England in utter ruin. A few victories yet, and Charles must yield, or—"

He did not conclude the sentence, but stared gloomily before him. He added only after a long pause:

"If the king succumbs, Parliament will get hold of the helm of government—Parliament, which is sitting quietly in London, and wrangling about trifles, while the soldier is shedding

"BEHOLD THE INSTRUMENT OF THE LORD!"

p. 2??.

his blood in the field. It seems to me the Spirit of God animates the assembly no longer, and their doings are vain. Many men, many minds. They lack a firm will, of which we have need at this juncture. Essex and Fairfax are not the men to achieve our great undertaking. The Lord will choose another servant to reveal His will. Whosoever he may be, he will take a heavy burden upon his shoulders, a task which only the best are able to accomplish. But the will of the Lord be done on earth as it is in heaven."

The moon illuminated the form of the praying general. His devotion was soon interrupted by the arrival of a squad of mounted men headed by old Henderson, whose wound had been carefully dressed.

"Behold the instrument of the Lord, the chosen leader of Israel!" exclaimed the fanatical Puritan, pointing to the kneeling general.

The soldiers greeted their commander respectfully. He seemed to awake from a profound dream, and looked around wonderingly, as though he had not noticed them before.

"Go," he said to them, "and do your duty. Pursue the enemy, and give him no quarter wherever you meet him. I shall pray for you while you are fighting."

CHAPTER XX.

LADY ALICE CARBURY—THE CASTLE BESIEGED.

Amid the mountains of Wales lay a green shady valley, through which flowed a limpid rivulet. The whole landscape resembled a large romantic park; a somewhat precipitous hill was surmounted by an imposing castle, which evidently dated from the commencement of the Wars of the Roses, but had since been greatly extended and improved. It had retained its original Gothic style, and looked imperiously down from its hills with its high tower and its bold projections and pillars. Surrounded by a strong wall, protected by a drawbridge, and covered by ramparts and other fortifications, it resembled a small fortress, well calculated to withstand even a numerous force during a protracted siege. Alice Egerton had lived here for several years by the side of her husband. After Milton's departure, the excellent girl had yielded to the persistent suit of the noble and brave Sir Robert Carbury, and accompanied him as his wife to his native country. She had no reason to regret the choice she had made, as her husband was one of the best men she had ever known, and tried to fulfil her every wish even before she had uttered it. Nevertheless, she was not able to efface the memory of Milton entirely from her heart. There were hours when his dear image appeared to her again and again, although, actuated by a stern sense of duty, she strenuously resisted all such temptations. Like many distinguished ladies she preserved the ideal of an early love in her heart, without thereby violating the faith she had plighted to her husband. She loved Carbury only the more, and sought to indemnify him by the most devoted tenderness and self-denial for these recollections which stole upon her in spite of herself. She had borne to him a son, who drew still closer the ties uniting his father and mother. To-day she was seated in the castle-garden, and by her side stood the cradle in which her little son was slumbering. A Bible, the constant companion of the truly pious Alice, lay open before her; but, while she was reading, the eyes of the tender mother wandered from the pages to the rosy babe. A sweet smile played round the lips of the little one, and the mother bent over him, not daring to kiss him, for fear of awakening the child. Her eyes feasted in an ecstasy of delight on the dear being, and she hearkened with reverence to the light breathing of the delicate breast which rose and fell with rhythmical regularity. While she was thus enjoying this delightful spectacle, she suddenly felt two vigorous arms encircling her.

"Alice, my dear sweet wife," whispered the well-known voice of her husband.

She turned and beheld Carbury, attended by his worthy chaplain. Her husband was in his travelling-dress, and his face, notwithstanding the forced smile illuminating it, wore an almost solemn expression.

"You are going away?" she asked, in surprise.

"Only for a short time. I trust I shall be back to-morrow. Our worthy doctor will stay with you in the mean time."

So saying, she pointed to the clergyman, whose gentle and intellectual face could not but inspire confidence. Nevertheless, Alice was greatly alarmed by this sudden departure.

"I can certainly," she said, "wish for no better protection, nor more agreeable company, than that afforded to me by Doctor Taylor's presence; and yet your resolve surprises me the more as it is taken at a time when dangers are menacing us from all quarters. You know that the army of the Parliament has invaded Wales, and is stationed only a few miles from our castle. Your sentiments and loyalty to the king are generally known."

"This is the very cause of my departure. I have been informed that a *coup de main* is in contemplation against us. The garrison of our castle is too weak to stand a vigorous and protracted siege. I therefore applied to the king for reënforcements, and although he himself is hard pressed on all sides, he has promised to send me the necessary troops. Your own brother is to lead them to me, and I am now going to meet them, because their failure to arrive before this time fills me with uneasiness."

"Then you look for a regular attack on our castle?" asked Alice, anxiously.

"I do not think any thing very serious will happen to us," replied Carbury evasively, "but will make all necessary dispositions for an emergency. When our enemies perceive that we are sufficiently prepared to receive them, they will not lose their time by entering upon a useless siege, by which, at the best, they can gain little or nothing."

"And my brother Thomas is to lead the reënforcements to us? It is a long time since I have heard any thing of him and the other members of my family."

"He was a long time in the service of the queen; but after she left England and escaped to France, he joined the king's army, in which he has already distinguished himself on more than one occasion."

"How glad I shall be to meet him, even though the cause of his visit is not very cheering."

"Never fear, my sweet wife. I hope that the storm will blow over this time also."

"God grant it!" added the pious and learned chaplain, with clasped hands.

Sir Robert Carbury took the most affectionate leave of his wife, and imprinted a kiss on the lips of his slumbering son, who, aroused from his sleep, started up weeping, and stretched out his tiny hands toward his mother. Alice quieted the crying babe by singing a lullaby to it, and soon the small blue eyes, which resembled those of the mother, closed again. The chaplain accompanied Carbury to the gate, and then returned to stay with the lady of the house. He found her occupied with reading the Bible. After a short time she laid the book aside.

"Is it not strange," she said, "that the same book which to me is a source of peace and consolation, should so violently inflame so many people? Catholics and Protestants, Independents and Presbyterians, as well as the Episcopal Church, claim the Bible as authority for their tenets, and fight in its name."

"Blessed are the peacemakers," replied the

chaplain. "True believers may be known by the charity and toleration with which they treat those who differ from them. When Abraham, according to the ancient legend, was seated at the door of his tent to invite, as he was in the habit of doing, weary travellers to come in, he beheld an old man, who, weighed down by his years and the fatigues of his journey, approached wearily. Abraham received him kindly, washed his feet, and invited him to sit down and partake of his food. But on noticing that the old man prayed neither before nor after the meal, he asked him why he did not worship God in heaven. The old man told him that he was a fire-worshipper and did not recognize any other God. This reply made Abraham so angry that he drove the old man from his tent and exposed him to the inclemency of the night and the dangers of the desert. After the old man was gone, God called Abraham, and asked him where the stranger was. He replied, 'I drove him away because he did not worship Thee.' But God said to him: 'I have borne for a hundred years with his neglect, and couldst thou not tolerate it a single night, although he did not offend thee in the least?' Then Abraham perceived that he had done wrong, hastened after the old man, begged his pardon, and took him humbly back to his tent!"

"And we will do so, too," said Alice, rising from the bench.

"I know many an excellent man who differs with me so far as religious matters are concerned, and yet I would not hate him for it. He who seeks for truth shall remain our friend, even though he should pursue another path than ours. All the virtuous and good will meet at the goal."

Alice passed her day, like all others, in faithfully discharging her duties. She had to attend to manifold household cares, and to direct and superintend the labors of a large number of servants. Tenants came and went; they brought the rents of their holdings, which Alice received and carefully entered in a book. Almost all of them complained of hard times, and demanded large or small reductions in the amounts they owed. Alice granted willingly all she could, and, by her kindness, increased the number of the friends and faithful adherents of the house, who, if need be, were ready to die for their landlord.

Toward evening she went, attended by the chaplain and her faithful maid, to the cottages of the poor and sick, spreading everywhere consolation and relief, and greeted by the blessings of those to whom she was an affectionate mother. After kissing her babe once more, she took from a private drawer of her bureau, which was neatly inlaid with ivory and silver, a book, to which she was in the habit of confiding her most secret thoughts, sentiments, feelings, and adventures. For years past she had given to herself a strict account of her doings and ideas; she examined herself in so doing, and these carefully-preserved pages were a mirror of her soul. Here she had also noted down the sweetest secret, her first love for Milton. Now she wrote the following words, which bore witness to her purity and amiability:

"September 15th.—My lord set out early this morning to make inquiries concerning the enemy, who is said to be only fifteen miles from our castle. He hopes to return with my brother and some royal troops. When he left me I grieved sorely, and took up the Bible to console myself. The chapter which I happened to open caused me to feel in the most vivid manner the goodness of God toward His weak and ignorant children. Thank God, no learning and talents are required to understand the Gospel! I believe that poor simple women often entertain better and healthier views of life than we with all our knowledge. I rarely see blind old Betty, whose cottage I visited again yesterday, without learning a great deal from her and being comforted by her example. She has lost her husband, and all her children except one son, who left her long ago, and of whom she does not even know whether he is still alive. Moreover, she has been blind for fifteen years past; and yet she is serene and full of confidence in God. This blind old woman sees better than I do with my eyes open. While I was thus reading and meditating, there came to me our good chaplain, who had accompanied my lord to the gate. He brought me greetings from my husband, and we spoke of toleration toward those who differ from us. The worthy clergyman shared my opinion, and I was glad to hear him utter such mild views. On this occasion I thought of the man who is still dear to my heart, despite my duties as a wife and mother. My little son was slumbering calmly, and I thanked God for the precious pledge He has intrusted to me. All my grief vanishes whenever I contemplate the smiling face of my child; every impure thought is silent in the presence of this sweet innocence. I feel purified and elevated by its aspect.

"At dinner I felt lonely, as my lord was absent. It is not only the force of habit that attaches me to my husband, but the most fervent esteem and love for the best of men. He conquered my heart by his virtues, and stifled every previous affection in it. For the companion of my youth I feel now only sincere friendship. It is my firm conviction that he has not forgotten me either. Last night I visited the dairy-farm, and found every thing in good order. Cicely is a faithful girl, and the cattle thrive under her care. I praised her, for praise from the mistress gladdens the hearts of faithful servants. Always be more sparing of your censure than your praise. The sheep are again covered with wool; they were shorn in May last. Poor animals! How they rebelled at first against the cold iron, and yet finally submitted patiently to their fate! The young lambs bleated; they seemed not to recognize their mothers in their altered garb. I returned through the park. Never did I see the chestnuts and beeches so beautiful in their autumnal foliage. A sunbeam gilded the red and yellow leaves, some of which rustled pleasantly at my feet. I thought of my death, but the idea did not frighten me; I only wished to pass away as gently and smilingly as parting nature.

"I settled all accounts with the tenants in my lord's absence. I am almost afraid that I devote too much attention to worldly affairs, and neglect the examination and improvement of my heart. Others may believe that I am doing my whole duty; for who penetrates the secret faults of the heart; who knows the reluctance, imperfection, and coldness with which I serve my Creator, the egotism and reprehensible motives prompting my benevolent actions? Since I am a mother, I must watch myself with redoubled attention. When, tired by settling all those accounts, and filled with apprehensions, I laid my babe on my breast, my gloomy, anxious face seemed to frighten the little one. The boy, notwithstanding his age, already pays close attention to the physiognomies of the persons surrounding him. The expression of my countenance must have startled him, for he cried violently. My smiles and caresses again quieted the little one, who laid his head on my breast and soon fell asleep. This incident is very trifling in itself, and yet it teaches me how necessary it is for us always to be careful of what we are doing. Now, if this duty is incumbent on us toward our children, and toward all men, how much more so toward Him who sees through our hearts and knows our most secret thoughts!"

On the following day Sir Robert Carbury returned with a small detachment of soldiers commanded by Thomas Egerton, whom the king had sent to him. Alice went to meet her husband and her long-wished-for brother with unfeigned joy; but she soon perceived an expression of ill-concealed grief in the features and conduct of the two men.

"Robert," she said to her husband, "what has happened? Do not conceal any thing from me. You know that I am not timid, and as your wife I have a right to share your sorrows as well as your joys."

"I am afraid," replied Carbury, after some hesitation, "that we must part. You must not stay any longer at the castle. The enemy is drawing nearer and nearer to it, and he may be here to-morrow and begin the siege. You will set out this very day, attended by a faithful servant, to Ludlow Castle, where you will be safe at the house of your parents."

"What! do you think I could leave you? My place is here at your side. No danger can tear me from your side. We have solemnly vowed not to leave each other to our last day."

"But I cannot, must not expose you to the terrors of such a siege."

"But I am not afraid. Put me to the test, and you will see that I shall not tremble."

"Think of our son. For his sake I beg, I implore you to leave the castle!"

"The duties of the wife are not less stringent than those of the mother. My life belongs to you as well as to my son. I shall not leave you."

Carbury's entreaties, and even orders, were in vain; Alice persisted in her determination to share all dangers with him. Thomas, who loved his sister tenderly, was likewise unable to shake her will. She therefore remained, and calmly awaited the impending siege.

In a few hours the castle had lost its peaceful aspect. The court-yard and the halls were filled with noisy soldiers. Two small pieces of ordnance, which had formerly only been used on festive occasions, were planted on the walls; the last time they were discharged was in honor of the birth of an heir, and they had since then lain unused in a corner of the castle. They were now taken out and loaded with pieces of lead and iron. Some servants were ordered to fell the old trees in the park, lest they should cover the besiegers. The decayed parts of the wall were hurriedly repaired and provided with loopholes. The drawbridge was raised, and the necessary sentinels were posted. Alice assisted her husband and brother in this emergency in the most vigorous manner; with her maids she attended to the wants of the garrison, and, so far as the time permitted, caused the tenants and laborers, who were devoted to her, to drive the cattle from the pastures into the court-yard, and convey as much corn as possible into the castle. The court-yard was soon filled with lowing cows and bleating sheep, and the store-rooms with corn and flour. A large fire was burning in the kitchen, and the cook boiled and baked all day long for the hungry garrison.

Sir Robert Carbury had sent out some stout lads to reconnoitre the operations of the enemy. The intelligence with which they returned was any thing but reassuring. The Parliamentary army, commanded by Fairfax, had taken by assault and destroyed most of the castles and fortresses of the country; a detachment led by Major Overton, had started for the possessions of Sir Robert Carbury, and was already so close to them that its appearance might be looked for on the following day. There could be no doubt whatever as to its destination, Sir Robert Carbury being considered one of the most zealous adherents of the king. The night passed amid gloomy apprehensions. On the following morning Sir Robert Carbury ordered all the women, children, and sick persons to be removed from the castle. Only faithful Cicely and two servant-girls remained, to assist their mistress in her numerous and arduous labors.

Immediately after dinner Thomas and Carbury ascended the tower to watch with spy-glasses the approach of the enemy. Toward three they descried, in the horizon, a cloud of dust approaching with considerable rapidity. Here and there flashed from it a glittering weapon, a musket, or the hilt of a sword. They also heard the noise and rhythmic tread of a detachment of soldiers. As yet the numbers of the force could not be ascertained, but, to judge from the size of the cloud of dust, it could not be insignificant. Thus the danger was drawing nigh, veiled, like a sombre secret, concealing in its bosom destruction and death. It was not till some time afterward that they distinctly perceived the whole column moving like a serpent amid the hills and valleys, now disappearing among the trees, now emerging again into the plain. At the head of the troops rode the commander, surrounded by a few officers; behind him marched several hundred soldiers, the Saints of Israel, as they styled themselves. On beholding the castle, they intoned a pious hymn, and advanced as calmly as though they were about to go to church instead of making an assault on a fortified place.

"I suppose," said Thomas, "the rascals indulge the hope that they will carry the walls of this castle, like those of Jericho, by their sanctimonious noise. Would it not be prudent for us to give them a more correct opinion of the situation by a well-aimed cannon-shot?"

"We shall have time enough for that hereafter," replied his brother-in-law. "We must save our powder; they are as yet too far from the castle to fear our cannon-shots. But, notwithstanding their singing, they are good men, and their whole bearing indicates that they are brave and well-tried soldiers."

"Hold on," interrupted Thomas, "the fellows seem to be more polite than I thought they were. By the Eternal! they are sending to us a flag of truce, probably in order to summon us to surrender."

"Come, we will receive the bearer of the flag of truce, and hear what he has to say."

After descending from the tower, Sir Robert Carbury met at the drawbridge a Parliamentary officer, who demanded an interview with him. He called upon Carbury to surrender the castle and submit unconditionally to Parliament, when his life, as well as those of the garrison, would be spared. Sir Robert declared that he was a loyal adherent of the king, and that he would defend himself to the last drop of blood.

"Your blood be upon your own head, then," said the Puritan officer, spurring his horse.

The enemy immediately encamped, and displayed the same evening the utmost activity. On reconnoitring his position from the tower, Sir Robert acquired the conviction that he had to deal with an adversary alike brave and skilled in military operations.

"We shall have a hard fight," he said to Thomas. "The commander seems to be a man who understands his business."

"I know him, and am glad to have an opportunity to settle an old account with him. This man, Overton, is still in my debt."

The approach of Alice and the chaplain now gave another turn to the conversation. She invited the men to supper, of which they partook in a grave and solemn frame of mind. Afterward Sir Robert posted the sentinels, and urged them to be as vigilant as possible; he himself did not go to bed, but remained awake all night long, in order to be on hand for any emergency that might arise. Alice stayed with her babe. Before falling asleep, she clasped her hands, and prayed God to avert the imminent danger.

CHAPTER XXI.

MARRIAGE OF THOMAS AND LUCY—CAPTURE OF THE CASTLE.

THE autumnal sun rose in golden radiance. The mists which were floating like airy veils round the hills and meadows vanished, and the landscape exhibited an aspect of wondrous beauty. Nothing indicated that savage war was raging in these rural scenes. Every thing was yet hushed; only the flocks of the departing migratory birds sounded their farewell notes. Alice had stepped to the window and gazed upon the scenery. At last she beheld the camp, with its gray tents, which, like a dark thunder-cloud, had descended on these peaceful fields. It was no dream, it was the stern reality of war that was staring her in the face. The silver sickle of the moon was yet in the heavens, and the morning-star twinkled comfortingly to her. Profound silence seemed to reign in the camp; but loud flourishes resounded suddenly, and in a few moments the whole scene was changed. Soldiers rushed from the tents and formed in line; scaling-ladders and fascines for enabling the troops to climb the walls and fill the ditches were brought up. The column moved, and advanced at the quick-step to within cannon-range of the castle, shouting wildly, "The sword of the Lord and of Gideon!" There was a fearful pause of several minutes, during which Alice heard nothing but the throbbing of her own heart. Meanwhile, Sir Robert Carbury was at the head of the besieged. He had likewise closely watched the operations of the enemy, and awaited his approach on the rampart. He now ordered his men, in a loud voice, to point the cannon and fire at the assailants. The next moment the booming of artillery shook the air, and Alice, from her position, was able to observe the destructive effects of the balls. Several of the Parliamentary soldiers had fallen, and considerable gaps were to be seen in their ranks. The latter closed up again, and the assaulting column advanced with the utmost firmness and intrepidity. The brave commander encouraged his men incessantly, and by his words and example immediately restored order in the ranks of his soldiers. The besiegers were soon so close to the castle as to be entirely out of the range of Sir Robert's artillery; they suffered at the most only by the musketry of the garrison, which, however, injured them but very slightly. By means of the fascines which they had brought along, they tried to approach the ditch and the ramparts, and to gain the drawbridge, by which they hoped to penetrate into the castle. Already the boldest had climbed up, and were preparing to cut with their axes the chains fastening the bridge, when it was suddenly lowered, and Thomas, at the head of fifty volunteers, rushed out and drove back the surprised enemies. The foremost were either killed or compelled to jump into the ditch, in whose muddy waters they perished, unless a bullet put a speedier end to their sufferings. A terrible *mêlée* took place in the middle of the bridge; the enemies fought hand to hand, and tried to push each other into the ditch. Overton brought up reënforcements, but they were likewise unable to force an entrance into the castle. The Parliamentary troops had to yield to the impetuous bravery of the besieged, and were compelled to retreat. Murderous volleys of musketry from the ramparts of the castle pursued the fugitives, and it was not until they were close to their camp that Overton succeeded in rallying his dispersed soldiers.

The first assault had been successfully repulsed, and Alice thanked God for her husband's victory. She hastened immediately into the court-yard, where she met Sir Robert and Thomas, who had been slightly wounded in the hand-to-hand conflict. A handsome youth, who seemed to be his servant, was engaged in dressing his wound. Alice did not at once recognize her friend Lucy Henderson, who attended to the wounded, and took good care not to look at her. But when she was about to withdraw, and turned her face toward Alice, the latter uttered a cry of surprise.

"Lucy!" she exclaimed, in dismay.

The poor girl dared neither to stay nor to leave. A deep blush of shame suffused her cheeks.

"Come with me," said Alice, who suspected that there was a secret at the bottom of this strange disguise.

Lucy accompanied her friend to her room. Amid a flood of tears she confessed to Alice her illicit love for Thomas, her escape from old Henderson's house, and all her adventures since the performance of "Comus" at Ludlow Castle.

"I am unworthy," she said, at the conclusion of her narrative, "to be addressed by a noble lady like you. Ah! I was filled with shame and confusion on beholding you; you must consider me the vilest creature on earth."

"God forbid!" replied Alice, mildly. "'Judge not, that ye be not judged.' The Saviour forgave the greatest sinner, and how could I condemn you? My brother is at least as guilty as you are. I shall speak to him about you."

"Do so, but do not drive me to despair. I feel that I can never leave him."

"And yet it is necessary that you should. But, above all things, you must doff your male attire, and put on a costume becoming your sex."

"I will do all, all that you ask; only do not tell me to leave Thomas."

"It is not I, but he, that is to decide what is to be done. He took your honor from you; he shall now restore it to you."

"What! Did I understand you right?" asked Lucy, as if awaking from a dream. "No, no, that is impossible. It can never be. Thomas, your brother, become my husband? You forget that neither my birth nor my fortune entitles me to such a position."

Alice tried to quiet the excited girl; but she was unable to prevent her covering her hands and feet with kisses and tears. She called Cicely, who assisted Lucy in changing her dress, and she soon reappeared in her former garb. The kind-hearted lady had furnished the necessary articles, which fitted Lucy exactly. Thomas was sent for, and his sister had a long and grave interview with him.

"You have to make amends for a grievous wrong," she said to him. "It is your fault that poor Lucy lost her honor. I know that she loves you; she has proved it to you by her boundless devotion. It is for you now to restore honor and reputation to her. Your *liaison* must cease, and be converted into a more sacred union."

Although Thomas fully shared the frivolous views of life entertained by the young cavaliers of his age, he was not bold enough to profess such principles before his noble sister. The virtue and purity of Alice filled him with profound reverence, and in her presence he did not venture to utter an unbecoming word or a frivolous jest. Up to this moment Lucy had not raised any such claims, and he did not by any means look upon his union with her as an illicit one. Such love-affairs were very common among the cavaliers of the time, and were not only tolerated but encouraged in their circles. Nevertheless, Alice's words seemed to make a deep impression upon the light-hearted young man. Perhaps the many touching proofs of fervent love on Lucy's part were exercising a decisive influence over him at this moment. He went to Lucy and held out his hand to her.

"The chaplain," said Alice, "is waiting for you in the chapel, in order to marry you this very night."

Weeping, overcome at once by shame and

joy, Lucy sank into the arms of the virtuous lady. Accompanied only by Sir Robert Carbury and his wife, who were present at the ceremony as witnesses, the young couple stood before the altar, where the pious chaplain addressed a few appropriate remarks to them, and then married them. The passionate bride was filled with an affection bordering on veneration for her new sister-in-law. After the ceremony was over, Alice kissed Lucy, but this did not satisfy the impetuous girl; she threw herself at her feet, and kissed her hands, notwithstanding Alice's entreaties not to do so.

Meanwhile the siege took its course. The troops of the Parliament had soon recovered from their first defeat, and burned with the desire of avenging their discomfiture as soon as possible. They requested their commander Overton to order immediately another assault, but he preferred to surround the castle more closely, and starve the garrison into a surrender. For this purpose he posted all around the castle detachments which rendered it impossible for Sir Robert to obtain supplies from the surrounding country. He also had heavy artillery brought up, in order to breach the walls, and then undertake another and more successful assault. What few supplies the garrison had were soon exhausted, and ammunition was also scarce. Sir Robert was under the necessity of tearing all the lead and iron from the roofs and windows, in order to make balls and bullets. The enemy's artillery daily made sad havoc; the walls were soon in ruins, and the castle itself had already been injured to some extent. The ranks of the garrison were thinned, many of its soldiers having been killed and wounded. Under these circumstances, a council of war was held, and the resolution taken to make a sortie in order to provision the castle, and, if possible, to compel the Parliamentary troops to raise the siege.

In the dead of night the intrepid garrison, driven to extremity, left the castle and approached the advanced line of the besiegers. A soldier of the Parliament, who was about to give the alarm, was slain by Thomas himself. Already they were in the open field when they met a strong picket, which attacked them. It was not until now that they used their firearms. The reports of their muskets aroused the whole camp, and Overton himself hastened up at the head of his troops, which he had hastily formed in line. A desperate struggle now ensued in the profound darkness, which was broken only by the flashes of the muskets and the glittering of the swords. It was a most savage and bloody hand-to-hand conflict. Friend and foe were scarcely able to distinguish each other in the darkness of the night. It was not until the moon rose and shed her pale light on the scene that Overton ascertained the insignificant number of his adversaries. They were soon hemmed in on all sides, and nothing remained for them but to surrender or force a passage through the ranks of the enemy, which, at the best, involved them in the heaviest losses.

"Follow me!" shouted Thomas, courageously. "Sell your lives as dearly as possible."

So saying, he rushed intrepidly at the iron wall of the enemy, in order to break it; his men followed him with desperate impetuosity. But Overton opposed him with his veteran soldiers. Twice they crossed their blades, and the old adversaries recognized each other in the dim moonlight.

"Take this for Haywood Forest!" cried Thomas, levelling at the Puritan's head a powerful stroke, which Overton parried with great skill.

"Surrender!" shouted Overton. "The Lord has delivered you a second time into my hands."

"Stop your sanctimonious phrases, which fill me only with disgust!"

They fought with extreme exasperation, and, as before, the two were surrounded by a circle of men who, attracted by the extraordinary scene, had ceased fighting. Both adversaries had already received several wounds, when Sir Robert Carbury, who had vainly tried to break the line of the enemy at another point, approached them. He rushed impetuously upon the Puritans, and the struggle became general again. In the *mêlée* now ensuing Thomas was separated from Overton. The victory remained long doubtful; the scales of success inclining now to one side, now to the other. Sir Robert performed prodigies of valor; surrounded by his most faithful servants, he succeeded again in opening a bloody passage through the ranks of the enemy; but the superior numbers of the latter rendered it impossible for him to follow up the advantages he had obtained here and there. His force was thinned more and more, and his brave men sank mortally wounded at his feet. Closer and closer became the net which he vainly tried to break. Hitherto he had managed to keep his back free by retreating to a small grove which was covered by a shallow ditch. With his rear protected in this manner, he was able to resist the superior force of the enemy for some time. Overton, however, with his habitual penetration, had not overlooked this natural bulwark: at his bidding, a small detachment of his soldiers forced a passage, sword in hand, through the bushes. The clash of the swords and the breaking of the branches informed Sir Robert of this new and imminent danger. After a few minutes the soldiers had removed all obstructions, and only the narrow ditch served him yet as a bulwark, which he resolved to defend at any cost. The besiegers waded the ditch and rushed up the opposite bank, which was only a few feet higher. Here they met with a truly desperate resistance. Carbury profited by the slight advantages of his position, and, aided by his faithful men, hurled the soldiers, as they were climbing up, again and again into the ditch. The ditch filled with the corpses of the slain, which formed à natural bridge for the living. They stepped over them to return to the charge. All efforts of Sir Robert were in vain; attacked both in front and rear, he was unable to prolong the fight. After resisting in the most heroic manner, he sank mortally wounded to the grouud. But his fall was the signal of a still more desperate struggle. Thomas, who had perceived from afar the danger menacing his brother-in-law, hastened up with the remainder of his men to rescue him from his perilous position. He came too late to save him, but determined at least to avenge his death. He attacked Overton and his troops with furious impetuosity. His grief added to his intrepidity, and the besieged fought for the same reason with redoubled valor. The soldiers of the Parliament began to give way, and Thomas succeeded in breaking their ranks and retreating with his men to the castle, without being pursued by the enemy. He had Sir Robert's corpse conveyed into the court-yard, where Alice met the mournful procession, and, uttering a piercing cry, threw herself upon the bloody bier.

Notwithstanding her profound grief at the terrible loss which had befallen her, Alice did not lose her presence of mind; she was determined to carry out the intentions of her lamented husband, and defend the castle as he would have done. After his remains had been interred in the family vault, she appeared in her weeds before the garrison, which was now commanded by Thomas. Her noble form was wrapped in a black veil flowing to the ground, and leaving free only her pale face. In her arms she carried her orphan son, who was playing unconcernedly with the dark ribbons on her bosom. Thus she addressed the brave little garrison, and called upon them to resist the Puritans with unflinching courage. Her aspect touched and fired the hearts of these valiant men; many an eye, which had seldom or never wept, filled with tears. All swore of their own accord to live and die for their mistress.

Despite Carbury's death, the besiegers met, as before, with an unexpectedly vigorous resistance. Accompanied by Lucy, Alice appeared at all hours of the day among her faithful defenders to fire their courage, and she never failed to do so. Wherever the danger seemed more imminent than anywhere else, there she was sure to be found. Her whole nature had undergone a sudden change. Hitherto timid and retiring, she had all at once become a heroine, avenging the death of her husband and keeping the faith plighted to her king. Like the heroic women of antiquity, she did not shrink from the terrors of war, the clash of arms, and the sight of the dead and wounded. After sharing by day all the dangers of her men, she walked by night through the halls to dress the wounds of the brave. She herself underwent the greatest privations, and as the lack of provisions became every day more distressing, she willingly deprived herself of her wonted food and comforts. The whole garrison, among whom there was not a single deserter or traitor, displayed a fidelity and perseverance unheard of in this war. Nevertheless, all efforts of the besieged were unsuccessful. The artillery of the besiegers had destroyed the larger part of the ramparts and walls, and the garrison was unable to repair the damages. Exasperated by this unexpected delay, Overton resolved to venture on another assault. At midnight, when the garrison, overcome by the fatigues of the incessant struggle, had fallen asleep, the Parliamentary troops scaled the walls, and, before the sentinels were able to give the alarm, they were slain.

The court-yard soon filled with soldiers, who attacked the surprised garrison from all quarters. But the besieged offered even now the most desperate resistance. Thomas had thrown himself with a number of determined men into the tower; there was also Alice with her child. The brave men fired from the windows at the enemy, and their bullets killed yet many a soldier of Parliament. A detachment of intrepid volunteers, armed with axes, approached to break in the iron doors leading into the tower. Several well-aimed volleys of the besieged, however, were sufficient to dislodge them. Overton himself led his men once more to the charge; they no longer listened to his orders, but gave way dismayed at the shower of bullets thinning their ranks. There remained only one means, to which their commander, from motives of humanity, had hitherto refused to resort; but now he ordered his men to fetch pitch and torches to set fire to the tower. Dense clouds of smoke arose after a few minutes, and the greedy flames, fed by straw and fagots, consumed the worm-eaten timber with great rapidity. The devouring conflagration rose from story to story, and soon threatened to burn the garrison. No escape seemed possible, and all prepared to die in the raging sea of flames.

"It is better for us," said Thomas, at last, "to fall sword in hand than to perish so miserably in the fire. Let us, at least, sell our lives as dearly as possible."

His proposition met with general approval. Thomas then signed to his men, who drew back the bolts of the iron door, and the besieged, now reduced to a very small number, rushed from the burning tower. In their midst were Lucy and Alice, who carried her son in her arms. The Parliamentary troops immediately surrounded them. Escape was hardly possible, but all the more desperate was the struggle. Thomas succumbed to the odds of the enemy, and was taken prisoner; the same fate befell such of his men as were not slain by the exasperated victors. The two women were more fortunate. In the darkness and general confusion they succeeded in effecting their escape without being perceived by the infuriated soldiers. Already they had reached a small gate leading to the park and the open fields, when the cries of the babe attracted the attention of a soldier, who immediately pursued them. It was no other than Billy Green, who, imitating the example of many similar adventurers, was now seeking for booty and promotion in the Parliamentary army, after his patron Pym had died, and his profession as a spy and informer was no longer so lucrative as at the outset. He took good care to keep out of danger, and watched only for an opportunity, after the fight was over, to fill his pockets with the spoils that fell into the hands of the victors. Such an opportunity seemed to have come for him now. Owing to the bright glare of the burning tower, he discovered the fleeing women immediately; and when he had to deal with women he was always exceedingly brave. He had soon overtaken Alice and seized her dress.

"Halloo!" he shouted. "My sweet little dove, you will not escape in this manner."

"For God's sake, let me go! What do you want of me?"

"What a foolish question!" laughed the villain. "You wear on your neck a golden chain which pleases me amazingly."

"Take it, then, and do not detain me any longer."

"There is also a little ring glittering on your finger. I should like to get it for my sweetheart."

"It is my wedding-ring," replied Alice, mournfully.

"Let me see whether it is worth any thing," was his unfeeling reply.

Billy grasped her hand in order to draw the ring from it. In doing so, he had approached so close to her that she recognized him as the impudent Comus of Haywood Forest. He seemed to remember her likewise.

"Thunder and lightning!" he cried out. "If I am not mistaken, I have caught a precious little bird. You and your child must accompany me. Give me the babe."

"I will die rather than do so," replied Alice, resolutely, pressing her little son firmly to her heaving bosom.

"No foolery," said Billy, gruffly. "You are the lady of the castle, and my prisoner. Do not resist me; you see that I know who you are."

Alice vainly implored him to spare her and her child. Already Billy stretched out his hand to seize the babe, when Lucy, of whom he had hitherto taken no notice whatever, rushed at the villain with the courage of an angry lioness. Before he was able to prevent her, she had snatched the pistol which he wore in his broad belt.

"Stand back!" she shouted to him in a thundering voice, "or, as sure as there is a God in heaven, I will instantly shoot you down!"

Billy, seized with terror, staggered back a few steps, and the livid pallor of cowardice overspread his features; but he was soon encouraged by the thought that he had to deal only with a feeble woman. He left Alice and turned to his new enemy.

"Stand back!" she shouted to him once more, cocking the pistol.

Whether the villain was ashamed of his former cowardice, or was impelled by the desire of effecting an important capture, and thereby securing a large reward, he disregarded the threat, and put his hand on his sword in order to intimidate Lucy and arrest her and Alice; but before he was able to carry his purpose into effect, Lucy aimed at him and discharged the pistol. Billy Green fell wounded, and shouted piteously for help. Before any of his comrades had heard his cries, Lucy had seized the hand of her sister-in-law and fled with her.

CHAPTER XXII.

EXECUTION OF CHARLES I. — CROMWELL AND THE LEVELLERS.

Misfortune after misfortune had befallen the king; his troops had been routed, his adherents were fleeing or imprisoned; he himself was wandering about from place to place with the demoralized remnants of his army. Thus deserted by all the world, he listened at last to the counsels of Montreville, the French ambassador, and repaired to the camp of the Scots. He preferred to intrust himself to his Scotch rather than his English subjects—counting, doubtless, partly on their generosity, partly on the jealousy constantly prevailing between the two nations. He soon, however, acquired the conviction that he had been mistaken. The Scots sold the king for the sum of four hundred thousand pounds to the English Parliament. The Presbyterians, who were still in the ascendant, seized the king, and conveyed him to Holmby, where he was strictly guarded by their commissioners, but still treated with the respect due to his exalted rank. Charles himself indulged once more the hope that, by negotiating with his adversaries, he would not only succeed in saving his crown, but by and by recover his former power and authority. In accordance with his usual duplicity, he seemed to listen readily to the terms and proposals of Parliament, while he was secretly trying to be delivered from their hands. He thought the fanatical Independents and the army would help him to recover his liberty. He hated the moderate Presbyterians, who were in favor of a constitutional monarchy, far more than the republican Independents. Despotism always inclines more toward extreme democracy than toward the constitutional friends of liberty.

No sooner was the struggle ended by the capture of the king, than the last tie which had hitherto connected the two hostile parties was broken. The discord between the Presbyterians and Independents broke out with undisguised fury. Both were intensely jealous of each other; the former preponderated in the Parliament, the latter in the army. To deprive their opponents of the support of the army, the Presbyterians resolved to disband a part of it, and send the remainder to Ireland, where the rebellion was still raging with unabated violence. The soldiers, to whose valor alone Parliament was indebted for its triumph, were extremely indignant at these measures. They held daily meetings of the most excited character in the camp, and appointed committees to maintain the rights of the army.

Old Henderson, who exercised considerable influence over his party, stood, a few days after the king had been delivered to the English, in front of his tent, surrounded by a number of soldiers who shared his opinions. Some had Bibles in their hands; others leaned on the hilts of their long swords. Their stern faces were even graver than usual; fanatical zeal reddened their cheeks, and gleamed from under their shaggy eyebrows. They resembled a congregation of ecstatic worshippers rather than a crowd of soldiers.

"Israel, arm!" shouted the old Puritan. "Gird on thy sword, and prepare for the struggle with the heathens. The Lord has vouchsafed a great victory to the lion of Judah, but the cowardly jackal is intent on depriving him of his well-deserved reward, and robbing him of the spoils that belong to him alone. While we were fighting, the idle babblers reposed in safety; while we were starving, they revelled in wine; while we were watching, they slept on soft cushions. Instead of thanking us, they mock and revile the warriors of the Lord. Woe, woe to them!"

"Woe, woe to them!" murmured the soldiers, grasping the hilts of their swords in a menacing manner.

"Are we to be insulted with impunity?" asked the fanatical speaker. "Are we to suffer them to deprive the industrious laborer of his wages, and defraud him of the fruits of his toils? Zephaniah, tell us your opinion, for I know that you are a wise and prudent soldier."

The soldier whom he thus addressed started up, unsheathed his sword, brandished it in the air, and then relapsed into his former brooding.

"I understand you," added Henderson. "The sword is to decide between us and them, between the victorious army and the ungrateful Parliament."

Zephaniah contented himself with nodding his head, to indicate that this was his opinion. Most of the other soldiers assented to it likewise. Only a cornet, named Joyce, made another proposition.

"The time has not come yet," he said, "for us to settle our accounts with Parliament. We have to deal with a bad debtor, and hence let us seize a pledge, that the reluctant debtor may remain at our mercy. Such a pledge is the king, whom Parliament is guarding. He who has his person has the power. I therefore advise you to start immediately for Holmby, and convey the king to the camp, either by a stratagem or by main force. Who is more entitled to Charles than the army which vanquished him? To it belong rightfully all advantages that may be derived from his presence; and if negotiations are to be entered upon with him, it is better that this should be done on the part of the army than on that of Parliament."

"The Lord inspires you to speak thus!" exclaimed old Henderson. "We will not hesitate to follow your advice immediately.—Mount your horses, soldiers; and you, Cornet Joyce, shall be our leader."

Shortly afterward a detachment of soldiers, headed by the cornet, set out for Holmby. Toward midnight they arrived at that place, and demanded to see the king. The commissioners of Parliament were not a little surprised, but they relied on the fidelity of their soldiers who were guarding the king. General Browne and Colonel Graves, who were in command of the troops, asked the cornet for his name, and what he wanted, before admitting him.

"I am Cornet Joyce," he replied, boldly, "and wish to see the king."

"By whose order?" they inquired.

"By my own."

The officers laughed.

"You need not laugh," he said, very gravely. "I have as good a right to see him as any one in England."

The officers told him to remove his soldiers, and apply on the morrow to the commissioners of Parliament.

"I neither need your advice," he replied, "nor have I to deal with the commissioners, but only with the king. I will and must see him immediately."

Browne and Graves ordered their soldiers to draw their swords, but they had already recognized some of their old comrades and come to an understanding with them. Instead of obeying their officers, they themselves opened the gate and welcomed the Puritan soldiers. After posting sentinels in front of the rooms of the commissioners, Joyce demanded, pistol in hand, an interview with the king. The four chamberlains informed Charles of what had occurred, but the king refused to see Joyce until the following day.

Early in the morning he admitted him. Joyce came into his presence armed with pistols, and told him that he must immediately go along with him.

"Whither?" said the king.

"To the army," replied Joyce.

"By what warrant?" asked the king.

Joyce pointed to the soldiers whom he had

brought along; tall, handsome, and well accoutred.

"Your warrant," said Charles, smiling, "is written in fair characters, legible without spelling."

The commissioners, who had been summoned in the mean time, were compelled to consent to the king's removal, and resolved to accompany him. Charles seemed not at all displeased with Joyce's mission. He had really more confidence in the army than the Parliament; he hoped he would now be able to enter into direct connection with the commanders of the troops, and gain them over to his side. In the first place he was conveyed to Hampton Court. His expectations seemed at first to be verified. On the way to his new place of confinement, he was allowed to embrace his children, the Dukes of York and Gloucester, and the Princess Elizabeth. The impressionable populace who witnessed this affecting interview were deeply moved by it. They strewed flowers and leaves at the feet of the royal family, and even his guards were so profoundly touched by this tender scene that they gladly permitted him to keep his children several days with him. At Hampton Court he did not live by any means as a prisoner; he resided in the most sumptuous rooms of the magnificent palace, and was attended by a numerous retinue. His adherents flocked to him from all quarters, and no one was denied access to him.

Presbyterians and Independents, Parliament and the army, every party and sect vied in their efforts to derive as much benefit as possible from the peculiar position of the king. All wished to come to an understanding with Charles, and bring about his restoration to the throne on as favorable terms as possible. Thus he became the centre of the most conflicting interests and all sorts of intrigues; he was courted and flattered by the leaders of the parties and the army. Members of Parliament, generals, and commissioners thronged in the apartments of Hampton Court around the person of the fallen monarch, as formerly at Whitehall, when Charles was still at the height of his power. Wily mediators went to and fro; the king used for this purpose his confidant Berkeley and his faithful adherent Ashburnham. Through them he negotiated now with the Parliament, now with the army, stirring hopes in both, making promises, and holding out prospects of rewards. So great was the charm of majesty, that, after having lost all, it yet possessed enough to excite the ambition, cupidity, and vanity of the victors. Even the shadow of this setting sun was yet surrounded with seductive splendor and imposing grandeur.

Notwithstanding his downfall, Charles was placed in a more favorable posture than during the war; but he did not know how to yield little things in order to gain great ones. His old obstinacy awoke again, and he deceived himself again as to the extent of his power. In his infatuation he ascribed the position which he owed to circumstances and to the mutual jealousies of the hostile parties, to his own person and his supposed innate and Heaven-given royal majesty. His old duplicity and treachery added to this infatuation: he sought to overthrow the Presbyterians by the Independents, the Parliament by the army, and *vice versa*, and get rid of one adversary by means of the other. For this reason he listened to all parties, and negotiated with all; now with the Scots, now with the English; with the commissioners of Parliament, as well as the commanders of the army. At the head of the latter were Generals Fairfax and Cromwell. It was chiefly with Cromwell and his son-in-law Ireton that Charles entered into clandestine negotiations. He made Cromwell promises brilliant enough to satisfy the ambition of the Puritan general. It was owing perhaps to Cromwell's dissatisfaction with Parliament that he listened to them; and yet he never ceased to look with the greatest distrust upon the king.

Cromwell and Ireton had learned from a spy that the king was keeping up a continuous correspondence with the queen, who had fled to France. They had been informed that a letter concerning them was to be forwarded from Hampton Court by a groom who had concealed it in a saddle. Henrietta had reproached her husband with negotiating with the "scoundrels" Cromwell and Ireton, and promising them titles and orders. Charles's letter contained his reply, and it was now all-important for the two generals to find out his true opinion.

For this purpose they watched at midnight at the gate of the palace for the departure of the messenger. The groom, who did not suspect that every thing had been betrayed, appeared at the stated hour, bearing the saddle on his head.

"Stand, villain!" thundered Cromwell to him.

"What do you want of me?" asked the groom, falling on his knees.

"What do you bear on your head?"

"A saddle, sir," replied the groom, trying to look unconcerned. "It is nothing but an old saddle which I am going to take to the saddler who is to repair it."

"At this hour of the night? Give it to us; we will save you the trouble."

"No, that would not do. I cannot let you have the saddle."

"You must," cried Cromwell, attempting to take it from him.

"Help, help!" shouted the groom, resisting him.

Before any one could hear him, Ireton had drawn his sword and stabbed him. The messenger sank to the ground without uttering a groan. The generals hastened away with the saddle; they opened it, and found in it a letter written by the king, containing the following words: "Never fear. You may leave to me the care of the negotiations, as I am familiar with the situation, and know precisely what to do under the circumstances. I have entered into relations with the scoundrels Cromwell and Ireton only in order to gain them over to my side for a short time. I am far from taking my promises seriously, and instead of the order of the garter, the halter which they deserve awaits them so far as I am concerned."

After reading these lines aloud, Ireton burst into imprecations against the king and his perfidy. Cromwell remained calm; only a wild peal of laughter indicated his intense hatred.

"I believe," he added, gloomily, "that his neck is in greater danger than ours. A traitor falls by his own hands. He shall presently tremble before the scoundrels."

After this event, a sudden change took place in the treatment of the king; he was kept again in stricter confinement; his guards were doubled; his adherents were removed, and many a liberty allowed to him hitherto was now denied. Charles deemed this change intolerable, and resolved to escape from Hampton Court, but he was chiefly incited to this determination by a mysterious warning that his life was threatened. A new political and religious sect, the so-called Levellers, had arisen in the army. They advocated an equal distribution of all property, the abolition of all distinctions of rank, and especially the overthrow of the royal throne. Henderson, Cromwell's old friend, joined these extremists, and so did several superior officers, such as the well-known Colonel Harrison, who dreamed, moreover, of a millennium, and a republic of the saints. These fanatics uttered loud threats against the king, and said they would seize his person. Charles had been warned of their plans, and this was the chief motive of his flight.

He had succeeded in deceiving his guards by means of a skilful disguise and escaping, attended only by a faithful servant. He was presently joined by his chamberlains, Berkeley and Ashburnham, who, informed of every thing, had been waiting for him on the road. Charles himself was at a loss where to go. At first he thought of repairing to London and intrusting himself to the city or the Parliament; but this step seemed too dangerous to himself; then again he resolved to escape to Jersey. Ashburnham finally proposed to him to go to the Isle of Wight, whose governor, Hammond, an old friend of his, he said, would surely befriend his majesty. The king was well pleased with this proposition, and dispatched his chamberlain to Hammond to ascertain more about his sentiments. Hammond professed great readiness to afford the king all necessary protection, and promised to call himself upon Charles and accompany him back to the isle.

No sooner had Ashburnham returned, than Charles regretted what he had done, and expressed fears as to the governor's fidelity.

"I am afraid," he said, "that Hammond will betray me."

"If your majesty has no confidence in him," replied Ashburnham, "you need not admit him."

"I have, moreover, dispatched Berkeley in your absence to Southampton, to find a vessel that can convey me to France, and look momentarily for his return. What are we to do when the governor comes?"

"If your majesty deems it best, I will kill him. I will conceal myself behind the curtain, and shoot him as soon as you sign to me."

"We will see," replied Charles, with his usual irresolution.

Hammond came, and was admitted. He assured the king so solemnly of his fidelity and attachment, that Charles's apprehensions disappeared. Ashburnham waited in vain for the sign which had been agreed upon. The king did not give it.

Charles embarked with the governor for the Isle of Wight, and accompanied him to Carisbrooke Castle, where he deemed himself perfectly safe. His faithful attendants, Ashburnham and Berkeley, did not leave him. Here, too, his position at the outset seemed by no means unfavorable. Both Parliament and the Scots sent commissioners to negotiate with him. With the latter he concluded a secret treaty, by which he recognized their rights, while they themselves engaged to restore him to his throne, if need be, sword in hand. He sent his faithful Berkeley to the generals of the army, to renew his former negotiations with them. As a matter of course, he met with a very cool reception.

Meanwhile the religious and political fanaticism of the Levellers had risen to such a pitch as to endanger the discipline of the army. Cromwell, with his wonted sagacity, penetrated the pernicious consequences of this mutinous spirit, which he himself had at first encouraged. He issued a proclamation forbidding his soldiers to hold meetings and present petitions. Nevertheless, the Levellers met secretly, and several regiments openly mutinied.

"We must make a severe example of them," he said to Ireton. "This mutinous spirit is spreading rapidly, and the Levellers will ruin the commonwealth."

"Are they not our friends?" asked his son-in-law, wonderingly. "Did they not drive the king to the Isle of Wight, where he can no longer escape us, and intimidate Parliament?"

"Friends may become burdensome to us, and do us more harm than good. We must no longer look on idly; otherwise this spirit of rebellion will involve us in general ruin. These saints injure the good cause, and turn the quiet citizens against us. They advocate a distribution of property, and abolition of all distinctions of rank. I do not intend to divide my property with them, nor to give up an iota of my vested rights."

"What are you going to do with them?"

"I will crush them before they are strong enough to resist me! Go, Ireton, and have the army formed in line for a review."

The army drew up in an open field. Cromwell soon appeared, attended by all the generals and staff-officers. With his usual tranquillity and impenetrable face, he rode down the line and stopped in front of the mutinous regiments. He knew the ringleaders, and ordered them to step forward. Among them was old Henderson.

"Seize them!" he ordered, in a loud voice.

The eleven men were instantly surrounded and given into custody. He summoned a council of war, which passed sentence of death upon the mutineers.

Cromwell approached them, and fixed his piercing eyes upon them. His gaze fell upon the Puritan, his former friend, but he feigned not to recognize him. After looking at them for a time, he pointed out two of the most violent Levellers.

"Take them and execute them," he said, in a loud voice.

Both were compelled to kneel down, and were shot in the presence of the whole army. No one dared to murmur; a salutary terror spread through the ranks. The other prisoners expected that they would be executed likewise. Henderson was the first of them; he was calm and composed. Already the muskets had been reloaded, and the sentence was about to be carried into effect; already the intrepid Puritan had knelt down to pray, when Cromwell waved his hand.

"It is sufficient," he said, with a peculiar smile. "Let this day be a warning to all. I tolerate no disobedience among my soldiers."

The army marched in silence and deep emotion past the general, whose energy and courage had thus stifled the mutiny and restored discipline among his soldiers. Old Henderson only remained inflexible, and his former attachment to Cromwell turned into a mortal hatred.

Shortly after this domestic triumph Cromwell was obliged to lead the army against a foreign foe. An insurrection had broken out in Scotland in favor of King Charles, and his partisans rose also in several parts of England, and particularly in South Wales. The general suppressed these risings in favor of the unfortunate king with his wonted bravery and sagacity. All these events added to the dangers menacing Charles. Cromwell became more and more satisfied that nothing but a bold stroke would restore order. Both he and his friends resolved to sacrifice the king, and abolish the royal throne. In Parliament, too, there were many who deemed this the most prudent course. People were tired of negotiating with Charles, whose duplicity had disgusted and exasperated all parties.

Governor Hammond, with whom Cromwell corresponded, received orders to deliver the king to Colonel Cobbett, who was instructed to convey him first to Hurst, and thence to London. On the road, Colonel Harrison, the fanatical champion of the millennium, joined the escort. It was not till he beheld the dreaded fanatic, that Charles lost the serene indifference which he had exhibited up to this time. However, the colonel treated the king with soldierly politeness, and his blunt though frank conduct and bearing gradually inspired him with confidence. He took his arm and conversed a long time with him.

"I have been told," said Charles, "that you intend to assassinate me."

"Your majesty has been misinformed," replied the colonel. "I may justly repeat what I have said so often, that the laws protect everybody, the noble and the lowly, the rich and the poor; and that justice must be done without regard to persons."

The king seemed offended by his frankness, and broke off the conversation after a while.

No sooner had Charles reached London, than the Parliament preferred charges against him. The trial of the king took place at Westminster Hall. The court consisted of one hundred and thirty-three members, among whom were Cromwell, Ireton, and Harrison.

The charges were read, and the king was called upon to defend himself. He did so with dignity and moderation, but without acknowledging the competence of the court. Above all things, he appealed to his inviolability as king, who, according to the English constitution, could do no wrong, and therefore could not be punished. His appeals, however, were unsuccessful. The court was determined to convict him, and sentence of death was passed upon him.

Three days were allowed the king between his sentence and his execution. All the steps taken by his friends and relatives in his behalf proved utterly fruitless. The people were indifferent, and manifested neither love nor hatred of him; they were intimidated, perhaps, by the presence of numerous troops in London. Charles passed this interval with great tranquillity, chiefly in reading and devotion. All his family that remained in England were allowed access to him. They consisted only of the Princess Elizabeth and the Duke of Gloucester; all the others had made their escape. Charles comforted and exhorted them, and tenderly embraced his weeping daughter.

"Tell your mother," exclaimed the unfortunate king, "that during the whole course of my life I have never once, even in thought, failed in my fidelity toward her, and that my conjugal tenderness and my life shall have an equal duration."

To the young duke, whom he held on his knee, he said: "Now they will cut off thy father's head."

At these words, the child looked very steadfastly upon him.

"Mark, child, what I say," he added. "They will cut off my head, and perhaps make thee a king. But mark what I say, thou must not be a king, as long as thy brothers Charles and James are alive. They will cut off thy brothers' heads when they can catch them; and thy head too they will cut off at last. And therefore, I charge thee, do not be made a king by them."

"I will be torn in pieces first," replied the boy. So determined an answer, from one of such tender years, filled the king's eyes with tears of joy and admiration.

On the morning of his execution, Charles rose early, and prayed in the presence of Herbert, his faithful servant, and Bishop Juxon, whom the Parliament had allowed to assist him in his devotions. The king then walked to the scaffold, where he uttered only a few words, justifying his conduct, and forgiving his enemies. When he was preparing himself for the block, Bishop Juxon called to him: "There is, sire, but one stage more, which, though turbulent and troublesome, is yet a very short one. Consider, it will soon carry you a great way; it will carry you from earth to heaven; and there you shall find, to your great joy, the prize to which you hasten, a crown of glory."

"I go," replied the king, calmly, "from a corruptible to an incorruptible crown, where no disturbance can have place."

He himself gave the signal of death by moving his hand.

A man in a black visor performed the office of executioner. At one blow was the king's head severed from his body. At the same moment the assembled spectators burst into deafening shouts, which indicated perhaps more compassion than approval.

The executioner held up to the spectators the head streaming with blood, and cried aloud, "This is the head of a traitor!"

BOOK III.

CHAPTER I.

MILTON AND DAVENANT—LADY ALICE'S DIARY.

MILTON had hitherto taken little or no direct part in public affairs; he lived mostly in quiet retirement, engrossed with the education of his pupils. It was not until the king had been executed that he was aroused from his tranquillity. He had joined the Independents almost against his will, as his former political friends seemed to profit by their victory only to menace anew that liberty to which he was so ardently devoted. Once a member of the extreme party, he did not shrink from any of the consequences of its principles. The bloody deed had been perpetrated; the people had availed themselves of their power, and killed Charles. But, as usual, death proved a great conciliator; the melancholy end of the unfortunate monarch caused the public to forget his faults, and the fickle multitude pitied him almost as much as it had formerly hated him. It was all-important now to enlighten public opinion and give it a definite direction, fix the vacillating sentiments and feelings, and pass a calm judgment amid the storm of passions. Milton took upon himself this arduous task, which might involve him in the greatest perils, without hesitation, without prospect of rewards or thanks, solely guided by his love of liberty.

A gloomy silence had succeeded the intense excitement of the nation, which now stood aghast at its own power and boldness. No one ventured to raise his voice and defend the execution of King Charles. So great was the awe inspired even by dead majesty, that the men who were now at the helm of government enjoyed the fruits and divided the spoils of their victory in silence.

Milton entered, without hatred of the king or of the monarchical system, upon an examination of the great problem of popular sovereignty, which he tried to solve with the dispassionate calmness of a philosopher. It was not till his adversaries, among whom the celebrated Leyden professor Salmasius played the most prominent part, overwhelmed him with the vilest invectives, that Milton retorted with a warmth which embittered all his later years. The success of his political pamphlets was as great as it was unexpected. The attention of the council of state, which was intrusted with the administration of the country, was called to the learned and enthusiastic lover of liberty, and it appointed Milton foreign or Latin secretary. In this capacity he wrote the correspondence of the new republic in Latin, which, since the peace of Westphalia, had become the language of the courts. In this manner he became acquainted with the leading men of the country, and Cromwell, who was already at the head of the administration, was on intimate terms with Milton.

A short time after Milton had been appointed to his new office, the witty poet Davenant was threatened with death. He had accompanied his patroness, Queen Henrietta, during her flight to France. At her request he had now returned to England to establish connections in favor of the exiled hereditary prince with the discontented royalists. His intentions were betrayed to Cromwell, who had him arrested, and examined him personally concerning the plans of his adversaries, The general approached the prisoner with a quick step, and threatened to pierce him with his keen eyes. Notwithstanding his dangerous predicament, the light-hearted poet had not lost his old humor.

"You are a self-convicted traitor," said Cromwell, in a stern voice, "and shall not escape your fate. I shall have you hung to-morrow."

"You need not be in a hurry about it; I am free to confess that I should like to wait a few years yet."

"Leave your jests, and prepare rather to die like a Christian."

"I have always been a good Christian, and am not afraid of death."

"A good Christian! Do you suppose, then, that I do not know you? Did you not write all the lascivious farces and masks that were performed at the court of Charles Stuart with such extravagant pomp and splendor? You deserve the halter for the life which you have led up to this time."

"If every one in this world were to be punished according to his deserts, all the halters in England would be insufficient."

"Enough said!" cried Cromwell, sternly. "I will send you my chaplain."

"For God's sake, don't! I hate nothing more intensely than water and priests. If you will do me a favor, send me a bottle of wine; it will comfort me much better than your chaplain."

Cromwell turned angrily from the incorrigible jester, and ordered the guard to take him away. On entering the anteroom, the doomed poet met Milton, with whom he had been slightly acquainted in former times.

"Davenant!" exclaimed Milton, in surprise. "Where are you going?"

"Where all go sooner or later—to death."

"You are under sentence of death? And why?"

"On account of my devotion to the queen. I have shared the days of her prosperity, and therefore could not forsake her in the days of her adversity; she fed me with her bread, and therefore I will give up my life for her. It is true, I have never paid my debts, but I am at least going to discharge this one."

"You must not, shall not die."

"Do not take any trouble to save me; I know that all will be in vain. Cromwell has pronounced my doom, and I look upon myself already as a dying man. Shake hands with me once more; perhaps we may meet again in a better life, where there are no Puritans and cavaliers, no soldiers and priests. To tell you the truth, I am not afraid of death; but I am sorry to leave the farce of human life at so early a stage. I should not have expected this tragic *dénouement*."

"I shall do all I can to save you."

"Accept my thanks for your kindness, which I appreciate very highly. Give me your hand, dear Milton! I always considered you a good-hearted, generous man. You are only somewhat too pious, and too zealous a lover of liberty. Believe me, it will result in nothing. The people expel one tyrant to exchange him for another who is a great deal worse; and the same thing is the case with religion. Sensible men, like you and me, should not meddle with such trifles at all. Do not be angry at this; I lack taste for such things, but

I really do not see why two sensible men should hate and persecute each other because they differ on certain points."

Milton shook hands with the poet, and promised to obtain a pardon for him from the general. He found Cromwell in a gloomy frame of mind. The young republic was at this juncture threatened from all quarters; foreign and domestic enemies united to overthrow it. Civil war was still raging in Ireland, and Cromwell's presence there was urgently demanded. The Scots had called the son of Charles I., Charles II., and conferred the crown of his father upon him, though on very rigorous conditions. The Levellers had been intimidated, but not crushed; they were again in open rebellion, and threatened to subvert law, order, and society. Add to all this the intrigues of the partisans of the late king, who were incessantly entering into new plots. The general sat frowning in front of a map, devising the plan of a new campaign, by which he intended to annihilate all his enemies. At Milton's entrance he gave a start, and looked around distrustfully. On recognizing him, however, he kindly held out his hand to him.

"It is you, Mr. Secretary," he said, with a winning smile.

"I bring you the letters to the Dutch Republic, and to Cardinal Mazarin."

"Put them on the table, and be seated. I wish to speak to you. You are an honest and pious man, in whom I may confide. Many others are not at all like you. The Lord has laid a heavy burden upon me."

"He knows what He does. To the strongest shoulders He intrusts the heaviest burdens. You are the only man capable of saving the country."

"I thank you for your good opinion, and would like to do something for you. Since I have acquired some influence, every one overwhelms me with requests and demands; you alone have not yet opened your mouth."

"I may hope the more, then, that you will not reject my prayer to-day."

"Tell me frankly what you want of me."

"I ask of you the life of a man whom you have just sent back to his prison."

"What!" said Cromwell, wonderingly, "you ask me to pardon Davenant, that infamous sinner? Do you know what he is charged with?"

"He has remained faithful to his queen, and to the cause he espoused. I esteem him more highly for this than many an apostate who has suddenly turned republican, whether from fear or self-interest."

"Bah! We must not judge our political friends too scrupulously. I know there are a great many rogues and hypocrites among us; but they do far less harm than the wrong-headed, stubborn, honest men. If I am not mistaken, your friend Overton is one of the latter. He and John Lilburn give me more trouble than the royalists. Give your friend Overton a hint to beware of me. I know that he sympathizes with the Levellers and rebels in the army."

"You assuredly do him injustice. It is true, he is an ardent enthusiast, but I do not believe that he shares the views of the Levellers and, like them, is bent on subverting law, order, and society. He loves liberty and the republic. This is certainly no crime after the royal government has been abolished."

"Of course not," said Cromwell, mildly. "A republican government is certainly a nice thing, provided it be understood correctly. Fools deem it a field where they may gratify their licentiousness; but wise men consider it a form of government like any other. But if I am not mistaken, we were speaking of Davenant."

"And I repeat my former request."

"He does not deserve to be pardoned. He is a miserable playwright, an immoral scapegrace."

"For that reason he is the more harmless; he is talented, and I should greatly regret to see him lose his head."

"As you intercede so warmly in his behalf, let him keep it, although I cannot comprehend how so virtuous a man can ask me to pardon such a sinner."

"He is a poet for all that, and as such at least he is entitled to my sympathy. I esteem divine poesy wherever I find it, and for the sake of the precious contents I would like to preserve the vessel, even though it should consist partly of base metal and be disfigured by many rents and holes."

"Well, I believe you are right," said Cromwell, with a sudden burst of mirth. "Davenant is a broken jar with many rents and holes. He has one hole which is very large, and his nose is gone."

The general then resumed his former dignified tone, and drew up the pardon for which Milton had applied.

"Go," he said, kindly, "and inform him personally that I consent to release him; but if he should enter again into a political conspiracy, nothing would save his head. I do not care if he writes farces and masks, but tell him to beware of meddling with politics. That is a dangerous, very dangerous game for such inexperienced hands."

So saying, the general dismissed Milton. He repaired immediately to the prison of Davenant, whom he found engrossed with a bottle of wine.

"I bring you your pardon," he said.

"Do you, indeed? Well, God bless you for what you have done for me! You see that I was already preparing for death. Wine is the best confessor and most efficient comforter. Nevertheless, I was unable to get rid of a somewhat unpleasant feeling. I must confess that I am a little ticklish, and when imagining a halter round my neck, I feel a very peculiar itching. You have relieved me of this unpleasant feeling, and I shall always be grateful to you for it. There may soon be an opportunity for me to prove my gratitude, for, to tell you the truth, I have very little confidence in this republic of the saints. The people feel at ease only when they have a master ruling over them. If his name is not Charles, it will be Cromwell. The general looks very much like a man who would not pass a crown if he should find it in his path."

"You misjudge Cromwell; his whole endeavor is to put an end to the civil war, and render England great and happy."

"I have no doubt of it; he will fatten the goose before killing it. But I do not want to exasperate you. You are an innocent, honest man, a genuine poet filled with illusions, and always seeking for some object of your enthusiastic admiration. I am precisely like you in this respect. We shall always be the fools of our enthusiasm, and fool others thereby. Farewell, my excellent friend in need."

"Where are you going now?"

"To my old mother, who is still keeping tavern and entertaining drinkers of all confessions. I shall await there quietly the end of your republic, write farces, and soon compose a coronation hymn for Charles II."

Davenant drank another glass of wine, and left his prison with that cynical indifference which had become habitual to him. Milton accompanied him a short distance, and then returned to his house. He found there his friend Overton, who had been expecting him for some time. The major was about to start for the army in Scotland.

"Before departing for the army," he said, after greeting Milton cordially, "I wished to see you once more."

"Where have you been so long?" asked Milton, kindly.

"Now here, now there, wherever the events of the war led me; to-day in the south, to-morrow in the north. A soldier is always on the wing, and it may be a long while yet before I shall be able to take repose."

"You seem to long for it."

"To tell you the truth, I am tired of this rough life. You know that I prefer science and the muses to any thing else. War, however just the cause for which it is waged, is always a very melancholy business. I have recently seen all its horrors in Wales."

"In Wales?" asked Milton, eagerly.

"I have fought there many a hard fight, and destroyed many a fine castle. It is true, I only did my duty, but I did it with a bleeding heart. The most painful duty imposed upon me was the destruction of Golden Grove. The garrison defended the castle with the most heroic intrepidity, and after the proprietor had fallen, his wife offered us a most unexpected resistance. I should have liked to spare her, but it was beyond my power. Nothing remained for me but to take the castle by storm. On this melancholy occasion I discovered accidentally that the distinguished lady must have formerly been on intimate terms with you."

"Her name was Alice Carbury," said Milton, deeply moved.

"Alice Carbury. Carbury was the name of her husband, and she herself was the daughter of the Earl of Bridgewater, formerly Lord President of Wales. I penetrated into the castle and passed several days there. The rooms of the lady had been ransacked; my soldiers had destroyed the furniture, torn off the hangings, and broken open the cabinets. This diary, which I found there, attracted my attention. I opened it, and saw your name on almost every page; this excited my curiosity, and I kept it in order to give it to you."

"But what became of the lady?" inquired the poet, anxiously.

"Unfortunately, I am unable to give you any satisfactory information on this point, although all that I ascertained about it leads me to the belief that she succeeded in making her escape. One of my men, a cowardly vagabond, asserted that he had seen her, and had even been wounded by her female companion on attempting to arrest them. I did not make any further inquiries concerning them, and, from regard for you, desisted from pursuing them. I should be very glad if the lady succeeded in making her escape. I will let you keep the diary, as it may be exceedingly interesting for you."

Milton received with profound emotion at the hands of his friend the pages which reminded him of the noble lady, and of his own youth. He thanked him by informing him of Cromwell's warning.

"I know that he is not partial to me," said Overton, with a sombre smile. "He is jealous of my influence, and afraid of the frankness with which I criticise his measures. I am a republican, and consider a republic our only salvation. According to his habit, the general tried to ascertain my opinions, and I did not conceal them from him."

"But you do not believe that he intends to restore the monarchy and recall the Stuarts?"

"He will assuredly not recall the Stuarts, but I should not like to pledge my word that he does not intend to convert our present government again into a monarchy. The general seems intent on becoming the tyrant of England; but before he is able to attain his ends, I and my comrades will oppose him and frustrate his plans."

So saying, Overton took leave of Milton. The poet held in his hands the diary, the first trace of his beloved friend with which he had met after so many years. A feeling of awe prevented him from opening it immediately, and he hesitated whether he had a right to penetrate into the secrets of this noble female heart. At last, it was not his curiosity that triumphed, but the tender interest which he took in Lady Alice's fate. In reading the diary, he felt anew that he once possessed and forfeited in her the supreme happiness of his life. What purity of heart, what innocence and cultivation of mind met him in her every line! He followed, with profound emotion, the noble woman's struggle between duty and love, until at last her heart turned entirely to her husband, and felt for Milton only a purified friendship, the sweet though melancholy memories of a blissful past. Every word he read bore witness to her noble heart, her profound mind, and her simple and gentle faith.

Milton was seized with the deepest grief, and his tears moistened the precious leaves, the only token of the fair friend of his youth, the only woman whom he had truly loved. He thought of her with mournful longing, and a deep sigh escaped his breast.

CHAPTER II.

LADY ALICE IN LONDON — MILTON AND SALMASIUS.

One day when Milton, according to his habit, was taking a walk in the environs of London, he beheld two women and a child; they were plainly, almost poorly dressed, and hotly pursued by a man who was about to overtake them. They tried to accelerate their steps, but the pursuer was already so close to them that he needed only to stretch out his hand in order to catch them, when one of the women uttered a loud cry.

"Save us!" she cried, in an anxious voice, which seemed well known to Milton.

Meanwhile the man had also come up.

"What do you want of these women?" asked the poet.

"Is that any of your business? I need not give you an account of what I am doing. These women must follow me; I arrest them in the name of the commonwealth."

"And by what right?"

"They are traitresses, for I have recognized them despite their disguise. They know me too, and that not to-day for the first time. Many a year has elapsed since we first met in Haywood Forest. Is it not so, Lady Alice?"

On hearing this name, Milton trembled with joyous surprise.

"These two ladies are under my protection," he said, with dignified firmness. "I will be their bondsman, and that you may know who I am, I will mention my name and official position."

"That is unnecessary," replied Billy Green, with his wonted impudence. "We are old acquaintances, Mr. Milton, and I hope to meet you and your *protégées* before long."

So saying, the vagabond left them.

The meeting of Milton and the lady he had loved so dearly was highly affecting. Alice's eyes filled with tears when she held out her hand to him.

"Little did I think that such a meeting was in store for us," she said, profoundly moved. "I am proscribed, a widow, persecuted by the officers of justice, or rather the minions of a victorious party. My poor brother, the husband of my companion, is imprisoned in the Tower, and looking for his impending execution. Life has no value for me, and but for this child I should long ago have surrendered myself voluntarily to my judges."

"I deeply deplore the mournful fate which has befallen you, and of which I have not remained wholly ignorant. I hope, however, to be able to alleviate your sufferings, as I have influential friends, and I myself am now holding an office in which I may be useful to you. For the present, pray accompany me to my house, where you shall stay until I have provided a safe asylum for you."

Milton succeeded by his influence in obtaining a pardon for Alice; and she was allowed to remain in London, as no danger was apprehended from a woman. Even a portion of her fortune was restored to her, so that she was sufficiently protected from want. Lucy, however, was unable to obtain a pardon for her husband. Thomas remained imprisoned in the Tower, and a delay of his execution was all that Milton could obtain by his intercession in his behalf. Alice passed her days henceforth in quiet retirement, mourning her heroic husband, and devoting herself exclusively to the education of her child. The only friend with whom she held intercourse was Milton, whom she now calmly saw coming and going. Notwithstanding their political and religious differences, she was still affectionately attached to him. Without timidly avoiding an exchange of their views, both took pains to meet on the neutral ground of art and poetry rather than in the arena of the wild struggle of parties. Each respected the other's convictions; the royalist and the republican exercised mutual forbearance, a mild toleration. So far as Milton was concerned, this intercourse exerted an extraordinary influence over his creative power as a poet, for Alice sought almost insensibly to lead him back to his original vocation. In her eyes his political labors were an aberration from the sublime task Nature had imposed upon him.

"You owe yet to me, or rather to the world, a more extensive work," said she once, half seriously, half jestingly. "But since you have been appointed foreign secretary to the Council of State, you have bidden farewell to the poor muses."

"You are mistaken, dear friend. Notwithstanding my manifold occupations, I do not lack leisure to think at least of divine poetry. I have conceived a great many plans; but I have not yet made up my mind whether to imitate the example of Shakespeare, or follow the sublime models of Homer, Virgil, and Tasso. I have already elaborated in my head several tragedies, the subjects of which I took from English history and from the Bible. Up to this time I have not felt inclined to write them, because I shrank from being compared with that immortal genius. For this reason I really prefer an epic, with which I have been engrossed for some time past."

"Would you inform me of the subject of this poem? Pardon my curiosity, to which I may assuredly give the nobler name of sincere sympathy."

"I will not conceal any thing from you. During my sojourn in Italy several years ago, I attended at Florence the performance of a play which, despite many imperfections and faults, made a deep impression upon me. The subject was the fall of man. I was powerfully struck at the time with the simple grandeur of that revelation. The subject seemed to me sublime, and worthy to claim the earnest efforts of a poetical mind, and it gave rise to innumerable conceptions in my imagination. I saw the wonders of Paradise, that garden of God, with its magnificent trees and golden fruits, with its fragrant flowers and shady groves. There lived Adam and Eve in undisturbed peace, in pure innocence, until the serpent came and beguiled Eve to eat of the fruit of the tree of the knowledge of good and evil. Thus Adam and his guilty wife were driven out of Paradise; death and sin clung to the heels of the sinners. The history both of mankind and of every individual is contained in that sacred tradition. Is not another Adam born in every man, and another Eve in every woman? Have we not all a lost paradise to weep over?"

"Entitle your epic 'Paradise Lost,'" said Alice, with a mournful smile. "You are right. Who has not a lost paradise to weep over? The innocence of childhood; the dreams of youth; our hopes and expectations, which are so often disappointed; the enthusiasm and ardor which prematurely succumb to stern reality; the still and calm peace, which is drowned by the noisy clash of arms; the lofty faith, which doubts and sneers try to undermine; love, with its divine transports, which pass away so swiftly; our most beautiful ideals: all are the lost paradises of poor humanity."

"But, above all things," replied Milton, "I intend to give prominence to the great and eternal struggles between the good and evil powers, between heaven and hell. Before my eyes stands the form of the fallen angel, who rebelled, first of all, against the Creator; I behold him, still beautiful, with hypocritical features and seductive form, not denying his divine origin even after his fall. Again and again he rises against the sway of the Eternal; and again and again he must acknowledge his impotence, for heaven and its angels always triumph over him."

The poet thus laid the outlines of his immortal epic before Alice, who listened to him in an ecstasy of delight; and he left her with the promise to carry out his plan as soon as possible; but the time for him to do so had not yet come.

Soon afterward, Milton received from the Council of State a mission with which he was obliged to comply. A few days after the king's execution, there had been published in England a book entitled "Eikon Basilike," or "The Portraiture of His Most Sacred Majesty." It was ascribed to Charles I., and contained the feelings, sentiments, meditations, impressions, and struggles, in short, the whole soul of the unfortunate monarch, and a history of his sufferings and trials, which caused him to appear in the light of a sainted martyr. The book created the most extraordinary sensation. The partisans of the king raised their heads again, and every reader of the book was seized with compassion and admiration. In spite of its prohibition by the government, it was rapidly circulated throughout the country, and Parliament trembled lest it should bring about a counter-revolution. One man only was able to neutralize its baneful effects, and that man was Milton. He was called upon to write a reply to the book. On assuming this task, he did not conceal from himself the painful consequences which would arise from it for him. He was to attack an unfortunate man, who was pitied by a vast majority of the people even in his grave, and, as it were, act as an intellectual executioner toward the beheaded corpse; he was to expose himself to the hatred and resentment of the royalists, who, in their blind vindictiveness, did not shrink from assassination, as was afterwards proved in many instances. But all these considerations exercised a less painful effect upon him than the thought of his relations to Alice. His fair friend worshipped Charles I., and had made the greatest sacrifices for him. Was he to lose again, by his own fault, her who had just been restored to him?

"I cannot refuse to fulfil my duty," he said to her, on informing her of the commission which had been intrusted to him. "I am almost afraid of losing thereby your friendship, my most precious boon; and yet I cannot act otherwise."

"Obey your convictions," replied Alice, respectfully. "You are a republican, and I am a friend of the king; but this must not prevent us from holding intercourse on the same terms as heretofore. No one can regret more intensely than I that you have entered this path, and thrown your talents into the scale of the enemy; but these party struggles shall not deprive me of my old and well-tried friend. I honor and esteem you as a man, even though I can never share your political views."

"I esteem you only the more highly," replied Milton, deeply moved by the lofty sentiments of the noble lady.

Both thus set a glorious example of toleration. Amid the general discord, they remained as devoted friends as ever. Pure humanity triumphed in them over the hatred of the hostile parties. However, before Milton left Alice, she fixed her eyes upon him with an expression of tender anxiety. Incessant toils had undermined his health, and especially injured his eyesight. It is true, his eyes seemed as lustrous as ever, but he himself had noticed that their strength had been failing for some time past, and had often complained of this evil to his compassionate friend. When he was now about to leave Alice, she was surprised at his being almost unable to see the door, and groping his way to it. She hastened after him in dismay, and conducted him into the street.

"Your health really makes me uneasy," she said to him, compassionately. "You must take better care of yourself, and, above all things, give the necessary repose to your eyes. For this reason, if for no other, I should like you to desist from writing that treatise."

"How can I? I must not delay writing it."

"Consider that you may lose your eyesight. Oh, I cannot bear the thought of your becoming blind!"

"I am not afraid of blindness, nor of the terrors of night, which are threatening me; for to me beams the faith in a kind Providence, the sympathy and tenderness of my friends, and, before all else, the conviction that I am doing my duty. These stars twinkle brightly in the darkness which will perchance surround me before long. 'Man doth not live by bread alone, but by every word that proceedeth out of the mouth of God;' why shall I not, therefore, content myself with the knowledge that my eyesight is not my only light, but that the guidance of God will illuminate me sufficiently? So long as He Himself looks forward to the future for me, so long as He takes care of me, as He has done all my lifetime, I will gladly let my eyes keep Sabbath, as such seems to be His will."

"But your adversaries and enemies may ascribe the loss of your eyesight to Divine visitation, and deride you for it."

"Let them do so, let them make me the sport of their sneers. They shall soon find that, so far from receiving my lot with repentance and despair, I strenuously adhere to my principles, neither fearful nor sensible of the wrath of God, but recognizing in this, as in all important events of my life, His paternal goodness and mercy. The consciousness of my rectitude will always sustain me, and I would not exchange it for all the riches of this world. If the cause of justice and truth requires me to give up my eyesight, I am willing and proud to make the sacrifice. Nay, if it were necessary for me to sacrifice my life for this purpose, I should not shrink from death. Between my duty and my eyesight I cannot hesitate a moment."

Animated with this spirit, Milton disregarded Alice's warnings, and took in hand a work which involved him in a number of violent controversies and proved most injurious to his health. Above all things, he took pains to refute the general belief that the king was the author of "Eikon Basilike," and tried to prove, in a very ingenious manner, that it must be the production of another writer; a supposition which seemed to be verified some years afterward, when the authorship was claimed by Dr. Gauden. Milton accomplished his task amid incessant sufferings, and opposed a true portrait of the king to the false image traced by Dr. Gauden, although he could not avoid introducing many an odious trait, and oftentimes used his pencil in too merciless a manner. At all events, his portraiture of the king did not conceal the failings and imperfections of Charles's character from the public gaze, and aroused the intense rage of the whole royalist party against him. Old and new adversaries arose against him; the celebrated Salmasius, a professor of Leyden, was the foremost among them. For two thousand gold-pieces Charles II. purchased the ever-ready pen of this great scholar to justify the memory of his father and abuse the whole English nation. Such, however, was the influence of the press already at that time, that the Parliament again took notice of the work written by Salmasius, and instructed Milton to publish a reply to it. It is true, the author's name added greatly to the importance that was attached to this pamphlet. Salmasius was considered the most learned man of his age; he spoke all living and dead languages, Latin and Greek, even Persian, Syriac, and Arabic. At the university he taught at the same time all sciences, theology, medicine, jurisprudence, and history. By means of his innumerable treatises, commentaries, notes, and learned prefaces, he had gained the greatest celebrity throughout Europe, and hitherto no one had ventured to dispute with him his supremacy in the learned world. He was courted by the most powerful monarchs; both Richelieu and Mazarin had taken the utmost pains to win him for France, and the eccentric Queen of Sweden succeeded only by means of urgent prayers in prevailing on him to comply with her invitation and come to Stockholm. When the celebrated professor was sick, or would not leave his house, owing to the cold climate of the north, Christina herself came to him, kindled the fire in the stove, cooked his breakfast, and often stayed for whole days at his bedside; so that the professor's wife became jealous of the queen, and compelled her learned husband to leave Stockholm and Sweden.

Such was the disputant with whom Milton now had to deal. All his friends were afraid lest this controversy should result in his signal discomfiture, and sought to dissuade him from entering upon it. Milton, however, was conscious of his strength, and knew that his ability was not only equal, but superior to that of a venal and pedantic polyhistor. Milton's learning was not merely a sterile and useless accumulation of indigested material, however well calculated to tickle his own vanity, or to impose upon the blind multitude. His knowledge had passed into flesh and blood, and become united with his whole character, and with his peculiarities of thinking and feeling. It was, therefore, under the promptings of a more exalted spirit that he entered upon this new task and wrote his "Defensio Populi." In this defence, he developed already, with surprising boldness, the principles which Rousseau afterwards only repeated in his "Contrat Social," and which were sufficient to shake the foundations of the whole civilized world. Milton rested his argument likewise on popular sovereignty, and contended that the nation had conferred power on the king solely for the sake of its own security. The sensation which his work produced was extraordinary. So eagerly and universally was it perused by the nation and throughout Europe, that fifty thousand copies were sold in the course of a few weeks. The foreign ambassadors congratulated Milton on this unexpected success; even the former patrons of Salmasius turned their backs disdainfully upon the discomfited professor, and lavished praise and flatteries on his victorious opponent. Queen Christina now derided her former favorite even more than she had once admired and revered him. Salmasius vainly made new efforts to wrest from his adversary his newly-gained laurels; every such attempt resulted in more profound humiliations for him. But Milton achieved his triumphs only at a heavy cost. Every word which he wrote, and by which he crushed the venal pedant, impaired his eyesight. A dreadful headache, with which he had often been affected from his earliest youth, added to the pains of his suffering eyes; but he paid little or no attention to the augmentation of his ills. Like a brave soldier, he continued the struggle with bleeding wounds, and, though fearfully injured, sternly refused to leave the field of battle.

The medieval tournaments had now given place to the scientific controversies of the most illustrious scholars, and the public took as much interest in them as in the knightly contests of former times. Princes and peoples were the spectators, and the power of the press had vastly extended the bounds of the formerly-restricted arena. A remnant of the knightly spirit of old lingered in these scientific combats, in which folio volumes took the place of cuirasses, and thick "Fathers of the Church" were used as lances and shields. The adversaries entered the arena well armed with quotations from classical authors, and with the ample stores of a learned arsenal; they fought with words instead of swords, and with theses and dogmas instead of battle-axes and spears. They fought not only for truth, but still more eagerly for honor and fame; hence, the war on both sides was oftentimes carried on with a degree of virulent abuse and personality which is calculated to strike a modern reader with amazement. The contest assumed mostly a personal character, and terminated only when one party or the other had been utterly defeated. The disputants did not shrink from inflicting the most painful wounds on each other, and the venom of slander and misrepresentation added to the pains of mortified vanity. The whole educated world took more or less interest in these intellectual tournaments, in proportion to the names and reputations of the disputants. Milton had entered upon such a duel with the learned Salmasius, and all Europe applauded the victor with the most rapturous acclamations. His reputation annihilated the moral authority of his opponent and hurled him from the throne which he had arrogated. Salmasius was mortally wounded, not only figuratively, but really; he survived his defeat but a short time, and died, because, as his friends asserted, Milton's severities had broken his heart.

Milton had conquered, but almost lost his eyesight in the struggle. To his triumph soon succeeded the everlasting night of blindness.

CHAPTER III.

DISPERSAL OF PARLIAMENT—CROMWELL MADE LORD PROTECTOR.

Meanwhile Cromwell, by his bravery, had delivered the new republic in the course of a few weeks from all its enemies. In the first place, he had subdued the rebellious Irish, and crushed their resistance by means of the most merciless measures. Next, he turned against the Scots, who had young King Charles II. in their midst. Worsted in two battles, the young prince wandered for some time about the country, and escaped only in an almost miraculous manner to France. After these victories Cromwell returned triumphantly to London. Surrounded by his officers, and followed by numerous prisoners, he made his solemn entrance into the capital. The Parliament, which acknowledged his deserts only with reluctance, and justly feared lest the victorious general should soon become a despotic usurper, sent four commissioners to meet him at Aylesbury, and salute him in the name of the assembly. In London he was received by the Speaker and a large number of members of the House, the president of the Council of State, and the lord mayor and aldermen of the city. Thousands of the most respectable citizens joined them and accompanied Cromwell to Whitehall, amid the booming of artillery and the jubilant acclamations of the people.

The general received all these honors with devout modesty; he spoke very little of his own merits, and ascribed his triumphs almost exclusively to the mercy of God and the valor of his soldiers. However, expressions of ill-concealed exultation and secret ambition burst from time to time from under the mask of this assumed modesty. He rewarded the commissioners sent to him by Parliament with princely munificence, presenting them not only with horses which had been taken during the war, but also with wealthy and aristocratic prisoners, who, it was to be expected, would pay a heavy ransom for their release. Thus he endeavored already to win for himself friends and devoted adherents. His bearing, his manners, and his language seemed to have undergone a complete change, and plainly exhibited the consciousness of his undisputed power. All these symptoms added to the apprehensions with which Parliament looked upon the influence and the schemes of the successful general, who, at the head of a victorious army, could demand and dare every thing. This distrust could not fail to lead sooner or later to an open rupture, and the struggle between the two sides seemed inevitable. Cromwell leaned upon the army, and counted upon the imprudence with which his opponents daily laid themselves open to his attacks. He did not hasten to strike the decisive blow, but prepared every thing in secret. Few great men have possessed the instinctive prudence and sharp-sightedness of this upstart. Seemingly inactive, he watched his enemies like a spider in its web. Like the latter, he was gifted with the finest scent for public opinion and for the sentiments of the people. Representing the wishes and ideas of the latter, he acquired a gigantic strength, a demoniacal power. Since the beginning of civil war, the whole authority of government had centred in the Parliament, which was held responsible for every public measure. It had governed too long already not to excite in the nation the longing for a change. Like every assembly of the same description, it was not free from the failings and weaknesses which always pertain to the exercise of power under similar circumstances. Adversaries were not wanting to it; among them, the quarrelsome John Lilburne was most prominent. Rarely has a politician enjoyed so much popularity; he was worshipped by the people, and especially by the lower classes of London. Already, during the reign of Charles I., he had gained the reputation of a martyr of liberty, and after the king's execution his restless spirit impelled him to oppose the Parliament with the same obstinacy. His contemporaries characterized his quarrelsomeness most aptly by saying that, if John Lilburne were to remain all alone in the world, John would enter upon a quarrel with Lilburne. However, it was not this innate peculiarity of his character that dictated his course, but he was guided far more by a strong sense of justice, and the conviction that the rights of every Englishmen must remain unimpaired, no matter what pretexts might be adduced for a contrary course. In the city, where he had passed his youth, and in the army, where he had served with honor and distinction, he had a host of friends, citizens, and apprentices, officers and privates, religious and political enthusiasts, who, like him, were ardently attached to democratic ideas and principles, and who cared neither for the requirements of social order nor the stability of the government, but were always ready to criticise and attack the latter when it did not come up to its demands and dreams, or pursued a course offensive to their pride or their convictions. Now, Lilburne possessed not only the talent of exasperating the public by means of his writings, but the still more dangerous gift of raising this exasperation to the highest pitch. He was indefatigable in getting up petitions, in holding seditious meetings, in influencing the temper of the army—in short, in all the democratic measures calculated to keep up a spirit of rebellion and to shake the power of the existing government. This remarkable man had succeeded in the course of time in discrediting the Parliament in the eyes of the multitude, and in undermining its influence and authority. In so doing, he served unwittingly the ambition of Cromwell, against whom he inveighed afterward with the same rancor and violence.

Cromwell profited by the unpopularity of the Parliament, to which he secretly sought to add as much as possible. For this purpose, he frequently assembled the most influential party leaders and the generals of the army, partly to ascertain their sentiments with his accustomed caution, partly to make sure of their assistance. Thus he gradually matured the plan which had long slumbered in his soul. However, before resorting to violent means, he wished to enter a peaceful path for getting rid of his adversaries. The people concurred universally in expressions of weariness and dissatisfaction at the so-called Long Parliament, which they said had outlived itself. A large number of pamphlets and scurrilous papers were levelled against it, and their tone became daily more insulting and aggressive. Contempt combined with hatred, and the weapons used were often those of scathing irony and mortifying scorn. In vain were all prohibitions and prosecutions of the offending authors; neither the wrath of Parliament nor the power of the Council of State was able to restore its influence, or to silence the enemies, who were well aware that Cromwell shared their opinions, and was a secret ally of theirs. The Parliament was already morally dead, and yet it was intent on continuing its semblance of life; it lacked alike moral and material power; neither the people nor the army, who agreed in their aversion to it, were willing to tolerate it any further. Under these circumstances, the leaders of the republican party themselves deemed it prudent to move the dissolution of Parliament and the holding of general elections; but they took measures in secret to secure their reëlection and the retention of the government in their hands. Cromwell was highly indignant at these intrigues, and made up his mind to frustrate them at any cost. The meetings of his friends at his rooms took place in a more rapid succession than heretofore; he used means to add to the number of his partisans, until he at last felt strong enough to throw down the gauntlet and disperse the Parliament by main force. What no King of England had ever attempted, what Charles Stuart, despite his despotic tendencies had never dared, was now unhesitatingly undertaken by Cromwell. When all was ready, Colonel Ingoldsby informed Cromwell, one day, that Parliament was sitting, and had come to a resolution not to dissolve itself, but to fill up the House by new elections. Cromwell in a rage immediately hastened to the House, and carried a body of three hundred soldiers along with him. Some of them he placed at the door, some in the lobby, some on the stairs. He entered the hall alone, without creating a sensation in the assembly. He wore a black coat and gray woollen stockings, as was his custom when not appearing in uniform. Cromwell took his seat and seemed to listen attentively to the debate; only from time to time a grin or sarcastic smile illuminated his stern features. Like an eagle, he was silent and calm before pouncing on his prey. Not a gesture betrayed his emotion, and yet his heart throbbed perhaps more impetuously to-day than it had done in many a bloody battle. He had arrived at the Rubicon; in the next moment he would be either a proscribed traitor or the sovereign ruler of three kingdoms.

His friend St. John spoke to him. It was not until now that Cromwell broke his silence, and told him that he had come with the purpose of doing what grieved him to the very soul, and what he had earnestly with tears besought the Lord not to impose upon him.

"PULL HIM DOWN!" CRIED CROMWELL.

But there was a necessity, in order to the glory of God and the good of the nation.

"I do not know what you refer to," replied St. John, "but God grant that whatever you do may redound to the good of the commonwealth!"

He went in dismay to his seat, and left Cromwell engrossed with his thoughts. Finally, the latter beckoned Harrison, and told him that he now judged the Parliament ripe for a dissolution. The intrepid soldier shrank from the great responsibility, and whispered to him:

"Sir, the work is very great and dangerous; I desire you seriously to consider before you engage in it."

"You say well," replied Cromwell; and thereupon sat still about a quarter of an hour. It was a quarter of an hour full of the greatest suspense and agitation for the general. He saw before him a scaffold and a crown; death at the hands of the executioner or the throne of England awaited him. Already the next minute might decide the matter. He muttered something sounding like a prayer, as though he wished to make God an ally of his plans. The most various thoughts and feelings stirred like wild waves in his bosom; ambition and sense of duty, pride and devout humility, truth and falsehood, alternated in rapid succession in his mind. He shrank from taking the decisive step, but not a moment was to be lost, for the speaker was ready to put the question.

He said again to Harrison, "This is the time; I must do it." He then rose and took the floor. Cromwell was not a good speaker; besides, he liked to conceal his thoughts under turgid phrases. Notwithstanding these defects, the assembly listened to him with the closest attention, his position and acknowledged merits commanding them to treat him with the greatest deference. At the outset, he spoke in respectful terms of the Parliament and its members, doing full justice to their zeal and activity; but he gradually changed his tone, and his expressions and gestures betrayed the most violent irritation. He frowned, and his large eyes flashed glances of inexorable anger at his adversaries. Finally, he loaded the Parliament with the vilest reproaches for its tyranny, ambition, oppression, and robbery of the public. Then stamping with his foot, which was a signal for the soldiers to enter—

"For shame!" he said to the Parliament; "get you gone! Give place to honester men, to those who will more faithfully discharge their trust. You are no longer a Parliament. The Lord has done with you; He has chosen other instruments for carrying on His work."

He crossed the large hall repeatedly with a noisy step, and then stood still once more with folded arms.

"Take him down," he said to Harrison, pointing to Lenthal, the speaker, who sat with a pale face in his chair.

The colonel called upon him to rise, which he refused to do.

"Pull him down!" cried Cromwell, inexorably.

Harrison obeyed, and dragged Lenthal from the chair.

Sir Henry Vane exclaiming against this proceeding, Cromwell cried with a loud voice:

"Oh, Sir Harry Vane, Sir Harry Vane! The Lord deliver me from Sir Harry Vane!"

He then turned to the other members, whom he reproached in the most scathing manner with their weaknesses and failings. "Thou art a drunkard," he said to one; "thou art an adulterer," to another; "and thou an extortioner," to a third. In this manner he preferred just or unjust charges against the members, who, from fear of the soldiers, or consciousness of their guilt, durst not defend themselves.

"It is you," he said to the House, "that have forced this upon me. I have sought the

Lord night and day, that He would rather slay me than put me upon this work."

He then commanded a soldier to seize the mace. "What shall we do with this bauble? Here, take it away."

Having commanded the soldiers to clear the hall, he himself went out the last, and ordering the doors to be locked, departed to his lodgings in Whitehall.

After the downfall of the so-called Long Parliament, Cromwell, who was now master of the situation, to preserve at least the semblance of liberty, ordered new elections. The Parliament, however, which met under his auspices, and consisted mostly of men destitute of ability and influence, dissolved itself, in the consciousness of its weakness and insignificance. It was an object of general ridicule, and the public gave it the nickname of Barebone's Parliament, because a worthy dealer in leather, Praise-God Barebone, was one of its most ludicrous members.

Four days afterward, a long procession moved between two lines of soldiers from Whitehall to Westminster. The lord mayor and aldermen of the city of London headed it, in their gorgeous gala equipages; next came Cromwell, attired in a black velvet coat, and with broad gold lace around his pointed hat. His guards, mostly veteran soldiers, and a large number of noblemen who had submitted to him, preceded his carriage, which was surrounded by the most distinguished officers, who held their drawn swords in their hands. On arriving at Westminster Hall, the procession entered the large hall, at the end of which had been placed a purple chair of state. Cromwell stood before the chair, and, after all the members of the procession had assembled around him, Major-General Lambert announced that Parliament had dissolved of its own accord, and demanded, in the name of the army, of the three nations, and of the requirements of the times, that the lord general should take upon himself the protectorate of England, Scotland, and Ireland. Although the whole scene had been preconcerted, and although the parts had been distributed beforehand among the actors, Cromwell, for appearance' sake, hesitated to make a definite reply, and yielded only to repeated and most pressing requests. One of the secretaries then read the new constitution, which he signed and solemnly swore to observe. Major-General Lambert knelt down and presented to him a sheathed sword, the symbol of civil authority. On receiving it, Cromwell took off his own sword and laid it down, signifying thereby that he would no longer govern by martial law. The lord keeper and the judges then invited him to take the chair of state. He sat down, and covered his head with his hat, while all the others stood bareheaded. After the ceremony was over, the procession returned to Whitehall, where a sumptuous banquet closed the festivities of the day. Heralds traversed the streets and announced the event to the people.

"Long live the protector!" shouted the multitude.

Only one man did not join in their acclamations. It was Henderson, the old Puritan.

"Oliver has betrayed us," he murmured, gloomily. "He has betrayed the Lord, and must die!"

CHAPTER IV.

THE LORD PROTECTOR'S COURT.

A NEW life began now at Whitehall. Cromwell put off his mask more and more, and seemed to manifest a desire to seize the crown of England. Cautious as usual, he first tried to ascertain the sentiments of his adherents before taking another step forward. Almost every day he had long interviews with his officers, as well as with the most influential citizens. In these interviews he took occasion to hint vaguely that England ought to have a monarchical government, and thus gradually prepared them for the change which he had in contemplation. He had vanquished the Presbyterians and Constitutionals by the Independents and Republicans, and overthrown these in their turn by means of the army, so that he only had to deal with the latter. It is true, he met here with unexpected resistance. Already his title of Protector excited discontent, and Colonel Harrison and Major Overton, Milton's friend, declared openly against it. They and their adherents threatened the usurper and opposed his schemes. Cromwell, however, headed them off, and before they were able to carry their plans into effect, he caused them to be arrested. Milton was not a little surprised on hearing of this event, and deemed himself in duty bound to ask the protector, at the first opportunity that should offer, to pardon his esteemed friend.

For this purpose he repaired to Whitehall, where Cromwell had taken up his quarters in the apartments of the executed king, and had already surrounded himself with a sort of retinue of courtiers. A special lifeguard was posted in front of his doors. The anterooms and staircases were crowded with persons who solicited favors and rewards at the hands of the new ruler. Generals and other officers, among whom were to be seen austere Puritans, who did not know how to adapt themselves to the change that had taken place, and still saw in Cromwell only their old comrade, were walking up and down in threadbare uniforms, and dragging their long swords noisily on the floor. It was evident that they considered as an abomination the splendor which surrounded them here. They cast distrustful glances on the young courtiers who, like flies in midsummer, had quickly made their appearance to buzz in the rays of the rising sun; they had now another idol to which they could bend their knees and whisper fulsome flatteries. Milton was not a little astonished on meeting here many an ex-cavalier, who but recently had applied to Cromwell the nickname of "Old Satan." All was forgotten now; the protector tried to conciliate the nobility, and had of late treated the aristocratic families with surprising lenity. They made peace with him, either from fear or from self-interest, and received at his hands, besides other substantial proofs of his favor, their estates, which the commonwealth had confiscated. Such being his course now, the nobility flocked to the new court, whose centre was composed of Cromwell's own family. A motley crowd now presented itself to the eyes of the beholder. In yonder corner stood an old Independent, or a fanatic expecting the fifth monarchy of God and the New Jerusalem, now grimly gazing upon the unwonted bustle. His awkward manners, his strange dress, which was very plain and dark-colored, and his language, interlarded every moment with Bible quotations, were secretly derided by the polished courtiers, who, however, dared only to smile furtively at them. At the other end of the hall some clergymen were engaged with a few officers in an animated controversy on theological questions, which were discussed with hair-splitting keenness on both sides, and in which the uncouth soldiers frequently got the better of their learned adversaries. Yonder, some young courtiers were conversing in a low tone about the love-affairs of his highness the protector, and tried to ascertain whether he gave the preference to the beautiful Lady Dysart or to the accomplished Lady Lambert. Soldiers and priests, aristocrats and republicans, the austere Puritan and the frivolous skeptic, were now united here by the will of the new ruler, or by their various interests, and blended together notwithstanding their differences. A very peculiar tone, therefore, reigned in the apartments of Whitehall. Democratic sullenness and aristocratic pliancy, fanatical enthusiasm and cool, sober selfishness, went hand in hand, and produced a truly wonderful effect.

While Milton was engrossed with such observations, he was frequently greeted and addressed by friends and acquaintances. Lord Broghill, the brother of the Countess of Ranelagh, shook hands with him. The poet Waller, a relative of the protector, and yet formerly a favorite of Charles I., spoke to him. He had just left Cromwell's cabinet, where the protector had given him an audience.

"Can I see the lord protector?" said Milton to him.

"I do not know," replied the merry but unprincipled Waller. "His highness has with him at this moment a saint, a shoemaker animated with the Holy Ghost. George Fox is the name of the queer fellow; he has already founded a sect called Friends or Quakers. He will no longer tolerate any clergymen, nor take off his hat to anybody, nor take oaths. He addresses every one with 'thou.' I tell you, it was rich to see him approach Cromwell and say to him, 'Peace be with thy house,' whereupon both entered upon a theological disputation. While his highness was putting on his trousers, there was a perfect shower of quotations from the Bible. I could no longer keep serious, and therefore left the room. The lord protector, in secret, also laughs at such wonderful saints; but what is he to do? As he told me in confidence, 'When you are in Rome, you must do as the Romans do.' You have no idea of the number of persons that call upon him. Last week Manasseh Ben Israel, the Jew from Amsterdam, was here, and presented in his own name, and in that of his fellow-Israelites, a petition, in which they begged leave to live and trade in London. What do you think of such impertinence?"

"In my opinion, the application of the Jews ought not to be rejected, but they should be received and treated with hospitality and toleration. They are, as it were, the trunk from which Christianity, that noblest blossom of humanity, has developed itself. Add to this that the chosen people display rare commercial talents and activity, and will assuredly bring riches into our country."

"That is just what the lord protector thinks. He immediately summoned a conference of merchants, theologians, and jurists, at which he himself presided, and warmly advocated the cause of his *protégés*."

"He is a great man in every sense of the word."

"Of course he is, and he lacks nothing of being a king but the royal title. To tell you the truth, I believe my worthy cousin will, before long, put the crown on his head."

"You must be jesting," said Milton, deeply moved.

"Not at all, sir; I have already written a coronation ode, and I should seriously advise you, for the solemnity of the coronation, to take your own Pegasus from the stable and mount him, which you have not done for a long time past."

"I cannot believe it."

"And yet it is only necessary for you to look around these apartments to be convinced that I have told you the truth. What is wanting, then, to the restoration of the monarchy? We reside at Whitehall, the royal palace; we have a splendid lifeguard, and a full retinue of courtiers. See, yonder stand the Earl of Warwick and Lord Broghill; and here comes, if I mistake not, Sir Kenelm Digby, to render homage to the new ruler of England."

"Sir Kenelm Digby, the Catholic, the exiled royalist?" asked Milton, wonderingly.

"Well, you need not wonder at it. He has obtained permission to return to England. We have need of him for secret purposes. Jews, Catholics, and Anabaptists, meet at our court, and I should not be surprised if the pope himself should come to Whitehall one day to put the crown on his highness's head."

So saying, the gay poet moved on and disappeared in the crowd. Milton remained, a prey to mournful thoughts and apprehensions. He feared more and more lest the republic, to which he was so ardently attached, should be on the brink of ruin. A new despotism, more intolerable than any other, because it rested on the brute force of arms, threatened to take the place of the former tyranny. Milton had hailed Cromwell as the liberator of his fatherland, the protector of freedom of conscience, the greatest man of his age; and now his ideal lay before his eyes broken and trampled in the dust. What he had revered he could not but despise; what he had loved he could not but hate. It is the greatest affliction that can befall a noble soul to be compelled to tear its idols with its own hands from its heart and hurl them from their exalted pedestals. It is not love deceived, but faith and trust betrayed and abused, that strikes the deepest wounds, because it envenoms man's heart and mind, and buries and destroys all his ideals at one fell blow. The poet's soul was filled with bitter grief, and he wept in secret not only over his country, but over the fate of the whole world. He asked himself if liberty was only an empty illusion, only the dream of a heated imagination. On gazing upon the unprincipled crowd about him, and observing their doings and aspirations, he felt doubts arising in his soul whether the people would ever be ripe for freedom. The degradation of human nature and the innate slavishness of the vile multitude impressed him with crushing force, and he experienced the disdain with which lofty spirits so often look upon the miseries and weaknesses of mankind. But soon these mournful thoughts gave place to the sense of his own dignity, which restored to him his faith in liberty and truth. He deemed himself in duty bound to utter his convictions fearlessly and unreservedly, even in the presence of Cromwell, and at the peril of incurring the wrath of the powerful ruler.

While he was engrossed with these thoughts, Sir Kenelm Digby, who recognized him, in spite of their long separation, approached him. After greeting him with seeming cordiality, he said to the poet:

"Well, Mr. Milton, I am sure you are likewise here for the purpose of saluting the sun that has lately risen over England. I am almost inclined to bet that you have in your pocket some poem written in honor of the great man."

"You are mistaken," replied the poet, indignantly. "I have come to Whitehall to wait on the lord protector in my capacity as Secretary to the Council of State."

"Then you have really followed my advice. You have bid farewell to poetry, and turned politician. Well, I am glad of it, and wish you joy of your new career. Beware only of being impeded in your path by your poetical vagaries. A politician must be cool, sober, and destitute of poetical illusions. I am afraid you still possess too much imagination and enthusiasm; at least, I have noticed these peculiarities in your late writings, which, as an old friend of yours, I read with a great deal of interest."

"I thank you for the sympathy which you vouchsafe to my writings, but I cannot share your views. In my judgment, a great and true politician must possess a heart throbbing for the liberty and welfare of the people. If he lack this, he will never exercise an enduring influence over public affairs, and, at the best, obtain only the reputation of a skilful intriguer. If Moses had not sympathized so profoundly with the sufferings of his people, if he had not revolted at the tyranny of its oppressors, he would never have performed the miracles which God caused him to do,

He was chosen by the Lord, because he had a heart for the sufferings of his people."

"Precisely like our lord protector," said Sir Kenelm Digby, sneeringly; "only, I believe, with this difference, that his highness will not content himself with viewing the land of promise from afar. Unless all symptoms deceive me, I believe we shall presently have a coronation in London, and in that case it would have been a better policy for you not to have so openly avowed your love of liberty and your republican sentiments. Believe me, my dear friend, liberty is nothing but a chimera of the poets, and a republic exists only till the right man arises to subvert it. Nowadays it is generally only a production of weakness and impotence, a sort of fever which closes with general exhaustion, and is cured by a skilful physician. But in talking politics, I forgot to communicate to you intelligence which concerns you personally. I have been at Rome and seen Leonora Baroni."

"Leonora!" echoed the poet, giving a start.

"I thought," continued Sir Kenelm Digby, "that you had not yet forgotten the signora. She fares no better than you; she told me to greet you, and I bring you, perhaps, her last farewell."

"She is dead?" asked Milton, mournfully. "Oh, tell me what has become of her."

"Shortly after your departure she was taken sick, she loved you so fondly. As she was growing weaker from day to day, she caused herself to be conveyed to a cloister. There I saw her; her cheeks were very pale, but her eyes beamed with heavenly radiance. She resembled a saint in her divine beauty. In devout contrition she repented of her past, and with fervent ardor turned her eyes from the joys of this world to the blessedness above. The signora will soon intercede for you in heaven. Ah! how anxious she always was for the salvation of your soul; with how touching an affection she thought of you! I left her on her death-bed, and had to promise her to visit you and convey her last greetings to you."

Milton's eyes filled involuntarily with tears, which he consecrated to Leonora's memory. This noble and artistic nature, then, which had once divided his heart with Alice, had also departed this life!

"Poor Leonora!" he sighed, forgiving her the pain which she had caused him.

CHAPTER V.

THE CROWN REFUSED BY CROMWELL.

Still profoundly moved by the news he had just received, Milton entered the cabinet, where the protector gave his audiences. Cromwell sat, with his eyes almost closed, and absorbed in his reflections. Before him lay an open Bible, in which he seemed to have just been reading. His eyes wandered from the sacred volume to the ceiling and the wainscoting of the walls. He contemplated musingly the golden crown and the royal initials which were everywhere to be seen in the room. This was the goal of his wishes. At present he was the most powerful man in England. Europe bowed to him; France courted his friendship, and the wily Mazarin flattered him in the name of his sovereign by means of complimentary letters and costly presents. The whole Protestant world looked upon him as its protector. His mere word had sufficed to intimidate the Duke of Savoy, who, with unheard-of cruelty, had persecuted the descendants of the old Waldenses in the mountain-valleys of the Alps for the sake of their Protestant faith. He stood, honored and dreaded, on the summit of an almost absolute power, to which he had risen solely by his merits and the strength of his mind. Nothing was wanting to him, except that crown which was here flashing toward him on all sides. It was only necessary for him to stretch out his hand for it, for the newly-summoned Parliament had voluntarily offered it to him, or rather sought to force it upon him; and yet he hesitated to accept it. He thought it was not time yet; public opinion had not been sufficiently prepared for this last and most decisive step. Through it he had become strong and powerful; to him it was the voice of God, to which, he said, he would never turn a deaf ear. This was on his part no hypocrisy, but his innermost conviction, for he regarded himself as an instrument of Providence, and as the chosen warrior of the Lord. His belief in his mission was deeply rooted in his soul, and this faith enhanced his greatness. Thus religious fanaticism was blended in this wonderful nature with a clear, sober understanding, which, in thinking of heaven, did not forget the earth and its worldly schemes; his fear of the Lord was coupled with a high sense of his own dignity and an insatiable ambition. Fanaticism and a spirit of intrigue penetrated one another, and thereby added to their mutual strength. But for his religious fanaticism, Cromwell would have remained a common schemer all his lifetime; and but for his cool, sober sagacity, he would have been a blind fanatic like Colonel Harrison. Possessed of these two antagonistic qualities, he was the greatest man of his age.

Milton's entrance put an end to his meditation. He drew his strong hand repeatedly across his broad forehead, as if to dispel the spirits that had haunted him. He feigned perfect tranquillity and indifference, which he dropped only in the course of the conversation. With a kind gesture he invited the poet to be seated. Although he himself had not enjoyed a very good education, he esteemed the more highly the learning and knowledge of others.

To the beholder the two men presented the most striking contrast. Cromwell was heavy-set; his body, in spite of the fatigues and privations which it had undergone during the war, seemed hewn out of granite; his flushed face indicated extraordinary strength of will, and on his coarse features was stamped a firmness commanding respect. Peculiar to him was his glance and the expression of his large, clear eyes, which now gleamed with enthusiastic fire, now seemed apathetic, as if turned inward and sunk into their sockets, until they suddenly and unexpectedly shot flashes and threatened to crush the beholder. On the other hand, the poet's figure was slender and almost feeble; fine dark-brown hair surrounded his delicate face and pale cheeks; from his high forehead beamed the noble expression of a profound thinker, and the traces of his intellectual toils and long-continued exertions were imprinted on his fragile frame. It is true, his suffering eyes had retained their old radiance, but the immobility of the pupils indicated the almost entire extinction of his eyesight. However, the light that was departing from them seemed now to float around his whole being; he resembled a transparent alabaster lamp illumined from within. Thus the two representative men of their time stood face to face—the energy of the ruler and the enthusiasm of the poet, the beautiful ideal and the stern reality.

Milton addressed the protector, and entreated him to pardon Overton, whom Cromwell had sent to the Tower.

"I should gladly grant your request," said the protector, "but your friend himself renders it difficult for me to do so. I call God to witness that I am a well-wisher of his, and that I am sorry to treat an old comrade with so much rigor. It is no fault of mine; but both he and Harrison have forced me to adopt this course. The Lord alone knows my heart, and will judge between me and them. Say yourself if I can act otherwise. They conspired against the government, and stirred up a mutiny in the army. Had they been royalists, I should have caused them to be beheaded; but, as they are old friends of mine,

I have contented myself with imprisoning them."

"So far as I know, their only crime consists in their intense devotion to the republic."

"Both are fanatics, incorrigible madcaps, bent on accomplishing impossibilities, and thereby breeding confusion and disorder. If their views were carried into effect, we should have no government whatever. They dream of a state of society that would be nothing but utter anarchy. This I cannot tolerate, and therefore nothing remained for me but to render them harmless. I swear to you that no harm shall befall either Overton or Harrison. God forbid that I should consent to the execution of such brave men, who shed their blood for the good cause! I will only keep them imprisoned until they have seen the errors to which they have yielded. Do not grieve, Mr. Secretary, and do not be angry with me, if I cannot grant this request of yours. You know that I am your friend, and am always glad to see you. If you wish to say any thing else to me, speak, for I regard you as a man alike wise and modest."

The protector thus unwittingly came to meet the poet, and Milton seized unhesitatingly the opportunity to lay his views before him.

"I grieve not only for the sake of my friend," he said gravely, "but still more for the fate of a fair woman, I might almost say the beloved of my youth."

"Ah, ah!" exclaimed Cromwell, in a playful tone. "Has our esteemed secretary for the foreign tongues also a sweetheart? For aught I know, you are married, and I have always heard you spoken of as a strictly moral man."

"I do not speak of a mortal woman, but of divine liberty and this republic. The general impression is that both are endangered."

"And by whom?" asked the protector, who was suddenly all ear.

"By a man whom Providence has raised higher than any other mortal, who delivered England from intolerable oppression, who achieved glorious victories in countless battles over the enemies of the people, and whom the grateful country calls the father of the people."

"And what do they say of this man now?"

"That he is stretching out his hand for a crown, and hankering after a title unworthy the transcendent majesty of his character. As yet the friends of freedom will not and cannot credit this rumor; they refuse to think the great man capable of such littleness. He will respect the fond expectations which we cherish, the solicitudes of his anxious country."

Milton paused to await the impression produced by his bold words. Cromwell, however, remained silent and seemed absorbed in deep thought. Carried away by his own enthusiasm, the poet discarded all timidity as unworthy of his character, and addressed the protector without further circumlocution.

"Respect," he exclaimed, with flushed cheeks, and in a voice of noble enthusiasm, "the looks and the wounds of your brave companions-in-arms, who, under your banners, have so strenuously fought for liberty; respect the shades of those who perished in the contest; respect also the opinions and the hopes which foreign states entertain concerning us, which promise to themselves so many advantages from that liberty which we have so bravely acquired, from the establishment of that new government which has begun to shed its splendor over the world, and which, if it be suffered to vanish like a dream, would involve us in the deepest abyss of shame."

"I am only an instrument in the hand of the Lord," interrupted Cromwell, as if to excuse himself to Milton, and to himself.

"Therefore, respect yourself. After having endured so many sufferings and encountered so many perils for the sake of liberty, do not suffer it, now it is obtained, either to be violated by yourself, or in any one instance impaired by others. Indeed, you cannót be truly free unless we are free also; for such is the nature of things, that he who trenches on the liberty of others is the first to lose his own, and become a slave. But if you, who have hitherto been the patron and tutelary genius of liberty—if you, who are exceeded by no one in justice, in piety, and goodness, should hereafter invade that liberty which you have defended, your conduct must be fatally operative, not only against the cause of liberty, but the general interests of piety and virtue. Your integrity and virtue will appear to have evaporated, your faith in religion to have been small; your character with posterity will dwindle into insignificance, and thus a most destructive blow will be levelled against the happiness of mankind."

Was Cromwell really moved? At all events he heaved a deep sigh. Milton continued, without taking any notice of his real or feigned emotion:

"I know full well that the work which you have undertaken is of incalculable moment; that it will thoroughly sift and expose every principle and sensation of your heart; that it will fully display the vigor and genius of your character; and that it will determine whether you really possess those great qualities of piety, fidelity, justice, and self-denial, which made us believe that you were raised by the special direction of the Deity to the highest pinnacle of power."

"I am only a weak man, an instrument in His hands," murmured the protector. "In truth, the Lord speaks out of your mouth; therefore, speak out fearlessly."

"At once wisely and discreetly to hold the sceptre over three powerful nations," added Milton, thus encouraged, "to persuade people to relinquish inveterate and corrupt for new and more beneficial maxims and institutions, to penetrate into the remotest parts of the country, to have the mind present and operative in every quarter, to watch against surprise, to provide against danger, to reject the blandishments of pleasure and the pomp of power—these are exertions compared with which the labor of war is a mere pastime; which will require all the energy, and employ every faculty that you possess; which demand a man supported from above, and almost instructed by immediate inspiration."

"What you say is true, very true," replied Cromwell. "The Lord Himself will illuminate me."

"I have no doubt that He is with you. But you will bear my feeble words in mind, and consider especially how you may discharge all these important duties in such a manner as not only to secure our liberties, but to add to them."

When Milton ceased, the protector rose from his chair and strode, as was his habit, up and down the room.

"Go, go," he said, laying his hand on Milton's shoulder. "You are an honest, excellent man, and I would I possessed your genius and virtue; but the Lord has endowed us all with different gifts. To you He has vouchsafed learning and eloquence; but to me—"

Cromwell did not finish his sentence. With a kind gesture he dismissed the poet, who left the great man with renewed hope and confidence. After he was gone, the protector became again absorbed in his reflections. In his mind arose once more that long struggle between his ambition and his sense of duty. The temptation was too strong, and the old demon soon seized him again. An old augury came into his mind. In his boyhood, in a Latin play performed by the pupils of Cambridge, and representing the struggle of the human limbs, he had played "the Tongue," and finally been crowned as victor, all his schoolmates kneeling down and paying homage to him. He involuntarily recalled all this, and it filled him anew with superstitious faith in his mission.

A private door in the wall opened noiselessly, and the head of a man looked cautiously into the room. His face, furrowed by a thousand small wrinkles and lines, his keen, twinkling eyes, and the pliable attitude of the bowed frame, indicated a shrewd and adroit servant. It was the protector's confidant.

"Thurloe, come in," said Cromwell. "We are entirely alone. What do you bring to me?"

"Glad tidings—the confidential deputation of Parliament to offer you the crown, and receive your definite reply. I preceded them to prepare your highness for their arrival."

"Thank you, thank you. But it is difficult for me to make up my mind. The matter is fraught with many difficulties."

"What! you hesitate to accept a crown?"

"New misgivings have arisen in my soul. A man who spoke to me on the subject has just left me. I confess that his words have made a deep impression upon me, although he is a half-blind enthusiast."

"You refer to Milton, the secretary to the Council of State?"

"I do. He is a very excellent and respectable man, and many people in England share his views."

"If you will listen to the Utopian vagaries of such fanatics, you will never reach the glorious goal beckoning to you."

"You are right, Thurloe. Admit the commissioners of Parliament."

Cromwell received them standing. They were headed by Lord Broghill, who addressed the protector, and, after enumerating once more all the arguments in favor of the restoration of a monarchical government, urged Cromwell to assume the royal title, after having so long been invested with royal authority and power. Cromwell's reply was long, vague, and interlarded with reflections, reminiscences, predictions, and allusions.

"Gentlemen," he replied to the deputation, "I have passed the greater part of my life in fire (if I may so speak), and surrounded by commotions; but all that has happened since I have meddled with public affairs for the general good, if it could be gathered into a single heap, and placed before me in one view, would fail to strike me with the terror and respect for God's will which I undergo at the thought of this thing you now mention, and this title you offer me. But I have drawn confidence and tranquillity in every crisis of my past life from the conviction that the heaviest burdens I have borne have been imposed upon me by His hand without my own participation. Often have I felt that I should have given way under these weighty loads if it had not entered into the views, the plans, and the great bounty of the Lord to assist me in sustaining them. If, then, I should suffer myself to deliver you an answer on this matter, so suddenly and unexpectedly brought under my consideration, without feeling that this answer is suggested to my heart and lips by Him who has ever been my oracle and guide, I should therein exhibit to you a slender evidence of my wisdom. To accept or refuse your offer in one word, from desires or feelings of personal interest, would savor too much of the flesh and of human appetite. To elevate myself to this height by motives of ambition or vain-glory, would be to bring down a curse upon myself, upon my family, and upon the whole empire. Better would it be that I had never been born. Leave me, then, to seek counsel at my leisure of God, and my own conscience; and I hope neither the declamations of a light and thoughtless people, nor the selfish wishes of those who expect to become great in my greatness, may influence my decision, of which I shall communicate to you the result with as little delay as possible."

Three hours afterward, the parliamentary committee returned to press for his answer. It was in many respects confused and unintelligible.

"Royalty," he said, "is composed of two matters, the title of king and the functions of monarchy. These functions are so united by the very roots to an old form of legislation, that all our laws would fall to nothing did we not retain in their appliance a portion of the kingly power. But as to the title of king, this distinction implies not only a snpreme authority, but, I may venture to say, an authority partaking of the divine! I have assumed the place I now occupy to drive away the dangers which threatened my country, and to prevent their recurrence. I shall not quibble between the titles of king and protector, for I am prepared to continue in your service as either of these, or even as a simple constable, if you so will it, the lowest officer in the land; for, in truth, I have often said to myself that I am, in fact, nothing more than a constable, maintaining the order and peace of the parish. I am, therefore, of opinion that it is unnecessary for you to offer, and for me to accept, the title of king, seeing that any other will equally answer the purpose.

"Allow me," he added, "to lay open my heart here, aloud, and in your presence. At the moment when I was called to this great work, and preferred by God to so many others more worthy than myself, what was I? Nothing more than a simple captain of dragoons in a regiment of militia. My commanding officer was a dear friend, who possessed a noble nature, and whose memory I know you cherish as warmly as I do myself. This was Mr. Hampden. The first time I found myself under fire with him, I saw that our troops, newly levied, without discipline, and composed of men who loved not God, were beaten in every encounter. With the permission of Mr. Hampden, I introduced among them a new spirit—a spirit of zeal and piety; I taught them to fear God. From that day forward they were invariably victorious. To Him be all the glory!

"It has ever been thus, it will ever continue to be thus, gentlemen, with the government. Zeal and piety will preserve us without a king. Understand me well; I would willingly become a victim for the salvation of all; but I do not think—no, truly, I do not believe that it is necessary this victim should bear the title of a king."

With this reply Cromwell dismissed the committee which had offered him a crown. When the members had left, his private secretary, Thurloe, asked him what his real opinion was.

"A crown," said Cromwell, plucking his confidant's ear, is "a nice thing, but a clear conscience is still better. The Lord will settle it all to our best. Come, let us go to dinner; the long speech has given me a good appetite, even though it may have greatly puzzled the gentlemen of the committee."

CHAPTER VI.

LADY CLAYPOLE—"KILLING NO MURDER."

Cromwell dined to-day with his favorite daughter, Lady Claypole, who exercised an extraordinary influence over her father. She was a lady of rare delicacy of feeling, endowed with accomplishments and understanding, faithful to her friends, magnanimous toward her enemies, and fondly attached to her father, of whom she always thought only with pride and solicitude. When Cromwell was exhausted by his public labors, and full of care and anxiety, he joyously sought relief and tranquillity in the society of a heart holding aloof from the ambitious struggles and violent deeds with which his life abounded. The very contrast in their two characters added to their mutual love. Lady Claypole was in secret an adherent of the proscribed Stuarts and the Episcopal Church, while her sister, the wife of Major-General Fleetwood, shared the republican principles of her husband. Thus the protector often met with resistance in the bosom of his own family, where were represented all the parties with which he had to struggle in public life. Many a supplicant applied to Lady Claypole, whose influence over her father was generally known.

The poet Harrington was now waiting in her room for a similar purpose. Cromwell had caused the manuscript of his "Oceana," which abounded with Utopian ideas, to be seized at the printing-office and conveyed to Whitehall. In vain were the efforts of the poet to recover his work. His last hope was the intercession of Lady Claypole. Her maid came in, accompanied by the little daughter of the lady, a sweet child three years old, with blond ringlets. Harrington took the little girl in his arms, and played with her until Lady Claypole came in.

"My lady," said the poet, putting down the child, "it is fortunate that you have come, for I was about to steal your sweet little daughter."

"Steal my daughter, and why?" asked the mother, pressing her darling to her heart.

"She will certainly make more brilliant conquests one day, but I will confess to you, my lady, that revenge, and not love, prompted me to steal her."

"And what have I done to provoke your resentment?" she asked, wonderingly.

"Nothing, my lady. I only wished to retaliate upon you, as your father has stolen from me a child of which I am as fond as you are of yours."

"Oh, my father is incapable of doing any thing of the kind. The protector is severe, but just."

"And yet he took my child from me. It is true, it is only a book, a sort of political romance, but its loss grieves me exceedingly."

Lady Claypole smiled at the *double entendre.* "I will speak to my father about it; he shall restore your child to you."

"Accept my thanks beforehand. I shall dedicate the work to the protector, and present the first copy to you, my lady."

The poet withdrew, and Lady Claypole went to meet her father, who arrived a few moments afterward.

"My lord protector," said the amiable lady, after tenderly embracing him, "permit me to intercede in behalf of a poor child which you have stolen from its father. Do you know Harrington, the poet?"

"I do, my daughter."

"I have promised him that you would give him back his manuscript."

Cromwell frowned, but his daughter stroked his forehead with her delicate hands, until it became smooth again.

"You are not afraid of a book, father?"

"I am not afraid either of the book or of the author, who would like to deprive me of my power and put his chimeras in my place; but no attack with a little paper-gun shall take from me what I have gained by the sword. I must assume the office of lord high constable to reëstablish peace between the hostile parties; for they cannot agree on any form of government, and use their power only to ruin themselves. For your sake I will let him print the book, and even accept its dedication."

At dinner Cromwell, as usual when he was at his daughter's house, was in very good spirits, and to-day his gayety was so great as to excite her surprise.

"Something very agreeable must have happened to you to-day," she said, sympathetically.

"The Parliament to-day offered me the crown for the third time. I believe I shall have to accept it, even if it were only to procure for you the title of royal highness."

Lady Claypole turned pale and heaved a deep sigh. Her uneasiness and paleness made a profound impression on the protector.

"My child, reassure yourself," he exclaimed, deeply moved. "I have not yet made up my mind. You will gradually accustom yourself to this idea."

"Never!" replied his daughter, resolutely. "The crown on your head would only be a misfortune for our whole house. Like my poor grandmother, I should be unable to sleep calmly for a minute; for I should always see the assassin's dagger raised against you. Oh, father, listen to me quietly, and do not be angry with me. I am only a feeble woman, and am unable to appreciate your lofty plans; but, if you love me, if you feel only the slightest tenderness for me, then content yourself with the greatness which you have already achieved, and do not aspire to a title which, as you say yourself, has no greater value than the plume on your hat. I feel that your accession to the throne would cause my death."

"No, no," cried Cromwell, in dismay; "you shall not, must not die. What would your old father do? Nothing would remain for him but to follow you immediately."

Tears moistened his cheeks, and the man to whom all England bowed, and who annihilated his enemies without mercy or compassion, trembled at the mere thought of such a loss. His paternal love drowned the voice of ambition, and those projects which the most influential and powerful men vainly sought to shake gave way, at least for the time, before the glance and the words of a feeble woman. But Cromwell was unable to give up every thing so abruptly. It is true, his feelings had overpowered him, but his understanding and his inflamed passions stirred up his ambition again. The prize beckoning to him was too tempting. So long as he was with his daughter, he forgot his ambitious schemes; in her presence he was nothing but a loving father; but no sooner had he left her peaceful company than he plunged anew into the whirlpool of intrigues and affairs, steadily keeping his goal in view. But he had to contend in his family not alone with the pious and tender objections of his daughter. His brother-in-law Desborough and his son-in-law Fleetwood, an ardent republican, opposed his plan in the most determined manner. When he conversed with them in his usual playful manner on the subject, and repeated his favorite phrase that the royal title would be only a plume on his hat, and that he could not but wonder at men refusing to let children rejoice in their playthings, they remained grave and persisted in their convictions.

"This matter," said Major-General Desborough, "is far more important than you seem willing to admit. Those who are urging you to take this step are not the enemies of Charles Stuart; and if you comply with their wishes, you will irretrievably ruin yourself and your friends."

"Both of you are too timid," replied Cromwell, laughing. "I cannot do any thing with you."

"If you assume the royal title, I shall consider your cause and your family as hopelessly lost; and although I shall never do any thing against you, I shall henceforth no longer do any thing for you."

They parted, angry and irritated. Cromwell, however, thought he might still overcome the resistance of his family; nor was he the man to drop so soon a resolution which he had once taken. Desborough, a prominent officer in the army, profited by his position, and caused his most distinguished comrades to sign a petition against the protector's assuming the royal title. This last step dashed the cup from Cromwell's lips; already so near the goal, he was hurled back from it, as he could maintain himself on the throne only by the assistance of the army. He therefore declined with an air of pious indifference the crown offered to him by the Parliament. He remained, as heretofore, Lord Protector of England. Nevertheless, the numbers of his enemies and opponents were constantly on the increase. Innumerable conspiracies against his life were discovered by his numerous spies, among whom Billy Green acted again a prominent part.

A pamphlet, entitled "Killing No Murder," was mysteriously circulated in the streets of London; it went from hand to hand; it spread everywhere like wildfire; it penetrated under various addresses into all houses, now concealed in a box, now in the shape of a letter. Women and children were engaged in circulating it. This pamphlet recommended the assassination of the protector, and commenced with an address to his highness, Oliver Cromwell. The unknown author wrote to him as follows: "I intend to procure for your highness that justice which no one as yet has been willing to let you have, and to show to the people how great an injury it would inflict upon itself and you if it should delay complying with my advice. To your highness belongs the honor of dying for the people, and the thought of the benefit which your death will confer on England cannot but comfort you in your last moments. Not until then, my lord, will you really have a right to the titles which you now arrogate to yourself; you will then really be the liberator of your people, and deliver it from a yoke hardly less oppressive than that from which Moses freed his people. Then you will really be the reformer that you now try to seem; for then religion will be reëstablished, liberty will be restored, and the Parliament will regain the rights for which it struggled so manfully. All this we hope to obtain by the speedy death of your highness. To bring about this blessing as soon as possible, I have written this pamphlet, and if it has the effect which I expect from it, your highness will soon be beyond the reach of human malice, and your enemies will only be able to level against your memory blows which you will no longer feel."

Cromwell was as indignant as he was dumfounded at this pamphlet, and instructed all his spies to strain every nerve in order to ferret out its author and circulators. Billy Green was fortunate enough to catch and arrest a woman who was engaged in circulating the dangerous pamphlet. The prisoner was waiting in the anteroom of the protector, who deemed the matter so important as to declare that he would himself examine her. He was resolved to treat her with extreme rigor, and nothing short of death seemed to him a penalty adequate to such a crime. He was pacing his cabinet with a rapid step; his forehead was covered with threatening furrows, and his whole face was flushed with anger and determination.

"Bring in the woman," he said to the officer of the day.

The prisoner came in; she bore calmly and composedly the threatening glance of the protector, which caused the most courageous men to tremble.

"You have committed a capital crime," he said, stepping close up to her.

"I know it, and am not afraid of death," she replied with a proud smile.

"But before dying, you will give me the names of your accomplices. Who gave you this pamphlet?"

"That is my secret, and no one will be able to wrest it from me."

"But suppose I should pardon you on this condition?"

"Life and liberty have no longer any value for me."

"You are young yet," replied Cromwell, struck by her firmness. "How comes it that life and liberty have no longer value for you?"

"Because sentence of death has been passed upon my husband, who is to be executed tomorrow."

"SPEAK! WHO IS THIS WOMAN?" p. 26[illegible]

"And what is your husband's name?"

"Thomas Egerton."

When the protector heard this name, the sympathy and compassion which had already begun to stir his heart died away again. He remembered his seduced daughter and the vengeance which he had sworn to wreak on her seducer.

"Thomas Egerton!" he cried, furiously. "Oh, I know him, and even though he had a thousand lives, he should lose them all. You are his wife, and shall die too. Heaven is just, and the Lord delivers into my hands His enemies and mine!"

"Your cruelty does not frighten me. To die at the same time with my husband was the dearest wish of my heart."

"It shall be fulfilled, but not in the manner you expect. You shall be executed before him, and in his presence."

"By adopting this course, you will in spite of yourself confer another benefit on me; for I shall not then have the grief of witnessing my husband's execution."

"This woman cannot be tamed," murmured Cromwell in impotent rage, and yet involuntarily admiring her conduct.

The longer he conversed with her, the more he was obliged to acknowledge her manfulness and courage; he felt the nearness of a kindred spirit. Her very features bore a certain resemblance to his own. In her whole appearance there was something that struck awe and terror into his heart, and he could not avoid shuddering the longer he contemplated her. He tried once more to wrest from her a confession in reference to the pamphlet, but she remained inflexible, and his threats were unable to intimidate her.

"Your blood, then," he said, "be on your own head. Remove her; she shall die with her husband."

"Thank you," replied the heroic woman, preparing to leave the room.

"Call Henderson," ordered the protector; "he shall take her to the Tower."

He turned indifferently to Thurloe, his private secretary, whom he instructed to pay a few gold-pieces to Billy Green for his services as a spy. Soon afterward old Henderson made his appearance. Cromwell gave him in an undertone instructions for the governor of the Tower. The Puritan approached the prisoner in order to take her away; on seeing him, she uttered a cry of surprise, which did not escape the protector. Henderson, too, seemed deeply moved, but he presently recovered his presence of mind, and his rigid features no longer betrayed the least emotion.

"Do you know this woman?" said the protector to his former friend.

"I do not."

"And yet she uttered a cry on seeing you. You lie, Henderson! But I shall find out the truth. All but these two will withdraw."

All the others left the room, in which Cromwell remained with the Puritan and the prisoner.

CHAPTER VII.

LUCY AND HER FATHER—CROMWELL'S LAST DAYS.

A VAGUE suspicion arose in the protector's mind. Profound silence, which no one dared to break, reigned in the cabinet. Seized with the most various feelings, the three stood face to face. Cromwell at last approached the Puritan.

"Speak! Who is this woman?" he asked, imperiously.

So saying, he gazed at the Puritan with those piercing eyes whose demoniacal power but few persons were able to withstand. Henderson also was unable to resist the charm, and, contrary to his original intention, he confessed the truth.

"You want to know it," he said, sullenly, and with a sinister smile. "Learn, then, that this woman is—your daughter!"

"My daughter!" echoed Cromwell, and buried his face in his hands. When he looked up again, the color had fled from his cheeks, and he trembled like an aspen-leaf.

"You lie!" he cried out. "I know that I have grieved you, and now you want to revenge yourself."

"I have never uttered a lie," replied the Puritan. "I speak the truth even now, though I intended to conceal it from you."

"You intended to let me kill my child?" asked Cromwell, divining the fanatic's purpose. "And then you would have stood before me and called me her murderer."

Henderson made no reply, but contented himself with nodding his head. Lucy had sunk at the feet of the father whom she had found so unexpectedly.

"Forgive me," she said in a heart-rending tone, "but I did not know that Oliver Cromwell was my father."

"You are not to blame," he replied, deeply moved; "I am the only guilty party. You are only an instrument in the hand of the Lord, who now punishes the sins of my youth. I forgive you."

"And my husband?"

"Your husband?" he asked doubtingly. "I always thought him your seducer, and hated him bitterly for it."

"He acknowledged the wrong he had perpetrated on me, and restored my honor and reputation. We have been married at the altar. I cannot live without him."

"I will pardon him for your sake, although he has richly deserved death. I shall, however, impose on you a condition; if you refuse to submit to it, the execution will take its course."

"To save him, I will submit to any terms, however rigorous they may be."

"You will never betray the secret of your descent either to him or to anybody else. Henderson will accompany you, and pledge me his word never to return."

"I will go, not because you order me to do so, but because the Spirit prompts me. The kingdom of the saints has not come yet; hence, I will leave the country and go to foreign lands. There is no longer any sympathy between you and me, for you are an apostate, and, by base defection from God, have betrayed your cause. He, therefore, will turn from you and your house, because you have become an abomination in his eyes."

Cromwell was long since inured to such language. Hence, he was not angry with the Puritan, and allowed him to depart in peace.

On the same day Thomas received his pardon. The long imprisonment and the imminent prospect of death had exerted a salutary effect upon his frivolous character; the heroic devotion of his wife, her fidelity and tenderness, had made another man of him. He left England with her, and returned only after the protector's death. From time to time Lucy received from a mysterious hand large sums of money, which covered all their expenses. This was the only sign of recognition which she received from her father. She faithfully kept the pledge she had given to him, and did not reveal the secret of her birth till after his death, when she communicated it to her husband.

The pamphlet which Colonel Titus had written, was only the forerunner of new and dangerous conspiracies, which now broke out against the protector in all parts of England. Charles II. had entered into negotiations with the malecontents of all parties, even with the republicans, and intended to make another descent upon England. The levellers and cavaliers, the ex-members of the Long Parliament and officers of the army, the most incongruous elements, had united to overthrow their common enemy. Even in London, and under Cromwell's eyes, the conspirators carried their boldness so far as to fix the day and the hour when they were to occupy the most important points of the city, arrest the lord mayor, set fire to the Tower, and, during the general confusion, seize the protector's person. Cromwell, however, redoubled his vigilance and the activity of his spies, whom he hired everywhere, even among the attendants and confidants of Charles II. So soon as he had obtained the necessary proofs, he acted with his accustomed firmness and energy. On the morning of the day when the blow was to be struck, at the very moment the conspirators were repairing to the posts assigned to them, their leaders were suddenly arrested, and all guards reënforced. Colonel Birkstead, the lieutenant of the Tower, marched with a strong body of troops and five pieces of artillery through the city, and arrested about forty of the conspirators, and as many apprentices. Among the former were Sir Henry Slingsby, an uncle of Lord Falconbridge, who had married Lady Mary Cromwell, and Dr. Hewet, a clergyman of the Episcopal Church, highly esteemed and revered by Lady Claypole. Both ladies took infinite pains to save these two men, upon whom sentence of death had been passed. Vainly did the favorite daughter of Oliver Cromwell overwhelm him with supplications and tears; on this occasion he remained inexorable; he was intent on intimidating his enemies, and, therefore, displayed the most inflexible rigor. Cromwell loved his daughter dearly, but his stern nature had no idea of the profound grief of this noble lady. She was a prey to indescribable anguish, and her feeble body began to succumb to it.

For the time being, the protector had attained his object; terror kept hatred at bay; but he himself and his tranquillity were the victims of this victory. Everywhere he thought himself surrounded by enemies menacing his life; henceforth he wore a hidden coat of mail to protect himself against the daggers of assassins; whenever he left the palace, several trusty attendants accompanied him in his carriage. In Whitehall he had several bedrooms with secret doors, and he never slept for two consecutive nights in the same room. This incessant emotion could not but undermine even his iron constitution. Old Henderson's curse seemed now to be fulfilled in him and his family. His beloved daughter, Lady Claypole, was taken sick. He had her sent to Hampton Court, that the country air and tranquillity might restore her health. When her sufferings grew worse, he himself went to her and nursed her with the most tender solicitude. His arm, which had caused the world to tremble, was now the support of a feeble woman; and it was from her sick-room that he governed three kingdoms.

"Poor, poor child!" he sighed, deeply moved, when she was in pain. "To save your life, I would sacrifice my whole power—all, all that I possess!"

She responded by that faint but charming smile which was peculiar to the noble lady, and denied with the self-abnegation of an angel the sufferings to which she was a prey.

"I am better, much better," she whispered, in a gentle voice, while the paleness of her cheeks and her lustreless eyes gave the lie to her words.

In such hours the soul of the great man rose high above the mists of ambition and egotism by which it was darkened, and from the earthly smoke burst forth the purified flame of his religious nature.

"The Lord will not forsake me," he said; "He will not take from me that which is dearest to me on earth. He has raised me to an exalted position, and chosen me as His instrument; what I did I did through and for Him. By God's help I have ended the bloody civil war, restored the greatness of England, protected our Protestant brethren, and defended our holy faith. He will not drop His faithful servant, nor disown His instrument. But His will be done, and not mine. If He has mercy on me, I will glorify His name, heal the wounds of this country, govern with the most conscientious justice, and dedicate the whole remainder of my life to His service, and to the welfare of my people. I feel that my task is not yet ended, and that I am called upon to achieve still greater things."

He remained for long hours on his knees, praying fervently for the recovery of his daughter; but Heaven turned a deaf ear to his appeals. Lady Claypole finally succumbed to her sufferings, and breathed her last in his arms. It afforded a melancholy enjoyment to the protector to surround his daughter's coffin with regal pomp. Her adorned remains lay in state at Westminster Hall, and were interred in a special vault amid the tombs of the kings.

After her death, the protector was subject to fits of the most profound melancholy. His health began to give way, and soon he was no longer able to leave his bed. His physicians were sensible of the perilous condition to which his disease had reduced him, but he himself would not believe that his life was drawing to a close.

"Why do you look so sad?" he asked the doctor, who was standing by his bedside.

"How can I look gay when I am responsible for the life of your highness?"

"You physicians think that I shall die," replied Cromwell, seizing the hand of his wife, who was sitting at his side; "but I tell you I shall not die of this distemper. I am well assured of my recovery."

Perceiving that the physicians were wondering at these words, he added:

"Think not that I have lost my reason; I tell you the truth. I know it from better authority than any which you can have from Galen or Hippocrates. It is the answer of God Himself to our prayers; not to mine alone, but to those of others who have a more intimate interest in Him than I have. You may have skill in your profession; but Nature can do more than all the physicians in the world, and God is far above Nature."

All the friends and adherents of the protector shared this firm belief. Not only in Whitehall, but in all the churches of London, prayers for his recovery ascended to heaven; but even his adversaries were filled with terror and anxiety at the thought of his death, and the confusion that would succeed to it. Hitherto, Cromwell had made no definite depositions as to his successor, and his friends, for this reason, were greatly embarrassed—even Thurloe, from various motives, hesitating to ascertain the protector's wishes in this respect. Cromwell himself, as his condition grew worse and worse, no longer took any interest in worldly affairs. His soul turned exclusively to heaven; it retired into itself, and occupied itself with other questions and problems than those which engrossed the mourners surrounding his bed. At the gates of eternity, which opened to him now, a sudden shudder seized him. Round his bed sat his chaplains, who henceforth did not leave him any more; he alternately prayed or conversed with them on religious subjects.

"Tell me," he asked, starting up from his meditations, "is it possible to fall from grace?"

"It is not possible," replied Sterry, one of the preachers.

"Then I am safe," said Cromwell; "for I know that I was once in grace."

He turned and commenced praying aloud: "Lord, though a miserable and wretched creature, I am in covenant with Thee through Thy grace, and may and will come to Thee for Thy people. Thou hast made me a mean instrument to do them some good, and Thee service. Many of them set too high a value upon me, though others would be glad of my death. Lord, however Thou disposest of me, continue and go on to do good for them. Teach those who look too much upon Thy instruments to depend more upon Thyself, and pardon such as desire to trample upon the dust of a poor worm, for they are Thy people too."

After uttering this fervent prayer, he sank into a stupor, which lasted until evening. Toward nightfall he became greatly excited; he spoke in an undertone, and very incoherently, and hesitated in the middle of the words and sentences:

"In truth, God is good; He will not—God is good—I should like to live for the sake of God and His people, but my task is ended.—— God will be with His people."

They asked him to drink, and then to sleep.

"I do not want to drink," he said, "nor to sleep. I think only of making haste, for I must depart very soon."

Thurloe, who did not leave his bedside, and the members of his family, deemed it indispensable to remind him of the necessity of appointing a successor. He uttered in a feeble voice the name of his son Richard. A terrific tempest raged at night, destroying vast amounts of property on land and sea. Morning dawned at last; it was the anniversary of his victories at Dunbar and Worcester, but Cromwell had already lost consciousness.

Between three and four in the afternoon he heaved a deep sigh; his friends and the members of his family hastened to his bedside and found that he was dead.

Profound silence reigned in the death-room, broke only by the sobs and low lamentations of the family, and of a few faithful servants.

"Cease to weep," said Sterry; "you have more reason to rejoice. He was your protector here; he will prove a still more powerful protector, now that he is with Christ, at the right hand of the Father."

CHAPTER VIII.

GENERAL MONK—MILTON AND LADY ALICE.

Important events occurred now in rapid succession. The little son of a great father ruled but a short time over England. Richard Cromwell was too weak for such a burden; he succumbed to the parties which, after the death of the mighty protector, delivered from the pressure of his iron hand, raised their heads again. The protector's generals, incited by their ambition, aspired to his power. They possessed, perhaps, his baser, but not his nobler qualities. Only one of them had inherited his calculating penetration and calm prudence; but the ardent enthusiasm, by which Cromwell had achieved such extraordinary successes, was wanting to him. General Monk marched his troops, who were blindly devoted to him, to London, where he restored tranquillity, and for the time being quietly watched the course of events. As usual, a state of exhaustion had succeeded to the protracted civil wars and the long-continued intense political excitement. Tired of party struggles, and deprived by Cromwell of the liberty for which the country had striven, a majority of the nation longed for tranquillity and enduring institutions. The youth hated the moral austerity of the Puritans, and were desirous of enjoying the forbidden pleasures of life. Thus the way was already fairly paved for the restoration of the Stuarts. Even during the existence of the republic, the pulpits resounded with appeals in favor of a monarchy, as they had formerly done against it. Large numbers of armed apprentices marched noisily through the streets, and cheered vociferously for Charles II. His agents now proceeded openly and fearlessly, and enlisted for him every day new adherents.

England's fate depended on one man, and he was the officer to whom we have already alluded, General Monk. Hitherto he had not revealed his intentions; he possessed the art of silence in the highest degree, and concealed his thoughts even from his own brother. Cool-headed and sober, he knew how to appreciate the state of public affairs and his own position; destitute of ardor and enthusiasm, the republic was as indifferent to him as the monarchy, and he concluded to espouse the cause from which he expected to derive most benefit. This man was now master of the situation. Cool calculation and prudent selfishness had succeeded to ardent fanaticism. Everything betokened the impending downfall of the republic. The ex-royalists exulted openly, while the friends of liberty mourned in secret.

No one grieved more profoundly than Milton. Since his last interview with Cromwell, he had taken heart again and hopefully looked forward to the future. Owing to his growing blindness, he was obliged to retire from public affairs; and, in accordance with his recommendation, Marvell, the young Englishman, whose acquaintance he had made in Rome, was appointed his assistant. The great poet was now again at liberty to pursue his private studies, and to realize the devout aspirations of his youth for an immortality of literary fame. In his lonely and sleepless nights he was at work upon his "Paradise Lost." Fragments of this great epic he communicated to his friends, who received the first books with rapturous admiration, and urged him to continue his work. Especially was Alice delighted with the passages which she had heard. He listened willingly to her advice, and her refined judgment and excellent taste, but more than all her innate piety exercised the greatest influence upon his immortal creation. No less happy was the effect which she exerted upon his spirits. His wife had died; in spite of their reconciliation, she had never been able to appreciate his worth and genius. Nevertheless, he mourned sincerely over his loss, which was the more painful to him as she left three half-grown daughters. His faithful friend was to him a devoted support, and to his children a mother. She took care of him and did not leave him. Owing to his constant intercourse with her, his mind assumed a milder tone; he learned from her involuntarily that gentleness and toleration with which the noble lady was animated. Without being recreant to his own convictions, he judged the views of others with greater forbearance than formerly. He reflected seriously on the reconciliation of the various Protestant sects, and in his conversations with her he frequently dwelt upon this subject.

"Such a reconciliation," he said to her one day, "is feasible only after the Church has gained its entire independence of the state."

"I doubt if it will ever succeed in so doing."

"And yet every argument supports my demand. It cannot be denied, being the main foundation of our Protestant religion, that we of these ages (having no other divine rule or authority from without us, warrantable to one another as a common ground, but the Holy Scripture, and no other within us but the illumination of the Holy Spirit so interpreting that Scripture as warrantable only to ourselves, and to such whose consciences we can so persuade) can have no other ground in matters of religion but only from the Scriptures. Hence it is obvious that neither traditions, councils, nor canons of any visible church, much less edicts of any magistrate or civil session, but the Scripture only, can be the final judge or rule in matters of religion, and that only in the conscience of every Christian to himself. Our doctrine prefers the Scripture before the Church, and acknowledges none but the Scripture sole interpreter of itself to the conscience. But if any man shall pretend that the Scripture judges to his conscience for other men, he makes himself greater not only than the Church, but also than the Scripture, than the consciences of other men; a presumption too high for any mortal, since every true Christian, able to give a reason of his faith, has the word of God before him, the promised Holy Spirit, and the mind of Christ within him; a much better and safer guide of conscience, which, as far as concerns himself, he may far more certainly know than any outward rule imposed upon him by others, whom he inwardly neither knows nor can know. Chiefly for this cause do all true Protestants account the pope Antichrist, for that he assumes to himself this infallibility over both the conscience and the Scripture."

"But if you deny all authority and church discipline, you throw open the door to heresy and infidelity," objected his orthodox friend.

"These dread words do not terrify me, although I know that they have been used for ages past as scarecrows to keep free and liberal minds from the field of truth. He who to his best apprehension follows the Scripture, though against any point of doctrine by the whole Church received, is not a heretic, but he who follows the Church against his conscience and persuasion grounded on the Scripture. How many persecutions, imprisonments, banishments, penalties, and stripes, how much bloodshed, have the forcers of conscience to answer for! Christianity in its original form is of a purely spiritual nature, and founded on unlimited liberty; for its growth and development, it has no need of the temporal power, which is manifestly subordinate to it, and whose yoke it cannot tolerate. It is a degradation of religion to deem such a support necessary to it; it is a perversion of its whole essence and character, and, what is worse still, an insult to divine truth."

"In my opinion, the state must have at least the right to superintend religious matters, so as to prevent blasphemy and immorality. This is its bounden duty."

"The protector becomes only too easily a tyrant. In pretending to protect religion against its enemies, he will ere long lay his hands upon the freedom of conscience and thought. He that seeks to compel an infidel to observe at least the outward forms of religion, or a conscientious man to act contrary to his conviction, will bring about the same result in the two cases, and make only hypocrites. I can see the salvation of our faith only in the entire independence of the Church from the state. It is not until then that we shall have that toleration which you, my friend, as well as I, desire for all men."

"God grant then that the day may soon dawn upon us, when every one shall practise the charity and forbearance which have animated us for many years past, notwithstanding our opposite views!"

"Amen!" said the poet. "And now let me recite to you the first lines of the third book of my 'Paradise Lost.'"

The poet spoke, in a tremulous voice:

"Hail, holy Light! offspring of heaven first-born,
Or of the Eternal co-eternal beam,
May I express thee unblamed? since God is light,
And never but in unapproached light
Dwelt from eternity; dwelt then in thee,
Bright effluence of bright essence increate.
Or hear'st thou rather, pure ethereal stream,
Whose fountain who shall tell? Before the sun,
Before the heavens thou wert, and at the voice
Of God, as with a mantle, didst invest
The rising world of waters dark and deep,
Won from the void and formless infinite.
Thee I revisit now with bolder wing,
Escaped the Stygian pool, though long detained
In that obscure sojourn; while in my flight
Through utter and through middle darkness borne,
With other notes than to the Orphean lyre,
I sung of chaos and eternal night;
Taught by the heavenly muse to venture down
The dark descent, and up to reascend,
Though hard and rare: thee I revisit safe,
And feel thy sovereign vital lamp; but thou
Revisit'st not these eyes, that roll in vain
To find thy piercing ray, and find no dawn;
So thick a drop serene hath quenched their orbs,
Or dim suffusion veiled. Yet not the more
Cease I to wander where the Muses haunt
Clear spring, or shady grove, or sunny hill,
Smit with the love of sacred song; but chief
Thee, Sion, and the flowery brooks beneath,

That wash thy hallowed feet, and warbling flow,
Nightly I visit; nor sometimes forget
Those other two equalled with me in fate,
So were I equalled with them in renown,
Blind Thamyris and blind Mæonides.
And Tiresias and Phineus, prophets old:
Then feed on thoughts, that voluntary move
Harmonious numbers; as the wakeful bird
Sings darkling, and in shadiest covert hid
Tunes her nocturnal note. Thus with the year
Seasons return, but not to me returns
Day, or the sweet approach of even or morn,
Or sight of vernal bloom, or summer's rose,
Or flocks, or herds, or human face divine;
But cloud instead, and ever-during dark
Surrounds me, from the cheerful ways of men
Cut off, and for the book of knowledge fair
Presented with a universal blank
Of Nature's works, to me expunged and razed,
And wisdom at one entrance quite shut out.
So much the rather thou, celestial Light,
Shine inward, and the mind through all her powers
Irradiate; there plant eyes, all mist from thence
Purge and disperse, that I may see and tell
Of things invisible to mortal sight."

Alice listened in profound emotion to the touching complaint which the poet uttered in regard to his own blindness. When he was through, she seized his hand and dropped a tear on it.

"Is my Muse weeping?" asked the poet. "Yes, you are my Muse, and stand as such before my dimmed eyes. In you I find again the divine nature of woman, which restores to us our paradise lost. Alas! I possessed it once, and forfeited it by my own fault. But Heaven was merciful to me, and sent to me in your person one of His angels, who opened to me the gates of a new and more beautiful Eden. That earthly passion has vanished, and only that heavenly love, which is now my comfort in gloom and adversity, has remained to me. Let me confess to you at this hour how fervently I once loved you, dear Alice. Time has purified and transfigured my love; free from all earthly desires, I may openly avow to you to-day what I formerly concealed with timid anxiety from the world."

"And I return your avowal in the same spirit," whispered Alice, deeply moved. "I loved you, also, in those beautiful days. Fate separated us, and I became the wife of another man. God knows how dear he became to me. It was not that intoxicating love that attached me to Carbury, but the highest admiration of his noble and manly nature. I grappled a long time with my remembrance of the past, and of you, until the fulfilment of my duty afforded me full satisfaction and tranquillity. I learned not only to esteem, but really to love my husband, and soon he was my most precious treasure on earth. For you, however, I preserved in my heart the most affectionate sympathy—an affection which, like yours, has remained free from illicit desires and impure thoughts."

"And thus was vouchsafed to me a happiness for which I scarcely ventured to hope. You have restored to me my faith in the better nature of woman; in you I learned to respect and revere that holy womanhood which I once considered a mere chimera. Let me confess to you that there was once in my life a time when I really believed that woman was made of baser stuff, and was inferior to man."

"How I deplore your error, and how you must have suffered in consequence! For a man who has lost faith in the exalted nature of woman cannot be happy on this earth. It is true, the Creator has given us weakness as our inheritance, but at the same time He has planted mildness in our hearts. If Eve deprived mankind of paradise, through another woman was given to us the Redeemer and the salvation of the world."

"In these words you have described my own fate. I also possessed once a wife resembling Eve. She destroyed the paradise of my wedded life, and I forgave her, as Adam of old forgave his wife, that great sinner. But now there has appeared to me another woman, who, free from all the weaknesses of her sex, soars high above this miserable world, and carries me from earth to heaven. Already I feel her blessed influence; already I feel that, despite my blindness, she fills my soul with radiant light, purifies me by her gentleness and toleration, reconciles me to the world, becomes a pattern for me by her piety, helps me to bear my grievous misfortunes, and, by her sympathy and refined judgment, encourages me in writing my epic, which, but for her advice, would perhaps never have been finished. Such a woman restores to me my lost paradise, and I praise the goodness of the Lord, who, even though so late, has had mercy upon me, and revealed to me the true and exalted nature of woman."

The blind poet felt a gentle, chaste kiss on his lips; but before he was able to return it, his muse had disappeared.

CHAPTER IX.

THE RESTORATION—MILTON'S CONCEALMENT.

Although Milton was thus restored to poetry, his heart was still ardently devoted to the liberties of his country, which at this juncture were more seriously threatened than ever before. General Monk, who, as we have said, was master of the situation, hesitated, it is true, to take the last decisive step; but all symptoms indicated the speedy overthrow of the republic. With profound affliction Milton saw his fondest ideals ruthlessly swept away, and he beheld the rapid return to power of a reactionary party, which, in anticipation of its overwhelming triumph, already exulted at the humiliation of its republican adversaries. As yet, however, he thought the cause that was so dear and sacred to him was not irretrievably lost; and as he had once spoken to Cromwell, so he resolved now to go to Monk and remind him of his duty. The blind poet caused himself to be conducted to the general, whom he found surrounded by the leading men of the different parties. All thronged about Monk to exercise a decisive influence over his resolutions. The haughty cavaliers in their rich costumes of silk and velvet, and the Presbyterian clergymen in their black Genevan gowns, dinned his ears; all sects tried to gain access to him, and either to fathom the intentions of the general or to lead them into a special channel. The fickleness and want of principle of the multitude became more and more apparent; and while Milton was waiting in the anteroom, he could not but notice that his old friends and acquaintances anxiously shunned him now that he had lost his former influence, and the current of public opinion was favorable to the Stuarts.

At last he was admitted. The general received him with the coldness and imperturbable equanimity which always give a shrewd, calculating mind the advantage over a fervent enthusiast.

"What do you want of me?" asked Monk, with his characteristic bluntness.

"Solicitude for the welfare of the country leads me to you; the fate of England is in your hands. At no time, perhaps, has so much been intrusted to a single man as to you, general. On your decision depends the weal or woe of England. A whole people looks up to you and holds you responsible for its fate. History, with uplifted pencil, stands ready to engrave your name on her tablets, either as the benefactor or the worst enemy of your country."

"Come to the point. Who sent you to me?"

"Who sent me to you? My love of liberty, general, and the voice of the Spirit. As the Lord of old raised up prophets in Israel when His people was in danger, so He calls forth to-day also men that will fearlessly proclaim the truth."

"The time of miracles is past," replied the general, sneeringly.

"And yet the events of the last fifteen years prove the falsehood of that adage. Has not a miracle happened under our own eyes? A throne fell before the mighty will of a nation, and the anointed head of a king was laid on the block. A man of lowly descent became ruler of England, and at the very moment when he was stretching out his hand for the crown, death overtook him. Is it not a miracle, too, that you yourself have reached a position where you may decide upon the future of three kingdoms?"

"And what are your views, your wishes? What do you advise me to do?"

"To preserve the republic and protect it against its enemies; to save to the nation those liberties which it has purchased with rivers of precious blood."

"Pray ask the people whether they want freedom; and ask yourself whether the multitude is ripe for it."

"In my opinion, freedom is not a gift of mercy, which must be solicited and humbly obtained, but it is the birthright of individuals as well as nations. I will not deny that it may be abused and degenerate into anarchy; hence, I demand wise laws and institutions to prevent such abuse of freedom."

"And who is to enact these laws?"

"An assembly of the best men, to be freely elected by the people."

"In that case we shall have another Parliament such as that of the miserable Barebone," said Monk, shrugging his shoulders.

"It is true, if the right of unrestrained suffrage were adopted, not wisdom and authority, but turbulence and greed would prevail, and would soon exalt the vilest miscreants from our towns and villages to the rank and dignity of senators. Should the management of the republic be intrusted to persons to whom no one would willingly intrust the management of his private concerns; and the treasury of the state be left to the care of those who lavished their own fortunes in an infamous prodigality? Should they have the charge of the public purse, which they would soon empty into private ones by their unprincipled peculations? Are they fit to be the legislators of a whole people who themselves know not what law, what reason, what right and wrong, what crooked and straight, what licit and illicit mean? who think that all power consists in outrage, all dignity in the parade of insolence? who neglect every other consideration for the corrupt gratification of their friendships, or the prosecution of their resentments? who disperse their own relations and creatures through the provinces, for the sake of levying taxes and confiscating goods? men, for the greater part, the most profligate and vile, who in a moment emerge from penury and rags to a state of splendor and wealth? Who could believe that the masters and patrons of banditti could be the proper guardians of liberty?"

Monk was silent, and his cold features did not betray the slightest symptom of sympathy; yet Milton continued to defend liberty in the most enthusiastic manner. To save the republic, no sacrifice seemed to him too great. He anticipated all possible objections, and even consented to concessions at which the members of his party took deep umbrage, and for which he was bitterly denounced by a great many. We have seen that he gave up universal suffrage; the members of the senate (the Parliament which he advocated) were to be elected for life, except some who were to lose their seats from time to time, and in whose places new members were to be elected. In return, he demanded freedom of conscience for all those who recognized the Bible as the foundation of their faith. He rejected emphatically the House of Lords, pointing to the influence of the large landed proprietors, an evil of the English constitution by which the country is injuriously affected even at the present time. Thus he strove to render good service to the republic, not as a mere enthusiast, but as a practical statesman, even at the moment when it was expiring, and when its adherents were exposed to grave dangers.

"If we return to kingship," he exclaimed at

the end of the conversation, "and soon repent (as undoubtedly we shall, when we begin to find the old encroachments coming on by little and little upon our consciences, which must necessarily proceed from king and bishop united inseparably in one interest), we may be forced, perhaps, to fight over again all that we have fought, and spend over again all that we have spent, but are never like to attain thus far as we are now advanced to the recovery of our freedom, never to have it in possession as we now have it, never to be vouchsafed hereafter the like mercies and signal assistances from Heaven in our cause, if by our ungrateful backsliding we make these fruitless; flying now to regal concessions from His divine condescensions, and gracious answers to our once importuning prayers against the tyranny which we then groaned under; making vain and viler than dirt the blood of so many thousand faithful and valiant Englishmen, who left us in this liberty, bought with their lives."

The general turned a deaf ear to these eloquent appeals; he was unable to discern the requirements and struggles of the future, and his sober mind did not rise above the questions with which he had to deal at the present moment. Milton's words made no impression upon him, and he dismissed the blind poet without revealing his intentions to him.

A few days afterward the general and the Parliament declared for Charles II. The people received this intelligence approvingly, nay, with manifestations of exultation. Tired of civil war, of military rule, and of the arrogance of the generals, they looked upon the restoration of the Stuarts as their only salvation, and as the safest road to the reëstablishment of law, order, and tranquillity. The change which public opinion had undergone became strikingly manifest at Charles II.'s solemn entrance into London. The most jubilant acclamations greeted him on all sides; the streets were strewed with flowers, and all the houses festively decorated. Charles rode by the side of his gloomy brother, the Duke of York. He kindly greeted the same populace which a few years before had hailed his father's execution, and had wished the same fate to be inflicted upon him. The merry, jovial king, jested and laughed with his companions and friends, among whom the licentious Buckingham rendered himself most noticeable by his coarse jests and his handsome appearance. Thus Charles repaired to the palace, surrounded by a brilliant suite and an innumerable multitude, which set no bounds to its rejoicings. His adherents now flocked to him from all quarters and rallied around him; and many of his former adversaries deserted their party and passed over to him. Now commenced that disgusting spectacle which is never wanting to a restoration. Many partisans of the republic, many Puritans dropped their masks, which they had worn only while they were benefited by so doing, and joined the court. The very noisiest democrats suddenly became the most enthusiastic adherents of the king, and persecuted their former friends and associates. Not only fellows like Billy Green, but men that had filled the most distinguished positions, gave the most unmistakable proofs of their venality and want of principle. Edmund Waller, the poet, who had celebrated Cromwell's death in one of his most vigorous and impressive poems, presented a congratulatory address to Charles II. The royal offering was considered inferior to the panegyric on Cromwell, and the king himself told him of the disparity.

"Poets, sire," replied the witty, self-possessed, and unprincipled Waller, "succeed better in fiction than in truth."

Charles smiled, and from that hour forward Waller was admitted to the circle of those dissolute courtiers who, by their vices and immorality, have gained a lasting though most unenviable name in the annals of English history. In a short time St. James's palace was converted into a rendezvous of indescribable licentiousness and corruption. Here were celebrated the orgies to which none but the intimate friends of the king were admitted. Frivolous women, such as the adventurous niece of Cardinal Mazarin, Barbara Villiers (Mrs. Palmer), afterward Duchess of Cleveland, and the accomplished but frail actress Nell Gwynn, played the most prominent parts on these occasions; the most notorious reprobates vied with them. Here reigned a tone and manners that defied the dictates of decorum and decency; obscene witticisms were levelled at the most sacred things, and the more vicious a man was, the more he was courted as a boon companion. At that time appeared first those frivolous *roués* who boasted of their vices, and lauded meanness and infamy as praiseworthy qualities. The very literature of that time was demoralized, and pandered to the basest lust. The most vicious plays were performed on the stage, and more lascivious utterances fell from the lips of the actresses than from those of the actors. This immoderate thirst for amusements and dissipation did not exclude the most vindictive spirit of persecution. The resentment of victorious reactionists knew no bounds. The king himself was not very bloodthirsty, but his courtiers urged him to commit a number of actions entirely at variance with his originally careless and indifferent nature. Sentence of death was passed upon the judges of his father, and they were executed amid the most excruciating tortures. The very grave did not shield the deceased republicans from the cavaliers, whose revenge extended beyond the bounds of death. The remains of Cromwell and Ireton, and even the corpse of the noble and magnanimous Lady Claypole, were torn from their coffins and hanged on the gallows. Death, imprisonment, or exile, menaced all the partisans of the commonwealth. Milton had occupied so prominent a position among them, that he could not hope to escape from the vindictiveness of the royalists. His friends were afraid lest sentence of death should be passed upon him, and advised him to conceal himself until the first storm had blown over. To mislead the persecutors, they even circulated the rumor that he was dead. While he found a quiet and safe asylum at Lady Carbury's house, a coffin, attended by a small number of mourners, was carried from his own dwelling to the cemetery. This stratagem saved him, at least, for the time being.

"I would," said the poet, during this sham funeral, "I were really dead and buried! Life has no longer any value for me since I have to lament the subversion of liberty, and this fearful demoralization prevailing everywhere."

"Why so gloomy?" replied Alice, who was seated at his side. "Resurrection succeeds to death. To-day they inter only Milton the politician, while Milton the poet celebrates his resurrection. You possess the greatest consolation in your poetical genius, which raises you above all earthly troubles. You should never have bid farewell to your Muse, never have plunged into the whirlpool of party-life; you would suffer less at this juncture."

"No, no! I followed only the dictates of my own conscience, and never shall I regret having courageously raised my voice in favor of freedom of conscience and thought. The true poet must not stand aloof from the world and its aspirations; he must not turn a deaf ear to the claims which life and his country make upon him. He is, at the same time, a bard and a prophet, a seer and an exhorter, enlisted in the service of truth. Life and art must commingle in him, and only if he serves humanity, takes part in its struggles, fearlessly enters upon the solution of great public questions, and undauntedly professes his principles and convictions, does he deserve the name of a poet."

CHAPTER X.

ARREST AND PARDON OF MILTON.

MILTON, therefore, was believed to be dead; but in his soul, as Alice had predicted to him, he celebrated the resurrection of poetry. In his safe retreat he worked at his "Paradise Lost," the great struggle of light with darkness, of truth with falsehood. Only from time to time his friends informed him of the events of the day. Parliament caused his "Defence of the People of England" to be burned by the public executioner. This act of baseness and resentment grieved him profoundly. His health began to give way under so many mournful impressions, and his voluntary loneliness produced a most injurious effect on his constitution. Gradually reassured in regard to his personal security, he left his asylum after nightfall and wandered through the streets of the city. Whenever he took such walks a shadow was noticed dogging his steps and seemingly watching his movements. He paid no attention to it, for life had lost all value in his eyes. He had long desired to see his daughters, and, contrary to Alice's advice, he went to his house in order to meet his children, who lived there under the care of his sisters. After spending a short time in their midst, he left the house again to return to his safe asylum. On stepping out of the door, he was surrounded by armed men headed by Billy Green, who had been lurking for him.

"You are my prisoner!" cried Cromwell's former spy, who was now in the service of the government.

The news of Milton's arrest spread like wildfire, and his friends were in great trepidation on his account. Alice hastened to the palace to intercede in behalf of the unfortunate poet. She vainly demanded admittance to the king; Charles II. was at dinner with his favorites, and had strictly forbidden his servants to disturb him. In vain the noble lady mentioned her devotion to the Stuarts and the great sacrifices she had made to their cause; the chamberlain was ordered not to admit her. Charles II. was utterly forgetful of the faithful services which his adherents had rendered to him, and they had often enough cause to charge him with ingratitude. Alice, however, was firmly determined not to leave the palace until she had seen the king himself and prevailed upon him to pardon Milton. While she was waiting in the anteroom, the poet Davenant came in on his way to the apartments of the king, with whom he was on the most intimate terms. Without knowing him, Alice hastened to meet him. On seeing her, Davenant involuntarily stood still.

"Pardon me if I detain you, and ask you to render me an important service."

"Ask of me all that you like, except money."

"I must see the king, and you must procure me an audience."

"I am afraid that that is altogether impossible; for, when his majesty is at the dinner-table with a full goblet before him, he does not allow himself to be disturbed, even though an angel should come from paradise to see him. Let me advise you to come back some other time."

"My business brooks no delay. I am here to obtain the pardon of a noble, magnanimous man, who is, moreover, so unfortunate as to be blind."

"I hope you do not refer to my friend Milton?" he asked eagerly. "If that is the case, I will myself speak to the king, and I pledge you my word I will get him pardoned!"

"Are you a friend of Milton?"

"Of course I am, although we bear no more resemblance to one another than the eagle does to the merry bullfinch. He is a republican, and I am a royalist; he is an enthusiast for ideals, and I am one for reality; he drinks water, and I drink wine; he loves the Muses, and I love pretty girls wherever I may meet them. This, however, shall not prevent my doing for him what he has done for me. He once saved me a very unpleasant sensation at the time that old Satan Cromwell was still alive. His highness was intent on hanging me, and I am indebted for my life to the intercession of my friend Milton."

"Oh, make haste, then, and save him!"

"Of course I shall; and in case his majesty should refuse to grant me this little favor, I swear to you, madam, that I shall commit suicide, and hang myself in despair, although I am exceedingly ticklish. But the king will not allow me to do so. I know him too well; he cannot refuse any thing to those who know how to take him, and least of all to a friend like me, who helps him to kill his time. Wait for me here, madam, until I return, and I will be a scoundrel if our friend Milton is not set at liberty this very night."

So saying, the frivolous Davenant hastened into the adjoining room, from which the laughter and shouts of a merry carousal penetrated to Alice. The king sat in the midst of his boon companions at a table loaded with dishes and decanters. The beautiful Nell Gwynn filled his glass, while the overbearing Buckingham told one of his funny stories, and, to the delight of his august patron, imitated, in the most ludicrous manner, the pedantic bearing and peculiarities of Lord Clarendon, the worthy president of the Council of State.

"Splendid! splendid!" cried Charles. "That is Clarendon to the life; only his big wig is wanting."

"Your majesty," said Buckingham, in the tone of his assumed *rôle*, "Providence has imposed on you the sublime task of making your people happy and contented. For this purpose you must, above all things, honor the Episcopal Church, and lead a virtuous and devout life. You must set a glorious example to your subjects, and be a pattern of morality."

"I suppose that is what I am," said the king, laughing, and imprinting a glowing kiss on Nell Gwynn's crimson lips.

"Besides, it is incumbent on your majesty, by wise economy and a prudent administration, to bring order into the unsettled finances of the kingdom. I deem myself also in duty bound to warn your majesty of those dissolute and extravagant men who, I regret to say, are to be seen but too often around my august master, such as the vicious Earl of Rochester, who is wallowing in the mire of lust, and Grammont, the Frenchman, an incorrigible rake."

"And, above all, the Duke of Buckingham," interposed Waller, the poet, "a man destitute of honesty and virtue, who runs after every wench in the streets, and from whom no woman in the three kingdoms is safe; a pattern of voluptuousness, a colossus of lewdness, the most vicious man in England."

"Better and better," laughed Charles, who liked nothing better than such coarse jests. "Long live the incorrigible Buckingham!"

"Long live the incorrigible Buckingham!" cried the whole chorus.

While the nobleman who had been cheered in so peculiar a manner returned thanks, in ludicrous words, levelling the shafts of his satire even at the king, Davenant entered the room.

"Ah," said Charles to him, "where have you been so long?"

"With some wench, I bet," said the Earl of Rochester, a well-known profligate.

"I do not like to hunt in your lordship's park," replied the poet, who was as witty as he was impudent. "Some harm might befall me there in the end."

"Then you have been at your mother's tavern, and tried to get sober after last night's carousal."

"You are not very happy in your guesses to-day. It would be advisable for you to send your wit to a cobbler and have it mended. It lacks point."

"Then it fares no better than your nose."

"*Requiescat in pace*," said the king, laughing. "Davenant, I want you to tell me where you have been so long."

"In your majesty's anteroom, where I had an interview with a lady."

"A lady who has had an interview with you is always suspicious to me."

"See her yourself and you will judge otherwise. She is waiting in the anteroom, and insists on being admitted to your majesty."

"Is she young and handsome?" asked the king, eagerly.

"She no longer possesses the charms of first youth, but in return she is gifted with that beauty which is imperishable, because it indicates a noble heart and a lofty mind."

"Davenant has gone mad," sneered Buckingham. "He must be confined in a lunatic asylum. In the interest of public security I move that he be sent thither."

"Hush! hush!" said Charles II. "Davenant's intellectual beauty begins to excite my interest. And what does the Platonic lady want of me?"

"She wants your majesty to pardon a prisoner, and I join my prayers to hers."

"She wishes doubtless to intercede in behalf of some accursed Roundhead," said Buckingham. "It is wrong in such supplicants to trouble his majesty during the most important hours of his life. The whole crowd should be hung at the same time, so that they may not disturb his majesty any longer."

"Buckingham is right," said the lazy king. "I do not want to be disturbed, nor do I want to hear any thing about the lady and her *protégé*. You are a tedious fellow, Davenant."

"Very well," replied Davenant; "I will go, then, and inform the lady that my gracious master has no memory for faithful services, nor ears for devoted friends."

"Well, I see that nothing remains for me but to listen to you. Tell me, therefore, what it is all about, but be brief. You see that our time is exceedingly limited. Who is the prisoner in whose behalf you intercede so strongly?"

"Milton, the poet."

On hearing this name, the guests burst into loud murmurs. The swarthy face of the king colored with indignation; he seemed to have awakened from his indolence.

"And you really ask me to pardon that man?" he said, sternly. "Do you not know that he reviled my father even in his grave?"

"He was a republican, and acted according to his convictions, as I did according to mine. Besides, he saved my life at the time I returned to England in compliance with your august mother's request. I am still in his debt, and your majesty pledged me your royal word to pay all my debts on your return."

"You are a rogue," said Charles, laughing at the witty pun. "But how does it come that Milton has not been arrested until now?"

"His friends said he was dead, and caused an empty coffin to be buried in his stead in order to protect him from punishment."

"A very good joke," said the king, whose good-humor had been fully restored by what Davenant had told him. "Justice has nothing to do with the dead, and punishment ceases with the grave."

"Your majesty, then, will pardon Milton?"

"Well, I believe I will."

"And to save your majesty all further trouble, I have drawn up these lines; all you have to do, sire, is to sign them."

With a quick stroke of the pen Charles ordered the immediate release of the prisoner, for which Davenant thanked him very warmly.

"But what about your lady?" asked the king, when Davenant was about to withdraw in order to convey the glad tidings to Alice. "You have not even told me her name. I am sure she is as bad a republican as your friend Milton, since she takes so lively an interest in his fate."

"Your majesty is utterly mistaken. The lady was the most loyal adherent of your lamented father, for whom her husband gave up his life. She herself fought like a heroine for the good cause, and in consequence lost the largest part of her estates. There is no more loyal woman in all England than Lady Alice Carbury, the daughter of the Earl of Bridgewater, Lord President of Wales."

"In that case it is my duty to see her. People in general reproach me with neglecting my old friends; but since my accession, God knows I have found so many old friends of my family that I could not satisfy their claims even though my treasury contained all the riches of the two Indies."

"So far as I know, Lady Alice Carbury is one of those friends who ask for nothing but an affable word and a kindly smile from your majesty. It will not cost you any thing, sire, to vouchsafe these to them."

"Well, we must display some gallantry toward ladies," said the king. "I will see her and pay my respects to her. Tell her that I shall await her in my cabinet to inform her in person that Milton's pardon has been granted. This room would not be a suitable place to give her an audience."

Davenant hastened to inform Alice of the king's will. Her loyal heart was filled with the utmost joy by this intelligence; she adhered to the royal cause with a rare fidelity bordering almost on fanaticism.

"All is well," whispered Davenant to her, "but his majesty is desirous of seeing you in person."

"God bless him for it!" she prayed, with fervent gratitude.

Charles II. came to meet her. She would have bowed her knee before him, but he prevented her doing so; he could not, however, prevent the kiss which she imprinted on his hand. The king, although he was not handsome, was able to display the most seductive amiability whenever he wished to do so. Full of disdain of human nature, although few monarchs ever received so many proofs of devotion at the hands of his subjects, he was yet naturally kind-hearted, and manifested on many occasions extreme affability and condescension. His frivolity was the source of his faults and virtues, if a certain indolent kind-heartedness and a sympathetic though superficial cheerfulness deserve to bear this name. Susceptible of every new impression, Alice's unfeigned devotion, and still more the intellectual beauty which she had preserved in spite of her mature years, won his heart.

"How does so devoted an adherent of the royal cause," he asked, in the course of the audience, "come to intercede in behalf of one of the most inflexible and dangerous republicans? Milton has injured our cause more than a legion of our other enemies, and yet you speak in his behalf."

"Because I esteem his character, and above all his genius, which I believe to be equal to that of the greatest poets of ancient or modern times."

"Very well. He shall live, then, and enter our service. We are fond of poets, and Davenant is aware that we know how to reward them."

"I doubt if Milton will accept so generous an offer, though I gratefully appreciate the spirit which has dictated it."

"And why should your *protégé* refuse to take a position at our court? Believe me, Lady Carbury, all men are venal, as soon as we know the price at which they will s[illegible] themselves."

In her loyalty, Alice did not venture to combat an assertion which the king made

HE WAS DICTATING TO HER.

p. 291

the rule of his life, and which rested especially on his experience during the first months of the restoration, a time when apostacy and shameless venality were fearfully prevalent. When the audience, during which Charles's respect for the noble lady had constantly increased, was drawing to a close, he alluded of his own accord to the sacrifices which she had made for the royal cause.

"Your noble husband died for us," he said, kindly. "You yourself have lost most of your estates by confiscation. It is meet, therefore, that so far as I am able, I should indemnify you for the losses which you have sustained. Golden Grove Castle and its domains, which were confiscated during the commonwealth, rightfully belong to you. I restore them to you and to your sons. They shall always be the property of your family."

"That is too much," faltered out Alice, in surprise. "I came to implore your mercy, not for myself, but in behalf of another."

"But it does not behoove the king," said Charles, in a dignified manner, which he saw fit to assume but very rarely, "to enrich himself with the property of widows and orphans. Go, Lady Carbury, and tell your republican friend that we princes are not so bad as he and his political friends paint us."

After this act of justice and magnanimity, the king returned to the banquet, where, intoxicated with wine and with the kisses of his mistresses, he soon forgot the lady who had stirred the better feelings of his heart.

CHAPTER XI.

SECOND MARRIAGE.

Alice, overjoyed, and accompanied by Davenant, hastened to Milton's prison to announce to him that the king had pardoned him. They found him in the company of his eldest daughter Anna, who had received permission to visit her father from time to time. He was just dictating to her a portion of his "Paradise Lost." Carried away by his enthusiasm, he did not notice the entrance of his friends, who, profoundly moved by the sublime spectacle, did not venture to disturb him. In prison, and exposed to the terrors of an ignominious death, he yielded fearlessly to the inspirations of his lofty imagination. He had just arrived at the description of the parents of mankind, whom he portrayed as follows:

"Two of far nobler shape, erect and tall,
Godlike erect, with native honor clad,
In naked majesty, seemed lords of all;
And worthy seemed; for in their looks divine
The image of their glorious Maker shone;
Truth, wisdom, sanctitude severe and pure,
Severe, but in true filial freedom placed;
Whence true authority in men: though both
Not equal, as their sex not equal, seemed;
For contemplation he and valor formed,
For softness she and sweet attractive grace;
He for God only, she for God in him.
His fair large front and eye sublime declared
Absolute rule; and hyacinthine locks
Round from his parted forelock manly hung
Clustering, but not beneath his shoulders broad;
She, as a veil, down to the slender waist
Her unadorned golden tresses wore
Dishevelled, but in wanton ringlets waved
As the vine curls her tendrils; which implied
Subjection, but required with gentle sway,
And by her yielded, by him best received,
Yielded with coy submission, modest pride,
And sweet, reluctant, amorous delay.
Nor those mysterious parts were then concealed;
Then was not guilty shame: dishonest shame
Of Nature's works, honor dishonorable,
Sin-bred, how have ye troubled all mankind
With shows instead, mere shows of seeming pure,
And banished from man's life his happiest life,
Simplicity and spotless innocence!
So passed they naked on, nor shunned the sight
Of God or angel, for they thought no ill:
So hand in hand they passed, the loveliest pair
That ever since in love's embraces met;
Adam the goodliest man of men since born
His sons, the fairest of her daughters Eve.
Under a tuft of shade, that on a green
Stood whispering soft, by a fresh fountain-side,
They sat them down; and, after no more toil
Of their sweet gardening labor than sufficed
To recommend cool Zephyr, and made ease
More easy, wholesome thirst and appetite
More grateful, to their supper fruits they fell,
Nectarine fruits, which the compliant boughs

Yielded them, sidelong as they sat reclined
On the soft downy bank damasked with flowers.
The savory pulp they chew, and in the rind,
Still as they thirsted, scoop the brimming stream:
Nor gentle purpose, nor endearing smiles
Wanted, nor youthful dalliance, as beseems
Fair couple, linked in happy nuptial league,
Alone as they. About them frisking played
All beasts of the earth, since wild, and of all chase
In wood or wilderness, forest or den:
Sporting the lion ramped, and in his paw
Dandled the kid; bears, tigers, ounces, pards,
Gambolled before them; the unwieldy elephant,
To make them mirth, used all his might, and
wreathed
His lithe proboscis; close the serpent sly,
Insinuating, wove with Gordian twine
His braided train, and of his fatal guile
Gave proof unheeded; others on the grass
Couched, and now filled with pasture, gazing sat,
Or bedward ruminating; for the sun,
Declined, was hasting now with prone career
To the ocean isles, and in the ascending scale
Of heaven the stars that usher evening rose."

It was not till Milton paused, that Alice and Davenant made known their arrival to the blind poet.

"You see," said Davenant, "how soon my predictions have been verified. To-day I return the visit which you paid me in prison, and am happy to inform you that you have been pardoned."

"You owe your life and liberty to this excellent gentleman," added Alice. "The king, whom may God save! was exceedingly gracious toward me, and toward you too."

"And it depends only on yourself," added Davenant, "to resume your former office as secretary to the Council of State. His majesty seemed greatly inclined to reappoint you to that office. If I were in your place, I should not hesitate a moment."

"Never!" replied Milton, with solemn earnestness; "never will I take such a step, and prove recreant to my principles. I will eat the dry crust of poverty rather than repudiate my convictions."

"Bah! one must not be so very scrupulous. Look about you: I could name a great many republicans who have now become ardent royalists. Believe me, my old friend, it does not pay to sacrifice one's happiness for a mere chimera. The first of all laws is self-preservation."

"I should think it was self-respect," replied Milton, and then turned the conversation into a different channel, Alice helping him kindly to do so.

Milton preferred his honorable poverty to the royal offer, and did not shrink from the sacrifices which he voluntarily imposed upon himself. Henceforth he lived in retirement in the environs of London, occupied exclusively with the completion of his great epic. His three daughters shared his retirement only with the greatest reluctance. They had inherited the character and predilections of their deceased mother, and requited his tenderness with coldness and ingratitude. Only his youngest daughter Deborah was an exception, and treated her father more affectionately than her undutiful and unkind sisters. The latter complained bitterly of the tyranny of Milton, who taught them to read and pronounce Latin, Greek, and even Hebrew, and caused them to read to him daily for several consecutive hours. He was now totally blind, "dark, dark, irrecoverably dark," and needed more than ever a support which he did not meet with at the hands of his undutiful daughters. With the assistance of the servant-girl they defrauded the blind helpless man by selling behind his back the most valuable books of his library, and extorted from him for household expenses a great deal of money which they spent for dresses and amusements. In this manner they indemnified themselves for the *ennui* which they felt in his company.

His good angel also left him. Alice was obliged to return to her estates, where her presence was indispensable. She deemed herself in duty bound to preserve from decay the inheritance of her only son, who had grown up in the mean time, and to rebuild the castle of his ancestors. She deferred as long as possible her departure, by which her friend was to be deprived of his last support. At last she informed him, profoundly moved, of her resolution.

"I must look after my neglected estates, and try to preserve to my son the inheritance of his ancestors. One idea only, that I must leave you here, grieves me profoundly. You have more than ever need of female care and solicitude, and your daughters fail to do their duty toward you."

"I am destined to drink the bitter cup of adversity to its very dregs," replied Milton, heaving a deep sigh. "My daughters resemble the unnatural children of King Lear. Oh, how truthfully did the great Shakespeare depict in his immortal tragedy the grief and despair of their poor old father! May God preserve me from madness!"

"I came to make you to-day a proposition, which, coming from my lips, may surprise you. I have struggled with myself a long time, and tried to find another expedient, but have been unable to do so. You must marry again."

"And *you* advise me to do so?" he asked, reproachfully.

"I know best the reasons which will render it difficult for you to make up your mind to take this step; but nevertheless you yourself cannot fail to perceive how necessary it is."

"And what girl would bestow her hand on a blind old man, the father of three daughters, who is not even rich enough to compensate her for the sacrifice she would make to him?"

"I know such a girl, the daughter of an excellent man, who has lived for some time past in my neighborhood, and shares my veneration for you. She herself has confessed to me her love for you, and is willing to become yours notwithstanding your blindness. At my hands you shall receive the wife who entertains no more ardent wish than to sweeten your life and become to you a stay and staff in your old age. If you consent to take her—and I am convinced that you will not turn a deaf ear to the voice of reason—you shall have this very day an interview with your intended at my own house."

"It is your wish, and I will comply with it, although my heart cannot love another woman."

"Let us forget the past, which is irrevocable for us two. We must submit to the requirements of life. I shall bid you farewell with less sorrow if I leave you under the tender care of this excellent creature."

Milton appreciated the sacrifice which Alice made to him unmurmuringly. Fate had sundered them forever, and vouchsafed to them only a spiritual and intellectual union. At Alice's house he got acquainted with the amiable girl she had destined for him. With womanly devotion and self-abnegation, the noble creature had resolved to sweeten the last days of the blind poet; free from all selfishness, she sacrificed to him her youth and a bright future. Alice was her friend, and, in her daily intercourse with her, she had inspired the young girl with love and veneration for Milton. She herself encouraged her to persevere in her intention.

"Can there be any thing more beautiful for a woman," she said, "than to accompany a man of genius on the thorny pathway of his life, to protect him from the cares of stern reality, and to belong to him? Were I not a mother, and had I not other duties to fulfil, I should have joyfully remained with him. But as it is, I must leave him, and he needs a helpmate. You, my daughter, are the only woman to whom I should not grudge his friendship and his affections."

"And I pledge you my word that I will be to him a faithful companion and assistant."

It was an affecting scene when Alice introduced to the blind poet the young woman who was to share the evening of his life. All three were profoundly moved.

"I accept your sacrifice," said Milton to the weeping girl. "Alas! I have become so poor that I have nothing to offer you, not even my love, which belongs to another woman."

"I know it, she replied; and yet I am proud of the name of your wife, for I revere in you the most sublime genius, the greatest poet. My only apprehension is, lest, with my feeble abilities, I should not fulfil your expectations. Never till now have I been so painfully alive to my own worthlessness."

"It is not knowledge, but love, that makes us rich," said Alice, putting the girl's hand into that of the poet. "God bless you!" she added, with tears in her eyes. "I shall be with you, even though you do not see me."

With a mournful embrace, and shedding bitter tears, she bade farewell to the beloved of her youth; however, she left him more calmly as she had given him a faithful wife, though her heart bled and grieved in secret.

CHAPTER XII.

MILTON AND THE DUKE OF YORK.

Milton's wife kept her word, and became a stay and staff to her blind husband. Peace returned to his house, although his unnatural daughters persisted in their heartless conduct toward their old father. New dangers and persecutions, however, threatened him from without; for his enemies were again intent on involving him in serious trouble. The attention of the king's brother, James, Duke of York, who afterward ascended the throne, and, owing to his tyranny, was deprived of his crown, was called to Milton. He dinned Charles's ears with entreaties, until the king allowed him to go and see the blind poet. Attended by Sir Kenelm Digby, with whom he was on terms of special intimacy, he repaired to Milton's house. They found him in an open bower, where he spent most of his time; he was engaged in dictating to a young man a letter to a distant friend. Hidden in the shrubbery, they listened to the words of the blind poet. Notwithstanding the twofold burden of age and adversity, his features had not by any means lost the noble intellectual expression for which they were distinguished. His gray hair fell in long ringlets upon his shoulders; from his high forehead beamed the majesty of his mind; and round his finely-chiselled lips played a melancholy smile, the only symptom of his sufferings, which he bore with manly resignation. His costume was simple, but neat; his slender, unbowed form was wrapped in a comfortable gray coat. Thus he was seated in the small garden where he used to pass most of his time during the fine season. The autumnal sun illumined his venerable face, and seemed to surround his head with a halo. The breeze whispered gently in the foliage surrounding the bower. Some late flowers bloomed in gay colors, while yellow leaves flitted from time to time to the ground. In the top of the linden a bird sang the melancholy notes with which he took leave of the parting season. The whole was a picture of peace, blended with a spirit of gentle melancholy. The poet, who was reclining in his easy-chair, involuntarily inspired the visitors, despite the hostile intention with which they had come, with a feeling of respect and admiration.

"I had formed a different idea of this enemy of religion and of our cause," said the gloomy Duke of York to his companion.

"And yet," whispered Sir Kenelm Digby, "no man in England has more fatally injured our sacred cause. You know his writings, which breathe the most intense hatred of Catholicism and of the Holy Father in Rome."

James, who had turned Catholic in France,

and become one of the most fanatical adherents of his Church, was irritated again by the insidious remark of Sir Kenelm Digby. The milder mood which had involuntarily seized him at the sight of Milton, gave place to his vindictiveness and spirit of persecution.

"It would be a downright outrage if such a heretic and republican should not suffer any punishment whatever. But, in the first place, I will speak with him, and enjoy the misfortunes which have so justly befallen him."

"He deserves his fate the more as he rejected in Rome the most brilliant offers made to him on the part of our holy Church. I myself took the greatest pains, and left no means untried, to prevail upon him to acçept them. Already I thought I had won him over to our side, when he escaped me, and rewarded my efforts by deriding and reviling me. Oh, I cannot tell you how intensely I hate that man, who has always frustrated my most important plans!"

"Depend on it, I shall revenge myself and you on him. The time is no longer distant when I shall openly proclaim my convictions, and annihilate our enemies."

"You really intend, then, to avow your adoption of the Catholic religion in the face of the whole world?"

"I have already too long deferred this. You yourself and our Roman friends advised me to proceed very cautiously; but the moment when I may put off the irksome mask is at hand. The throne has been so firmly reëstablished that nothing is able to shake it. My brother, too, is secretly attached to our Church. However, he cannot yet openly adopt our faith; and, besides, his mind is too frivolous to fathom and appreciate the sublime task imposed upon our house. I for one am firmly resolved to subvert Protestantism in England for all time to come. I swear that I will do so as soon as I have ascended the throne! The task of my life will be accomplished then. The innocent blood of my father, who died for his faith, will no longer cry to Heaven, and my vengeance will be fully satiated."

"We will commence avenging your father's death upon this fanatic. Come, I will speak to him, but he shall not learn immediately who I am."

So saying, the duke and his companion approached the poet, who heard them, and rose from his easy-chair.

"Who is there?" he asked.

"A good friend," said Sir Kenelm Digby, with feigned cordiality. "I have long intended to afford myself the pleasure of visiting you in your retirement."

"I bid you welcome, Sir Kenelm; but you have brought a companion with you?"

"You cannot wonder that an admirer of your genius has accompanied me in order to pay his respects to you."

"Sir Kenelm tells you the truth," added the duke, with a sinister smile. "Already long ago I wished to get acquainted with the celebrated poet and republican, who has sworn everlasting hatred to kings."

"Not to kings, but only to tyrants and unjust princes."

"Moreover, you are the standard-bearer of Protestantism, and the sworn foe of the Roman Church."

There was in the tone of these words a bitterness which could not but attract Milton's attention, the more so as the speaker had come with Sir Kenelm Digby, whose attachment to Rome was generally known. Hence Milton avoided at first making any reply to the remark. Soon, however, the duke no longer contented himself with these covert attacks; both he and Sir Kenelm put off their hypocritical masks more and more.

"You have attained your object now," said Digby, sneeringly; "your high-flying dreams and expectations have been fulfilled in a most remarkable manner. What has become of you and your republic? The very children laugh it to scorn. Admit now that you acted the fool. In truth, when I think of the time we spent together in Rome, and compare the present to it, I am almost inclined to take compassion on you. At that time the world lay admiringly at your feet; beauty, wealth, and power offered themselves to you. All you needed to do was to stretch out your hands for them. Why did you not follow my advice? With the eye of a seer I divined events as they have come to pass. Instead of your so-called liberty, the throne stands firmer than ever; and in a few years, as is to be foreseen with absolute certainty, all England will return to the faith of its fathers."

"And you can really hope to bow my courage?" asked Milton. "It is true, I am poor, unfortunate, and weighed down by adversity; but I do not despair for all that. Out of the shipwreck of my life I have saved my most precious treasure, the consciousness of having remained true to myself, and of never having denied my convictions. I know full well that man is not infallible, but the Lord forgives errors arising from thirst for truth. God will be a mild judge to me. Now I am sitting here like Job, whom Heaven had given into the hands of the tempter. My houses have sunk into ruin, my gardens are devastated, my children have forsaken me; my enemies are triumphant, my very friends deride me; but, like him, I am firm in my faith. Therefore, the all-merciful Father will not forsake me, but sustain me in my sore distress."

"But I believe you have not yet experienced the full extent of the sufferings which you have brought upon your head," remarked the duke, exasperated at the firmness which Milton still displayed amidst his misfortunes.

"What more can befall me?" asked the blind poet. "Since I have become blind, I am no longer afraid of any thing. The greatest loss which I have sustained is that of my eyesight. To be blind, oh! that is worse than imprisonment, poverty, or the infirmities of age; for a blind man is at the same time a prisoner, buried in everlasting night, poorer than the most wretched beggar, and more decrepit than the feeblest old man. The lowest animal is better off; the worm creeps in the dust, but it sees, while I live in darkness. O darkness! darkness! And I know that the golden sun is now shining in the heavens. This terrible gloom deprives me of all hope and joy. And why is the noblest of boons intrusted to an organ so delicate and weak as the eye?"

In this touching manner the poet lamented over his fate. Even Sir Kenelm Digby was profoundly moved; but the Duke of York had no compassion on him. With his innate cruelty he gloated over the sufferings of the unfortunate man, which he tried to sharpen by his bitter taunts.

"And do you not see yet," he asked, sneeringly, "that your blindness is only the just penalty of your misdeeds?"

"I am not sensible of any guilt," replied Milton, with the calmness of a clear conscience.

"You forget entirely your sins against the late king, whom you reviled even in his grave. Do you confess your guilt?"

"I do not, for I acted only in accordance with my convictions."

"You do not know with whom you are speaking," whispered Sir Kenelm to the poet. "Beware! your imprudent utterances might still endanger your life."

"I am afraid of no man," replied Milton, aloud.

"Not even of me?" asked the duke.

"Not even of you, even though you were the king himself."

"I am not the king," replied James, frowning, "but his brother, the Duke of York. I repeat it to you, that Heaven is just. He has deprived you of your eyesight, because you, an incorrigible republican, insulted my late lamented father even after his assassination. You deserve your fate; the vengeance of Heaven has overtaken you."

Milton was not frightened by this unexpected visit, nor did he humble himself before the most powerful of his enemies. With a calm smile he rose from his chair, and saluted the duke by bowing slightly to him.

"If your royal highness," he replied, "is of opinion that our misfortunes are evidences of the wrath of God, and that they befall us only in consequence of our crimes, how do you explain the death of your father?"

The duke turned pale with rage; muttering a terrible threat between his clinched teeth, he left the inflexible republican, a prey to the most violent agitation.

"By the bloody head of my father!" he exclaimed, on leaving the house, "this blind monster shall find out that a worse fate than the loss of his eyesight is in store for him."

Flushed with excitement and vindictiveness, he went to the king, his brother. Charles II. was promenading in his park with his boon companions, and engaged in his favorite pastime of feeding the ducks in the pond of St. James's. While the birds were snapping greedily at the crumbs which he threw to them, he made all sorts of witty remarks as to their haste and the manner in which one duck tried to deprive another of the morsels destined for her.

"They are my parasites," said the king, who was in excellent humor. "Look, Buckingham, how they are fighting for a few crumbs! If this goes on for any length of time, my pockets will soon be empty, and I shall not have a morsel left. These parasites will utterly impoverish me. Do you not think so too, Rochester? How loud they scream! I suppose they are relating how well they have served me. I bet that old drake is an excellent cavalier, who believes himself justly entitled to my gratitude; and that waddling duck yonder is urgently requesting me to promote and reward her young ones. All my favors have been distributed for to-day, and I am sorry that I can no longer do any thing for the birds."

The courtiers joined in these playful sallies, and delighted the king by applying to the ducks the names of well-known office-seekers. Meanwhile the Duke of York had approached. On perceiving his brother, Charles said to him in a kind tone: "Come, James, we are giving an audience in the open air, and conferring orders and offices on our faithful subjects in the pond."

"Will you do me a favor?" said the duke.

"Well, I do not care if you get a crumb too, though you are in want of nothing, because you have always been more economical than I."

"I do not ask for money, but for the punishment of an offender."

"Always the same old strain," said the king, more gravely; "always the same old cry for revenge. Do you know, James, that your vindictiveness begins to be tedious? I think we have done enough, and you may be satisfied."

"There lives as yet one of the most infamous adversaries of our lamented father—a man who, in my eyes, is more criminal than the regicides. Sire, it is your fault that old Milton has not yet been hanged."

"Then you have been at his house?" asked Charles, throwing the rest of his crumbs with a careless air into the pond.

"I have had an interview with him."

"And in what condition did you find him?"

"Bowed down by age, and, it seemed also, very poor."

"And he is blind, too, is he not?"

"He is totally blind."

"Go, go, James," replied the king; "you are a downright fool to believe that the gallows would be a punishment for such a man.

Why, it would at once put an end to his sufferings, and confer upon him a great blessing. If he is old, poor, and blind, he is sufficiently punished, and we may spare his life."

In spite of his brother's remonstrances, Charles adhered for once to his resolution not to take any further steps against Milton. But, in return, the bloodthirsty James wrested from him an order for the execution of the younger Vane, although the king had solemnly promised to the latter that no harm should befall him. Indemnified by this victim, the duke left St. James's Park, and gloated over the agony to which the king's perfidy would subject the prisoner.

CHAPTER XIII.

PUBLICATION OF "PARADISE LOST"—MILTON AND DRYDEN.

Henceforth Milton was safe from further persecutions, and he had ample leisure to complete his immortal epic. He dictated it alternately to his daughters and young Ellwood, who had been recommended to him, and who now lived at his house. Ellwood was a Quaker, and by his modesty, and the reverential homage which he paid to the blind poet, he won Milton's friendship and esteem. Perhaps Milton secretly entertained the desire of making him his son-in-law; but his youngest daughter Deborah, his only child that had never treated him in an undutiful and disrespectful manner, and whom he had destined to his young friend, left her parental home and eloped to Ireland, where she married. This event, however, did not dissolve the intimate relations between the master and his pupil; and when the plague which had broken out in London made sad havoc among the inhabitants of the capital, Ellwood rented for Milton a small cottage at Chalfont, in Bucks, where the poet, in the healthy country air, and protected from all disturbing influences, completed his "Paradise Lost."

The young Quaker was in an ecstasy of delight when Milton permitted him to read the manuscript. On returning it to him, he expressed the warmest thanks.

"In truth," he said, with the frankness peculiar to his sect, "thou hast created a work which will outlive all thy other writings. Thou hast descended to hell and ascended to heaven, and forcest the reader's soul to follow thee with transports or horror wherever thou mayst lead it. Through thee we become acquainted with the terrible majesty of Satan, who, in spite of his wickedness, still exhibits traces of his divine origin. We see the prince of hell a prey to the most violent grief and looking up to heaven with intense longing; only his still unbroken pride sustains him and fans the flames devouring his bosom. Guided by thy hand, we walk in an ecstasy of delight through Paradise, and rejoice in the innocence of Adam and Eve, in their pure love, in their devout prayers, and in the sweet charms of the scenery surrounding them. We tremblingly see the evil one, in the shape of a seductive serpent, approach the credulous Eve and tempt her to eat of the forbidden fruit. We take compassion on the fallen woman, and, although she has delivered mankind to sin and death, we forgive her, as did Adam, touched by her prayers and supplications. We follow Adam and Eve as they are driven out of Paradise, and listen with solemn awe to the teachings and prophecies of the messenger of God, who reveals the fate of his descendants, until he finally promises them, in the name of the Lord, that He will send them a Redeemer to deliver the human race from the bondage of sin."

"I am glad," replied Milton, to the enthusiastic youth, "that my poem has pleased you so well, and that you have so clearly penetrated its spirit and object. My only merit is the firm confidence that, in the struggle between the good and evil powers, truth and liberty must triumph over all the wiles and arts of hell."

"For this reason I do not consider thy work complete. Thou hast given us only the promise, but not the fulfilment; thou hast shown us 'Paradise Lost,' but not 'Paradise Regained.'"

Milton made no reply to the honest Quaker; he sat for a time absorbed in his reflections, and in his soul dawned the plan of a new epic, the subject of which was to be the salvation of mankind.

No sooner had the plague ceased raging in the metropolis, than the poet returned thither to find a publisher for his work. He applied to Samuel Simmons, a well-known bookseller, to whom he offered the manuscript. After reading the poem, Simmons returned it to the poet.

"The poem is not so bad," said the bookseller, "but it is not suitable to the times. A few years ago I should have gladly given you ten times as much for it as I can offer you now. The times are changed, and taste is changed with them. The public no longer cares for religious books; nobody buys them nowadays. There is no demand for grave and learned treatises. Ah, if you had written a satire or a witty farce, I might pay you a round price for it. I want such works as Butler's 'Hudibras,' of which thousands of copies have been sold, and which every one wants to read. I admit that it is a low and scurrilous book; but we publishers have to humor the wishes of the public."

"Then only scurrilous books and farces meet with purchasers nowadays?"

"That is the difficulty, and I cannot help it. But in order that you may see how willing I am to help talented men, I will take your poem on liberal terms. It is true, I know beforehand that it will not sell, but I will do the best I can."

"Tell me what you will give me for it. I do not like to haggle about the price, although I greatly need the money."

"Well, I will give you five pounds," said the penurious bookseller. "That is a handsome sum, and I will pay it to you immediately. Are you satisfied with it?"

"Nothing remains for me but to accept your offer."

"And you will receive the like sum as soon as a new edition is issued. You shall see that I am not niggardly, and treat authors in a generous manner."

A melancholy smile played over the poet's lips when he delivered his immortal work, the fruit of years of toil and reflection, to the avaricious publisher for this ridiculous sum. Simmons immediately drew up a contract, which Milton, who stood in need of the money, signed with a deep sigh.

When the book was issued from the press. the predictions of Mr. Simmons seemed to be fully verified. The public appeared insensible to the merits of the divine poem then entering on its course of immortality. Taste was changed indeed. Literature, which always reflects the time and its sentiments, languished in the midst of the general decay and corruption which had seized the whole English nation. The greatest licentiousness and most shameless immorality reigned at that period in the productions of the poets, and on the stage, which had become the scene of all vices and extravagances. Obscene wit levelled its shafts at all that was sacred and venerable. Innocence and truth were mercilessly derided, and lewdness was of itself considered a sign of talent. Only the books of authors who pursued this course, and penned the most dis graceful things, were bought, and eagerly de voured. Hardly any notice was taken of Milton's sublime epic, which was kept out of sight by the rankling weeds of contemporary literature. The publisher was dissatisfied with the small sales, and dinned the poet's ears with his complaints.

"Yes, yes," said Mr. Simmons, "such are the results of the desire of writers to immortalize themselves, and of their contempt of the present. What do I care for immortality, when the present does not care about us? What does the future concern us? Posterity will not pay me a penny for all your poetical works."

"You must not grow impatient," said Milton, to comfort the dissatisfied bookseller.

"Besides, the purchasers complain of the blank verse of 'Paradise Lost.' This is, indeed, a very serious fault of the work. Such innovations should not be countenanced. We should always adhere to that which is well established and used by everybody else."

"That is what I have done, for both Homer and Virgil wrote their poems in blank verse."

"What do I care for Homer and Virgil? They did not know any better; but culture has advanced since then, and as the public does not want any but rhymed poems, the poets should comply with its demands."

"But I am sure you do not want me to change the whole poem?"

"Of course I do not, for in that event it would have to be printed anew; but something should surely be done.—Hold on! I know what you must do. You must write a preface to your work, and excuse in it, to the best of your ability, your having written 'Paradise Lost' in blank verse, and not in rhyme."

"I think there is neither rhyme nor reason in your suggestion," said Milton, sarcastically.

"Then you refuse to comply with it? Very well, sir; then nothing remains for me but to write such a preface myself."

"I cannot object to that," said the poet, shrugging his shoulders.

Milton relented, however, and added to the second edition of the work a short and spirited explanation of his reasons for departing from the 'troublesome bondage of rhyming.' We do not know whether or not the idea of the bookseller had the wished-for results; but gradually 'Paradise Lost' met with more admirers and purchasers. Sir John Denham, a gentleman distinguished for his taste and learning, took the poem with him to Parliament, in order to read it in the intervals of the sessions. On being asked by his acquaintances what book he was reading, he expressed the most enthusiastic admiration for it.

"It is," he said, "the best poem ever written in any language or in any age."

The Earl of Dorset, an influential courtier happened one day to enter with a friend the book-store of Milton's publisher. He inquired for the latest productions of literature, and caused them to be shown to him. Among them was Milton's "Paradise Lost." The earl took up the book and read the title.

"A work by John Milton!" he exclaimed eagerly. "Is that the same Milton who was foreign secretary to the Council of State during the time of the commonwealth?"

"The same," replied the bookseller: "I bought the manuscript from compassion for the poor blind man; but it was a bad bargain for me. If the public does not soon commence buying the book, I shall lose heavily by the transaction."

While Simmons was giving vent to his complaints, the earl had seated himself and begun to read the book. The book-stores at that time were also reading-rooms, and no one purchased a book without having thoroughly examined its contents. Already, after reading the first pages, the earl perceived the rare merits of the poem.

"Magnificent! magnificent!" he exclaimed rapturously. "This is a perfect gem."

"Good heavens!" sighed the bookseller. "For two weeks past, I believe, I have not sold a single copy. Shall I send a copy to your lordship's house?"

"I will take one along."

The earl left, and his delight increased with every page he read. He communicated his discovery to Dryden, the poet, who lived at the court of Charles II., and was generally considered the greatest poet of his time, from whose imperfections, it is true, he did not keep himself entirely free, although he pursued a more praiseworthy course than most of the contemporary authors. Like Milton, John Dryden had been an ardent adherent of the republic during the time of the commonwealth, and had sung hymns in honor of Cromwell. When monarchy was restored, he went over with the tuneful throng to welcome in Charles II., and some time afterward he was appointed poet-laureate. During the reign of James II. he embraced the Roman Catholic faith. In direct contrast with Milton, he distinguished himself by his want of principle; nevertheless, he had remained enough of a poet to fully appreciate the vast importance and the extraordinary beauties of "Paradise Lost." After reading the book, he was asked by the Earl of Dorset what he thought of it.

"This man," he said, in a tone of admiration, not entirely devoid of envy, "eclipses us all, and the ancients also."

Afterward he sought an opportunity to get acquainted with Milton, of whom he begged permission to dramatize "Paradise Lost." He also offered his protection at court to the blind poet, whose pecuniary circumstances were then by no means brilliant.

"I am obliged to you," said Milton. "The court is not a proper sphere for me. In my opinion, a poet must be free above all things, and he cannot be free when his Muse is in the service of a prince. I value my independent poverty much higher than all the splendor which I might purchase at the expense of my convictions."

"You should at least devote your attention to the drama," advised Dryden, kindly; "the stage holds out to you far better prospects than the book-trade."

"If the stage is to fulfil its exalted task," replied Milton, "and be a school of life, it needs freedom before every thing else. At present the theatre only serves to amuse aristocratic rakes and the low rabble, who digest there comfortably, and desire to be diverted by the obscene jests of the actors. Rather than stoop to write such things, I would starve to death. The drama, that noblest blossom of art, is affected by the general corruption and decay; and no poet, however talented he may be, can restore it to its purity unless a change should take place in our whole moral and political atmosphere. The putrid sap circulating in the trunk produces rotten fruits; only a healthy people and a moral age can possess a true and great drama."

On receiving this reply, Dryden took his leave, somewhat irritated and offended. When he complained of Milton to Davenant, the latter burst into laughter.

"My friend," said the merry poet, "you must not wonder at this reply. Milton is like an oak, which is bent neither by the violent storm nor by the gentle zephyr. On seeing him, I always feel as if I behold one of the old prophets, predicting the doom of Jerusalem or Babylon! Allow him this harmless pleasure, and come with me and drink a glass of malmsey. At all events, we cannot change the world."

CHAPTER XIV.

ENGLAND UNDER CHARLES II.—OLD HENDERSON'S INSURRECTION.

MILTON thus lived in an age of general corruption, one of the few men of that period who remained faithful to their convictions, and whose names were unsullied by venality and apostasy. The court had become the centre of the most disgraceful licentiousness. Amusement succeeded to amusement—now a play, represented in the most lavish and extravagant manner; and now a ball, resplendent with flowers, lights, and frail beauties, or a tea-party, still at that time a rare and expensive entertainment. Splendid masquerades, at which the ladies appeared in the most transparent and lascivious costumes, alternated with ballets and concerts, which Saint-Evremond and the Duchess de Mazarin had brought over from France and rendered fashionable in England. Charles occupied himself with feeding his dogs and ducks, or was present at cock-fights and bear-baitings, while the bloodthirsty Duke of York never failed to be present at the executions, feasting his eyes on the agony of the Puritans and republicans who were put to death. To this laxity of morals corresponded the evident decline of the national character; skepticism and indifference took the place of the fanaticism and enthusiasm which only a short time since had reigned in England. A vain, flippant literature, to which not wit, but depth of principle and conviction, was wanting, supplanted the manly, bold poetry and courageous prose of the past. Instead of the intrepid spirit of investigation, with which England had formerly ventured to enter upon the solution of the most important questions, only frivolous subjects were treated of, and French patterns were copied in a manner alike servile and superficial. The great and eternal principles, for which, during the Revolution, the most eminent men had entered the lists, seemed to be forever forgotten and relinquished; freedom of thought, of conscience, and of speech, reform of parliamentary elections, and improvement of public instruction, were stifled, and silence was imposed on their friends and advocates. The press groaned under new fetters, and bribery bought up the votes of such parliamentary orators as were still to be feared. The persecution of the republicans was carried on as vindictively as ever; the triumphant party had not yet satiated its resentment, although it had already shed rivers of blood to avenge the execution of Charles I. The enthusiastic Harrison, and the younger Vane, one of the most eminent men of his time, suffered death for their convictions. Milton wept over the premature end of his friend, to whom he was chiefly indebted for his appointment to the secretaryship, and for whose talents and fervent zeal he entertained the highest respect. Profound grief gnawed at the poet's heart, and his soul revolted at this high-handed act of injustice and tyranny. He himself was poor, infirm, and blind; forsaken by nearly everybody, and deeply afflicted by the ingratitude of his own children. Weary of life, he tottered through the streets of London, holding the hand of a boy who was employed to guide his steps. A crowd was gathered at the corner. There stood a man with a livid face and wan, hollow cheeks. Covered with rags, he held in his hand a broom, which he brandished in the air. It was the visionary Harrington, the author of that Utopian work "Oceana." Banished to a desert island without a lawful trial, he had gone mad. The sufferings endured in his captivity impaired his intellectual faculties, and he sank into incurable insanity.

"What!" cried the maniac, brandishing his broom in the air. "What! you will not vanish, devouring thoughts? There they are coming again, chirping and humming like little birds and bees. How they sing and whistle, buzz and croak! Begone! Let me alone with your horrible cries! I have fed you on my life-blood, and you have feasted on it until I became a mere skeleton; and you are not yet satisfied! Air! air! The vapor stifles me. It smells of corpses; my thoughts are the worms creeping out of my petrified brain. A plague upon the vermin devouring an honest man while he is still alive! Oh, would I had never thought, never thought!"

Such were the wails and ravings of the madman, who, with his broom, incessantly sought to dispel his thoughts, which seemed to him to be flying about him in the shape of little birds and insects. A large crowd surrounded him, and brutally derided the poor man, whom his sister accompanied, and vainly sought to draw from the spot. Milton approached her in profound emotion, as he had formerly been intimately acquainted with Harrington.

"Poor friend," he said to the maniac, in a tremulous voice, "do you not know me?"

On hearing Milton's voice, Harrington gave a start; his eyes beamed strangely, and his reason seemed to return for a moment.

"You?" asked the maniac. "Why should I not know you? You are also dead and a corpse. Every thing is dead—the republic, liberty, the protector, and the king! The grave swallows us all; we then moulder, and new thoughts arise from our putrefying remains. There they are! Do you not see them? As yet they are as small as gnats; but they are constantly growing larger and larger, until they become eagles, and soar to the sun. Ah, how unfortunate we two are for having thought too much! Thinking brings misfortune upon us, and may drive a sensible man to the verge of insanity. Beware—beware!"

Profoundly moved by this heart-rending spectacle, Milton went away; and at a distance he still heard the cries of the maniac, "Why did we think, think?"

Not less deplorable was the fate which befell Milton's most faithful friend, Major Overton. Although he kept perfectly quiet when monarchy was restored, yet the mere reputation of his love of liberty sufficed to make him suspected. He was likewise imprisoned without a trial, and kept in a dungeon for long, long years. Such persecutions and cruelties could not but drive the republicans to despair; but their courage was gone, and they lacked, above all things, a sagacious and prudent leader. Isolated insurrections, which broke out from time to time, were speedily suppressed.

After Cromwell's death, old Henderson had returned to England. In vain did his former foster-daughter Lucy, and her husband, who were now living again at Ludlow Castle, offer him an asylum; he preferred to wait with his political friends for the rise of the fifth monarchy and the New Jerusalem. But when monarchy was restored, and the Puritans and other dissenters were persecuted with extreme rigor, Henderson joined a band of similar fanatics who intended to establish the kingdom of God sword in hand. Although they were only sixty strong, these madmen undertook to overthrow the king and carry their hair-brained plans into execution; they thought themselves invincible.

"It is not numbers," said the Puritan, at a meeting of the fanatics, "but our faith, that will enable us to achieve a brilliant victory. The Saviour Himself will be our leader, and render our arms strong and our bodies invulnerable. Therefore, never fear the odds of our enemies. Even though their number were legion, we should vanquish them; for the Lord is with us. He beckons, and they are annihilated; He commands, and they disappear like chaff before the wind. Who can withstand His people, or injure the elect? Onward! The sword of the Lord and of Gideon!"

Such was the battle-cry with which the fanatics rushed, sword in hand, into the street; every one fled before the infuriated men. Among the fugitives was Billy Green, who hurriedly tried to escape. Henderson had recognized the hateful spy, and pursued him at a furious rate.

"Stand and surrender, son of Belial!" he shouted to him.

Seized with indescribable terror, the villain rushed toward the nearest house, where he thought he would find an asylum. Already he had reached the door, and knocked loudly for admittance, when the Puritan's sinewy hand seized him by the neck.

"The judgment of the Lord," cried Henderson, savagely, "shall overtake all sinners! Confess your sins, villain, for your soul is as black as that of the evil one."

"Mercy!" gasped Billy, while the fanatic's hand clutched his throat so violently that his small, cunning eyes protruded from their sockets. "I am innocent, and never wronged you in my life."

"You are innocent? Then Satan in hell is a saint! Have you not always served vice and infamy? Have you not been the boon companion of the most black-hearted scoundrels? You see, I am not ignorant of your character. You have deserved death a hundred times, because you have always been an impudent, Heaven-defying reprobate. Did you not strut about in heathenish costumes, an abomination in the eyes of the just? Did you not serve the tyrant who, on account of his sins, lost his head on the block?"

"I perceived the error of my ways, and if Mr. Pym were still alive, he would bear witness to the zeal with which I afterward served the cause of the republicans."

"Miserable hypocrite! For the sake of filthy lucre, you were intent, under the mask of a saint, a wolf in sheep's clothing, only on promoting your own interests. Did you not turn your back on us as soon as young Stuart returned to England? You were his pointer, and helped him to pursue the noble game of the pious Puritans. On your head is the blood of the martyrs, which cries to heaven for vengeance."

"Mercy!" groaned the unfortunate spy. "I will make amends for all the wrongs that I have perpetrated; I will do all that you demand. If you will let me go, I will communicate an important secret to you. The Duke of York has embraced the Catholic faith, and a French priest privately reads mass to King Charles II. I know a great many other things, and will tell you all if you will let me go."

In his anguish, Billy Green had clasped the Puritan's knees, and lay writhing at his feet, while Henderson was brandishing his sword over his head.

"Down with the traitor!" shouted the infuriated fanatic, and his flashing sword cleft the spy's skull. Billy Green died without uttering a groan, while Henderson coolly turned from him.

"The Lord has judged him," he said, pushing aside the corpse, whose glazed eyes stared after him.

At the head of his men, he marched triumphantly from street to street, proclaiming the kingdom of Jesus, the invisible leader of this pious and devout insurrection. The authorities attempted to disperse the insurgents by main force, but the assailants were driven back by the irresistible valor of the fanatics, who defended themselves with the most heroic intrepidity. Many a member of the militia was killed or wounded by them, until the whole force that had been sent to disperse them, seized with a panic, took to flight, although its numerical strength was perhaps ten times superior to that of the insurgents.

No sooner had the militia fled, than old Henderson intoned a triumphant hymn. Baring his gray head, and brandishing his blood-stained sword, he sang exultingly:

"Great is the Lord, and they who trust in Him will be invincible. The enemies approached in countless strength, like locusts descending on a harvest-field; and yet we did not succumb, for He is our shield. We struck them, and they sank to the ground; with the keen edges of our swords we mowed them down like stubble. The Lord be praised, the

God of Israel, who does not suffer His people to perish in distress. Sing to Him, and give praise to His glory!"

Singing a psalm, as they had done at Dunbar and Worcester on rushing upon the enemy, the enthusiastic Puritans marched through all London without meeting with any serious resistance, so great was the cowardice of their adversaries, and their own confidence in divine assistance. They firmly believed in the triumph of their cause, and expected every moment the appearance of the Saviour, whom they proclaimed King of the world. It was not until the following morning, when the danger grew more and more alarming, that the royal guards were sent against the fanatics, who had retired in good order and taken position in a remote part of the city. From thence they made several sallies into the old city of London, which was nowise prepared for their attacks. They produced there not a little confusion, and the wealthy merchants believed that the turbulent times of the commonwealth had returned, and left in timid haste their counting-houses and the riches stored in their warehouses. Finally, assailed from all quarters, and hemmed in, the fanatics threw themselves into a neighboring house, where the troops were obliged to enter upon a regular siege against them. Their ranks were fearfully thinned by the volleys of the soldiers, and at last only a few of them were left. In vain quarter was offered to them if they would surrender voluntarily. In their fanatical faith in divine assistance, they rejected all the offers of their adversaries.

"Stand firm," cried old Henderson; "the Lord cannot and will not forsake His people. Follow me, and nobody shall hurt a hair of your heads."

The small band, headed by the Puritan, rushed unhesitatingly upon the troops. The soldiers at first fell back in dismay; but on perceiving the small number of their assailants, they advanced again and attacked the intrepid enthusiasts on all sides.

"In the Saviour's name," shouted Henderson to his men, "do not budge an inch! This is our last trial, and he who shall pass through it will enter heaven and the new Jerusalem."

A bullet pierced his breast and struck him down. Already darkness veiled his eyes.

"Do you see?" murmured the mortally wounded Puritan. "The day is ours. The gates are unlocked, heaven opens to us, and the Saviour descends from it. Legions of saints, martyrs, and angels, surround Him; they lift me up and carry me to heaven. Already I am floating in their midst. Ha, give me my sword! There stands the evil one, the archfiend of mankind! I will—"

He did not conclude. In his last struggle he still convulsively grasped the hilt of his sword as if to redeem the world at a blow. And thus the fanatic departed this life. Most of his men were killed; only a few surrendered, and were ignominiously executed on the scaffold.

Not far from Henderson lay Billy Green's mutilated corpse: the stern, consistent Puritan, and the unprincipled, fickle apostate; both productions of the same stormy commotion which carries virtue as well as vice to a colossal development, far overstepping the ordinary bounds of human nature.

Such was the last flicker, the last desperate attempt of a party which, at first persecuted and oppressed, had gradually risen to almost absolute power, which it was to wield only for a very short time. The Puritans did not venture upon another rising, and left the field to others, who afterward entered the list for liberty, and, during the reign of James II., achieved the final victory over despotism.

Milton shared the principles and aspirations of these political and religious fanatics only so long as they themselves groaned under the grinding yoke of their oppressors, and met their persecutors with valor and manly courage. His common-sense and innate poetical spirit preserved him from their violent excesses. After conquering their adversaries, the Puritans were as intolerant and prone to persecution as the royalists, although they distinguished themselves most advantageously from the latter by their morality and fervent piety. Nevertheless, the maintenance of their supremacy would have done more harm than good to England, inasmuch as, from their narrow-minded point of view, they were intent on converting the state into a house of prayer, and the nation into a pious conventicle. A reaction was the inevitable consequence of this system, against which the people could not but rebel in the interest of individual liberty.

CHAPTER XV.

MLLE. DE QUEROUAILLE—ALLIANCE WITH LOUIS XIV.

At the royal court had arrived a guest who carried to the highest pitch the licentiousness and immorality already prevailing there. This was the beautiful and accomplished but frail Henrietta of Orleans, the sister of Charles II., and sister-in-law of Louis XIV., and doted upon by both. She was one of the amiable ladies of that period, who combined with the utmost frivolity a polished mind and an extraordinary spirit of intrigue. They were the diplomatists in petticoats, the forerunners of those arrogant mistresses who, toward the end of the seventeenth and the beginning of the eighteenth centuries, exercised at almost all courts a decisive influence over the political affairs of the time. These ladies coupled love with politics, coquetry with diplomacy; from a tender *tête-à-tête* they went to a cabinet meeting, and tied and untied with their delicate white hands the threads of political intrigues; reclining carelessly on their swelling divans, they contracted alliances and waged wars; by a smile, by a glance, they often decided the most important questions. Their whole life was a net-work of intrigues, in which now the heart, and now the interests of the state, played the most prominent part.

Henrietta was exceedingly skilled in this intricate game, and Louis XIV. was perfectly justified in intrusting her with a confidential mission to England. Under the mask of a mere visit to her native country, she was to enter upon the most important negotiations, whose object was nothing short of a total change in the foreign policy of the country. England, which had hitherto stood at the head of the Protestant states, and had but recently concluded an alliance with Sweden and the Dutch Republic for the protection of the Reformation, and as a measure of safety against the thirst of France for conquest, was to dissolve this "triple alliance," which the nation had hailed with the utmost enthusiasm, declare war against the Dutch Republic, and assist Louis XIV. in his plans for destroying the equilibrium of Europe. Both the triumph of Catholicism and the supremacy of absolution, whose most prominent representative, and, as it were, incarnation, was the King of France, was to be achieved by this arrangement. The fate of the world was at stake, and every thing depended upon the decision at which Charles II. should arrive. Circumstances greatly facilitated Henrietta's task. The king had rewarded the faithful services of his pedantic but honorable minister, Clarendon, by ignominiously depriving him of his office, and sending him into exile. The men to whom the government was now intrusted were a set of frivolous and unreliable profligates. Clifford, Ashley, Buckingham, Arlington, and Lauderdale, were the unprincipled servants whom the king called into the cabinet and appointed to the most responsible offices. From the initial letters of their names the people made the word "cabal," which is still used to stigmatize a system of falsehood, rascality, and infamy. Surrounded and influenced by such men, Charles lost the last trace of shame and scrupulousness. Engrossed only with his pleasures, he left the whole government in the hands of his ministers.

Henrietta was familiar with her brother's weaknesses, and, to profit by them, she had brought with her a female ally. This was Mlle. de Querouaille, one of the most beautiful ladies of France. No sooner had the king beheld her, than he fell in love with her. His sister had foreseen this, and given beforehand the necessary instructions to the beautiful lady.

At St. James's palace a most brilliant festival was given in honor of the guests. The apartments and halls were resplendent with fairy-like magnificence. Costly hangings, splendid Gobelins, covered the walls with their artistic embroideries; on the wainscoted ceilings hung large lustres, shedding a flood of light over the gorgeous scene. The tables were loaded down with viands and liquors, which were served up in silver and golden vessels. Immediately after the banquet, commenced the ball, which the king opened with the beautiful Mlle. de Querouaille. They were followed by the extravagant and reckless Buckingham with the charming Henrietta of Orleans, and the other dancers. The gloomy fanatics and rude warriors were supplanted by licentious and supercilious courtiers, who imitated the example of their sovereign. They turned in the mazes of the dance until they sank exhausted upon their chairs. The gentlemen lavished on the ladies the most gallant compliments, which, like their whole costume, they borrowed from France. Here and there some old cavalier, who had fought under Prince Rupert or the Duke of Newcastle, wore his own gray hair, and the ancient uniform to which he had become partial; but the younger generation covered their heads with the enormous wigs purchased in Paris, which was then, as now, the leader of fashion. The coats were adorned with costly embroidery, and the elegant hanger which the gentlemen wore threatened entirely to supplant the heavy broadsword. Gay-colored ribbons floated down from the shoulders, and the large number of rosettes fastened to the attire of the gentlemen imparted to them an effeminate appearance.

The ladies at the court of Charles II. wore light, transparent dresses; they unhesitatingly displayed the charms which their mothers had carefully veiled, and took pains, if possible, to outstrip their French patterns. English gayety combined with French coquetry into a strange mixture, which, like champagne and porter mixed together, gave rise to a doubly heavy intoxication, and degenerated into the most licentious frivolity. To the ball succeeded a mask, specially written for the occasion by Dryden, who gradually eclipsed the already superannuated Davenant, and, with Waller, shared the special favor of the king and his courtiers. On the stage appeared nearly all the gods of Olympus, represented by ladies and gentlemen of the court, who celebrated the arrival of the Duchess of Orleans with the most fulsome flatteries. Already, for several days previous to the performance, all the actresses were in the highest state of excitement in regard to the interesting question which of them would be selected to play the part of Venus. This was a matter of the highest importance for the ladies of the court, as the selection would be equivalent to a public declaration which of them was generally considered the most beautiful. All the mistresses of the king believed themselves justly entitled to the *rôle*, and left no means untried to attain their object. Prayers and threats, blandishments and tears, were resorted to, and none of them were willing to renounce their claims, but rather determined to carry matters to extremities. Charles was greatly puzzled, and the affair engrossed him and his cabinet far more than the most important political questions. Finally, after innumerable consultations and secret conferences, it was resolved to bestow upon Mlle. de Querouaille the *rôle* of the goddess of love, whereby she was, as it were, elevated to the position of the king's favorite mistress. The whole court had watched these important deliberations with the utmost suspense, and it was now filled with the most intense curiosity, assembled in front of the stage.

The curtain rose. A number of inferior genii announced the approach of the Olympian gods, at last appeared the procession, amid the brilliant notes of a solemn march. At the head of the procession strode Ashley, a member of the "cabal," representing Jupiter, wearing a golden crown on his head, and holding a sceptre in his hand. At his side appeared Lady Arlington as Juno, seated in a chariot of gold drawn by peacocks. Then followed the other gods and goddesses, who were greeted with more or less applause by the audience, and gave rise to all sorts of witty remarks and exclamations.

"Good faith," said a courtier, rather loudly, "there comes Grammont as Apollo, with his thin legs, which look precisely like walking-sticks. A man must be very bold to walk on them."

"And yet," whispered another, "he has padded them with more than twenty pounds of wool. What do you think of Lady Clifton as Diana?"

"As she has no Actæon, she has placed antlers on her husband's head. But hush! if I am not mistaken, Venus and the Graces are about to step upon the stage."

"Mlle. de Querouaille! By Jove, she is beautiful!"

"You need not hope for any thing in that direction. That game is reserved to his majesty, and no loyal subject is allowed to hunt and kill game in the royal park."

A general burst of surprise and admiration greeted the appearance of the goddess of love. Surrounded by Cupids, a silver chariot, adorned with shells and drawn by two doves, moved across the stage. A surpassingly beautiful woman carelessly reclined in it. Like small serpents, countless black ringlets curled round the white forehead, under which two dark eyes were burning. The most precious pearls and diamonds, flashing around her charming head, were to represent the water-drops clinging to the goddess, who had just risen from the foam of the sea. A blue gossamer mantle surrounded her slender form, and served to unveil rather than hide her charms. At her side strode the Earl of Rochester, representing Mars, and clad in a magnificent cuirass; while Lord Wilmot, as Vulcan, limped after them. A beautiful boy, Amor, accompanied her, and handed her from time to time a gilded arrow, which she sent from her small bow into the midst of the audience.

Great was the admiration excited by this goddess of love; especially were the king and the other gentlemen in ecstasies at her loveliness and grace, while the ladies gave vent to their envy by all sorts of malicious remarks. Mlle. de Querouaille was about to recite the lines which she was to utter as Venus, when suddenly there emerged from behind the scenes a similar chariot, likewise drawn by doves. From it descended another goddess of love, wearing the same costume, and who was no other than Barbara Villiers, the king's former mistress. The slighted mistress could not bear the idea that a stranger should be preferred to her; therefore, at the risk of incurring the king's anger, she had chosen the same mask, and appeared so unexpectedly to dispute with her the palm of beauty. Both the spectators and actors were not a little surprised at this spectacle. All fixed their eyes on Charles, who, speechless with astonishment, seemed at first to be at a loss whether to laugh or be angry at this improvisation.

During this piquant scene, the two fair rivals looked daggers at each other. Mlle. de Querouaille, however, did not lose her self-possession, and commenced reciting the lines in broken English. No sooner, however, had she concluded, than Barbara Villiers recited a few verses perfectly adapted to the situation. Thus a most charming contest of love and grace took place between them in the presence of the whole court, which followed with undisguised interest the developments of the strange scene. At last the king rose and put an end to the mask which had been interrupted by Barbara's appearance. He took the hands of the two ladies, and whispered into the ear of each a word sounding half like an entreaty, and half like an order. The rivals then approached and embraced each other before the audience, which burst into loud applause. Peace seemed momentarily restored; but in the hearts of the two jealousy fanned as before its devouring flames.

It was not until late in the evening that the king succeeded in getting rid of the irksome Barbara, and in holding an undisturbed *tête-à-tête* with Mlle. de Querouaille. Henrietta of Orleans had instructed her beforehand as to the course she was to pursue in regard to the king. Every favor which she should grant to Charles was to be sold at an exorbitant rate. In a remote cabinet the king lay at the feet of the goddess of love. A discreet lamp shed its rosy lustre over her charming form. The distant notes of seductive, voluptuous music penetrated faintly into the room.

"I will give my crown," said Charles, "for you and your love."

"I do not ask for it," replied the French lady; "moreover, it no longer belongs to you, but to your consort."

"Do not remind me of the sacrifice which I was obliged to make to circumstances. We poor princes are entitled to your compassion."

"Poor king!" jested the lady.

"I cannot offer you any thing save my heart."

"Which I should have to share with a hundred other women—among them with Barbara Villiers, Nell Gwynn, and so forth."

"You are cruel. But I swear to be faithful to you."

"Do not commit perjury. I have been warned of your oaths. The king, I have been told, is constant only in inconstancy."

"Put me to the test, and ask of me whatever you please," cried Charles, whose desires were still more inflamed by her resistance.

"I am a good Catholic, and, therefore, solicitous for the salvation of my soul. A heretic never can be my lover. My Church would not forgive such a sin."

"For your sake, then, I will embrace the Catholic faith."

"That is quite acceptable," she replied, with charming coquetry. "At least I should do something for my Church, and would be less guilty. Tell me, are you in earnest about your promise?"

"As sure as my name is Charles, and as I am King of Great Britain. Like your Henry IV., I say, 'Such a woman is worth a mass.'"

"He said, 'Paris is worth a mass.'"

"I would give Paris and London for a kiss from your rosy lips."

"You will not attain your object so very fast. I am not only a good Catholic, but also a good Frenchwoman. So long as you side with the heretical Swedes and Dutch, and oppose France, you shall not touch the tip of my little finger."

So saying, she withdrew her delicate white

hand from that of the king, and pouted so charmingly that Charles entirely lost his presence of mind, and would have consented to all that she asked of him.

"I envy your king, not for his glory, but for the fair subject who so warmly advocates his cause; but you do not know what you ask of me. I am to dissolve the triple alliance, that is to say, defy the public opinion of all England, which, in consideration of this alliance with the Protestant powers, overlooks all my other weaknesses and faults. Do not look at me so wonderingly with your large blue eyes, to which I cannot refuse any thing; but it would be no joke for me if all parties should rise against me, and stun my ears with their cries. It would be a dangerous, very dangerous step; for, to tell you the truth, the people submit to a great many things so long as I do not act contrary to their Protestant convictions. In this point they are like a restive horse, prancing and perhaps throwing off his rider, if he should not sit well in the saddle."

"I always thought you a good horseman, and able to manage your charger."

"What will Parliament say?" asked Charles thoughtfully; for, notwithstanding his frivolity, he possessed sufficient understanding to see his position in its true light. Only his passions blinded him, and to them he mostly sacrificed his better conviction.

"Parliament?" smiled Mlle. de Querouaille, playing with her fan, and gently waving it; "you will chase it away if it should incommode you, just as I chase away the fly buzzing around me at this moment."

"That is not so easy as you seem to imagine. Parliament is not a fly, but a wasp which knows how to sting."

"Then you will kill the wasp. Do what the King of France did with his Parliament. He silenced its members, riding-whip in hand."

"But there is a vast difference between England and France. Our government is only a limited one, and hitherto no king has succeeded in governing without a Parliament."

"Then you must be the first to do so. I have been authorized to promise you the assistance of his majesty King Louis, who will furnish you all the means you need for imitating his example."

So saying, the beautiful woman drew from her bosom a treaty fully drawn up, and containing all the points which she had mentioned. With a seductive smile, the ambassadress handed the enamoured king the paper which she wished him to sign. Charles read it, and seemed to hesitate. In spite of his recklessness, he shrank from a plan aiming at nothing less than the restoration of England to the Catholic faith, and the abolition of Parliament. It is true, he was perfectly indifferent in religious matters, and looked upon the repeal of the constitution only as a removal of an irksome restraint; but at the same time he was fully alive to the dangers in which such a step might involve him. Too indolent to make up his mind on so important a subject, he possessed not sufficient courage and energy either to accept or to reject the offer. Mlle. de Querouaille watched with anxious suspense the features of her lover. On perceiving that he hesitated, she seized his hands, and with caresses and blandishments pressed into it the pen with which he was to sign the treaty.

"You do not know what you ask of me."

"A proof of your love. It is only on this condition that I can belong to you."

The lovely woman bent over his shoulders as if to read the contents of the important document. Her fragrant breath intoxicated him; her silky ringlets touched his cheeks, and her electric contact fanned the fire burning in his heart to a devouring flame. Her eyes gazed so longingly and beseechingly into his own, that he was scarcely able to withstand her. He himself did not know exactly how it happened, but her hand moved the pen which he yet held in his hand, and with her assistance he mechanically affixed his royal signature to the treaty. By a stroke of the pen the fate of England had been decided; and he had become a vassal of Louis XIV., from whom he henceforth received an annual stipend, which he used in gratifying his expensive passions. The tender embrace and the burning kisses of the female diplomatist stifled the rising misgivings of the king.

At such a price Charles bought the love of Mlle. de Querouaille, whom he afterward created Duchess of Portsmouth.

CHAPTER XVI.

"SAMSON AGONISTES."

HENCEFORWARD England sank deeper and deeper from the lofty position which she had hitherto occupied. At home, the reactionary party put off its hypocritical mask and no longer disguised its despotic intentions; abroad, the government, owing to its humiliating dependence on France, forfeited what little respect it had enjoyed up to this time. The "cabal" continued in power, while Charles gratified his licentiousness the more eagerly, as Louis XIV. furnished him with the necessary funds. As a matter of course, general discontent prevailed among the people, and, despite the demoralization reigning throughout the country, there stirred in the nation a growing sense of its humiliating condition, which was intensified by the consciousness of having forfeited its honor, and by gloomy forebodings of dangers menacing the security of England. It is true, Charles did not possess sufficient energy to take a decisive step toward carrying out the treaty which he had concluded with France. He contented himself with making new promises when he was reminded of his engagement, or with underhand half-measures against the British constitution, which he dared not openly attack. An event, not very important in itself, characterizes most strikingly the course he pursued toward Parliament, and betrayed his real intentions. The Parliament contemplated imposing a tax upon actors. The court party opposed this measure, objecting that the actors were servants of the king, and were kept for his majesty's pleasure. On this occasion a highly-respected member of the House of Commons inquired whether they referred to the actors or actresses. This was evidently an allusion to two actresses who were favorite mistresses of Charles II. The king was furious at this insult, and resolved to revenge himself in a manner entirely unworthy of his exalted office. Some officers of the lifeguards took upon themselves the task of chastising the offender. They assailed him in a most cowardly manner, and, notwithstanding his determined resistance, mutilated him by slitting his nose. The Parliament was highly indignant at this cowardly outrage, and, supported by the violent exasperation of the whole country, demanded due satisfaction for it.

The people, however, were aroused to still greater excitement by their apprehensions regarding the restoration of the Catholic faith. The king was not unjustly suspected of leaning toward the Roman Church. The Duke of York, his brother, had already publicly admitted that he had embraced Catholicism. Sir Kenelm Digby, who had meanwhile died during a journey to France, had not unsuccessfully worked, both in secret and openly, for the faith of his executed father. Protestantism was seriously menaced, and religious liberty had to fear the worst at the hands of the gloomy and bigoted James.

The mournful posture to which England was reduced made upon no one a deeper impression than upon Milton. His domestic afflictions added to his grief at the distress of his country. He had witnessed the greatness of his nation, which was now so deeply humiliated. Liberty, for which he had once entered the lists, was gone, destroyed, and reviled. His political friends had expiated their honest convictions on the scaffold or in prison. Perfidy and meanness were triumphant. Moreover, he had grown old and blind, and his own daughters had deserted him. Profound dejection had seized him, and he longed to die. Poesy alone had remained faithful to him; but it no longer appeared to him as a divine comforter, but in a mourning-garb, and with tears in the extinct eyes. He exhaled his grief in a drama which he published a short time previous to his death, under the title of "Samson Agonistes." This was an outburst of his deep anguish.

In the person of the blind hero of the Israelites he lamented his own misfortunes. Milton himself was the blind Samson, derided by the Philistines and idolaters, betrayed by a perfidious woman, deserted by all, and despairing of the mighty God of his fathers. Like this Biblical hero, he had fought and struggled, and now he was prostrate, chained, and crushed.

While depicting his sufferings in this drama, he was cheered from time to time by a visit of his faithful friend Marvell. This honest man was one of the few who had remained true to their convictions, and had disdained all the offers of Charles, who recognized his worth, and sought to win him over to his side. With this friend Milton shared the remainder of his fortune; with him he recalled the eventful past, and he communicated to him his new poem, which was to appear in dramatic form.

"Dryden," said the poet, "asked me to write a drama, and I have done so; but I am afraid it has little prospect of being performed at court."

"And what subject have you chosen, my venerable friend?"

"Blind Samson is my hero."

"Blind Samson," repeated Marvell, mournfully.

"Blind like myself, deserted like myself, but full of hope in the Eternal. Thus he sits under the gate of Gaza, while the Philistines are feasting and celebrating orgies in honor of their contemptible idols. Listen to his complaints:

'Oh, that torment should not be confined
To the body's wounds and sores,
With maladies innumerable
In heart, head, breast, and veins;
But must secret passage find
To the inmost mind.
There exercise all his fierce accidents,
And on her purest spirits prey,
As on entrails, joints, and limbs,
With answerable pains but more intense,
Though void of corporal sense.
My griefs not only pain me
As a lingering disease,
But finding no redress, ferment and rage;
Nor less than wounds immedicable
Rankle, and fester, and gangrene
To black mortification.
Thoughts, my tormentors, armed with deadly stings,
Mangle my apprehensive tenderest parts,
Exasperate, exulcerate, and raise
Dire inflammation, which no cooling herb
Or med'cinal liquor can assuage,
Nor breath of vernal air from snowy Alp.
Sleep hath forsook and given me o'er
To Death's benumbing opium as my only cure;
Thence faintings, swoonings of despair,
And sense of Heaven's desertion.
I was His nursling once, and choice delight,
His destined from the womb,
Promised by heavenly message twice descending.
Under His special eye
Abstemious I grew up, and thrived amain:
He led me on to mightiest deeds,
Above the nerve of mortal arm,
Against the uncircumcised, our enemies;
But now hath cast me off as never known,
And to those cruel enemies,
Whom I by His appointment had provoked,
Left me all helpless, with the irreparable loss
Of sight, reserved alive to be repeated
The subject of their cruelty or scorn.
Nor am I in the list of them that hope:
Hopeless are all my evils, all remediless.
This one prayer yet remains, might I be heard,
No long petition: speedy death,
The close of all my miseries, and the balm.'"

"Poor Samson!" cried Marvell, seizing the

poet's hand in profound emotion. "Is there no other consolation left to thee? We must submit, and bear with patience that which cannot be helped."

"I possess such patience, and, above all things, confidence in the government of Divine Providence. Nevertheless, I am in pain, and no one will blame my Samson for crying out under his heavy burden, and praying God to end his life."

"But will you not continue?" begged Marvell; "that is, if the recitation does not exhaust or excite you too much."

"Samson's complaints are replied to by the chorus of his Israelite friends, which I arranged in accordance with the rules of the Greek tragedy:

'Many are the sayings of the wise,
In ancient or in modern books enrolled,
Extolling patience as the truest fortitude;
And to the bearing well of all calamities,
All chances incident to man's frail life,
Consolatories writ
With studied argument, and much persuasion sought,
Lenient of grief and anxious thought:
But with the afflicted in his pangs their sound
Little prevails, or rather seems a tune
Harsh, and of dissonant mood from his complaint;
Unless he feel within
Some source of consolation from above,
Secret refreshings, that repair his strength,
And fainting spirits uphold.
God of our fathers, what is man,
That Thou toward him with hand so various,
Or might I say contrarious,
Temperest Thy providence through his short course!
Not evenly, as thou rulest
The angelic orders, and inferior creatures mute,
Irrational and brute?
Nor do I name of men the common rout,
That, wandering loose about,
Grow up and perish, as the summer fly,
Heads without name, no more remembered,
But such as Thou hast solemnly elected,
With gifts and graces eminently adorned,
To some great work, Thy glory,
And people's safety, which in part they effect:
Yet toward these, thus dignified, Thou oft,
Amidst their height of noon,
Changest Thy countenance, and Thy hand, with no regard
Of highest favors past
From Thee on them, or them to Thee of service.
Nor only dost degrade them, or remit
To life obscured, which were a fair dismission;
But throwest them lower than Thou didst exalt them high;
Unseemly falls in human eye,
Too grievous for the trespass or omission;
Oft leavest them to the hostile sword
Of heathen and profane, their carcasses
To dogs and fowls a prey, or else captived;
Or to the unjust tribunals, under change of times,
And condemnation of the ungrateful multitude.'"

Here Milton paused, profoundly moved by his own words. He thought of the fate of his unfortunate friends. In his mind he saw the scaffold on which the noble Vane had bled, the dungeon in which his friend Overton was still groaning—all the banished and persecuted men, his political friends. He remembered with great bitterness the fickleness of the foolish people, who were to-day kneeling again before the idols they had once upset: who denied and derided the principles to which they had adhered only yesterday with the ardor of fanaticism, and who heaped the most poignant contumely and mortification on their former favorites and friends. A tear of indignation and just anger trembled in the eyes of the poet when he continued:

"If these they 'scape, perhaps in poverty
With sickness and disease Thou bowest them down,
Painful diseases and deformed,
In crude old age;
Though not disordinate, yet causeless suffering
The punishment of dissolute days: in fine,
Just or unjust, alike seem miserable,
For oft alike both come to evil end.
So deal not with this once Thy glorious champion,
The image of Thy strength and mighty minister.
What do I beg? How hast Thou dealt already?
Behold him in this state calamitous, and turn
His labors, for thou canst, to peaceful end.",

While Milton was reciting these lines, which lamented his own fate in the person of Samson, the cold wind moved the leafless trees, and accompanied the mournful words with its melancholy tones. The summer was at an end; the fields had been mown, the flowers were withered, the joyous notes of the birds had died away. A profound, gloomy silence reigned all around. The parting rays of the pale sun illuminated the gray head and wan face of the poet. He had grown old and feeble; blind and sick he sat there, a broken, crushed hero like his Samson; but in his heart there lived yet the courageous spirit of poetry, the unexhausted vigor of the soul. Without an effort he recited his poem to the end. In stirring lines he depicted at the conclusion the vengeance which blind Samson wreaked upon his enemies, the terrible strength with which the hero shook the pillars of the house in which his adversaries were feasting, and the fall of the roof, under which he simultaneously buried them and himself. He raised his voice on reciting the triumphant chorus of the Israelites:

"'But he, though blind of sight,
Despised, and though extinguished quite,
With inward eyes illuminated,
His fiery virtue roused
From under ashes into sudden flame,
And as an evening dragon came,
Assailant on the perchèd roosts
And nests in order ranged
Of tame villatic fowl; but as an eagle
His cloudless thunder bolted on their heads.
So Virtue, given for lost,
Depressed and overthrown, as seemed,
Like that self-begotten bird
In the Arabian woods embost,
That no second knows, nor third,
And lay erewhile a holocaust,
From out her ashy womb now teemed,
Revives, reflourishes, then vigorous most
When most unactive deemed;
And, though her body die, her fame survives
A secular bird ages of lives.

* * * * * *

All is best, though we oft doubt
What the unsearchable dispose
Of Highest Wisdom brings about,
And ever best found in the close.
Oft He seems to hide his face,
But unexpectedly returns,
And to His faithful champion hath in place
Bore witness gloriously; whence Gaza mourns,
And all that band them to resist
His uncontrollable intent:
His servants He, with new acquist
Of true experience from this great event,
With peace and consolation hath dismissed,
And calm of mind, all passion spent.'"

Like one of those prophets of the Old Testament, the poet poured out in awful words his grief, his wrath, and his hopes. His form seemed to grow; he had risen and drawn himself up to his full height, an intellectual Samson, shaking once more the edifice of despotism, ready to die, and even in death clinging to the faith of his whole life.

CHAPTER XVII.

MILTON'S DEATH.

This was the last flicker of his surpassing genius before its utter extinction. Long-continued sufferings of the body and soul confined Milton at last to his bed; he felt that his life was drawing to a close. His wife nursed him with the greatest devotion; his brother, who did not share his political views, also hastened to him. The brothers met after a prolonged separation, and forgot their political differences, at least during the first few moments. Milton held out his emaciated hand to his faithful brother.

"Dear Christopher," he said, in a feeble voice, "I see that you still love me. How glad I am to see you after so many years; how glad I am that you have come! You will help me to set my house in order."

"I will gladly do so," replied his brother, deeply moved.

"My fortune is but small, for poets gather no riches. I am sorry that I can leave so little to my wife. I should have liked to free her from care; she deserves it by the tender solicitude with which she has nursed me, and by the love and patience with which she has always treated her poor blind husband; but I did not know how to amass large sums of money."

"I understand you have many claims outstanding."

"My debtors are even poorer than I; most of them are political friends of mine, who lost their fortunes at the restoration it is not in consonance with my wishes that you should collect these claims."

"And your children, your daughters?" asked Christopher, as delicately as possible.

"I have no children," said Milton, mournfully. "They have forsaken me. I am lonely and deserted."

At these words the door opened noiselessly. A matron, whose face still bore the traces of surpassing beauty, entered the room. She was accompanied by a young man with noble features. It was Alice, with her son. She had completed the education of the youth at her country-seat, far from the pernicious influence of the court. No sooner had she heard that her friend had been taken dangerously sick, than she hastened to him; but she had not thought that his end was so close at hand. The tears of his heart-broken wife told her that such was the case. Although she had entered as noiselessly as possible, the keen ears of the blind poet had heard her arrival.

"Who is there?" he asked, eagerly.

"A friend—Alice," replied the matron, hardly able to repress her tears.

A gentle smile kindled Milton's face; a touching gleam of joy flushed his pale cheeks.

"Welcome," he cried, profoundly moved, "spirit of my youth, genius of the poet! I knew that you would come, and that I should meet you once more before bidding farewell to this world."

"And I am not alone; I bring with me a son, who has come to receive your blessing."

"Approach," said the dying poet to the young man.

He touched with his hands the noble lineaments of the youthful face, which seemed to please him. He nodded with an air of great satisfaction.

"God refused a son to me," sighed Milton. "I have no children to perpetuate my name."

"You have immortal sons and daughters; your works, 'Comus,' 'Paradise Lost,' 'Paradise Regained,' 'Samson Agonistes,' and all those magnificent creations of your genius."

"Oh, they are not sufficient. I would willingly give all my works for a son, a child of flesh and blood, to whom I might bequeath my name, my spirit, and my sentiments."

"Take my William, then, and bequeath your love to him."

The young man, who shared his mother's attachment to her illustrious friend, bent his head before the dying poet and asked his blessing.

"I shall not leave this world, then," said Milton, "without leaving a son in it. God bless you, God bless the youth of England, from whom alone I expect the salvation of our poor country! I depart with the hope that the seeds which we have scattered will not utterly perish. A later generation will harvest the fruits. It was not vouchsafed to us to set foot in the land of promise. Like Moses, we were allowed only to see the promised liberty from afar. The Israelites had to wander through the wilderness for forty years before reaching the sacred soil of Canaan. The Lord will not allow us to perish either. The spirit which He stirred in us cannot die. We may compare the present time to a wilderness, in which we are wandering about without knowing the right path. The people are still dancing around the golden calf, and turning their backs upon the true God, who veils Himself majestically in his clouded heavens; but the nation will surely acknowledge its fault, forsake the false gods, and turn again toward the Almighty."

The sufferer paused, exhausted by the effort; language failed him, but his soul, which was already beginning to free itself from its earthly shell, took a loftier prophetic flight; it soared unfettered above time and space. After a long pause, he added:

"The struggle is not yet over, the struggle between heaven and hell, between the good and evil powers. There stands the fallen angel, with his infernal host; he is preparing anew for war with truth. Here Comus is grinning at me—Comus, the god of lust and worldliness. The Philistines are roaming everywhere, and boasting of their victory over the God-sent hero. All is in vain, all their efforts are fruitless. I know and feel that hell will not triumph. Already I saw the Messiah coming, before whom falsehood vanishes. The Holy Ghost descends upon the nations, the Holy Ghost of knowledge, humanity, and toleration. The guardian angel of virtue and innocence expels the lustful Comus, who must give up his prey. There will be better times and other soldiers of truth, who will triumph in the end. Arm, ye chosen ones; never tire, never give up the contest! Victory will not always flee from you or from the just cause. As for you," he added, turning to Alice's son, "I enlist you now for the new army which is to fight out the old contest. Be faithful to the religion of your fathers, to your convictions, and to truth. God bless you!"

A profound, reverential silence reigned during these words of the dying poet. The fine-looking youth, overcome by his feelings, knelt down at the bedside to receive the blessing of the illustrious sufferer. He was profoundly impressed with the grave importance of the moment which was to exercise a decisive influence over his whole life. Milton held out his hands to his faithful wife, and the beloved of his youth, who were standing like angels at his bedside.

"Do not weep," he said to them. "It is true, my life has abounded in sufferings. I have stood at the grave of that liberty which I helped to establish. My convictions have been derided, my opinions reviled, my writings burned by the public executioner. My friends have been persecuted, imprisoned, and executed. I have had to deplore the loss of my eyesight, and become a poor, miserable, blind man. Fate has taken much from me, but it has also given me much. It was vouchsafed to me to live in a great period, and take part in the greatest event of the century. I fought and labored faithfully during the great struggle. The first minds of my time joined hands with me, and the spiritual bond of friendship and esteem united me with the noble and eminent men of all countries. Princes and nations listened to my words, which became deeds, and inspired thousands with love of liberty and truth. But all this is nothing compared with the love which two of the noblest women bestowed upon me—you, my dear wife, and you, Alice, my Muse, my genius. I thank you and God for it at this last hour. God bless you!"

The tears of the two women moistened his hands. Gradually he became nearly unconscious, and the marked change in his features indicated the impending extinction of the dying flame. His cold hands still grasped those of Alice and his wife. During the brief and almost painless agony, his physical blindness disappeared for a moment; he seemed to see all the bystanders in the most wonderful illumination; they appeared to him free from earthly admixture, as heavenly forms in the light of transfiguration. The phantoms which seemed to crowd around his death-bed became more and more numerous; the friends of his youth, the men who had toiled and suffered with him, the women who had loved and revered his surpassing genius, passed as a glorious procession before his eyes ere he closed them forevermore. A serene, blissful smile illuminated his countenance. When Alice bent over him, his sublime spirit had already fled.

She imprinted a kiss, her last love-offering, on the pale, noble forehead of the poet, and then sank weeping into the arms of his wife.

A large number of mourners accompanied Milton's remains to St. Giles's Church, near Cripplegate, where he was buried close to the altar.

It was not vouchsafed to him to witness the victory of the liberal cause under James II., and the triumph of his principles, which took place a few years after his death. Alice's son took a leading part in the subsequent struggle, and sided most energetically with the party which rebelled against the tyranny of a bigoted and cruel king. His mother lived in quiet retirement, and always cherished and honored the memory of her illustrious friend. She still enjoyed the happiness and satisfaction of witnessing the rapid growth of his renown.

Like most eminent men, Milton did not receive the full meed of his fame until after his death; but it is not altogether just that it should rest chiefly on his "Paradise Lost." His prose works bear as much the stamp of his genius, despite their faults, which were those of their pedantic age rather than of their author. The more do they deserve our admiration and attention, as they treat almost every great question of humanity, and all the political and social problems whose solution has been attempted by the most eminent men up to the present time. In these writings we find Milton to be the most indefatigable champion of liberty, and the great precursor of Rousseau and the French Revolution. He stands on the doctrines of the new era, an intellectual giant, adorned with the radiant crown of the poet, whose splendor eclipsed for a time the merits of the publicist. The poet never forgot that he was a man and citizen. He did not live in egotistical seclusion from the world, but took part in its struggles, its aspirations, and sufferings. He sacrificed all to his convictions, and shrank from no dangers when struggling for the ideas which he advocated. He rested firmly and immovably on his faith in Christianity. From religion, from the eternal truths of the Bible, he derived the necessary strength. He looked upon his task as a sublime, divine mission; hence, the stern, moral earnestness, the lofty energy, and the inspired zeal which did not forsake him even when he advocated principles and defended views which belonged to a narrow-minded, and, in many respects, a bigoted age. He knew how to preserve a certain dignity in his controversies, in which the war on both sides was carried on with a degree of virulent abuse and personality which, though common in the age of the disputants, is calculated to strike a modern reader with astonishment. But we cannot but esteem him even in his errors, because they arise from his ardent thirst for truth. He was the sworn foe of restraint, whether in education or in domestic life, in the state or Church. In his eyes every man was born free, and, to fulfil his task before God and man in a becoming manner, should enjoy the whole extent of his freedom. He therefore demanded that all the natural rights of man should be scrupulously respected; he advocated the separation of the Church from the state, free investigation of the truths of the Bible, liberty of speech, of the press, of education, and of matrimonial relations. In his prose works, Milton has traced, as it were, the outlines of a new social system. There are few of the questions agitating the public mind, even at the present time, to which he did not give his attention. The deliverance of Greece, the reform of parliamentary elections, the improvement of public instruction, and of the laws regulating divorce—in short, all the hopes and wishes of our times, were foreseen and dwelt upon by his prophetic mind. Like a prophet of the Lord, he saw into the most remote future, and his genius, transcending the circumstances surrounding him, outstripped not only his times, but in many respects even our own.

None of his contemporaries equalled his intellectual strength, his moral worth, and his firmness of character. In the midst of general corruption and apostasy, he remained true to himself and to his principles. His faults and errors belong to the age in which he lived; his virtues and his genius to himself alone.

THE END.

The Conversion of the Roman Empire. The Boyle Lectures for the Year 1864, delivered at the Chapel Royal, Whitehall, by CHARLES MERIVALE, B. D., Rector of Lawford, Chaplain to the Speaker of the House of Commons, author of "A History of the Romans under the Empire." Large 12mo. Price, cloth, $2.

Principles of Political Economy, with some of their Applications to Social Philosophy. By JOHN STUART MILL. From the fifth London edition, 2 vols., small 8vo, handsomely printed. Cloth, $7; half calf, extra, $12.

The Vegetable World; being a History of Plants, with their Botanical Descriptions and peculiar Properties. By LOUIS FIGUIER, author of the "World before the Deluge." Illustrated with 446 Engravings interspersed through the text, and 24 full-page Illustrations, chiefly drawn from Nature, by M. FAGUET, Illustrator to the Botanical Course of the Faculty of Sciences of Paris. 1 vol., 8vo, beautifully printed. 584 pages. Cloth, $6; half calf, $8.50; full calf, $10.50.

Thirty Years' View; or, a History of the Working of the American Government for Thirty Years, from 1820 to 1850; chiefly taken from the Congress Debates, the private papers of General Jackson, and the Speeches of ex-Senator Benton, with his actual view of men and affairs. With Historical Notes and Illustrations, and some notices of eminent deceased contemporaries. By THOMAS H. BENTON. 2 vols., 8vo. Cloth, $8; half calf, extra, $13.

The Harvest of the Sea; a Contribution to the Natural and Economic History of the British Food Fishes. By JAMES G. BERTRAM. With fifty Illustrations. 1 large vol., 8vo, 520 pages. Cloth, $7.50; half calf, $10.

The Harmonies of Nature; or, the Unity of Creation. By Dr. G. HARTWIG, author of "The Sea and its Living Wonders," and "The Tropical World." With eight full-page Drawings, and nearly two hundred Woodcuts. 1 vol., 8vo, 406 pages. Cloth, $7.50; half calf, extra, $10; full calf, extra, $12.

History of the Romans under the Empire. By CHARLES MERIVALE, B. D., late Fellow of St. John's College. 7 vols., small 8vo, handsomely printed on tinted paper. Price, cloth, $21; half calf, extra, $35.

Haydn's Dictionary of Dates, relating to all Ages and Nations, for Universal Reference. Twelfth edition. Revised, Enlarged, and Corrected to February, 1866. By BENJAMIN VINCENT. 1 vol., large 8vo, 833 pages. Cloth, $7.50.

Metallurgy. Embracing the Elements of Mining Operations, and Analysis of Ores; a full description of all Smelting and other Operations for the production of Metals from the Ores. By T. OVERMAN. With numerous Wood Engravings of Machinery, Furnaces, and Apparatus. A vol., 8vo, of over 600 pages. Cloth, $8.

The Works of Lord Macaulay. Complete. Edited by his Sister, Lady TREVELYAN. With Portrait, engraved on steel, by W. Holl. 8 vols., large 8vo. Cloth, $40; half calf, extra, $56.

Correlation and Conservation of Forces; a Series of Expositions by Prof. Grove, Prof. Helmholtz, Dr. Mayer, Dr. Faraday, Prof. Liebig, and Dr. Carpenter; with an Introduction and brief Biographical Notices of the chief Promoters of the New Views, by EDWARD L. YOUMANS, M. D. Cloth, $2.50.

Appletons' Cyclopædia of Biography, Foreign and American, embracing a series of Original Memoirs of the Most Distinguished Persons of all Times. Edited by FRANCIS L. HAWKS, D. D., LL. D. With over 600 Engravings. 1 very large vol., 8vo. Cloth, $7; sheep, $8; half calf, extra, $10.

Cyclopædia of American Eloquence: a Collection of Speeches and Addresses by the most eminent Orators of America; with Biographical Sketches and Illustrative Notes. By FRANK MOORE. Two handsome volumes, large 8vo, embellished with the finest steel-plate Portraits. Cloth, $8; half calf, extra, $13.

History of Civilization in England. By HENRY THOMAS BUCKLE. With copious Index (not in the English edition). Two large volumes, 8vo, beautifully printed. Cloth, $8; half calf, extra, $13.

Made in the USA
Monee, IL
20 October 2026

66035290R00181